THE
ULTIMATE
DINOSAUR

PAST ◆ PRESENT ◆ FUTURE

THE
ULTIMATE DINOSAUR
PAST · PRESENT · FUTURE

BYRON PREISS AND ROBERT SILVERBERG
EDITORS

PETER DODSON
SCIENCE EDITOR

HOWARD ZIMMERMAN AND WILLIAM R. ALSCHULER
ASSOCIATE EDITORS

MARTIN H. GREENBERG
CONSULTING EDITOR

A BYRON PREISS BOOK

BANTAM BOOKS
NEW YORK · TORONTO · LONDON · SYDNEY · AUCKLAND

To my wife Sandi, with love.
— B.P.

For my father, for museum days long ago.
— R.S.

THE ULTIMATE DINOSAUR
A Bantam Book / October 1992

*Thanks especially to Jessica Steinberg and Sally Arbuthnot for keeping
the ball rolling ahead of the dinosaur's footfall.*

*Book design by Alex Jay/Studio J
Typeset by Pica Images Typography*

Library of Congress Cataloging-in-Publication Data

*The Ultimate Dinosaur: past * present * future /
edited by Robert Silverberg and Byron Preiss
p. c.m.
ISBN 0-553-07676-0
1. Science fiction, American. 2. Dinosaurs–Fiction.
3. Dinosaurs. I. Silverberg, Robert. II. Preiss, Byron.
PS648.S3U35 1991
813'.087620836–dc20
91-33829 CIP*

Published simultaneously in the United States and Canada

*Bantam Books are published by Bantam Books, a division of Bantam Doubleday
Dell Publishing Group, Inc. Its trademark, consisting of the words "Bantam Books"
and the portrayal of a rooster, is registered in the U.S. Patent and Trademark Office
and in other countries. Marca Registrada. Bantam Books, 666 Fifth Avenue, New York,
New York 10103.*

PRINTED IN THE UNITED STATES OF AMERICA

0 9 8 7 6 5 4 3 2 1

Page i: Deinonychus, *a predatory theropod ("beast foot"), and the lizard-hipped dinosaurs* Oviraptor *and* Apatosaur. *By Wayne D. Barlowe.*

Pages ii and iii: A herd of Diplodocus, *the giant sauropods, wandering on a Jurassic plateau. By John Gurche.*

Page iv: A Late Cretaceous bird-hipped dinosaur, the thick-skulled Pachycephalosaur. *By Brian Franczak.*

CONTENTS

INTRODUCTIONS

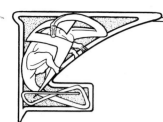
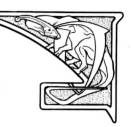

KINGDOM OF THE TITANS

ROBERT SILVERBERG

AMONG THE GREATEST TREATS OF MY CHILDHOOD IN NEW YORK WERE THOSE SUNDAY afternoons when my father would take me to the American Museum of Natural History to see the dinosaurs. Goggle-eyed with fascination and delight, I would wander from room to room staring at the *Tyrannosaurus* and the *Brontosaurus* and the *Stegosaurus* and the *Pteranodon* and all the other bizarre and grotesque and unforgettable giant creatures as though I had been given the key to a magic world. I knew all their jawbreaking names; I could tell you (and would, if you gave me half a chance) which ones were Triassic and which were Jurassic and which were Cretaceous; I let it widely be known that I was going to be a paleontologist when I grew up; I drew crude little crayon sketches of dinosaurs in school, and when I was seven or eight I laboriously jigsawed out a crude plywood sauropod which — nearly fifty years later — I still possess. It's on the desk before me as I write this. Perhaps it looks a little more like a camel (a purple camel, with yellow stripes!) than a sauropod, but I know what it was intended to be, and what I meant to express by making it in that far-off time.

My childhood obsession with dinosaurs was hardly unique, of course. Virtually every small boy — and a good many girls also — goes through a period of falling under the spell of the great saurians, is drawn to them just as I was, and for a time is utterly mesmerized by the notion that such stupendous creatures once walked the earth. The dinosaur wall paper in children's bedrooms, the cuddly dinosaur toys that populate every toy store, the animated monsters that roar on Saturday morning television — they all testify to the perennial and almost irresistible appeal of these strange extinct beasts. To a child they are the dragons of myth and folklore; but to the mythic power of their size and shape is added the astonishing realization that there was a time when they actually walked the earth, that huge herds of them wandered once unchallenged through what now is the domain of humankind.

So powerful is that appeal that it often proves ineradicable even in adulthood. Every professional paleontologist I have known, without exception, became entranced by the dinosaurs at an early age and never let the wonder fade. And although I myself somehow changed my career track in my teens from paleontology to science-fiction writing, I am quite sure that my visionary contemplation of the Age of Dinosaurs in my childhood was one of the things that led me to science fiction in the first place, and I still respond to the sight of some majestic fossil with the old awe and wonder. When I left New York to take up a new life in California, some three decades after the first of those Sunday afternoon trips with my father, one of the last things I did was to pay a last visit to the Museum of Natural History and offer a quiet farewell to the bony idols of my childhood. That was how important to me those memories of the early museum visits were. The giant reptiles have figured more than somewhat in my fiction, too — beginning with my very first novel, *Revolt On Alpha C*, in 1955,

Above: A re-creation of carnosaurs looking for prey, as they wander along the great Clayton sauropod trackway. By Doug Henderson. Preceding spread: Tyrannosaurs *attack the heavily armored ankylosaur,* Edmontonia, *on a Late Cretaceous plain. By Brian Franczak.*

when I populated an entire planet of our closest stellar neighbor with a complete Mesozoic biota. So it was with great pleasure indeed that I agreed to work with Byron Preiss and Martin Harry Greenberg on this unique collection of stories, articles, and illustrations designed to bring back to life as well as words and pictures are capable of doing the era of the mighty saurians.

There is more, of course, to the appeal of the dinosaurs than the great size of the most familiar species and the fantastic strangeness of their form. The enormous intellectual puzzles posed by the existence and sustained survival of these extraordinary beasts are some of the most stimulating and challenging scientific mysteries of the twentieth century.

How, for example, did they manage to dominate their world for so phenomenally long a time? We know that the earliest dinosaur-like creatures were present on earth at least 225 million years ago, inaugurating a reign that would endure for some 160 million years. We can barely comprehend an era so lengthy — we who can trace our own ancestry back a paltry few million years to the protohuman primates of the late Pliocene, and who did not reach something approximating our present evolutionary form until just a few hundred thousand years ago. The whole period of mankind's existence is just a tick of the clock compared with the length of the dinosaurs' stay on earth.

And if the riddle of their extraordinary durability is a mystifying one, what about the enigma of their extinction? After having ruled the world so long, they appear to have vanished totally, some 65 to 70 million years ago, within a period of no more than a few million years. That is in itself no brief moment, of course; but on the geological scale of things it is an incredibly short time for the wiping out of a race as hardy as the dinosaurs. So not only the problem of their extended survival but also the puzzle of their relatively swift disappearance has been a major concern of scientists.

More recently, with the development of modern analytic techniques, speculations of the most startling sort have been put forth concerning the nature of dinosaur metabolism and intelligence. Were they, as has long been thought, mere sluggish dull-witted behemoths, helpless prisoners of their environments like all cold-blooded creatures? Or is it possible that they were intelligent and adaptable warm-blooded animals far more capable of coping with life's challenges than the early paleontologists ever suspected? This astonishing theory — elaborately buttressed with a variety of scientific evidence — has touched off one of the liveliest scientific controversies of modern times.

In *The Ultimate Dinosaur* we have brought together a spectacular group of scientists — Dr. Anthony Fiorillo of the Carnegie Museum of Natural History, Dr. Philip Currie of Canada's Tyrrell Museum, Dr. Ralph Molnar of Australia, and many more — to provide a richly detailed survey of the latest discoveries and hypotheses along the dynamic frontiers of paleontology. Then we have invited some of science fiction's most distinguished writers to contribute that dimension of imaginative vividness that is their special province — such people as Ray Bradbury, L. Sprague de Camp, Poul Anderson, Harry Harrison, and Gregory Benford, to name only a few. Finally, a roster of artists famed for their visual recreation of other times and places has done a dazzling series of illustrations — Doug Henderson, William G. Stout, John Gurche, Wayne D. Barlowe, and others whose work has enlivened the walls of many museums and the pages of any number of books.

What you hold in your hands, therefore, is the collaborative effort of forty or fifty people who in one way or another have responded over many years with intense imaginative and intellectual effort to the mystery and splendor of the dinosaurs. We offer it to you with great pride and satisfaction — knowing that you, too, have experienced the same shivers of wonder, the same rapture of awe, that these wonderful creatures have called forth in each of us since the first moment we became aware of their existence.

— ROBERT SILVERBERG

DINOSAURS FOR ADULTS

PETER DODSON

THE NEWS IS THAT DINOSAURS AREN'T JUST FOR KIDS. WE ADULTS HAVE RECLAIMED THEM. The kids can have their mutated turtles and their Muppets. Dinosaurs fill a need in the human psyche for the exotic, the bizarre, the exciting. Anyone who doubts the dragons of the mind has never visited the great gothic cathedrals of France to see the tortured figures frozen in stone around their buttresses and spires. Adults too fond of the Brothers Grimm may be subject to scrutiny, but dinosaurs have a cachet of social respectability—not only are they fantastic but they are real! We didn't have to invent them. Indeed they are firmly within the domain of natural science. When such a distinguished scientist and public figure as Stephen Jay Gould says "bully for *Brontosaurus*!," who are we to resist?

A convincing case can be made that we are now living in the golden age of dinosaur paleontology. The evidence is both scientific and popular. Scientifically, for the past twenty years new dinosaurs have been described at the rate of one every eight weeks. There are three times that number of dinosaur paleontologists active today around the world then there were sixty years ago. More than forty percent of the three hundred kinds (or genera) of dinosaurs that we recognize today were unknown before 1970. Discoveries of brainy, active, small meat-eating dinosaurs such as *Deinonychus* spawned ideas that dinosaurs, at least some of them, may have been warm-blooded, and that birds sprang from dinosaurs—indeed may even *be* dinosaurs. Particularly exciting areas where major discoveries are being made today include Argentina, Mongolia and China. Dinosaurs were unrecorded from Antarctica until 1987, when an ankylo-saur was reported by a scientific party from Argentina, and in the winter of 1991 a prosauropod discovery made it onto the front pages of our newspapers. Major discoveries of arctic dinosaurs in Alaska appeared in scientific reports in 1987. I predict that our knowledge of new kinds of dinosaurs will continue to grow for 200 years, and that by the year 2200 we will have found more than 700 kinds of dinosaurs. I also believe that the actual number of kinds of dinosaurs that have ever lived is between 1000 and 1200 genera. So there is still lots more work for us (and our children).

Not only is a scientific flowering of international scope underway, but the fruits of this work are available to an interested public as never before. In England 150 years ago, Richard Owen announced the name "dinosaur" in a bold speech before a distinguished scientific audience. Whatever the reaction of the sages, his message was entirely inaccessible to the British public. Owen's bold inference was based on only a few handfulls of fossils—no one had yet seen anything like a complete skeleton. It was ten years later, when Owen worked with the colorful artist and sculptor Waterhouse Hawkins, that dinosaurs began to take vivid shape. The Crystal Palace monsters were life-sized hypothetical reconstructions in plaster of Mesozoic reptiles. Victorian Londoners flocked there in droves, and "dinosaurmania" has been with us ever since. The powerful tradition of the artist working with the scientist is evident today as a whole corpus of beautifully executed art brings new scientific work to life. In 1977 artist Ely Kish worked with paleontologist Dale Russell to bring a vanished world to life, the dinosaurs of Western Canada. More recently Doug Henderson worked with paleontologist Jack Horner to trace the life history of the duckbill *Maiasaura* from eggs in the nest to adulthood, and John Sibbick worked with Dr. David Norman to illustrate the entire spectrum of dinosaurs. Other artists whose work combines attention to scientific detail with sometimes breathtaking liveliness and imagination include such artists as John Gurche, Mark Hallett, and Brian Franczak, with new artists bowing every day. With leading paleontologists and conscientious journalists writing for the public and illustrating their works with fine art, the trickle of information once available is now a torrent. A Dinosaur Society consisting of leading dinosaur paleontologists, along with representatives of art and writing, has now been formed, one of whose goals is to help insure that the public receives accurate, up-to-date information.

In that vein, we are pleased to present an overview of dinosaur paleontology as seen through the eyes of a group of paleontologists that represent the diversity of our dynamic field. Our writers come from the United States, Canada, Poland, India and Australia, are early in their careers or are more established, are male and female, are conservative or less so. Sankar Chatterjee writes about the remote world when dinosaurs were first beginning. The world was very different then, with the continents joined in a huge supercontinent called Pangaea. The earth was recovering from an ice age, dryness was widespread, and there were no colorful flowering plants. Not long ago Chatterjee electrified the paleontological community with the claim of the first bird, from Triassic rocks of Texas, 75 million years earlier than the previous candidate, *Archaeopteryx* from Germany. His find is controversial but extremely interesting. Catherine Forster details the evidence of earliest dinosaurs, especially those from Argentina and Brazil. She recently had the privilege of digging early dinosaurs in Argentina. The new specimens she talks about will help us define more precisely exactly what a dinosaur is.

Teresa Maryanska is a Polish paleontologist who works on dinosaurs of Mongolia, where she has dug many times. She provides an overview of the kinds of dinosaurs throughout the entire Mesozoic, and what the principle characteristics are by which we may distinguish them. David Gillette has made his mark by discovering what may be the largest dinosaur in the world, *Seismosaurus*, a sauropod possibly 140 feet long from Jurassic rocks of New Mexico. He describes a world in which the continents began to split apart, in which crocodiles, turtles and mammals flourished, and the greatest dinosaurs of all time roamed about. Tony Fiorillo has worked among the giant dinosaurs at the Carnegie Museum in Pittsburgh. He has dug in the sauropod beds of the American west, and has done field paleontology on two other continents as well. He describes the most fascinating dinosaurs of all, the giant sauropods, as well as their contemporaries. China is now known to be a major center for Jurassic dinosaurs, with more kinds of stegosaurs than anywhere else on earth. Like Maryanska, Halszka Osmolska is a Polish paleontologist specializing in Mongolian dinosaurs, especially small meat-eaters. She describes every-

A herd of Muttaburrasaurs *wanders by a Lower Cretaceous antarctic lake shore. By William G. Stout.*

one's favorites, the predators, including *Tyrannosaurus, Deinonychus,* and a bizarre new horned carnivore from Argentina, *Carnotaurus.* Ralph Molnar left the United States for Australia more than 15 years ago, but his thoughts about dinosaurs roam all over the world. Here he brings meat-eating dinosaurs to life, fleshing out their bones with fascinating musings on how they used their teeth, the strength of their bones, their running speeds and body temperatures.

Willian Gallagher is expert on the fossils of the Atlantic Coast, where America's first dinosaur skeleton, *Hadrosaurus,* was found in 1858. He writes of a world becoming modern, a world of flowering plants, mammals and birds. Ron Rainger is a historian who specializes in American 19th century paleontology. He narrates some of the colorful and slightly disgraceful history of our paleontological forefathers. I hope we behave a little better today! Don Lessem is a science journalist and founder of the Dinosaur Society. He has traveled to China and Mongolia to tell the tale of the dinosaur. He portrays the Late Cretaceous world still populated with dinosaurs, including *Tyranno-*

saurus and *Triceratops*, among the last and greatest of the dinosaurs. Phil Currie has worked for 15 years in some of the richest dinosaur beds in the world, those of western Canada. He has co-directed the Canada-China dinosaur project that has taken him to some of the most remote and exotic dinosaur terrains on this planet. Currie develops interesting new ideas about dinosaur behavior, distribution and migration, some of which follow from the new discoveries of polar dinosaurs.

Ken Carpenter has collected dinosaurs for almost as long as he can remember, and is one of leading mounters of dinosaur skeletons. He reminds us that not all great reptiles of the Mesozoic were dinosaurs. There were many kinds of great marine reptiles that were distantly related to dinosaurs, while the flying pterosaurs were close relatives of dinosaurs. David Archibald is expert on non-dinosaurian vertebrate fossils, especially turtles and mammals that span the time period when dinosaurs became extinct. He offers a real shocker—he tries to convince us that dinosaurs did *not* become extinct, but survive today as the birds on our front lawns. His scheme is completely rational. But are you convinced?

This is our bill of fare. Browse and chew on the essays. Challenge yourself. Relax and enjoy the imaginative fiction. Admire the art. Bring yourself up to date. Dinosaurs aren't just for kids anymore.

— PETER DODSON

1.
THE DAWN OF THE DINOSAURS
ESSAY BY SANKAR CHATTERJEE
SPECULATION BY L. SPRAGUE DE CAMP

THE DAWN OF THE AGE OF DINOSAURS

SANKAR CHATTERJEE

THE TRIASSIC PERIOD OF EARTH HISTORY, SPANNING FROM 245 TO 208 MILLION YEARS AGO, WAS THE INITIAL period of the Mesozoic and a time of major change for the world's land animals.

The Triassic began after the most catastrophic mass extinction event in geologic history. Perhaps as much as 96 percent of all species disappeared at the end of the Permian. The main land-based victims were the therapsids, advanced mammal-like reptiles. There were drastic geographic changes as the Permian drew to a close. Plate movements, mountain building, violent volcanism, and regression of the seas produced major changes in the global distribution of continents and oceans that destroyed the habitats of many organisms. Climates became more severe, with marked seasonal changes and aridity in many areas. All these catastrophes contributed heavily to the breakdown of stable ecological communities and disrupted the biosphere. In the aftermath of the Permian extinctions, some forms of life rebounded. Groups of animals that formerly played minor roles now assumed prominence, and new groups appeared.

By the Late Triassic, archosaurs (thecodonts, crocodiles, and dinosaurs) had replaced therapsids as the dominant land vertebrates. This was a time when mammals originated from small therapsids, while the aerial vertebrates such as pterosaurs, kuehneosaurid lizards, and possibly birds first appeared to conquer the last frontier of ecospace. The Triassic also witnessed the emergence of frogs, turtles, and crocodiles. It was a crucial period in the history of vertebrate evolution and radiation.

BIRTH AND BREAKUP OF PANGAEA

When the Triassic Period began, all of the major continents of the world were joined into a single colossal supercontinent called Pangaea. It allowed animals the opportunity to migrate back and forth from continent to continent. Pangaea was surrounded by Panthalassa, the ancestral Pacific Ocean, and was composed of two landmasses: Laurasia in the north, and Gondwana in the south. A narrow bay of the Tethys Sea, comparable to the present Mediterranean, lay between Indo-Africa and Eurasia. Today, the former position of the Tethys is marked roughly by the Alpine-Himalayan mountain belt. One of the most remarkable features of the Triassic was the widespread emergence of continents and the subsequent recession of seas from the continents, as well as the extensive spread of nonmarine deposits, composed largely of redbeds. These redbeds were deposited in a complex river-deltaic-lake system in many parts of the world. Today, they are known from India, Argentina, Brazil, South Africa, East Africa, Germany, Great Britain, China, the United States, and Canada, and have produced a rich record of Triassic vertebrate fauna.

The unity of Pangaea was short-lived. At the end of the Triassic, Pangaea began to break apart, and the continents ultimately shifted to their present positions on the globe. During this initial fragmentation, a rift was opened in the southwest Indian Ocean, moving South America and Africa away from Antarc-

tica-Australia. The Atlantic Ocean was beginning to open. When the Atlantic opened, huge fractures in the crust of Nova Scotia, New Jersey and Connecticut served as conduits for great outpourings of lava. The ancestral Gulf of Mexico began to take form farther south. While the rifting was occurring, a large meteorite fell to Earth in the wilds of central Quebec to produce the giant Manicouagan Crater, about 100 kilometers across (half the size of Connecticut). It was a time of major environmental disruption. Another mass extinction struck both in the ocean and on the land at the end of the Triassic. It eliminated a wide range of land vertebrates. Surprisingly, the dinosaurs went unscathed, and proliferated after this crisis to dominate terrestrial habitats.

FLORA AND PALEOCLIMATE

The Permian had been characterized by extremes in climate. While the northern landmasses were relatively warm and sometimes arid, the southern Gondwana continents exhibited scars of widespread glaciations. At the advent of the Triassic, *Glossopteris* flora of Gondwana disappeared. The topography and climate became more uniform, since Pangaea was symmetrically disposed above and below the equator. The paleoclimate was dominated by monsoonal circulation. Dense forests and swamps covered the land from the equator to high latitudes. Many of the land plants in the Permian Period such as conifers, sphenopsids, ferns, and seed ferns continued into the Triassic, while other gymnosperms such as cycads, cycadeoids and ginkgos appeared for the first time. Cycads were tall, tropical trees with rough columnar branches, superficially resembling palms. Cycadeoids, which were closely related to cycads, are now extinct. The ginkgo has the characteristic fan-shaped leaf, and is extensively used as a street tree in Washington, D.C., New York City, and other urban areas. No other plant has so effectively captured the imagination of people, from the standpoint of its past history, as has the ginkgo, because of its association with some early dinosaurs. It has the longest lineage of all trees, and is a true living fossil.

The cycads, cycadeoids, conifers, and ginkgos formed the tropical forests in many parts of the world during the Triassic Period. We have collected abundant plant fossils from the Triassic deposits of Antarctica, which include the seed fern *Dicroidium*, horsetails, and ferns. The *Dicroidium* flora flourished in Gondwanaland during the Triassic. Today horsetails and ferns inhabit the banks of streams and lakes and typically exist in temperate and tropical regions where there is abundant moisture. Their presence in Antarctica indicates that the temperatures in the polar region were probably warm and temperate in order to support such lowland, swamp-like vegetation.

In the United States, we get two glimpses of the Triassic flora — one in the foliage preserved in the dark shales of the Newark group in the east coast (Virginia and the Carolinas), the other in the petrified logs of Arizona. The first was a swamp of ferns and horsetails, much like is seen in parts of the Everglades today. The Petrified Forest National Park of Arizona, on the other hand, has yielded chiefly petrified logs of conifers along with leaf impressions of ferns and cycads. The floral community was composed of a dense canopy forest of conifer trees with an understory of ferns. The conifer trees were composed entirely of *Araucarioxylon*, which were over 200 feet tall, with straight, more or less unbranched trunks under a canopy of small leafy branches at the top. The Triassic landscape of Arizona resembled the modern redwood forests of the Pacific Coast.

At the end of the Triassic, the environment became more savanna-like with a shift to drier and more arid habitats. This is reflected by the occurrence

Above: Coelophysis *roams a barren plain east of the Rockies, volcanic smokers in the background. By Doug Henderson. Preceding spread: Among the* earliest of the meat-eaters, these Coelophysis *are hunting along a Late Triassic forest floor. By Brian Franczak.*

of dune sands over a large area found in the interior of several continents. Evaporite deposits of anhydrite and gypsum were formed in the circum-Atlantic rifting and circum-Tethyan zones, and evoke a picture of coastal deserts such as near the modern Red Sea. The vegetation became sparse; consequently, competition for food and resources must have become intense among the vertebrates.

RISE OF THE REPTILES

The Triassic was an extraordinary time in reptilian history. Conquest of the land by reptiles, begun in the Late Carboniferous coal swamp, was accomplished during the Triassic. Both on the land and sea reptiles became the ruling vertebrates. The record of their spectacular radiation, which includes the genesis of birds and mammals, is one of the fascinating histories in the evolution of life.

THERAPSIDS

In the Early Triassic, the therapsids quickly rebounded from their severe losses in the Permian to dominate the Pangaean landscape. The therapsids early on cleaved into two major lines: a herbivorous side branch, of which the dicynodonts are the most prominent members, and one of mainly carnivorous forms leading essentially in a mammalian direction. The dicynodonts became worldwide in distribution in the Early and Middle Triassic. They ranged from the size of a squirrel to that of an ox. A short, heavy neck, a broad barrel-shaped body, and a tiny tail were the distinguishing external features of these animals. Most were terrestrial, but some lived in holes like prairie dogs, while others were aquatic like the hippopotamus. These "two-tusked" herbivores were the dominant four-limbed animals in the Early and Middle Triassic, but became extinct at the end of the Triassic. Some dicynodonts lacked tusks; their absence may have been a sexual characteristic of females of some species.

Lystrosaurus, one of Early Triassic dicynodonts, has been recovered from South Africa, Antarctica, India, China, Indochina and Russia. Their broad distribution indicates that these animals could migrate back and forth across Pangaea. *Lystrosaurus* was about the size of a sheep, with a robust body, rather short, thick legs, a very short tail, and a peculiar skull in which there were just two teeth, consisting of a large tusk on each side. The toothless jaws were obviously sheathed with a horny covering, like the beak of a turtle, which was helpful in tearing tough plants. The food was pulverized entirely by shearing. *Lystrosaurus* was replaced by similar large, tusked mammal-like reptiles, such as *Kennemeyeria* and its relatives, in the Middle Triassic. Their fossils have been found in North and South America, Africa, Australia, India, China, and Russia. The wide distribution of dicyno-

donts supports the theory of plate tectonics and is evidence of the existence of a single land mass before the plates bearing the modern continents moved apart. The remains of *Placerias*, the last survivor of the dicynodonts in the Late Triassic, were found in abundance in the Petrified Forest of Arizona.

In many parts of the world, fossils of dicynodonts have often been associated with those of carnivorous therapsids, like cynodonts, indicating a predator-prey relationship among the communities. Cynodonts may be compared with wolves in modern ecosystems. They were stubby-bodied animals—short neck, short tail, short legs. The front and hind limbs were nearly equal in length, in contrast to those of the ruling reptiles. They possessed incisors, canines, and molar-like teeth. They display several mammalian traits such as complex cheek teeth, secondary palate, enlargement of the lower jaw bone (dentary), and an expanded adductor chamber allowing for powerful muscles to work the jaw. They were probably warm-blooded, and were capable of killing and dismembering prey as large as dicynodonts. One of the Early Triassic cynodonts, *Thrinaxodon*, has been found in Africa and Antarctica, suggesting a biotic link between these two continents. Another, larger form, *Cynognathus*, has been found in South America and South Africa, indicating a similar continental connection. For paleontologists, cynodonts are among the most fascinating of fossils because they provide the evolutionary link between reptiles and mammals. Some cynodonts, such as traversodonts and tritylodonts, evolved back to become herbivorous and were widely dispersed. Traversodonts continued to survive nearly to the end of the Triassic, with the tritylodonts persisting into the Middle Jurassic as the last surviving therapsids. Tritylodonts were highly specialized cynodonts with molarlike cheek teeth showing multiple roots as in mammals.

LEPIDOSAURS

Lepidosaurs are by far the most diverse of modern reptiles, consisting of lizards, snakes, and sphenodontids, but their fossil record is poorly documented in the Triassic. There are approximately 6,000 different species of lizards and snakes living today, chiefly in tropical regions. Unlike other reptilian groups, the snakes are still a rapidly evolving assemblage; their earliest records are known from the Cretaceous Period.

The earliest lizard, *Paliguana*, is known from the Permo-Triassic boundary of South Africa. However, the fossil record of lizards remains blank for most of the Triassic. By the Late Jurassic, modern lizards appeared in many parts of the world, and they continue to be important elements in the world fauna. In the Late Triassic, some lizards, such as kuehneosaurids, developed gliding abilities. They were characterized by the elongation of the ribs to support a membrane that allowed this reptile to sail from tree to tree, much as does the modern lizard, *Draco*, of the Orient. The "wingspan" was about 12 inches. When the rib wings were folded, they formed a crest over the animal's back.

Sphenodontids, which appeared in the Late Triassic, still survive in New Zealand as an endangered species, the *Sphenodon* or tuatara. The modern form shows very little change from its Triassic ancestor, and is called a living fossil.

PRIMITIVE ARCHOSAUROMORPHS

Some Triassic reptiles, such as protorosaurs and rhynchosaurs, were traditionally grouped with lepidosaurs. Recent work shows that these reptiles are more closely related to archosaurs and may be included in a larger assemblage called the archosauromorphs.

The protorosaurs appeared in the Late Permian, and were very successful during the Triassic Period,

being recorded from all continents except South America. They were small, gracile, long-necked animals, similar to lizards in size, proportions, and inferred activities. They show a skull configuration similar to lizards. The similarity of protorosaurs to lizards is superficial, and is an example of convergent evolution. Some of the protorosaurs adapted to marine life. Others became bipeds like the modern basilisk lizard, and could run effectively.

Rhynchosaurs were widely distributed reptiles during the Triassic, and have been recorded from Europe, North and South America, India, and East Africa. They were small quadrupeds in the Early Triassic, but became progressively bigger and more heavily built in the Middle and Late Triassic. They were then about the size of a large pig, with sprawling limbs and large claws, while the skull was short and broad with a pair of bony beaks in front. Rhynchosaurs have highly specialized dentition with multiple tooth rows in the upper jaws, separated by a central groove. The lower jaw forms a sharp cutting edge that fits into the groove of the upper jaw like a chopper. The diet of rhynchosaurs probably included various fruits, seeds, rhizomes, or even mollusks. The teeth have long roots and were fused to the bone. I have named this unusual tooth implantation in rhynchosaurs "ankylothecodont." The most remarkable feature of the teeth is that they were not regularly replaced as in most reptiles, but were continually added backward as the jaws grew.

Another peculiar Late Triassic archosauromorph is the trilophosaur, known mainly from the American Southwest. The skull has a toothless beak, presumably horn-covered, but the cheek teeth are transversely widened and three-cusped, well suited to munching thick leaves, soft stems, and fruits. The teeth suggest an affinity with rhynchosaurs. Unlike other primitive archosauromorphs, trilophosaurs had a solid cheek.

THECODONTS

Thecodonts have long been recognized as the stock from which all other archosaurs (such as dinosaurs and crocodilians) were derived. They arose in the Late Permian and diversified throughout the Triassic Period. They can be distinguished from the primitive archosauromorphs by the presence of an opening in the skull in front of the eye, the antorbital fenestra.

Thecodonts are a diverse assemblage and their interrelationships are not fully known and agreed upon by experts, but, as a whole, they show the initiation of archosaurian tendencies. I have recognized three distinct lineages of thecodonts based on the configuration of ankle structure: Proterosuchia, Pseudosuchia, and Ornithosuchia (for the latter see Chapter 2). In these groups the nature of articulation of two large ankle bones, the astragalus and calcaneum, is the basis for classification. In Proterosuchia, these bones are firmly articulated without any movement between them. This is the most primitive lineage, and includes various early forms such as *Archosaurus, Proterosuchus*, and *Erythrosuchus*. Proterosuchians were powerful, big-headed predators, with sprawling limbs similar to the crocodilians.

In the pseudosuchian lineage, there is a peg and socket joint between the two ankle bones allowing rotational movement between them. The peg is on the astragalus, and the socket is on the calcaneum. This pattern of ankle joint is also recognized in modern crocodiles and is referred to as the "crocodile-normal" pattern. Phytosaurs, aetosaurs, and rauisuchians are included within the Pseudosuchia. Phytosaurs were long-snouted aquatic animals similar to modern gharials in India. Aetosaurs were heavily armored herbivores with erect gait (all four limbs directly under the body) and superficially resembled the ankylosaur dinosaur. Rauisuchians were the largest terrestrial carnivores during the Middle and Late Triassic with lengths of up to 20 feet, and a developed erect posture. Some of

the rauisuchians, such as *Postosuchus*, were highly specialized bipeds, with a swivel wrist joint as found in very advanced theropod dinosaurs and birds, and looked like a scaled-down version of *Tyrannosaurus*. *Postosuchus* was the lord of the predators in the American Southwest. The pseudosuchian lineage eventually gave rise to crocodilians, probably in the Late Triassic.

TRIASSIC WARFARE: COMPETITION AND EXTINCTION

Darwin considered the struggle for existence in a wide sense, including the competition of organisms for possession of common places in nature, as well as their destruction of one another. When food is abundant and the food chain is stabilized, different animals may coexist without much interference. However, when food is in short supply, animals with similar ecologic requirements will compete with each other. Consequently, one competitor will inevitably exploit the resource more efficiently and will increase numerically at the expense of the other. In general, the progressive types prevailed, and the archaic forms disappeared under the pressure of competition. The history of Triassic vertebrates depicts three such episodes of interspecific competition and subsequent replacement of one species by another.

The replacement of therapsids by thecodonts is the first evidence of competitive exclusion in the Triassic. In the Permian, therapsids were the dominant predators in the ecosystem. In the Early and Middle Triassic, the therapsid monopoly on the large predator role was broken in a series of steps by the adaptive radiation of thecodonts. Thecodonts became larger, and developed erect posture. Their skull was fairly large, equipped with the sharp teeth of a formidable carnivore. Bipedality developed in several thecodont lines, which permitted them to move about more quickly than the sprawling therapsids. The forelimbs, being freed from locomotory function, were used for capturing and killing prey. Cynodonts could not compete with thecodonts for food and were soon replaced by them.

The second wave of extinction may be related to over-predation of many species. In the early part of the Late Triassic (Carnian stage), thecodonts and dinosaurs coexisted in tropical forest environments in many parts of the world. The lush vegetation must have supported abundant food for herbivores, as well as cover and camouflage for a variety of prey and predators. A large number of prey species was available to thecodonts and theropods (the carnivorous dinosaurs), as evident from the fossil record. Dicynodonts, rhynchosaurs, protorosaurs, and trilophosaurs are the most common groups in the adequately known fauna. They were slow and defenseless and were accessible to predators. I have recovered rhynchosaur and protorosaur remains in the stomach contents of phytosaurs (early theropods). On the other hand, lizards and sphenodontids were small, and could hide or escape from predators by climbing or digging. The aetosaurs were heavily armored for protection and could only be subdued by large predators such as rauisuchians with their stabbing teeth. Thecodonts were more robust and larger than the contemporary dinosaurs and at this era were still able to compete successfully with dinosaurs wherever they came into extensive contact with them.

At the end of the Carnian, a major crisis developed in terrestrial ecosystems. Most of the accessible prey species such as rhynchosaurs, large trilophosaurs, and dicynodonts became extinct in response to over-predation. Both thecodonts and theropods contributed heavily to the decline and extinction of these groups. The food chain became unbalanced, and prey-switching became inevitable. Competition for food may have become more intense among large predators.

The third wave of extinction can be seen at the end of the Triassic, when thecodonts were replaced by dinosaurs. The crisis was compounded at this time, as arid climates became more widespread, and the environment became more open savanna. Due to scarcity of vegetation and decline of prey populations, the struggle for existence became severe, and the balance of competitive advantage between thecodonts and dinosaurs shifted. In an open-country environment, great speed and endurance were advantageous for survival. Although some thecodonts approached erect posture, they walked flat-footed and were relatively slow in locomotion. In contrast, early dinosaurs were fully erect, gracile bipeds, and walked on their toes like birds. The early dinosaurs could run faster with longer strides than the contemporary thecodonts. The refined locomotion and running adaptation of both herbivorous and carnivorous dinosaurs allowed them to roam large territories for food. The herbivorous dinosaurs were swift and agile and could easily escape from most predators. They exploited new resources for foraging. With long necks and tripodal pose (long hindlimbs and stout tail for support), they could reach high up in the foliage and pluck vegetation. They had specialized dentition for dealing with resistant plant material, the type that would be expected in drier climates.

In contrast, the herbivorous thecodonts such as aetosaurs foraged mainly on the ground. Their chance of survival deteriorated as the lowland plants became scarce in the more arid climates. With the emergence of the running prey population, thecodonts were unable to meet their food requirements. They could not escape direct interactions with the dinosaurs during the condition of extreme stress. They began to decline and soon became extinct at the end of the Triassic. Morphological novelties such as locomotory refinement, improved foraging techniques, and exploitation of new resources seem to have given dinosaurs a competitive edge over thecodonts.

CROCAMANDER QUEST

L. SPRAGUE DE CAMP

PLEASE, MS. BROWNLEE! I ASSURE YOU I HAVE NOTHING AGAINST WOMEN. I'VE BEEN MARRIED to one — the same one — for twenty-odd years, and we get along fine.

Even if I'm not a male chauvinist, though, I bloody well won't change my rule against taking ladies on time safaris, at least along with men. Not that women can't rough it in the outback as well as men. But when you mix the sexes in a small, close group, you're asking for trouble. When people are thrown together so intimately, they either form close attachments or come to hate one another. Adding the sexual factor merely makes a difficult situation impossible. I'll tell you how we once tried such a mixed party and what came of it.

If your women's-rights organization would like to get up an all-woman time safari, we'll consider it. Of course I should have to see how my wife would take it. When she heard I had signed up five clients, including a woman, to the Triassic, she said:

"Reginald Rivers, what on earth are you thinking of? Having a quickie in the cycads with this bird? You're asking for problems."

I assured her I had nothing of the sort in mind, but in the end she could have said: "I told you so!" Not that the dear girl ever said it aloud; but I knew she was thinking it.

About the time Aiyar and I launched this mixed safari... that's Chandra Aiyar in the photo on the wall, the dark chap with the dead dinosaur. I call him "Raja" because he's the hereditary ruler of some little place in India named Janpur. Of course that's purely honorary nowadays, like the title of that Frenchman, the Comte de Lautrec, who had his head taken off by a flick of the tail of a sauropod he annoyed.

I'd been getting some flak about our men-only policy; so the Raja and I thought we'd try a mixed safari once to see how it worked. There was a couple named Alvarado, Tomás and Inez, who wanted to go back to the Age of Reptiles. Tom Alvarado was a stout Spaniard who made his living singing in operas. He must have been bloody good at it, to be able to afford a time safari. They weren't much interested in hunting or trophy collecting; but they were ambitious travelers, who had covered all the continents and most of the countries of the present-day Earth and were looking for something new. They weren't even going to take a gun; but I persuaded them to rent a nine-millimeter Mannlicher. Otherwise the party would have been a little too lightly armed for safety.

It jarred me a bit when Tom introduced Mrs. Alvarado as "my former wife, Inez." (He pronounced it to rhyme with "Macbeth.") When I asked him about this later, he said: "Oh, yes, Inez and I have been divorced for years. We could not stand living together; but then we found we liked each other better than anyone else around. So we do what *americanos* call 'going steady'."

Well, I didn't consider his private arrangements, no matter how bizarre, any of my business. Inez was a Yank of, I believe, Mexican antecedents; quite a stunner in a black-haired Latin way.

The Raja and I decided we wouldn't send them to the Jurassic or Cretaceous, when one finds the most spectacular dinosaurs, because of the risk. We also had a prospect who was keen to get to the Triassic but couldn't afford to do it solo, because his grant from the Auckland Museum of Natural History wouldn't cover the fees. We had to charge high to include the costs to Professor Prochaska's laboratory, since the time machine uses fantastic amounts of electric power.

This third sahib was a New Zealander, Professor Doctor Sir Edred Ngata, a paleontologist. He was a picturesque bloke, two meters tall, built like a locomotive, with a leather-brown skin and bushy black hair just beginning to gray. He must have been at least three-quarters Maori. I was glad to have a Kiwi along, who wouldn't poke fun at my accent.

The reason Ngata was keen for the Triassic, where the wildlife is less spectacular than it becomes later, is that he wanted to study all the little lizardy creatures to find out which were the ancestors of the reptiles and mammals of later times. He told me:

"Also, Mr. Rivers, I want to study the distribution of the later rachitomes—"

"Excuse me," I said, "the racket *whats*?"

"Rachitomes, or their offshoot the stereospondyls. They're orders of amphibians, in decline in the Triassic but still abundant and including some large creatures like *Paracyclotosaurus* from your own Australia. Imagine a newt or salamander expanded to crocodile size, with a huge head for catching smaller fry, and you'll have the idea."

"Might call it a 'crocamander,' eh? At least that's easier to say than the name you just gave it."

Ngata chuckled. "True; but the short, easy Latin names have been pretty well used up by now."

"I see," I said. "Trouble is, I no sooner get one of those jaw-breaking names memorized than you blokes go and change them, or at least change the classification. But why particularly crocamanders?"

He explained: "They help to date the breakup of Pangaea."

"You mean that super-continent that, they say, once included them all?"

"Right-o. The breakup started in the Triassic. First the northern half, which we call Laurasia, separated from the southern, or Gondwanaland, when the Tethys Sea formed between them. So if we find one of your—ah—crocamanders very similar to one of ours in the southern continent, in the land that became North America, we can be fairly sure that the land connection between the two parts of Pangaea still existed."

"Why couldn't crocamanders swim from one to the other, the way the saltwater crocodile does?"

"Because most amphibians can't take saltwater, with those soft, moist skins."

The fourth sahib was an American, Desmond Carlyle, who knew the Alvarados. He was a good-sized fellow, well-set-up with sandy hair and a little blond mustache. He had done a bit of mountaineering and had the old idea that it proves one's manhood to hang the stuffed heads of large wild animals on one's wall. I've outgrown that sort of thing myself; but I don't discourage it because it keeps clients coming in to the firm of Rivers and Aiyar, Time Safaris. Carlyle hoped to work up to a Cretaceous safari for a *Tyrannosaurus* head but thought a Triassic jaunt would be a good way to get broken in.

Last to join was a young man named Willard Smith. He was from one of those complicated families where both parents had been divorced and remarried ever-so-many times. One of his many stepfathers had given him the time trip as a present on his graduation from college. I've always heard that such extended families are a sure way to produce juvenile delinquents, addicts, and criminals; but young Smith didn't show any such symptoms. He did, however, confide:

"Mr. Rivers, I hope you won't mind that I'm a klutz."

"Eh?" I said. "What's that? Some sort of secret society, demanding compulsory birth control for comedians or something?"

"No, no, nothing like that. It's Pennsylvania Dutch for an awkward, clumsy person."

That gave me pause. I said: "Well, I don't know. If you're that kind of gawk, how do I know you won't trip over a root and blow somebody's head off?"

"Oh, I'm not interested in shooting," said Smith. "I'll be quite happy just tagging along and taking pictures. That's my real enthusiasm."

A little against my better judgment, I let Smith's registration stand. I told myself to keep an extra-close watch on young Willard. In former geological eras, if you gash yourself with a skinning knife, or shoot yourself in the foot, or step in a hole and break your leg, there's no telephoning the ambulance to come fetch you to the hospital. But if Smith didn't carry a gun, at least he couldn't accidentally shoot any of the rest of us.

Hunting dinosaurs isn't especially dangerous *if* you make all your moves smoothly and correctly, and don't commit foolish mistakes like catching a twig in the mechanism of your gun, or stepping on the tail of a sleeping carnosaur, or then climbing a small tree the dinosaur can pluck you out of. Even clumsiness isn't fatal if you have sound judgment, are in complete control of yourself, and take whatever extra care is needed to make up for your lack of coördination.

So on a fine spring day we gathered with our gear at Professor Prochaska's laboratory here in St. Louis. The service personnel were our longtime herder Beauregard Black, two camp helpers, and a cook. By then the Raja and I were experienced enough so we didn't feel that both had to be along on every safari. One could stay behind to hold down the office; that's why I'm here now, while the Raja takes a group back to the Eocene.

This time, however, we agreed that the Raja should come along, because the period was new and also because it was our first safari mixed as to sex and therefore an experiment. The Raja is better at human relations than I. He can calm down an excited man — excuse me, person — or cheer up a despondent one, or jolly along a bad-tempered one in a way I've always envied.

On other safaris we had taken the party coasting about the local area, breaking camp and setting it up again half a dozen times. We decided that this time, since we had some decided tenderfeet, one a female, we had better leave the camp where we first pitched it and merely make one-day walkabouts in different directions. So we didn't need a train of packasses to haul our gear around the country.

Eh? Why don't we use off-trail vehicles? In the first place, we could take only those of the smallest kind — practically toys — because of the size of the transition chamber. In the second, there's no source of petrol in case we run low on fuel. In the third, Mesozoic country is often so overgrown and poorly drained that even the most versatile vehicle would have a hard time. And lastly, if your jeep breaks down or skids into the river, it's done for; you can't get it back to the transition chamber. The asses, on the other hand, can live off the country; and in dire straits you can eat them — if some hungry carnivore doesn't beat you to it. You can't eat a petrol-powered vehicle.

The sahibs, the sahiba, the Raja and I crowded into the transition chamber with our guns and packs. It was policy for the guns to go first, not knowing what sort of reception committee might be waiting for us. The operator squeezed in after us, closed the door, and worked his buttons and dials.

I had told the laboratory people to set the timer for May first, 175 million B.C. So the chamber wallah set his dials for that date and pressed the red button. The lights went out, leaving the chamber lit by a little battery-powered lamp. The sahibs gave some grunts and groans at the vertigo and vibration, and that horrid feeling of being in free fall. But the Raja and I had been through all this before.

When the spinning dial hands stopped, the operator checked his gauges to make sure he could safely set the chamber down. It wouldn't do to land it in an inland sea or on the side of a cliff. Sometimes he has to move the chamber back and forth in time by half a million years or so to find a soft landing. This time we were lucky to come down on fairly level soil. Another button opened the door.

As usual, I jumped down first, my gun ready. I hadn't been in the Triassic before, but I'd read up on the period. I saw rolling country with water in the distance, and a fairly heavy growth all around of trees and shrubs you find nowadays only in the form of little "living fossils," they call 'em, like horsetails and ferns. For real trees we had araucarias, trees of the ginkgo type, and cycads looking much like palms. No grass, of course; that didn't evolve for another hundred million or so, and likewise no flowers.

The only sample of the fauna I saw on that first look-around was one little lizardy fellow running away on a pair of long hindlegs. I was watching it disappear into the ferns when Sir Edred Ngata shouldered me aside, whipped up his shotgun, and fired, *bang-bang!* at the vanishing two-legger. I said:

"Hey, Sir Edred! You agreed to shoot only when I told you to!"

"I say, I'm frightfully sorry!" said Ngata. "But it looked like a thecodont, one of those that evolved into the big dinosaurs. One of my objectives is to get some specimens to mount or dissect. I suppose I missed; but please, let me go look!"

He started off, but I said: "Damn it, Sir Edred, reload your gun first! And keep heavy buckshot in one barrel!"

He turned back with a shamefaced grin. "You're right, of course. And forget the 'Sir.' Just call me 'Edred,' will you, old boy?" Ngata was an amiable sort of bloke whom it was hard to stay angry with for long.

Meanwhile the rest of the party came out of the chamber, which vanished back to the present to pick up Beauregard and his crew and the kit. All this took a bit of time, during which I scouted around to pick a campsite near a stream.

As soon as camp was pitched, our first job was to get fresh meat. Being unfamiliar with the period, I asked Sir Edred for advice. We wanted an animal, preferably a plant-eater, not too large (which would rot before we got it eaten) or too small (in which case there wouldn't be enough to go round). Ngata said:

"If I were you, I'd try for a dicynodont. I think you'll find them on the higher ground."

"What's a dicynodont like?"

"Just imagine a hairless, saber-toothed sheep and you'll come close."

Since it was too late in the day to start out, we stayed in camp. The service personnel had set up one big tent for themselves and four small ones for the rest of us. I put Ngata and Alvarado in one tent, Carlyle and Smith in another, and gave one to Inez Alvarado. The Raja and I took the remaining tent, since we should have to consult on managing our party. Also, since we went watch-and-watch, there was no use waking up one of our lambs every time we changed watch.

If the Alvarados had been a normal married pair, I should have given them a tent to themselves. But I didn't know if they were currently on a screwing basis — excuse me, Ms. Brownlee — and it's not the sort of thing one cares to ask people right out.

Sleeping proved not so easy as one might think. Besides the big cockroaches, whom the smell of food brought swarming into the camp, the insects included a huge cricket whose chirp sounds like a burglar alarm going off.

Next morning we set out on our routine meat hunt. We went uphill, pushing through vast fern beds; there didn't seem to be any game trails. A heavy growth of ferns can give you a real workout to wade through, so we were soon filthy and drowning in sweat. Besides, the ground is so broken by nullahs that every walk is an up-and-down scramble.

We saw a pair of coelophysids — slender, long-tailed, bipedal flesh-eating therapsids weighing about as much as a small man — ah — person. They were prowling through a fern brake, looking for smaller creatures to snap up in those narrow, toothy jaws. As soon as they saw us they took off and vanished. Carlyle, our one really dedicated hunter, sent a shot after them but missed.

When we got to higher ground, the ferns thinned out. All the while, Smith clicked his camera this way and that. Ngata dashed excitedly about, banging away with his little 28-gauge shotgun. Now and then he came back holding up some little lizardy fellow before popping it into his collecting bag. Once I said:

"There's a little one!"

I pointed to a stubby lizardlike animal, no bigger than a rat. Ngata brought up his shotgun; then said:

"No, better not. It looks like an ictidosaur, and I might shoot one of my own ancestors!"

"At which point, I suppose you'd vanish like a blown-out match flame?"

"Or all of us might," he said.

"More likely, we should all be snatched back to our own times and torn to pieces in the process," I said, "to prevent a paradox. That's what actually happened to one client of mine, who tried to occupy the same time slot twice."

After a couple of hours' hiking, the Alvarados complained of sore feet. So I split up the party, bring-ing Carlyle and Ngata, as the ones most hardened to such stress, along with me, and leaving the others to take a spell with the Raja.

As we climbed, the landscape opened out, with more bare spaces between clumps of trees, mostly looking much like ginkgos, and conifers resembling the modern monkey-puzzle pine. People who expect a Mesozoic landscape to be colorful are apt to be disappointed, since all the plant life is pretty much the same dark, somber green, without flowers. Through one of the gaps in the forest we could see, beyond the next few rises, the big conical shape of a volcano, with a plume of smoke and vapor coming out the top.

Soon after leaving the others, I heard noises of animal life. Ngata began to burble and would have dashed ahead if I had not caught his arm.

"Easy, easy!" I said. "We want to see what we're getting into first."

"But there aren't any *Allosauri* or *Tyrannosauri* in this period...."

"I know," I said, "but from what I've read, some of the carnivores are still big enough to kill you."

So I led the way, peering ahead through the shrubbery and holding my rifle ready. The Raja and I were using .375 magnums. We had left our six-nought-noughts, our real dinosaur killers, back home, figuring that nothing we were likely to meet required such heavy artillery, which is a cow to drag through the bush.

At last we arrived at a little glade in which four dicynodonts were feeding. I crept up, keeping a clump of cycads between me and the animals, until I got a good view through the gaps. Carlyle had lagged behind us, and for some minutes I didn't notice his absence.

There was one male, distinguished by his tusks, and three females. I can't say they reminded me of hairless sheep. Hairless they were, but stoutly built, about the size and shape of your American black bear, with pot-bellied bodies tapering aft to thick reptilian tails. Their heads began with horny beaks like those of turtles, plus those saber tusks on the male.

All four were chomping away at leaves and fronds. Bloody ugly things, I should call them; but then I suppose we should seem equally so to them. When I got ready to shoot, Ngata touched my arm.

"Wait a bit," he said. "I want to observe them first."

So we stood watching, though seeing an animal simply eat, eat, eat soon loses its entertainment value. I was again getting ready to shoot, when Ngata whispered:

"Hold it, Reggie; something's coming!"

The something turned out to be another male dicynodont. The resident male looked up from its eating and uttered a warning grunt.

The newcomer grunted, even louder. For most of a minute these two beggars stood glowering at each other, if anything so expressionless can be said to glower, and grunting.

Then the newcomer yawned, exposing his tusks. The resident male then yawned, too; and all the while they continued to grunt. During this time, Carlyle caught up with us, mumbling something about having to retie his bootlace.

The newcomer moved closer, yawning and grunting. The two circled each other until I was no longer sure which was the newcomer. At last one of the two, whichever it was, made a shambling dash at the other and slashed with his tusks. He laid open a gash in the other's shoulder; and the other backed off, still yawning and grunting. When the wounded one had put enough distance between them, he turned and waddled away. That was all there was to this clash of the titans, if you want to call it that. All the while, the three females kept on munching vegetation as if this duel were no business of theirs.

"Can't leave all three ladies husbandless," I said, and to Carlyle: "Your shot. Take the one on the left."

He fired at the nearest female, and down she went. The remaining three looked around in a vague sort of way but showed no disposition to flee.

"They've never developed a flight reaction to gunfire," said Ngata. "I fear we shall have to chase them away."

He picked up a cycad frond and advanced on the dicynodonts, yelling and waving the frond. Carlyle and I came with him, shouting and waving; and soon the three survivors turned and shambled off in no great hurry.

By the time we reached the carcass, Ngata fell to measuring and writing notes. While he was so engaged, the Raja called from the bush, and presently he appeared with the rest of our party. Young Smith was shooting pictures.

The Raja and I got out our knives to clean the animal, to lighten it for carrying back to camp. I had a folding magnesium carrying pole in my pack. But when I started to cut out the guts, Ngata cried:

"I say, Reggie! You're not going to leave all those lovely intestines here?"

"Certainly," I said. "What's the point of lugging an extra thirty kilos of inedible stuff back to the camp?"

"I need to study all those organs! Don't you realize that nobody has ever described the internal anatomy of a therapsid before? All we've had to work with were bones! It's as if we had stepped out on another planet!"

"Well, if you want to shovel that pile of guts into your specimen bag—"

"I can't do that! The bag's full already!"

"I'm sorry, but we do what we can. What we can't, just doesn't get done. And you'll have other chances. Come on, give me a hand with tying this bugger's feet to the pole!"

By coaxing and bullying, the Raja and I got Sir Edred calmed down enough to lash our beast's feet together so we could carry it suspended from the pole.

Since Ngata and I were the biggest men of the party, it fell to us to bear the pole. The Raja carried my rifle as well as his.

Halfway back, I asked Willard Smith to take my end of the pole, he being the youngest and almost my size, and I not so young as I once had been. I had forgotten about his being what he called a "klutz." But we hadn't gone another fifty meters when Smith tripped over his own feet and fell at on the trail. Since Ngata remained upright, the dicynodont slid down the pole on top of Smith, who got pretty bloody.

So I took back the pole for the rest of the hike. We got back in time for billy, with enough time left over to clean up before a dinner of dicynodont steaks. Our cook, Ming, has learned never to be surprised by the creatures we bring into camp and tell him to cook for us.

While our tucker was cooking, we sat around the fire, telling stories and enjoying a lot of whiskey, while Mrs. Alvarado sat with her feet in a bucket of warm water. Alvarado and Carlyle and Smith also wanted to soak their feet; but there was only one bucket, so I gave Inez the first crack at it.

As for the whiskey, I had served out pretty potent portions; but then Desmond Carlyle demanded seconds.

"No, sorry," I said. "I told you, that one's *it* for tonight."

"Liquor flows like glue here," he grumped. "I could put away half a liter and not feel it."

"Sorry about that," I said. "Our supply is calculated to last the fortnight. I don't want to run short before the chamber returns."

Actually I was more concerned with what might happen if one of my lambs got too disinhibited from liquor. I'd seen that happen on other safaris, where the imbiber did something silly like picking a fight. You never can tell how a person will react to liquor. Some

get talkative, some amorous, some despondent, and some belligerent. The only way to find out is to get them drunk, and the risks were too great in these surroundings, a couple of hundred million years from help.

Carlyle's drink was strong enough, however, to get him talking. He told a fanciful tale of hunting a lion in Africa. From what I know of Africa, it wasn't much of a hunt; there isn't any more of that, really, there. Somebody ran a lion farm and then, when a would-be hero with enough money showed up, he would turn one lion loose in a big private preserve and send the man in with a gun.

Since the lion was semi-tame and had never learned either to attack or to fear a human being, it just lay or stood quietly while the joker walked up and shot the poor beast. A pretty poor idea of sportsmanship, if you ask me. But then, I suspected Carlyle of being a skite with a lot of fictitious adventures he liked to trot out to impress the women.

Then my attention was drawn to Sir Edred Ngata. He was squatting in front of a cloth on which he had laid out a score of specimens he had brought down with birdshot. Except for one primitive tortoise, they were all lizardlike, looking pretty similar to my unscientific eye. The astonishing thing, though, was that tears were running down Ngata's big brown face.

"Edred!" I said. "What's the matter, mate?"

He looked up, choked back a sob, and took a swallow of his drink. "You wouldn't understand, Reggie. I'm suffering from information overload."

"So what? I never heard that too much news was anything to cry over."

"No; it's just that there's such a damned colossal job here to be done, and only one man — me — to do it. I can't even scratch the surface. It's as if you were, say, a historian, and were sent back in time with a copying machine to the Library of Alexandria in the days of the Ptolemys and told you could photocopy all the lost manuscripts you could do in one hour. You'd know you couldn't copy more than a fraction of one percent in the time allowed; and how could you choose among them? I'm in a similar fix."

"Well, hadn't you better get those specimens into the alcohol jars before they begin to stink?"

"Good-o," he said, wiping away the tears.

The party was tired enough from the day's hike so there was no argument over turning in early. In our headquarters tent, the Raja and I talked. It was unlikely there were any very spectacular sights to see within the radius of one-day excursions, such as a huge waterfall like your Niagara. There was that volcano we had seen from where we bagged the dicynodont; but I think volcanoes, like the larger carnosaurs, are best admired from a respectful distance.

So we decided simply to box the compass, taking our lambs out in a different direction until we had covered them all in the two weeks allowed. Then the Raja said:

"Reggie, I have an uneasy feeling about our female time traveler."

"Afraid she'll collapse on the trail?" I said.

"No; she's in good physical shape, even if she got sore feet the first day out. But it's the sexual thing. The way she was trading long, speculative glances with some of the men — well, it gave me qualms. We had better keep an eye on her."

Understand, Ms. Brownlee, I'm no wowser. Got nothing against sex. Marvelous institution and all that, but not when it interferes with the smooth operation of Rivers and Aiyar. So I said:

"Right-o, Raja!"

You see, the Raja's one of these intuitive chaps. I've learned that, when he warns of problems building up in the human sphere, I'd better listen.

• • •

As I said, I had given Inez Alvarado a tent of her own. So I was surprised next morning, when I was making rounds just before dawn at the end of my watch, to see that great, hulking Maori, Sir Edred Ngata, coming out of the tent I had assigned to Mrs. Alvarado.

"What the hell?" I said, giving him a sharp look. "I thought you were in with Tom."

He gave a kind of giggle, like a child caught out, and held the tent flap back to show the tent was empty. He finally said, between giggles:

"Well — ah — Inez begged me to change places with her. And — ah — what gentleman could refuse a lady such a simple request?"

"You knew they were an ex-couple?"

"Yes, I heard that. But some religions say, once married, always married. So I figured — ah..."

"Oh, cut it out, mate," I said. "I have enough problems bringing my lambs through these safaris alive without trying to manage their sex lives as well."

So I went about my business. When Inez came out of Alvarado's tent, I just looked through her as if she weren't there.

The Raja and I decided our lambs were bushed enough from the previous hike, so we went nowhere that day. Ngata spent it happily examining his specimens, dissecting those of which he had duplicates and getting blood up to his elbows, and explaining to anyone who would listen that this one was probably a rhynocephalian, while that one was more likely an eosuchian, like those ancestral to the dinosaurs.

"Aren't there any real dinosaurs in this period?" asked Inez Alvarado.

"That depends," said Ngata. "In one sense, it's a matter of where you draw the line between the dinosaurs and their thecodont ancestors. Most of my colleagues put the coelophysids, which we saw yesterday, in with the dinosaurs. In other words, it's a question of definitions.

"From another point of view, I could say no, there weren't, on the ground that there really are no such things as dinosaurs."

"What?" said Inez, startled. "But what about all those big skeletons in the museums? I know there's that preacher who goes around arguing that all those fossil bones are just a hoax by Satan to destroy men's faith. . . ."

"What I mean," said Ngata, "is that the first paleontologists to dig them up, in the nineteenth century, assumed that all those giant reptiles belonged to the same order, which they called Dinosauria. Now we know that they fall into two long-separated orders: the Saurischia and the Ornithischia, no more closely related than, say, we are to bats. The difference lies in the shape of the pelvis. That difference goes way back, to some thecodont common ancestor in a period earlier than this one. My job is to try to straighten out these obscure family trees.

"You've seen an example of an early saurischian in those little coelophysids, which aren't big enough to bother you. We call that bipedal, flesh-eating stem of the saurischians the theropods, the coelophysids, being one branch and the carnosaurs, like the famous *Tyrannosaurus*, the other. The other saurischian stem is made up of plant eaters ancestral to the sauropods, which became the biggest land animals ever. Those from this period look a little like long-necked versions of those cow dicynodonts we saw yesterday. All the rest of the so-called dinosaurs are herbivorous ornithischians.

"True, in the later Triassic beds one finds fragments of carnosaurs, such as the European *Teratosaurus*, large enough to be dangerous. But I don't know that such organisms existed at the time we are now in; and even if they did, whether they ever got to these lands before Pangaea broke up."

As we sat around, talking and examining equipment and listening to Sir Edred lecture, I began to sense a restlessness among the sahibs. After a number of these safaris—an Arab client on one of them said the correct plural was *safariin*—one comes to recognize the symptoms. Carlyle in particular seemed out of sorts, prowling about, cleaning and recleaning his gun, and generally acting like a caged animal. I heard him mutter:

"I've got to kill something!"

The Raja and I decided to lead the party next day northwest. We had gone pretty much due north on the meat hunt; so by going round the compass we could cover the territory within a radius of twenty or twenty-five kilometers from our base camp.

That night went off peacefully enough, if you don't count the shrieks of those giant crickets advertising for a mate and the other rustles, grunts, and hisses of a Mesozoic night.

Next day we hiked as planned. We saw more dicynodonts, in fact whole herds. When we had finished our lunch and were plowing on a little farther before turning back, Inez Alvarado said:

"Reggie, would you mind taking the rest on without me for a bit? I'll catch up."

"All right," I said, knowing that ladies, too, have calls of nature. We set out at a leisurely pace but had been out of sight of Inez for not more than ten or fifteen minutes when we heard her shriek:

"Help! Help!"

We raced back through the brush. She was standing before a little group of cycads, swinging her rifle—the nine-millimeter Mannlicher I had rented the Alvarados—by the barrel at a group of three quadrupedal flesh-eaters, which Ngata identified as rauisuchids. They were the size of a large dog, with thicker limbs and a body that tapered lizardwise into a thick tail. They had heads like carnosaurs of that size, with a mouthful of fangs.

Carlyle proved the fastest runner. When I puffed up after him, he already had his gun up. At the first bang, one rauisuchid flopped over, writhing and snapping. Bang! Down went another. The third seemed to get the idea, because it ran off. When I came up, I said:

"For God's sake, Inez, why didn't you shoot?"

"When I reached into my ammunition pouch, I found I'd left all my cartridges back at the camp. I'm sorry to be so stupid."

I just sighed. This is the sort of thing one has to put up with in my trade, and fussing and fuming won't help. "Oh, well, it's time to start for home anyway. Want a trophy, Desmond?"

"You bet!" said Carlyle, and got to work on one of the carcasses with a big sheath knife.

Pretty soon, with help from the Raja, he had the head off. We set out with him carrying it in a scarf he wore. The scarf got blood-soaked; but since the animal lacked hair and external ears, there wasn't any other easy way to hold it.

I suppose he could have put his fingers into the open mouth; but reptiles don't die all at once. This fellow's jaws kept snapping now and then for at least a quarter-hour after its head had been cut off. Or he could have whittled a point on a stick and impaled the head on it. The thought, when it came, reminded me unpleasantly of those French revolutionaries who made such a point of carrying people's heads around on the points of spears. Bad taste, eh?

This time everybody was tired enough by cocktail time so that it was a subdued safari that sat around drinking our medicinal whiskey. The camp helpers had packed the rauisuchid's head in salt.

Alvarado gave us a song. Carlyle told how he'd almost been eaten by a great white shark off an Australian beach. I know from the way he described the beach that he had never been near the place, but I thought it better not to say so. If he entertained the others, it didn't much matter whether his tales were true.

• • •

This time there was no problem with getting everyone tucked into bed early. As usual, the Raja and I took watch-and-watch through the night. When the sky was lightening before dawn, who should pop out of Inez Alvarado's tent but young Willard Smith!

"Hey!" I said, "What the devil...?"

"Just me," said Smith, "getting up to take a piss." (Excuse me, Ms. Brownlee.)

"But what were you doing in that tent?"

He scuffed his feet, twisted his hands, and generally acted as if caught in the act of breaking all ten commandments, including worshiping graven images. If the light had been stronger, I'm sure I should have seen him blushing.

"Ah — Mr. Rivers," he choked out at last. "There wasn't anybody in that tent."

"You were," I said.

"Sure. But that was just because Mrs. Alvarado asked me to trade places with her. So I — well, what else could I do?"

"You could have asked me before making any change," I began, "and let me as leader decide —"

Just then an angry shout aroused the camp, followed by yells and curses. Some sort of commotion was going on in and around the tent assigned to Smith and Carlyle. I got there in a dead heat with the Raja, who had been taking his turn to sleep.

The tent was heaving like a hooked fish, and as we arrived it collapsed. Out from the wreckage crawled Tom Alvarado and Desmond Carlyle, both in their underwear. No sooner had they cast off the folds of canvas than Alvarado sprang at Carlyle, grabbing for his throat.

As I said, Alvarado was a bit on the corpulent side, while Carlyle was in whipcord-tight physical shape, being in fact something of a fitness fanatic. Carlyle blocked Tom's attempt to strangle him and knocked him down. Alvarado landed on something hard. He felt around beneath his body and came up with Carlyle's big sheath knife. In no time he had it out and was lunging at Carlyle.

Meanwhile, Carlyle grabbed an edge of the canvas and threw it back, reaching for his rifle. In casting off the canvas he also uncovered Inez Alvarado, curled up on one of the bunks and naked as a frog. Before Alvarado got within stabbing distance, Carlyle stood up with his rifle.

The Raja tackled Alvarado, while I grabbed Carlyle's gun and twisted it to point up. It went off with a bang, fortunately without hitting anything, and with another wrench I got it away from him.

I stepped away to cover both. The Raja had wrested the knife from Alvarado, though he got a cut on the arm in doing so.

"All right, you idiots!" I said. "Stand with your hands clasped behind your necks, or by God I'll shoot off a member or two! Now, what's the story? You first, Tom!"

Tom was so enraged that for the moment he forgot his excellent English. "¡Este cabrón coge a mi mujer!" he shouted, waving his fists and dancing about. He followed it with a translation, which I won't trouble a lady's ears with. Then Mrs. Alvarado, who stood up with a sheet wrapped around her, screamed:

"¡Ya no estoy su mujer! Hago lo que quiero!"

The two kept shouting until they ran out of breath. She argued that as a single woman she had the right to a trot in the sheets whenever and with whomever she liked. Besides, Tom had been pestering her to marry him again, and she wanted to sample the field to have a standard of comparison.

When his turn came, Carlyle shrugged the whole thing off. "What do you expect?" he said. "I knew they weren't married. Even if they had been, what normal man would turn down such an offer?"

The Raja and I agreed on the following judgment: that everyone should thereafter stick to his or her own tent. If we found any more trading beds, we would tie up the culprits and leave them in camp while the rest of us went exploring. Ngata said confidentially:

"I'm just as glad, Reggie, that she never got down her list to me. I don't know that my hot Polynesian blood would have let me turn her down!"

Most of the rest of the trip went off in a routine way, with nothing notable on the part either of my sahibs or the rest of the fauna. Alvarado and Carlyle were formal with one another, calling each other "mister" when they had to communicate. Ngata collected and dissected more pseudo-lizards.

Carlyle shot a big knobby-headed anomodont with a parrot-like beak and hauled its head back to camp. Smith and the Alvarados took scads of photographs. We got soaked by a heavy thunderstorm, but that was all in the game.

Towards the end, I led our lambs westward, down a long slope to the water we could see in the distance. The Raja, whose arm was still bandaged from that cut, stayed in camp to supervise the packing up for departure.

The water proved a bend in a big river, which meandered through flat country with a lot of swamps and oxbow lakes alongside it. The going got really bushy, with masses of ferns as high as your head to hack your way through, and squilchy mud underfoot. If our sahibs thought they had got hot, sweaty, and dirty before, they soon learned it was nothing compared with this.

We finally found an area where we had a good view of the river and a bit more open country stretching back from it. The river gurgled and the insects swirled and buzzed and chirped. Desmond Carlyle said:

"Hey, Reggie! Look at that croc! Bet it beats any of those you have in Australia!"

Sure enough, on a meter-high bank on the edge of

the river was a big pseudo-crocodile, which Ngata identified as a phytosaur, dozing under a small conifer. It looked for all the world like the gavial or garial of modern India, except that its nostrils opened in a bump on its forehead instead of at the end of its snout. Ngata said:

"I don't know, Desmond. The salt-water croc grows up to five meters, and I don't think this one's over four. Of course this may not be the largest of its kind."

"Dangerous?" said Alvarado.

"Not really. Those narrow jaws say it's a complete fish-eater. Of course if you walk up and kick it in the ribs, it's likely to retaliate."

Carlyle said: "May I shoot it, Reggie? I want the skin for my wall."

"All right," I said, "if you'll skin and haul it. Be sure to sever the spine, or it'll scramble into the water and be lost."

Desmond stalked the phytosaur with his gun ready. At about thirty meters the brute saw him, opened its toothsome jaws, and hissed. Carlyle raised his gun, took his time, and squeezed off a round.

The phytosaur rolled over, writhing and thrashing. About half its length went off the bank and into the river; but Carlyle, running up, caught the end of its tail and pulled it back on shore. Being a reptile, it continued squirming and snapping long after it was officially dead.

Young Smith ran up, hopping around to get camera shots from different angles. The others also took pictures.

"Will!" said Carlyle commandingly, pulling out his big knife. "Can you lend a hand with the skinning?"

"If you'll show me what to do," said young Smith doubtfully. "I suppose you know how?"

"Oh, sure! I'm an old hand with alligators and crocodiles, and I'm sure these guys work the same way." He began to slit the skin from chin to belly. "Now catch hold here and pull the skin back...."

Skinning any animal is a gory spectacle, though one gets used to it. But it's also pretty dull. After the other lambs had taken all the pictures they wanted, Ngata fell to studying the guts of the phytosaur as Carlyle and Smith uncovered them. The Alvarados had been having some argument in an undertone. Tom Alvarado said:

"Reggie, if you do not mind, I will take a little walk with Inez. We have family matters to discuss."

"Just don't get out of sight," I said, and turned back to watch Carlyle and Smith struggle with that huge hide.

Time passed, and insects buzzed. They had the skin almost all off when young Smith, stepping back from the carcass, backed off the bank and slid down into the water, knee-deep. Carlyle said:

"Oh, you idiot!"

I said: "Get out of there fast, Will! You don't know what's—"

Smith was already scrambling back up the bank; but then he gave a shriek: "Something's got me!"

With a convulsive effort, he managed to clutch the trunk of the tree on top of the bank. I grabbed my gun and looked over the edge. Something had his right foot in its jaws—something with a wide head over a meter long, with a pair of goggle eyes on the flat upper surface.

"It's a big stereospondyl!" yelled Ngata. "Hold on, Will, while I study it! It proves that Pangaea—"

"Study it, hell!" I said and fired. The bullet splashed right over that great head; but the crocamander seemed not to notice. Behind the head I could dimly make out a barrel body, four stout legs with webbed feet, and a long tail flattened for swimming. The animal must have been at least four meters long. You know how a creature like a snake or a newt swims, with undulating curves moving from front to back? Well, this bugger was undulating from back to front. In other words, it was trying to back water, to pull Willard Smith in with it.

"I think it mistook Will's foot for a fish," said Ngata.

Carlyle and I fired again and again, to no apparent effect. One trouble was that the crocamander was under water, and even high-velocity bullets lose their speed fast in water. Besides, a cold-blooded life-form like that can take a lot of punishment without fatal effect.

"Grab his arm," I told Carlyle, "and I'll take the other, and we'll pull him up. . . ."

Then I heard a shriek from inland. When I looked around, Inez Alvarado was legging it toward us. Behind her came Tom Alvarado, and behind him came a dinosaur — and never mind that Ngata claimed there were no such things. This was an unmistakable carnosaur, the same group that includes monsters like *Tyrannosaurus* and *Epanterias*.

This one was much smaller but still big enough to kill and eat a man, just as a lion or a tiger could. It must have been about four meters long from nose to tail. When it ran on its hindlegs, with its body horizontal, it came up to about belt height; but when it stood up, bracing itself with its tail like a roo, it towered up to Sir Edred's height of two hundred centimeters.

I got ready to shoot; but I had to make sure neither of the Alvarados was in line with the carnosaur. This was a problem, since both were headed straight for me, and the carnosaur was pursuing them in as straight a line as if it were following a tape laid out on the ground.

While I stood there for some seconds, with my gun raised but unable to shoot, I heard yells and splashing behind me; but I didn't dare turn to look.

Then Tom Alvarado stopped, whipped off his bush jacket, and waved it at the approaching carnosaur in matador style. Just before the creature reached him with jaws agape, he hopped to one side. The carnosaur went right past him.

Any carnosaur, large or small, can work up a fair turn of speed on a straightaway, but they can't make quick turns. In other words, they're not agile; something to do with the structure of their leg joints.

After three or four strides the bugger got it into its little reptilian brain that its prey was no longer before it; and it skidded to a stop, swinging its head this way and that. Seeing Alvarado waving his jacket behind it, it charged him again; and again he stepped nimbly aside. When I got a momentary clear view, I pulled the trigger. I got only a click, because I'd shot off my whole magazine at the stereospondyl.

This time the carnosaur did not overshoot its mark by such a wide margin. I started reloading; but Inez came up and grabbed me around the neck, squealing: "Help! ¡Ayúdame!"

I pushed her off, a bit roughly I'm afraid, saying: "God damn it, sister, will you get out of the way and give me a clear shot?"

Meanwhile Tom and the carnosaur had gone through their toreador routine for the third time. This time the carnosaur was only a few steps from Alvarado when it turned, so that one stride would bring it to a position to reach out and bite his head off. As it started forward, I got it into my sights and fired. The impact knocked it down, where it lay thrashing and snapping. When it started to get up, I gave it two more rounds. This time it stayed down, though it continued to jerk and thrash.

I turned back to see how poor young Smith was doing. You can fancy my relief when I saw him sitting at the base of the conifer with his back against the trunk, muddy but apparently unharmed. Carlyle explained:

"I couldn't pull Will away from the beast alone, and Edred was loaded only with birdshot." (Ngata either forgot or ignored my order to carry buckshot in one barrel.) "So he jumped off the bank, waded out, and bashed the creature over the head with his gun butt. About the third bash, it got the idea that it wasn't wanted and swam off."

"How's your foot?" I asked Smith.

"Sore," he said, pulling up his wet trouser leg. His boot and thick sock had taken most of the punishment, but a few of the crocamander's sharp little teeth had gone through and punctured his skin, where a pair of big purple bruises was forming from the pressure of those jaws.

I hauled out the tube of disinfectant and the roll of bandage that I carry. We never did learn whether the crocamander had really mistaken Smith's foot for a fish or was trying, like a real croc, to pull him in to drown him. A crocodile would then cache him and eat him later when the corpse had softened enough to come apart easily.

"And what of you people?" said Carlyle, while I worked on Smith's bleeding ankle. "What's that beast?" He pointed to the carnosaur.

"By God!" cried Sir Edred, examining the carcass. "I'm damned if that isn't a close relative of *Teratosaurus*! I want as much of it as we can take back with us!"

"Oh, no, you don't!" said Carlyle. "I need the head for my wall!"

"I need the whole thing to study!" said Ngata.

Those two had a rare old row until I stepped in. "Now look here, fellas, you needn't argue the toss. I shot the bugger, so I can do what I like with the remains. Since you, Desmond, have already got the phytosaur skin, I hereby give the carcass of the carnosaur to Sir Edred, to do with as he likes. If you two decide exchange your trophies, that's all right with me, so long as everyone's agreed."

Carlyle looked sober. "We-ell, come to think, my walls are going to be pretty crowded already. So Edred can have the dinosaur and I'll take the pseudo-croc."

"Willard," said Ngata to young Smith, "How about giving me a hand with this carcass? Skin and skeleton both."

Limping but game, Smith did not object, since I suppose he was feeling guilt about having fallen into the river from sheer clumsiness. Ngata said to Alvarado:

"I say, old man, where did you learn to dodge slavering predators like that? I knew carnosaurs were not good at quick turns, but that's not a theory I'm keen to try out personally."

Alvarado grinned. "When I was younger, I wanted to be a bullfighter. So I trained for it, but I also practiced my singing. Now singing gives a man a big appetite, and so I got too fat for the *corrida*. At least, my *torero* training was not time wasted!"

There's little more to tell. On the way back to camp, the Alvarados acted like honeymooners, and that night I avoided noticing any changes in sleeping arrangements. Next day the transition chamber appeared, right on schedule. We loaded the gear and service personnel in first, leaving the sahibs and the guns for last in case something inimical showed up at the site. It took an extra trip by the chamber to fetch back all the bones and hides and pickled heads and other specimens to the present.

Eh? About Tom and Inez? No, so far as I know the Alvarados did not remarry. I'm sorry I can't give the tale a proper happy romantic ending. Despite all their endearments on the way back to camp, the last I saw of them, as they left Prochaska's laboratory, they were quarreling furiously over something, but in Spanish too fast for me to follow. Watching them made me happy to have just a nice, steady, easy, humdrum domestic relationship. I get all the excitement I need on these time safaris.

So now you can see why I won't mix the sexes on these expeditions. It's not the dinosaurs and other animals that cause the main problems; it's the human beings. It was more by luck than by management that neither Tomás Alvarado stabbed Desmond Carlyle, nor did Carlyle blow Tom's head off. You can reason and argue all you like; but when the primitive sexual instinct takes over, anything can happen. One of those in a lifetime is quite enough, thank you.

I'll admit that not even an all-male group is proof against such outbursts. Once I had an all-male party, of whom three — though I didn't know it when I signed them up — formed the corners of a homosexual love triangle, which came within a whisker of another murder. But that's another story.

2.
The First Dinosaurs

Essay by Catherine Forster

Speculation by Charles Sheffield

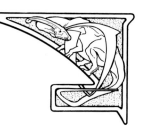

THE FIRST DINOSAURS

CATHERINE A. FORSTER

OUR CURRENT KNOWLEDGE OF THE FOSSIL RECORD SHOWS THAT DINOSAURS APPEARED IN THE FIRST half of the Late Triassic as rare members of animal communities that were largely populated by other groups. These first dinosaurs are known from a small number of mostly incomplete specimens that so far have been found in only two locations in South America. From this beginning, the dinosaurs increased in numbers and diversity and spread to all corners of the earth by the close of the Triassic. By Jurassic times dinosaurs were

the most numerous land animals on earth, while most of the animal groups contemporary with the first dinosaurs had dwindled or gone extinct.

Although much mystery remains concerning the origin of the dinosaurs, recent work by a number of paleontologists has shed new light on how and from what these first "terrible lizards" evolved. Here we examine the first dinosaurs, their evolution, and their closest relatives, as well as the varied groups of animals that existed side by side with the earliest dinosaurs. We also discuss the world of the Late Triassic, which had a climate and continental map very different from ours.

ARCHOSAURS AND THE ORIGIN OF THE DINOSAURS

Dinosaurs are members of a larger group of reptiles called the Archosauria. Most archosaurs went extinct long ago, although two groups remain today: the crocodiles and the birds. In the Middle and Late Triassic, however, the archosaurs were a numerous and diverse group of reptiles both large and small including herbivores (plant eaters) and carnivores (meat eaters), crocodiles and crocodile-like forms, squat four-legged armored forms, and the flying pterosaurs. Out of this

varied group of Triassic archosaurs arose the dinosaurs which, though initially rare, spread, diversified, and eventually completely dominated the animal communities of the world over the next 150 million years.

But from where within this large grab-bag of archosaurs did the dinosaurs arise? By studying both fossil and living archosaurus, paleontologists have shown that the archosaurs split into two branches, or lineages, in the Early Triassic. These lineages were the Crocodylotarsi ("crocodile-ankle"), and the Ornithosuchia ("bird-crocodile"). The Crocodylotarsi lineage led to the crocodilians, while the Ornithosuchia lineage terminated in the dinosaurs and birds. To better understand the placement of the dinosaurs within the Archosauria, and their nearest relatives and contemporaries, we need to recall the discussion in Chapter 1 and here take a closer look at the second of these lineages as it relates to the dinosaurs.

THE TRIASSIC ARCHOSAURS:
THE ORNITHOSUCHIA
The Ornithosuchia form the second branch of the archosaurs and include the ornithosuchids, pterosaurs, the species *Lagosuchus* and its close relatives *Lagerpeton* and *Pseudolagosuchus*, and the dinosaurs and birds. The Ornithosuchia share certain birdlike char-

acteristics, which include new kinds of foot and hip structures. This shows that these animals are each other's closest "cousins."

The ornithosuchid family is known from Late Triassic rocks in South America and Great Britain. They were medium-sized, quadrupedal carnivores that superficially resembled the rauisuchids. Like the rauisuchids, they had large, deep skulls with long, sharp teeth.

Lagosuchus, *Lagerpeton* and *Pseudolagosuchus* were slender, long-limbed carnivores from the Middle Triassic Ischichuca Formation (layer of rocks) in Argentina. These closely related animals were about the size of a hare, with long, narrow skulls and small sharp teeth. Their forelimbs were rather short, implying that they may have gotten up to run on their hind limbs. Their long, slender hind limbs indicate they were swift and agile runners, chasing and capturing small prey.

Some paleontologists have speculated that *Lagosuchus* or one of its relatives may have been the ancestor of the dinosaurs. They possess many of the features thought to be present in oldest dinosaurs, and they also are found in sediments that underlie the formation containing the first dinosaurs. However, only partial remains have been recovered of *Lagosuchus* and its kin, so there is much left to learn about them. *Lagosuchus* is at least closely related to the ancestors of the dinosaurs, though probably not the ancestor itself.

The pterosaurs arose in the Late Triassic and persisted alongside the dinosaurs until they both went extinct at the end of the Cretaceous Period. Although pterosaurs are usually thought of as flying reptiles, the earliest pterosaurs were small, land-bound animals (but see Chapter 10 for more information on this unique group of archosaurs).

The pterosaurs are the closest known relatives of the dinosaurs. They share with the dinosaurs a subset of characteristics evolved in only those two groups. Pterosaurs are not ancestors of the dinosaurs, but appear to be their first cousins.

NON-ARCHOSAUR CONTEMPORARIES OF THE FIRST DINOSAURS

Although the many different kinds of archosaur formed a large part of the communities early dinosaurs lived in, three other reptile groups were also very important and well represented in the first half of the Late Triassic. These include animals called rhynchosaurs, cynodonts, and dicynodonts.

Rhynchosaurs apparently existed in great numbers and are often the commonest animal found in Triassic rock formations. Cynodonts were small to medium-sized reptiles that belonged within a larger reptile group called the Therapsida. Dicynodonts, another of the therapsid groups, were the largest herbivores in the Late Triassic.

The vast array of archosaurs and non-archosaurs from the early part of the Late Triassic formed the bulk of the known animal communities in which the earliest dinosaurs appeared. With the players known, and the scene set, we are ready to look at the earliest dinosaurs.

THE FIRST DINOSAURS

The earliest known dinosaurs are from the early part of the Late Triassic. These rare dinosaurs were rather small, a far cry from some of their later, enormous relatives. So far, the earliest known dinosaurs have been found in Argentina and Brazil. They are called pisanosaurs and herrerasaurs, the latter including the staurikosaurs.

Dinosaurs are usually divided into two groups: the

Preceding page: A pair of Plateosaurs, *the first large dinosaur. These early prosauropods ate high leaves from the cycads of the Late Triassic. By Brian Franczak.*

Saurischia ("lizard-hipped"), and the Ornithischia ("bird-hipped"). However, when the first herrerasaurid was discovered in Argentina and studied in 1963, paleontologists realized it was neither. The herrerasaurids lack some of the features that exclusively characterize the Saurischians, but possess many dinosaur features shared by both the Saurischia and the Ornithischia. Because of this, paleontologists feel the herrerasaurids are too primitive to belong to either of these groups, and instead they are related to their common ancestor. That is, they belong to a family of dinosaurs that existed before the dinosaurs split into saurischians and ornithischians.

Because they are not saurischians or ornithischians, some paleontologists originally argued (and still believe) that the herrerasaurids are not dinosaurs at all. Most paleontologists now feel that we simply need to stop considering the Dinosauria as being composed of only the Saurischia and Ornithischia. Since the herrerasaurids do have many "dinosaurian" features, they are considered to be the earliest, most primitive known dinosaurs. This early confusion as to whether herrerasaurids are dinosaurs or not shows how little we really know about the early evolution of these creatures, and in particular, the evolution of the dinosaurs before the saurischian-ornithischian split.

PISANOSAURUS: THE FIRST ORNITHISCHIAN

Pisanosaurus mertii is the earliest known species of ornithischian dinosaur. It was discovered by Galileo Scaglia in the middle section of the Ischigualasto Formation in La Rioja Province, Argentina. *Pisanosaurus* was originally described and named by an Argentine paleontologist, Dr. Rosendo Casamiquela, in 1967.

Pisanosaurus is known from only one very poorly preserved and fragmentary skeleton. This skeleton was very badly weathered; that is, it was broken up and partially washed away by the elements as it lay on the ground. As a result of this erosion, only parts of the jaws, some vertebrae, a piece of the shoulder blade, and parts of the hind legs remained by the time it was discovered. Also found with the skeleton were the impressions in the rock of parts of the hip bones and one front foot, although the actual fossil bone that once filled the impressions had been washed away.

Even though so little of the skeleton remained, it is thought that *Pisanosaurus* is a very early ornithischian dinosaur because of the type of teeth in its upper and lower jaws. These teeth are small and blunt, lie side by side in the jaw, and have tiny bumps, or "denticles," along their edge. This type of tooth is characteristic of ornithischian dinosaurs, and is not found in either herrerasaurids or saurischian dinosaurs. However, some paleontologists are not convinced that *Pisanosaurus* is an ornithischian dinosaur, but feel that it, like the herrerasaurids, may have originated before the saurischian—ornithischian division.

Like all early dinosaurs, *Pisanosaurus* was quite small and lightly built, probably only as big as a medium-sized dog. The teeth of *Pisanosaurus* indicate that it was a herbivore, but it is not known whether it walked on two or four legs. However, the type of front foot *Pisanosaurus* had suggests that it may have been bipedal.

By the Early Jurassic other genera, such as *Heterodontosaurus*, had appeared which were already rather advanced ornithischians. Their exact relation to *Pisanosaurus* is still unclear.

THE HERRERASAURIDAE

Much more is known about the Herrerasauridae, since unlike *Pisanosaurus*, the remains of herrerasaurids are more numerous and far more complete.

The first specimen of *Herrerasaurus* was discovered by Victorino Herrera in the Ischigualasto Formation in the Valle de la Luna area of San Juan Province,

Argentina, in May of 1961. Mr. Herrera was a rancher who traversed the area with his herds, often finding fossils during his travels. This first specimen was fragmentary, consisting of part of a hind limb, pelvis, and jaw. An Argentine paleontologist, Dr. Osvaldo Reig, named this newly discovered dinosaur *Herrerasaurus ischigualastensis*, meaning "Herrera's reptile from Ischigualasto."

The first and only complete, articulated skeleton ever found of *Herrerasaurus* was discovered in 1988 by a joint U.S. — Argentine expedition to the Ischigualasto Formation in San Juan Province, Argentina. A well-preserved skull with the lower jaws still in place was found with the skeleton. This specimen is the earliest whole dinosaur skeleton known and has provided paleontologists with their first complete picture of what one of the first dinosaurs looked like. Partial remains of *Herrerasaurus* were also found during this expedition.

Two other specimens have been found in the Ischigualasto Formation which paleontologists initially named as new herrerasaurids. One specimen was named *Ischisaurus cattoi*. This specimen was quite fragmentary, consisting of portions of a front limb, hind limb, and pelvis, some vertebrae, and parts of the jaws. Another specimen, which consisted of fragments of a skull and some tail vertebrae, was named *Frenguellisaurus ischigualastensis*.

Because *Ischisaurus*, *Frenguellisaurus*, and *Herrerasaurus* were known previously from only incomplete remains, paleontologists were not able to compare them closely. This made it difficult to determine if they were really different animals. Since the discovery of the complete *Herrerasaurus* specimen in 1988, paleontologists have been able to study and compare all the known specimens. Prevailing opinion is that *Herrerasaurus*, *Ischisaurus*, and *Frenguellisaurus* are all the same animal. Because *Herrerasaurus* was named first, this name has priori-

ty, and thus all of the remains can now be referred to as *Herrerasaurus*.

Herrerasaurus was a carnivorous, bipedal dinosaur that stood about four or five feet tall. Its skull was narrow and moderately deep, with strong jaws lined with curved, serrated teeth. It had relatively short but strong front legs with long, grasping hands that ended in large, curved claws. Its rather light build and long hind legs indicate that it may have been a fast runner and an active predator. *Herrerasaurus* was not the largest carnivore in the Ischigualasto community (it was exceeded in size by the rauisuchid *Saurosuchus*), but it was probably the quickest.

A fragmentary specimen of a second species, *Staurikosaurus pricei*, has been reported from the Ischigualasto Formation, making it a contemporary of both *Herrerasaurus* and *Pisanosaurus*. Another specimen was found in a slightly older formation in Brazil. It thus may be the oldest dinosaur. *Staurikosaurus* is smaller than *Herrerasaurus*, but is otherwise very similar in body form, being a small, quick, bipedal carnivore with sharp teeth and long hind legs.

Though first collected in 1936, it wasn't until the 1960s that *Staurikosaurus* was finally studied by paleontologist Edwin Colbert. Dr. Colbert quickly realized it was an early dinosaur and described and named it in 1970. *Staurikosaurus* means "reptile of the cross," alluding to the constellation of the Southern Cross seen in the southern hemisphere.

Because of the fragmentary nature of the known *Staurikosaurus* specimens, paleontologists have been unable to determine with certainty if it does or doesn't belong in the hererrasaurid family. Many paleontologists consider *Staurikosaurus* to be a herrerasaurid, while others feel it should be in its own family, the Staurikosauridae. Regardless, all agree that like *Herrerasaurus*, *Staurikosaurus* is neither a saurischian nor an ornithischian, but is an earlier, more primitive kind of dinosaur.

THE WORLD OF THE EARLIEST DINOSAURS: THE ISCHIGUALASTO FORMATION

The Ischigualasto Formation of San Juan and La Rioja Provinces, Argentina, contains a rich and varied animal community that includes the earliest dinosaurs. A look at this extraordinary community gives us a glimpse of what life was like for the first dinosaurs.

The dinosaurs of the Ischigualasto fauna, *Herrerasaurus*, *Pisanosaurus*, and *Staurikosaurus*, have all been found in the lower half of the formation. These dinosaurs are quite rare, although other animals are extremely common. The most common animal found in the lower one-third of the Ischigualasto Formation is the rhynchosaur *Scaphonyx*, which accounts for about 60 percent of all remains. Toward the middle part of the formation, *Scaphonyx* disappears and plant-eating cynodonts, such as *Exaeretodon* and *Ischignathus*, make up most of the fauna. These abundant herbivores may have formed a large part of the diet of *Herrerasaurus* and *Staurikosaurus*.

Many other animals can be found throughout the dinosaur-bearing beds, including two aetosaurs *(Aetosauroides* and *Argentinosuchus)*, a huge dicynodont *(Ischigualastia)*, a carnivorous cynodont *(Chiniquodon)*, a very large rauisuchid *(Saurosuchus)*, a crocodylomorph *(Trialestes)*, an ornithosuchid *(Venaticosuchus)*, and two amphibians *(Promastodontosaurus* and *Pelorocephalus)*. Another member of the fauna is *Proterochampsa*, a primitive type of large, aquatic, meat-eating archosaur with a crocodile-like appearence.

Herbivorous cynodonts and rhynchosaurs dominated the fauna by their sheer numbers, leaving *Pisanosaurus* a minor constituent of the plant-eating community. While the herrerasaurids were probably slightly more common, they were exceeded in both size and number by the non-dinosaur carnivores *Saurosuchus* and *Proterochampsa*. These new, rather rare dinosaurs managed to gain a strong foothold however, multiplying in number and variety, while their early contemporaries eventually waned or went extinct for reasons unknown.

DINOSAURS AT THE CLOSE OF THE TRIASSIC

Although dinosaurs are extremely rare in the early part of the Late Triassic, sediments from the close of the Triassic contain a wide variety of dinosaurs. By the end of the Triassic or Early Jurassic new groups of dinosaurs (prosauropods, fabrosaurids, heterodontosaurids, and coelurosaurids) had spread worldwide in an ever-increasing array of species and numbers.

No one knows what happened in the transition period between the beginning and end of the Late Triassic. For example, the Los Colorados Formation, which directly overlies the Ischigualasto Formation in Argentina, contains the large prosauropod, *Riojasaurus*; what happened between *Herrerasaurus* and *Riojasaurus* is still unknown. What we do know is that by the close of the Triassic, dinosaurs had spread worldwide and multiplied in number and variety, a harbinger of what was yet to come.

THE PROSAUROPODA
The prosauropods were the first major group of dinosaurs to evolve, diversifying in both geographic extent and number of genera. At least seventeen genera of prosauropod dinosaurs have already been discovered in Europe, Great Britain, North America, Argentina, southern Africa, and China. Prosauropods are quite common in some areas and have occasionally been found in great numbers (for example, large numbers of *Plateosaurus* skeletons have been dug from the Trossingen quarry in southern Germany).

Prosauropods arose at the end of the Late Triassic and lived through the Early Jurassic; they were the first large group of true saurischian dinosaurs. The earliest prosauropods were bipedal, but later forms appear to have walked either occasionally or habitually on all four legs. Prosauropods had long necks, bodies, and tails, strong front legs, and enormous claws on their thumbs that may have been used as defensive weapons or possibly for digging.

All prosauropods were herbivorous and had leaf-shaped, serrated teeth for shredding plant matter. Concentrated masses of small stones within the rib cages of some specimens of *Massospondylus* indicate that the prosauropods may have also used gastroliths ("stomach stones") to help break up the plant matter, as in modern birds.

Since all prosauropods appear to be descended from a common ancestor, they must have evolved and spread very rapidly around the ancient world. Exactly what the ancestors of prosauropods were, what they looked like, and where the prosauropods evolved is still a mystery. Although the name prosauropod, meaning "before-sauropods," implies they were the ancestors of the enormous sauropods, paleontologists now believe they did not give rise to the sauropods. They were already too specialized to have developed into the sauropods. The prosauropods and sauropods instead shared a common, yet unknown, ancestor, giving them a first cousin relationship.

THE COELUROSAURIDAE

The coelurosaurs were the first true theropod dinosaurs. Coelurosaurs had nearly as wide a distribution as that of prosauropods, but have been found in large numbers only in New Mexico, where mass accumulations of *Coelophysis* have been excavated from the famous Ghost Ranch locality. Coelurosaurs were a very successful group of early predatory dinosaurs and lasted into the early part of the Cretaceous

period. The known coelurosaurs include *Halticosaurus* (West Germany), *Procompsognathus* (West Germany), *Syntarsus* (Zimbabwe — possibly Early Jurassic), *Saltopus* (Scotland), *Lukousaurus* (China — possibly Early Jurassic), and an as-yet-unnamed form from Argentina.

Coelurosaurs were small, bipedal meat eaters with narrow skulls and large eyes, long arms with grasping hands, and slender hind legs. Their two lower jaws were lined with long serrated teeth and were rather loosely bound together in front, allowing flexibility for eating large prey items. Coelurosaurs were apparently swift and agile predators, possibly using their grasping forelimbs to capture small prey.

TWO LATEST TRIASSIC FAUNA: THE CHINLE AND THE UPPER KEUPER

The cosmopolitan nature of dinosaur fauna at the close of the Triassic allows us a much broader view of the dinosaur world at that time. By examining two separate fauna, the Chinle from the U.S.A. and the Upper Keuper from Germany, which spans the Late Triassic, we can observe the similarities and differences that were already becoming apparent in dinosaur evolution.

The Chinle Formation is found in Colorado, Utah, Arizona, and New Mexico, and has produced many animal and plant fossils from the end of the Late Triassic. The most famous exposure of the Chinle Formation is Petrified Forest National Park in Arizona, where thousands of fossil tree stumps and logs can be seen on the surface.

The Chinle Formation has also revealed one of the most famous mass dinosaur graveyards in the world. The Ghost Ranch Quarry in New Mexico has produced many specimens, of all sizes and ages, of the ceratosaur *Coelophysis*. This wonderful accumulation of skeletons has allowed paleontologists to thoroughly study this early dinosaur. No other kinds of dinosaurs have been found in the Chinle Formation.

Although *Coelophysis* has been found in abundance at the Ghost Ranch site, it is much rarer in other locations in the Chinle Formation. The most common animals include a large amphibian called *Metoposaurus*, and two large phytosaurs, *Phytosaurus* and *Rutiodon*. Also found in the Chinle Formation are four different aetosaurs, a dicynodont, two primitive archosaurs, an unnamed rauisuchid, and many types of fish including lungfish and coelacanths (the famous "living fossils").

More than fifty species of plants are also known from the Chinle Formation, including lycopods, ferns, ginkgos, conifers, and cycads. These plants, as well as the great abundance of aquatic forms such as the amphibians and the phytosaurs, suggest a wet and tropical environment in Chinle times.

The Upper Keuper rocks are located in Central Europe, and are part of a thick sequence of Triassic strata. More dinosaurs have been found in the Upper Keuper strata than in the Chinle Formation.

Two plateosaurs, *Sellosaurus* and *Plateosaurus*, are found in the Upper Keuper. *Plateosaurus* remains are common and have been recovered in great abundance in Germany, Switzerland, and France. Large accumulations of *Plateosaurus* skeletons were found in a quarry outside of Trössingen in Bavaria. This quarry was excavated in three separate operations beginning in 1911 and ending in 1932, and many complete and partial *Plateosaurus* skeletons recovered.

Two coelurosaurs, *Procompsognathus* and *Halticosaurus*, have also been found in the Upper Keuper rocks. Like *Coelophysis* in New Mexico, these two dinosaurs were small predators who probably relied on their agility and speed to capture prey. Unlike *Coelophysis*, these coelurosaurs have never been found in mass accumulations.

Many other animals have been found in the Upper Keuper beds, including three amphibians (*Cyclotosaurus*, *Plagiosternum*, and *Metoposaurus*), the earliest turtle (*Proganochelys*), an unnamed phytosaur, an aetosaur (*Aetosaurus*), a rauisuchid (*Teratosaurus*), and a crocodylomorph (*Saltoposuchus*).

There are many similarities between the Chinle and Upper Keuper communities. Both contain small coelurosaurs, aetosaurs, dicynodonts, phytosaurs, and rauisuchids. They also contain the same large amphibian, *Metoposaurus*. Although the specific genera are different in most cases, the basic kinds of animals are the same, so the two communities were probably very similar. The most conspicuous difference between the two formations is that while prosauropods are very common in the Upper Keuper, they are absent in the Chinle.

CONCLUSIONS

The first dinosaurs, *Herrerasaurus*, *Staurikosaurus*, and *Pisanosaurus*, are known only from the Ischigualasto Formation in Argentina, and the Santa Maria Formation in Brazil. Although they have been found only in South America so far, the earliest dinosaurs may have been present in other places as well. At present we certainly don't know either the true geographic extent of all early dinosaurs, or know all of the early dinosaurs.

To begin to understand how dinosaurs came to dominate the Mesozoic world, the animal groups with which the earliest dinosaurs lived are important to consider. Why did the dinosaurs succeed and the others fail? This puzzling question will perhaps be answered as new dinosaur specimens are found, and other archosaur and non-archosaur groups become better understood. But whatever the reason, we do know the dinosaurs started with a whimper, but closed the Triassic with a bang.

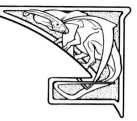

THE FEYNMAN SALTATION

CHARLES SHEFFIELD

HE WORM IN THE APPLE; THE CRAB IN THE WALNUT... COLIN TRANTHAM WAS ADDING FINE black bristles to the crab's jointed legs when the nurse called him into the office.

He glanced at his watch as he entered. "An hour and a quarter the first time. Forty minutes the second. Now he sees me in nine minutes. Are you trying to tell me something?"

The nurse did not reply, and Dr. James Wollaston, a pudgy fifty-year-old with a small mouth and the face of a petulant baby, did not smile. He gestured to a chair, and waited until Trantham was seated on the other side of his desk.

"Let me dispose of the main point, then we can chat." Wollaston was totally lacking in bedside manner, which was one of the reasons that Colin Trantham liked him. "We have one more test result to come, but there's little doubt as to what it will show. You have a tumor in your left occipital lobe. That's the bad news. The good news is that it's quite operable."

"Quite?"

"Sorry. *Completely* operable. We should get the whole thing." He stared at Trantham. "You don't seem surprised by this."

Colin pushed the drawing across the table: the beautifully detailed little crab, sitting in one end of the shelled walnut. "I'm not an idiot. I've been reading and thinking cancer for weeks. I suppose it's too much to hope it might be benign?"

"I'm afraid so. It is malignant. But it appears to be primary site. There are no other signs of tumors anywhere in your body."

"Wonderful. So I only have cancer *once*." Trantham folded the drawing and tucked it away in his jacket breast pocket. "Am I supposed to be pleased?"

Wollaston did not answer. He was consulting a desk calendar and comparing it with a typed sheet. "Friday is the twenty-third. I would like you in the night before, so we can operate early."

"I was supposed to go to Toronto this weekend. I have to sign a contract for a set of interior murals."

"Postpone it."

"Good. I was afraid you'd say cancel."

"Postpone it for four weeks." Wollaston was pulling another folder from the side drawer of his desk. "I propose to get you Hugo Hemsley. He and I have already talked. He's the best surgeon east of the Rockies, but he has his little ways. He'll want to know every symptom you've had from day one before he'll pick up a scalpel. How's the headache?"

The neurologist's calm was damping Colin's internal hysteria. "About the same. Worst in the morning."

"That is typical. Your first symptom was colored lights across your field of vision, sixty-three days ago. Describe that to me..."

The muffled thump on the door was perfunctory, a relic of the days when Colin Trantham had a live-in girlfriend. Julia Trantham entered with a case in one hand and a loaded paper bag held to her chest with the other, pushing the door open with her foot and backing through.

"Grab this before I drop it." She turned and nodded down at the bag. "Bought it before I thought to ask. You allowed to drink?"

"I didn't ask, either." Colin examined the label on the bottle. "Moving up in the world. You don't get a *Grands Echézeaux* of this vintage for less than sixty bucks."

"Seventy-two plus tax. When did you memorize the wine catalog?"

"I'm feeling bright these days. When a man knows he is to be hanged in a fortnight, it concentrates his mind wonderfully."

"No points for that. Everybody quotes Johnson." Julia Trantham pulled the cork and sniffed it, while her brother was reaching up into the cabinet for two eight-ounce glasses.

"You're late." Colin Trantham placed the thin-stemmed goblets on the table and watched as Julia poured, a thin stream of dark red wine. His sister's face was calm, but the tremor in her hand was not. "The plane was on time. You went to see Wollaston, didn't you, before you came here?"

"You're too smart for your own good. I did."

"What did you find out?"

Julia Trantham took a deep breath. Colin had always been able to see through her lies; it would be a mistake to try one now. "It's a glioblastoma. A neuroglia cell tumor. And it's Type Four. Which means — "

"I know what it means. As malignant as you can get."

Colin Trantham picked up his glass, emptied it in four gulps, and walked over to stand at the sink and stare out of the kitchen window. "Christ. You still have the knack of getting the truth out of people, don't you? I had my little interview with Dr. Hemsley, but he didn't get as honest as that. He talked *procedure*. Day after tomorrow he saws open my skull, digs in between the hemispheres, and cuts out a lump of my brain as big as a tennis ball. Local anesthetic — he wants me conscious while he operates."

"Probably wants you to hold tools for him. Like helping to change a car tire. Sounds minor."

"Minor for *him*. He gets five thousand bucks for a morning's work. And it's not *his* brain."

"Minor operation equals operation on somebody else."

"One point for that. Wish it weren't *my* brain, either. It's my second favorite organ."

"No points — that's Woody Allen in *Sleeper*. You're all quotes today."

Colin Trantham sat down slowly at the kitchen table. "I'm trying, Julia. It's just not . . . easy."

The casual brother-sister jousting shattered and fell away from between them like a brittle screen. Julia Trantham dropped into the seat opposite. "I know, Colin. It's not easy. It's awful. My fault. I'm not handling this well."

"Not your fault. Everybody's. Mine too, same problem. You go through life, build your social responses. Then you get a situation they just don't cover. Who wants to talk about *dying*, for Christ's sake?" There was a long silence, but the tension was gone. Colin Trantham stared at his older sister's familiar face, unseen for half a year. "I'm scared, Julie. I lie awake at night, and I think, I won't make old bones."

Little brother, hurt and crying. We're grown-ups now. We haven't hugged in twenty years. "Social responses. I'm supposed to say, don't be scared, Col, you'll be fine. But while I say it I'm thinking, you're scared, no shit? Of course you're scared. Me, I'd be petrified. I *am* petrified."

"Will you stay until the operation's over?"

"I was planning to. If it's all right with you, I'll hang around until you're out of the hospital. Write up a paper on extinct invertebrates that I've had in the mill for a while." She poured again into both glasses, emptying the bottle. "Any girlfriend that I need to know about, before I embarrass her by my drying panty-hose?"

"Rachel. Just a now-and-again thing." Colin Trantham picked up the empty bottle and stared at the layer of sediment left in the bottom, divining his future. "Should we have decanted it? I hardly tasted that first glass. I'll try to sip it this time with due reverence." The raw emotion was fading, the fence of casual responses moving back into position. "No problem with Rachel. If she finds you here with me I'll just pretend you're my sister."

The waiting room was empty. Julia dithered on the threshold, possessed by conflicting desires. She wanted news, as soon as it was available. She also wanted a cigarette, more than she had ever wanted one, but smoking was forbidden anywhere in the hospital.

Dr. Wollaston solved her problem before she could. He approached along the corridor behind her and spoke at once: "Good news. It went as well as it possibly could go."

The nicotine urge was blotted out by a rush of relief.

"Minimum time in the operating room," the neurologist went on. "No complications." He actually summoned a smile. "Sedated now, but he wanted you to see this. He said that you would know exactly what it means."

He held out a piece of paper about five inches square. At its center, in blue ink, a little figure of a hedgehog leered out at Julia, cheeks bulging. She could feel her own cheeks burning. "That's me — according to Colin. Private family joke."

"Drawn right *after* the operation, when Hemsley was testing motor skills. Astonishing, I thought."

"Can I see him?"

"If you wish, although he might not recognize you at the moment. He should be sleeping. Also" — a second of hesitation, picking words carefully — "I would appreciate a few minutes of your time. Perhaps a glass of wine, after what I know has been a trying day for you. This is" — Julia sensed another infinitesimal pause — "primarily medical matters. I need to talk to you about your brother."

How could she refuse? Walking to the wine bar, Julia realized that he had talked her out of seeing Colin, without seeming to do so. Typical James Wollaston, according to Colin. Gruff, sometimes grumpy; but smart.

His eyes were on her as they settled in on the round cushioned stools across a fake hogshead table, and she took out and lit a cigarette.

"How many of those a day?"

"Five or six." Julia took one puff and laid down the burning cigarette in the ashtray. "Except I'm like every other person who smokes five — a pack lasts me a day and a half."

"You're going to regret it. It's murder on your skin. Another ten years and you'll look like a prune."

"Skin? I thought you were going to tell me about my heart and lungs."

"For maximum effect, you have to hit where it's least expected. You ought to give it up."

"I was going to. I really was. But you know what happened? Since Mother died, Colin and I have called each other every week."

"Sunday midday."

"That's right. How'd you know?"

"I know a lot about you and Colin."

"Then you know Colin's not one for overstatement. He hadn't said a word about…all this. When the evidence was in, he hit me with it all at once. It floored me. I'd got up that morning determined that I was through, that was *it* for cigarettes. I'd just thrown a near-full pack away." She laughed shakily. "Looks like I picked a hell of a day to quit smoking."

"That's from *Airplane*. No points, I think your brother would say."

"My God. You really do know a lot about us."

"When it was clear to me that Colin might have a serious problem, I put him through my biggest battery of tests, checking his memory and his reflexes and his logical processes. We also went over all his background. As a result I know a great deal about you, too, your background, what you do." He paused. "I even understood about the hedgehog, though it didn't seem the best time and place to mention it. Anyway, how's the paleontology business?"

"Just scratching out a living. Sorry. Programmed response. In a very interesting state. You see, every few years there's a major upheaval — facts, or theories. New radioactive dating, punctuated equilibrium, Cretaceous extinctions, mitochondrial DNA tracking, the reinterpretation of the Burgess Shale. Well, it seems we're in for another one. A biggie."

"So I have heard."

"You have? Well, not from Colin, that's for sure."

"True. I read it."

"Fossils bore him stiff. He says that *Megatherium* was an Irish woman mathematician."

A moment's thought. "Meg O'Theorem?"

"That's her. He was all set to be a mathematician or a physicist himself, till the drawing and painting bug took hold. He's the talented one, you know — I'm just the one who wrote papers and stayed in college forever. Anyway, first he started to paint in the evenings, and then — " She stopped, drew breath, and shook her head. "Sorry, doctor. I'm babbling. Nerves. You wanted to talk."

"I do. But I like to listen, too — unless you're in a big hurry?"

"Nothing in the world to do but sit here and listen."

Wollaston nodded. The wine had arrived and he was frowning at the label. "I hope this isn't too lowbrow. It's certainly not one of the *grand crus* that you and your brother like to sample. It's a naive domestic burgundy without any breeding, but I think you'll be amused — "

"— by its presumption. No points. But I get one for finishing the line."

"I need practice, or I'll never be a match for the two of you." He poured the first splash of wine, and in that instant seemed to become a younger and more vulnerable person. "A successful operation. That was the first stage. It is now behind us. Did your brother discuss with you what might happen next?"

Julia shook her head. Colin had not raised the subject, nor had she. Somehow it had not seemed significant before the operation. "Chemotherapy?"

"Not with the conventional anti-metabolites. They have difficulty crossing the blood-brain barrier. The normal next step would be radiation. But a glioblastoma is fiercely malignant. Bad odds. I want to try something that I hope will be a lot better. However, I wanted to obtain your reaction before I discussed it with Colin." Another pause, words chosen carefully. Julia nodded her internal approval. A good, cautious doctor. "I'd like to put him onto an experimental protocol," continued Wollaston. "An implanted drug-release device inside the brain itself, with a completely new drug, a variable delivery rate, and an internal monitor sensitive enough to respond to selected ambient neurotransmitter levels. It's tiny, and there will be no need to reopen the skull to install it."

He was not looking at her. Why not? "Price isn't an issue, Dr. Wollaston, unless it's out of this world. We have insurance and money. What are the side effects?"

"No consistent patterns. This is too new. And the implant would be done free, since your brother would be part of a controlled experiment. But" — the kicker, here it came, he was finally looking into her eyes —

"Colin would have to fly to Europe to get it. You see, it's not yet FDA approved."

"He'd have to *stay there?*"

His surprise was comical. "Stay there? Of course not. He could fly over one night, have the implant performed the next day, and as soon as the surgeon there approved his release he'd turn right around and come back. But I'm not sure how Colin will react to the idea. What do you think? It's doesn't have FDA approval, you see, so — "

"I don't think. *I know*. Colin doesn't give a tinker's damn about the FDA. He'll do it." Julia stubbed out her cigarette, which had burned its whole length unnoticed in the ashtray. "Of course he'll do it. Colin wants to live."

She took a first sip of wine, then two big gulps. "What next?"

"On medical matters? Nothing. I'm done. More wine. Relax. Your turn to talk." He was smiling again. "I hope you don't have to run off right away." Julia was staring all around her. His smile vanished. "Do you?"

Julia was still scanning the wine bar. "Where are all the waiters? You know, I didn't eat one thing all day. I'm absolutely famished. How do you order food in this place?"

Walking back to Colin's apartment through the mellow April evening, Julia Trantham was filled with guilt. Ten hours ago a malignant tumor the size and shape of a Bartlett pear had been removed from the brain of her brother. He was lying unconscious, gravely ill. While she...

For the past three hours she had managed to forget Colin's condition — and in the company of James Wollaston she had enjoyed herself hugely.

Concorde, Heathrow to Dulles; seventy thousand feet, supersonic over open ocean.

Colin Trantham sat brooding in a left-side window seat, staring out at blue-black sky and sunlit cloud tops.

The plane was half-empty, with no one between him and the aisle. Occasional curious looks from flight attendants and other passengers did not bother him. He was beyond that, accepting their stares as normal, just as he accepted the head bandages and bristly sprouting hair. If his appearance were enough to stir curiosity, what would people say if they knew what sat *inside* his head?

Maybe they would be as unimpressed as he had been. Colin had been shown the device before its insertion, and seen nothing to suggest its powers: a swollen iridescent disk no bigger than his fingernail, surrounded by the hollow legs of sensors and drug delivery system. Super-beetle. An unlikely candidate to be his savior. He felt nothing, but according to the London doctors it had set to work at once. The battle was going on now. Deep within his skull, bloated with slow poison, the scarab was stinging the crab's microstases in silent conflict.

And the chance that it would succeed? No one would give him odds. Bad sign.

"Make a note of thoughts that strike you as unusual." Wollaston, on their last meeting before Colin flew to England, had maintained his imperturbability. "We can watch your stomach at work, or your gall bladder. But you're the only one who knows how normally your brain is functioning. Record your dreams."

"My *dreams?* Doctor Wollaston, even before I got sick, my dreams never made much sense."

"They don't have to. Remember what Havelock Ellis said: 'Dreams are real while they last; can we say more of life?' I want to know about them."

Colin was beginning to agree. Dreams and life, life and dreams; he had felt like telling Wollaston that his whole life had become one waking dream, on that morning when a headache came and grew and would not go. Since then nothing had been real. The pain had gone with the operation, but in its place was a continuous foreboding. *Never glad confident morning again*. He did not recall a real dream of any kind since the operation. And he did not want to write notes on his condition; he wanted it never to have happened.

The flight attendant had paused by Colin's row of seats and was staring at him questioningly. He did not want to talk to her; to avoid it he stared again out of the window. The sun was visible in the dark sky, farther toward the rear of the plane. At Mach Two they were outpacing it. Time was running backwards. *Call back yesterday, bid time return.*

Colin shivered at a slow stir of movement, deep within his brain. Something there was waking from long sleep. He stared straight at the sun. His pupils contracted, his hands relaxed. Fully awake, he began to dream.

I was standing on a flat shore, watching the sea. Or maybe I was sitting, I can't tell because I had no sense of feeling of legs and arms. I just knew I was there. Enjoying the sunshine on my bare back, feeling good. More than good, absolutely terrific. Cold, perfect day, I could feel the blood running in my veins. Something must have died a mile or so offshore, or maybe it was a school of fish, because thousands of flying things were swooping and turning and settling. I decided I would swim out there and see for myself...

Julia Trantham looked up from the third sheet. "Does it just go on like this for all the rest? Because if it does, I can't help. It's not specific enough."

"I know." Wollaston nodded. "It would have been nice if you could have said, hey, that's where we spent my fourteenth summer. But I didn't expect it would ring any particular bells. Keep reading, if you would — I want you to have the context for something else."

"And I thought you asked me here for dinner."

He did not reply. She went on in silence until she reached the last page, then looked up with raised eyebrows. "So?"

He took four pages of 20″ × 14″ unlined paper from a folder and slid them across the table. "Colin found what he had written as unsatisfactory as you do. He says he's an artist, not a writer. Pictures, not words. What do you make of these?"

The drawings were sepia ink on white background. Julia glanced for a few seconds at the first couple of sheets and put them aside, but the other two occupied her for a long time. James Wollaston watched her closely but did not speak or move.

"If you tell me these are all Colin's, I'll have to accept that they are." She tapped the first two pages, spread out on the table of Wollaston's dining room. "But these ones sure don't look like it."

"Why not?"

"Not detailed enough." She picked up one of the sheets. "When you ask Colin to draw something, he draws it *exactly*. It's not that he lacks imagination, but he never cheats. Once he's seen it, he can draw it. And he sees more than you or I."

"He didn't see these. He dreamed them."

"You're the one who's been telling me that dreams are as real as anything else. Anyway, compare the first two pages with the others. These must be birds, because they're flying. But they're cartoon birds, vague wings and bodies and heads, almost as though Colin didn't care what they looked like. And now look at these other two, the tidal shellfish and crabs and worms. Precise. Every joint and every hair drawn in. See this? It's *Pecten jacobaeus* — a scallop. Look at the eyes on the fringed mantle. You could use it as a textbook illustration. That's Colin's trademark. Same with the two lugworms. You can tell they're different species. But those first two pages are just *wrong*." She paused. "You don't see it, do you?"

"I can't argue with you." Wollaston stared at the pages as though he were seeing them for the first time. He had taken off his tie and draped it over a chair back, and now he picked it up and rolled it around his forefingers.

"But you don't like it," said Julia, "what I said about the first two sheets?"

"I do not."

"It's a bad sign?"

"I don't know. I know it's not a *good* sign. In Colin's situation the best change in behavior is no change."

"Do you think it's coming back?"

"I'd love to say, no, of course not. But I don't know. God, I hate to keep saying it to you. I don't know, I don't know. But it's the truth." He came closer, half a step nearer than convention permitted. "Julia, I wish I *could* say something more definite. It could be the treatment—new drug, new protocol, new delivery system."

"But you don't think it is."

"I think these drawings may be the effects of the treatment." He slid the sheets back into the folder. "But they're not the whole story. I go more by look and sound and sense. My gut feel says it's something more than side effects. I think Colin has problems. How long are you staying?"

"I've been wondering. I could stay the whole summer. It's late to do it, but if I moved fast I could even make part of next year a sabbatical. Should I?"

She was tense, hearing the question behind the question, not sure she wanted to hear the answer.

"I think you should." James Wollaston looked more miserable than an objective physician had a right to look. "I think you should stay, until—Well, stay as long as you can."

The northern bedroom of the ground-floor apartment had been converted to a studio, its bare expanse of window looking out onto a paved courtyard where weeds pushed up between cracked stones. The studio lay at

the end of a corridor, far from the entrance to the apartment. Julia stood and listened as she came through the front door.

Total silence. That was odd. For the past three months her arrival had always produced a call of "Hi!" and a quick appearance in the kitchen to discuss dinner plans. He must be really deep into his work.

She slipped off her shoes and stole along the corridor.

Colin was in the studio, standing at the easel with his back half-turned to her. He was working in acrylics, and she saw a vivid flash of colors on the big board. She studied him as she came in. The hair on the back of his head had regrown completely, it must be two inches long now; but he was terribly thin, just gaunt bones, and the skin on his temple had a pale, translucent look. She saw that the food on the tray table beyond the easel was untouched. He must have eaten nothing since she left, over ten hours ago.

"Col?"

He did not seem to hear. He was painting furiously, brush strokes as rapid and sure as they had ever been. She came to his shoulder to examine the picture, but before she reached the easel she glanced up at his face. His gray eyes were unnaturally bright, and there was a smile of exquisite pleasure on his gaunt face. But it was not for Julia. He did not know that she was there. He was smiling away into some private space.

"Colin!" She touched his arm, suddenly frightened. The brushstrokes faltered, the moving hand slowed. He blinked, frowned, and turned toward her.

"Julie—" he said. "I'm through one barrier. It's wonderful, but now there's another. Bigger. I can't see a way past it yet." His hand jerked up and down, a quick chopping movement with the paintbrush. "Like a wall. If I can just get through this one..."

The expression of ecstasy was replaced by surprise. He swayed and groaned, his lips drawing back from his teeth. Julia saw his gums, pale and bloodless, and the veinless white of his eyes. The brush fell to the floor. She grabbed for his arm, but before she could catch him he had crumpled forward, pawing at the painting and easel before falling heavily on top of them.

"I don't care *what* you tell Colin. I want your prognosis, no matter how bad it looks."

It was long after working hours. Julia Trantham was sitting at one end of the uncomfortable vinyl-covered couch in the doctor's reception room. Her face was as pale as her brother's had been, twenty-four hours earlier.

"At the moment Colin doesn't want to hear anything. Doesn't seem to care. That's not as unusual as you might think." Wollaston had been standing, but now he came to sit next to her. "People hide from bad news."

"And it *is* bad news. Isn't it?"

"It's very bad. And it's not a surprise." He sighed and leaned his head back on the smooth yellow seatback. At dinner he had switched to martinis instead of the usual wine. Julia could see the difference. He was more talkative than usual, and he needed her to be an audience.

"I wonder what it will be like a hundred years from now," he went on. "The physicians will look back and think we were like medieval barbers, trying to practice medicine without the tools. All the cancer treatments except surgery are based on the same principle: do something that kills the patient, and hope it kills the cancer a bit faster. The anti-metabolite drugs — like the ones in Colin's implant — kill cancer cells when the cells divide. But a few resistant ones survive, and they go on and multiply. I've seen it a thousand times. You start chemotherapy, and at first the patient does well, wonderfully well. Then over the months . . . the slip back starts."

"That's what's happened to Colin — even with this new experimental treatment?"

He was nodding, eyes closed and the back of his head still against the couch. "Experimental treatments are like lotteries. You have to play to win. But you don't win very often." He reached out blind and groped for her hand. "I'm sorry, Julia. We're not winning. It's back. Growing *fast*. I can't believe the change since the last CAT scan."

"How long, Jim?"

"I don't know. Pretty quick. Colin can come out of the hospital if he wants to; keeping him in won't help. A hospice might be better. A day or two, a few weeks, a month. Nobody knows."

"And there's no other treatment you can try?"

He said nothing. Julia stared across at the wall, where Wollaston had hung one of Colin's post-operative drawings, a lightning sketch of half a dozen lines that was clearly a picture of some kind of bird feeding her chick, the beak inside the little one's gaping bill and halfway down its throat.

"When did Colin draw the picture on the wall there?"

"About two weeks ago." Wollaston stirred. "It's wonderful, isn't it? Have you seen all the others — the ones he's done since the operation?"

"I haven't seen any. It's a habit we got into years ago. I wouldn't look at Colin's work when he was getting ready for a show or a delivery until the end, then I'd give him my opinion of the whole thing. He didn't like me in his studio."

"Maybe it's just as well. Some of the recent ones have been . . . strange."

"You mean he's losing his technique? God, to Colin that would be worse than dying."

"No. The *technique* is terrific. But the animals don't look right. For instance, he drew a pair of seals. But their flippers were too *developed*, too much like real legs. And there was one of a zebra, except it wasn't quite a zebra, more like a funny okapi. I wondered at first if the pictures could tell me something about what's going on in Colin's head, but they haven't. I'd say he's feeling strange, so he's drawing strange." He patted her hand. "I know, Julia, 'Colin draws just what he sees,' don't say it."

"Real legs, you say? And there's *wing claws* on that bird, that's what's odd. But it's not a baby hoactzin."

The hand was pulled from his. There was a rapid movement of the couch next to him. Wollaston opened his eyes. "Julia?"

But she was no longer by his side. She was over at the wall, gazing with total concentration at Colin's drawing. When she turned, her mouth was an open o of confusion and surmise.

"There they are." Julia Trantham patted a stack of papers, boards and canvases. They were in Wollaston's office, with the big wooden desk swept clear and the table lamp on its highest setting. "Every one we could find. But instead of grouping according to medium and size, the way you usually would, I've rearranged them to chronological order. There are eighty-nine pictures here, all signed and dated. The top one is the first drawing that Colin made when he was flying back from England. The last one is the painting he was working on in his studio when he passed out. I want you to look through the whole stack before you say anything."

"If you say so." James Wollaston was humoring her, knowing she had been under terrible stress for months. It was close to midnight, and they had spent the last hour collecting Colin Trantham's pictures, pulling them from medical records and apartment and studio. Julia would not tell him what game she was playing, but he could see that to her it was far more than a game. He started carefully through the heap: pen and ink drawings, charcoal sketches, oils and acrylics and pencils.

"Well?" Julia was too impatient to wait for him to finish. She was staring at him expectantly, although he was on only the tenth picture.

"Did he always draw nothing but nature scenes?" said Wollaston. "Just plants and animals?" He was staring at sheet after sheet.

"Mostly. Colin is a top biological illustrator. Why?"

"You insist he drew from life, from what he had seen. But in these pictures that doesn't seem to be true."

"Why not?" Julia pounced on him with the question.

"Well, I recognize the first drawings, and they're terrific. But this" — he held out the board he was examining — "it looks wrong."

"It's not wrong. That's *Castoroidinae* — a rodent, a sort of beaver. Keep going. What's that one?"

"Damned if I know. Like a cross between a horse and a dog — as though Colin started by drawing a horse's head, then when he got to the body and legs he changed his mind."

"You were right about the horse. That's *Hyraco-therium*. To the life. *Keep going.*"

But Wollaston had paused. "Are you sure? It looks strange to me, and I have a pretty good grounding in comparative anatomy."

"I'm sure you do." Julia took a painting from the stack. They were less than halfway through the heap. Her hands were trembling. "*Current* anatomy, Jim. But I specialize in *paleo*-anatomy. Colin has been drawing real plants and animals. The only thing is, some of them are *extinct*. *Castoroidinae* was a giant beaver, big as a bear. It was around during the Pleistocene. *Hyracotherium*'s a forerunner of the horse; it flourished during the Lower Eocene, forty or fifty million years ago. These pictures are consistent with our best understanding of their anatomy based on the fossil record."

She was shaking, but Wollaston did not share her excitement. "I'll take your word for it, Julia. But I want to point out that none of this is too surprising, given your own interests and the work you do."

"That's not true!" Julia fumbled out a cigarette, lit it, and inhaled hard enough to shrivel the bottom of her lungs. "It's more than surprising, it's *astonishing*. I told you the first time we had a drink together, what I do bores Colin stiff. He doesn't know beans about it and he doesn't care. There's *no way* he got these drawings from me. And do you realize that these pictures are in *reverse chronological order*? Fossil dating is a tricky business, I'm the first to admit that; but in this set, the more recently Colin did them, the older the forms represented."

"What are you *saying*, Julia?" The concern in Wollaston's voice was for sister more than brother. "If you're suggesting…what it sounds like you're suggesting, then it's nonsense. And there's a perfectly rational explanation."

"Like what?"

He reached forward, removed the cigarette from her fingers, and stubbed it out. "Julia, the longer you study the human brain, the more astonishing it seems. You say that what you do bores Colin. Probably true. But do you think that means he didn't even hear you, when you talked and talked paleontology all these years? Do you think he never picked up one of your books? They're scattered all over the apartment, I've seen them there myself. It's no wonder you recognize what Colin has been painting because you put all those ideas into his head *yourself*."

"I didn't, Jim. I know I didn't. And here's why." She was turning the stack, moving down towards the bottom. "Now we're beyond the K-T barrier — the time of the Late Cretaceous extinction. See this?"

The painting was in subdued oils, browns and ochers and dark greens, crowded with detail. The viewpoint was low to the ground, peering up through a screen of ferns. In the clearing beyond the leafy cover crouched three scaly animals, staring at a group of four others advancing from the left. The sun was low, casting long shadows to the right, and there was a hint of morning ground mist still present to soften outlines.

"Saurischians. Coelurosaurs, I'd say, and not very big ones." Julia pointed to the three animals in the foreground. "The pictures we were looking at before were all Tertiary or later. But everything beyond that is Cretaceous or *earlier*. I'd place this one as middle Jurassic, a hundred and sixty million years ago. No birds, no flowering plants. I know those three animals — but the four behind them are completely new to me. I've never seen anything like them. If I had to guess I'd say they're a form of small hadrosaur, some unknown midget relative of *Orthomerus*. That flat hulk, way over in the background, is probably a crocodile. But look at the detail on the coelurosaurs, Jim. I couldn't have told Colin all that — I couldn't even have *imagined* it. Look at the scales and wrinkles and pleats in the mouth pouch, look at the eyes and the saw-toothed brow ridges — I've never seen those on any illustration, anywhere. The vegetation fits, too, all gymnosperms, cycads and ginkgos and conifers."

James Wollaston laughed, but there was no suggestion from his face that he found anything funny. He was sure that Julia Trantham was practicing her own form of denial, of reality avoidance. "Julia, if you came in to see me as a patient and said all that, I'd refer you for immediate testing. Listen to yourself!"

But she had moved to the final drawing, smeared where Colin Trantham had fallen on top of it before it was dry. "And this is earlier yet." She was talking quietly, and not to Wollaston. He stared at her hopelessly.

"Something like *Rutiodon*, one of the phytosaurs. But a different jaw. And there on the left is *Desmatosuchus*, one of the aëtosaurs. I don't recognize that other one, but it has mammalian characteristics."

She looked up. "My God, we must be back near the beginning of the Triassic. Over two hundred million years. These are thecodonts, the original dinosaur root stock. He's jumping further and further! Jim, I'm scared."

He reached out for her, and she clung to him and buried her face in his jacket. But her words were perfectly clear: "First thing in the morning, I've got to see Colin."

What James Wollaston had heard with incredulity, Colin Trantham listened to with a remote and dreamy interest. Julia had taken one look at him, and known that no matter what the neurologist might say, Colin would never be leaving the hospital. It was not the IV's, or the bluish pallor of his face. It was something else, an impalpable smell in the air of the room that made her look at her brother and see the skull beneath the skin.

Whatever it was, he seemed oblivious to it. He was grinning, staring at her and beyond her, his face filled with the same ecstasy that she had seen in the studio. His conversation faded in and out, at one moment perfectly rational, the next jumping off in some wild direction.

"Very interesting. The implant and the drugs, of course, that's what's doing it. Has to be." From his tone he might have been talking of a treatment applied to some casual acquaintance. "Did you know, Julia, if I were a bird I'd be in much better shape than I am now? Good old Hemsley operated on me, and he got most of it. But he must have missed a little bit — a bit too much for the implant to handle. Poor little scarab, can't beat the crab. But if I'd been a *bird*, they could have cut away the whole of both cerebral hemispheres, and I'd be as good as ever. Or nearly as good. Wouldn't know how to build a nest, of course, but who needs that?"

And then suddenly he was laughing, a gasping laugh that racked his chest and shook the tubes leading into his fleshless arms.

"Colin!" The fear that curiosity had held at bay came flooding back, and Julia was terrified. "I'll get the nurse."

"I'm fine." He stopped the strained laughter as quickly as he had started it and his face went calm. "Better than fine. But I'm a robot now. I, Robot."

She stared at him in horror, convinced that the final disintegration of mind was at hand.

"You know what I mean, Julie." Now he sounded rational but impatient. Don't go stupid on me. Remember what Feynman said, in physics you can look on any positron as an electron that's traveling backward in time. You tell me I've been jumping backward —"

"Jim says that's nonsense. He says I'm talking through my hat."

"Jim?"

"Dr. Wollaston."

"So it's *Jim*, is it. And how long has that been going on?" He narrowed his eyes and peered up at her slyly. "Well, you tell *Jim* that I agree with you. I'm going backwards, and I can prove it. And according to Feynman that means the electrons in my brain are positrons. I've got a *positronic brain*. Get it?" He laughed again, slapping his skinny hands on the bedsheets. "Positronic brain. I'm a robot!"

"Colin, I'm getting the nurse. Right now." Julia had already pressed the button, but no one had appeared.

"In a minute. And you know *how* I can prove it? I can prove it because I feel absolutely wonderful."

His face had filled again with that strange bliss. He reached out and held her hand. "Remember how it felt when you were four years old, and you woke up in the morning, and you knew it was your birthday? That's how it used to be, all the time for all of us. But ontogeny recapitulates phylogeny: immature forms pass through the evolutionary stages of their ancestors. And that applies to *feelings* as well as bodies. Little kids feel the way all the animals *used* to feel, a long time ago. That's the way I am when I'm there. Fantastic, marvelous. And the further I go, the better it gets. You looked at my pictures. If I've been going back, how far did I get?"

Julia hesitated. She was torn. Half of her wanted to believe her brother, to see more of those marvelously detailed drawings and to analyze them. The other half told her she was dealing with a mind already hopelessly twisted by disease.

"Your last picture shows the period of the earliest dinosaurs. They're all thecodonts, nothing that most people would recognize. The fossil record is very spotty there. We don't know nearly as much about them as we'd like to."

"And what would be next — going backward, I mean?"

"The Permian. No dinosaurs. And at this end of the Permian, over ninety percent of all the life-forms on earth died off. We don't know why."

He was nodding. "The barrier. I can feel it, you know, when I'm trying to jump. I went through one, when all the dinosaurs died off. This one is bigger. I've been trying to fight my way through. I'm nearly there, but it's taking every bit of energy I have."

"Col, anything that tires you or upsets you is *bad*. You need rest. Why are you climbing imaginary walls?"

"You don't know the feeling. If I could jump all the way back, right to the first spark of life, I bet the intensity of life force and joy would be just about too much to stand. I'm going there, Julie. Across the barrier, into the Permian, all the way to the begin-

ning. And I'm never coming back. *Never*."

As though on cue, the thin body arched up from the bed, arms flailing. The mouth widened to a rictus of infernal torment and breath came hoarse and loud. Julia cried out, just as the nurse appeared. Wollaston was right behind her.

"Grand mal." He was bending over Colin, grabbing at a rubber spatula and pushing it into the mouth just as the teeth clenched down. "Hold this, nurse, we don't want him swallowing his tongue."

But the spasm ended as quickly as it had started. Colin Trantham lay totally at ease, his breath slow and easy. His face smoothed, and the fixed grin faded. In its place came a look of infinite calm and blissful peace.

"Dr. Wollaston!" The nurse was watching the monitors, her hand on Cohn's pulse. "Dr. Wollaston, we have arrhythmia. Becoming fainter."

Wollaston had the hypodermic with its six-inch needle in his hand, the syringe already filled. It was poised above Colin Trantham's chest when he caught Julia's eye.

She shook her head. "No, Jim. Please. Not for one month more pain."

He hesitated, finally nodded, and stepped away from the bed.

"Dr. Wollaston." The nurse looked up, sensing that she had missed something important but not sure what. She was still holding Colin Trantham's wrist. "I can't help him. He's going, doctor. He's going."

Julia Trantham moved to grip her brother's other hand in both of hers.

"He is," she said. "He's going." She leaned forward, to stare down into open eyes that still sparkled with a surprised joy. "He's going. And I'd give anything to know where."

3.
THE DINOSAUR RADIATIONS

ESSAY BY TERESA MARYANSKA
SPECULATION BY DAVE WOLVERTON

THE DINOSAUR RADIATIONS
TERESA MARYANSKA

I DON'T KNOW ANYBODY WHO COULD NOT IN A MORE OR LESS PRECISE WAY GIVE THE ANSWER TO THE question: what is a dinosaur? However, when we ask another question, namely: what distinguished dinosaurs from other contemporary or present-day reptiles, many people have problems with giving the right answer. Fascination with the often gigantic size and the shapes of dinosaurs is what generally dominates in all those answers. To provide the right answer to both questions, one ought to examine the basic differences in the anatomic structure of skeletons of dinosaurs and other reptiles as well as the consequences of these differences.

Let's take a look at the results of recent paleontologic research which has yielded important new information about dinosaurs. The new data has led to great advances in understanding. However, we have to be aware of the fact that many problems concerning the development of dinosaurs and their biology will never be completely solved. Even the most fascinating results of each year's paleontological expeditions and scientific research on fossil materials could only be compared to small bricks or at the most to a fragment of a wall which is itself a part of some big construction which started in the 1820s, but which will never achieve completion.

Is it surprising? No! Dinosaurs appeared on the earth about 225 mybp (million years before present), in the second half of the Triassic Period of the Mesozoic Era, lived through the Jurassic, and died about 65 mybp (at the end of the Cretaceous), tens of millions of years before the appearance of humans on the earth. Only scraps of information about organisms from past geologic epochs reach our times in the form of fossils. This incompleteness was caused by many complex geologic processes going on throughout the earth's history. Among other factors, it was the successive changes of the distribution of seas and oceans which forever wiped out the remains of animals once inhabiting the land.

DINOSAURS DEFINED: THE SKELETON SPEAKS

Before we go on to discuss the diversity and the distribution of dinosaurs, we need to agree as to what a dinosaur really was. Recent research results allow us to determine quite precisely the features that are shared by dinosaurs and at the same time distinguish them from all other reptiles. For example, the fact that dinosaurs were exclusively terrrestrial animals is generally better known than the fact that they were reptiles capable of walking and running extremely efficiently, with upright posture and erect gait. These capabilities developed as a result of anatomic changes in the structure of the limbs, especially of the hindlimbs, and changes in the hip joint and the backbone structure. Some of these characters were inherited from their archosaur ("ruling reptile") ancestors, others were unique to dinosaurs, but the combination of these characters is known only in dinosaurs.

The most significant change concerns the position of dinosaur limbs: they were held underneath the body (so-called erect posture, resulting in erect gait) and not, as in a great majority of reptiles, out to the sides (so-

50

called sprawling posture and gait). Such a position of limbs allowed dinosaurs to raise their bodies significantly above the ground, which consequently increased their ability to walk and run. Erect posture is associated with the changes in the structure of the upper leg bone (the femur) and the hip joint. For example, the femoral head is clearly offset from the shaft by a narrowing (called the femoral neck) which directs it towards the socket in the hip joint. This socket (acetabulum) in dinosaurs is perforated at least partially. The structure of the ankle joint is also a result of important anatomical modifications. All dinosaurs possess the so-called mesotarsal joint, in which the axis at the ankle joint runs straight between the two adjacent ankle bones and the other foot bones, providing the toed dinosaurian foot with great mobility. Additional features distinguishing dinosaurs from other reptiles include: the division of the vertebral column into several regions, a long and mobile neck, and at least three sacral vertebrae in contact with the pelvis. There are also differences in the forelimb structure in comparison with other reptiles. The fourth and fifth fingers in the hand were shortened. Due to this, the hand became asymmetrical. The appearance of the asymmetrical hand in the oldest dinosaurs made it possible to shift the forelimbs from their function of support and locomotion over to food manipulation.

These are, in summary, the most important dinosaur features. I am fully aware that among these features I did not include gigantic size, for it is not true that all dinosaurs were giants. Gigantic size characterized only some groups of dinosaurs. Many of these animals were medium or even relatively small-sized, though none were diminutive adults. Thus, their size range could be fully comparable to the size diversity of the contemporary fauna of land vertebrates.

At the time when the first dinosaurs appeared, all continents were merged into a single supercontinent called Pangaea, and that is exactly what promoted the spread of dinosaurs. Beginning at the end of the Triassic and lasting through Jurassic and Cretaceous times, the splitting of the supercontinent into our present land masses, separated to a greater or lesser extent by seas and oceans, caused the isolation and divergent evolution of the dinosaur fauna living on different continents. Likewise, changes in the flora which occurred simultaneously influenced dinosaur development and radiation. In the Late Triassic, when the first dinosaurs reached their worldwide distribution, ferns, seed ferns, horsetails, lycopods, ginkgos, and conifers were the dominant plants. The presently widespread angiosperms (flowering plants) first appeared in the Early Cretaceous and became the dominant terrestrial plants during the Late Cretaceous. As we will see later, this transition greatly affected the Late Cretaceous radiation of dinosaurs.

THE MAJOR DINOSAUR CLASSES

Among the earliest dinosaurs, one can observe that there were two main groups. Before a more detailed discussion of the dinosaurs' diversity, let's concentrate on this general division.

From 1841, when the British anatomist, Richard Owen, coined the name Dinosauria (meaning "terrible lizard") for what were at that time scarce and huge reptile remains, dinosaurs were regarded as a single group of reptiles. Another British anatomist, Harry G. Seeley, was the first to notice that dinosaurs could be divided into two groups depending on their hip arrangement. In 1887, he introduced the name Ornithischia ("bird-hipped") for one group and Saurischia ("reptile-hipped") for the other. Since the time of Seeley's division of dinosaurs, many authors have thought that each group evolved independently, from different archosaurian ancestors. Today, this view has been modified radically, and almost all researchers

Preceding page: A group of Australian dinosaurs from various parts of the Early Cretaceous. They signify the radiations of dinosaurs into many types and to distant climes. In the foreground are two large Muttaburrasaurs, *a* Fulgotherium *(herbivores), and behind them the ferocious* Rapator. *By Mark Hallett.*

believe that both groups, Ornithischia and Saurischia, are closely related and that all dinosaurs form a so-called monophyletic group, originating from a common ancestor.

What distinguishes saurischian and ornithischian? Since the basis for the first distinction of these two groups was the pelvic structure, let's start by examining the differences in this structure. As in all tetrapods (land vertebrates), the pelvis of dinosaurs consists of three paired bones: the ilium, the pubis, and the ischium. These three bones join together in the area of the hip socket (acetabulum). The ilium, the upper hip bone, joins the pelvis and also indirectly the hindlimb with the backbone. In the Saurischia, the pubis is directed forward and the ischium backward, which makes the pelvis similar to that of other reptiles. This is where the name "reptile-hipped" comes from. In the Ornithischia, the pubis position is different from what we normally see in reptiles; it is directed backward and runs parallel to the ischium. Such an arrangement of bones characterizes birds, and thus the name "bird-hipped" came about. If the pelvic structure were the only difference between the Saurischia and the Ornithischia, it would have to be rejected in the light of recent discoveries, for we know already that there exist some members of the Saurischia (very few, but they exist), in which the pubis also points backward. However, in both Saurischia and Ornithischia, we notice many other traits unique to their members, which allow us to easily decide which a given animal belongs to.

What is unique for all — beginning with the oldest — representatives of the Saurischia, for example, is the elongation of the neck vertebrae (in consequence, the neck is relatively long); the presence of additional intervertebral articulations between trunk vertebrae; the considerable asymmetry of the hand, with the second finger the longest and the first, very heavy finger exhibiting a large claw. Another unique feature of the

Saurischia was an advanced development of muscles of the temporal (cheek) region of the skull. Their attachment sites spread toward the front of the skull. The saurischian dinosaurs contain both carnivorous and herbivorous forms. Relations between particular subgroups of the Saurischia have often been controversial and even today various conflicting hypotheses are still put forward.

What is an ornithischian? What are the features which allow us to classify an animal as belonging to the bird-hipped dinosaurs? Aside from the position of the pubis turned to the back (we do not know a single member of the Ornithischia that has the pubis directed forward), its shape is different from the pubis in the Saurischia. Among other things, that is due to its elongated, slender, rodlike shaft and to the appearance of the additional spur directed forward, called a prepubis. Characteristic of ornithischians are, among other skeletal features, the presence of ossified tendons along the vertebral column and the presence of at least five sacral vertebrae in contact with the pelvis. Many unique features can also be seen in the structure of the skull, jaws and teeth. Among them, for example, are the presence of a toothless bone called a predentary at the front of the lower jaw and a toothless forward end of the upper jaw. The roughened, external surface of the predentary and the front portion of the upper jaw are an indication of a once-present horny bill in front of the snout. By contact, in the Saurischia, the front of the snout in both jaws is toothed. Unlike in the reptile-hipped, the teeth in bird-hipped dinosaurs exhibit a clear neck separating the root from the crown of the tooth. The crowns are leaf-shaped. This tooth structure provides a clear proof that all members of the Ornithischia were herbivorous. All dinosaur skulls exhibit a characteristic bony indentation (antorbital fossil) situated on the side of the skull between the nostrils and orbits (eye openings). There is an opening (fenestra) at the bottom of the fossa, which is a

A general scene of predators and prey from the Lower Cretaceous in Antarctica based on the few fossils now known and the Cretaceous fauna of South America. By William G. Stout.

feature inherited from an archosaurian ancestor. In the Saurischia, this indentation is large and carries at least one fenestra, whereas in the Ornithischia the fossa as well as its fenestra are significantly reduced or missing.

In the course of evolution, these defining features of the Saurischia and the Ornithischia underwent many modifications, and the state of these changes together with appearance of other, new anatomic features characterize different subgroups of the two main dinosaurian lines.

The fact that ornithischians have descended from a common ancestor has not stirred up controversy since the time it was first proven. Much debate, however, dealt with mutual relationships among smaller groups within the Ornithischia, and especially the role played by the Ornithopoda in the development of the bird-hipped dinosaurs. However, before we pass on to a more detailed discussion of dinosaur diversity, a short note about the classification principles adopted here is necessary.

SISTER GROUPS AND SPECIALIZED CHARACTERS

Since ancient times, classification of the animal world has been based on overall similarities. A new methodology stressing the importance of specialized characters (called derived characters) was devised about thirty years ago. This method is named phylogenetic systematics or cladistics. Two or more animal groups may share a number of characters, but some of these are inherited from remote common ancestors and, thus, do not tell us about the degree of relationship between the groups of interest. But the derived characters shared by the members of the two groups reveal their close relationship. A special name, sister groups, was coined for two groups that share a number of specialized characteristics. When I talk about sister groups, the reader should understand that I refer to two groups descending from a common ancestor and being more closely related to each other than to other mentioned groups.

A major reclassification, based on shared, derived characters, was recently presented by two American paleontologists, Jacques Gauthier and Paul Sereno, in order to distinguish different groups within the Saurischia and Ornithischia. Even though certain details of the suggested classification are still controversial and can be changed, Gauthier's and Sereno's proposals are almost universally accepted.

I could go on to discuss the diversity of the Ornithischia and Saurischia (and now I can say that they are sister groups) if not for the fact that there are several South American Late Triassic dinosaurs which cannot be placed in either group. Apparently, they represent the geologically oldest verified dinosaur remains, and at the same time they are the most primitive dinosaurs known so far. Represented by scarce and incomplete skeletons (until a recent discovery by Sereno), they are called the Herrerasauridae and are considered a sister group to all other dinosaurs (i.e., Ornithischia and Saurischia).

THE BIRD-HIPPED DINOSAURS

Now, let's look at the diversity of the Ornithischia. Late Triassic ornithischian dinosaurs, because of the fragmentary nature of their remains, cannot definitely be placed among any recognized subgroup of the Ornithischia. However, their presence among the fossil vertebrates from the Upper Triassic sediments proves that primitive bird-hipped dinosaurs first achieved their worldwide distribution during the Late Triassic. To the primitive members of the Ornithischia belong the best-known Early Jurassic fabrosaurids, the *Lesothosaurus* from South Africa. The presence of many primitive features allows us to say that these creatures differ only slightly from the common ornithischian ancestor. Because of this, we may call them basal ornithischians. But this does not mean that *Lesothosaurus* is the ancestor of other ornithischians. Today, it is believed that it represents an independent, Early Jurassic line of ornithischians that form a sister taxon (or branch group) to all other bird-hipped dinosaurs.

The basic differences between fabrosaurids and all other members of the Ornithischia is that the cheeks are missing, though they are present in all other reptiles, recent reptiles included. Cheeks are present in other ornithischians, which are therefore called Genasauria ("cheeked" dinosaurs). In all Genasauria, cheek cavities were formed due to a displacement of teeth rows from the side of the face toward the middle of the mouth cavity. The appearance of cheek cavities and cheeks (which are formed by muscles) was certainly linked with the ability to provide a space for collecting chewed-up plants before swallowing.

Already in the Early Jurassic, there was a high degree of diversity among "cheeked" dinosaurs. They were represented by primitive Thyreophora ("shield bearers") and fleet-footed Ornithopoda. Let's now take a close look at the history of the two groups. We will start with the description of the Thyreophora, because all evidence seems to suggest that they formed a sister taxon to the all other "cheeked" ornithischians. Among the derived features which distinguish all members of the Thyreophora (i.e., features which must have been present in their common ancestor) from other ornithischians are rows of plates covering their bodies. The oldest representatives of the Thyreophora are known from the Lower Jurassic sediments of Europe and North America. They were relatively small, about 3 meters long, called scelidosaurids. Advanced thyreophorans first appeared in the Middle Jurassic and are represented by two different groups: Stegosauria and Ankylosauria.

STEGOSAURS

The Stegosauria were medium to large quadrupedal (four-legged) animals (up to 9 meters in length) with small skulls, weak dentition, short and massive forelimbs, long columnar hindlimbs, hooflike nails, and a system of vertical plates and spikes on both sides of the backbone. The earliest remains of the Stegosauria occur in the Middle Jurassic sediments in China and Europe. This group flourished in the Late Jurassic. At that time, they constituted the dominant group of bird-hipped dinosaurs in parts of Europe, China, and Africa, and were especially numerous in North America. They are also known from a few Lower Cretaceous deposits, mainly from China and Europe, and some fragmentary Upper Cretaceous remains from India.

Closely related to stegosaurs are ankylosaurs. These were quadrupedal animals whose whole bodies as well as their skulls were covered with a bony armor. Among numerous structural features of the skull and the rest of the skeleton that distinguish ankylosaurs from other dinosaurs is the distinctive shape of the upper hipbone, which has a very long front portion and a very short rear portion. Ankylosaurs can be clearly divided into two groups: the Nodosauridae (more lightly built) and the Ankylosauridae (more heavily built), whose tail bears a large club at its end. The oldest, rare, Late Jurassic remains of nodosaurids are known from Europe. Later remains occur commonly in Cretaceous sediments of Europe and North America and are also known from Australia. So far they have not been reported in Asia. Ankylosauridae are exclusively a Late Cretaceous group, and their very numerous remains, many with whole skeletons, are known from North America and Asia. Recently armored dinosaurs have even been discovered in Antarctica.

ORNITHOPODS

The next large taxon of bird-hipped dinosaurs, more diversified and numerous than other ornithischian groups, is the "bird-footed" Ornithopoda, exhibiting specialized teeth. All representatives of this group share, among other features, a very long prepubic process directed forward. The Ornithopoda consist of the heterodontosaurs, hypsilophodonts, iguanodonts, and hadrosaurs.

Heterodontosaurs form a sister group to all other true ornithopods and were a short-lived group, restricted to the Early Jurassic. They were small (one meter in length) bipedal animals with massive skulls, relatively large hands, and jaws containing large caninelike teeth near the front. Their very rare remains occur only in South Africa.

Among the other, true ornithopods, the hypsilophodonts ("high ridged tooth") were a group of small to medium sized (1 to 5 meters in length) bipeds with small skulls and robust lower jaws. Their closely arranged teeth formed a continuous sharp cutting edge in each jaw. They also exhibited grasping hands and distinct bony tendons along the tail vertebrae. They are known from the Mid-Jurassic to the Late Cretaceous of Europe, North America, China, Australia and Antarctica. Most species, however, are represented by single skeletons or their parts. The genus *Hypsilophodon*, numerous in the Lower Cretaceous sediments of the British Isles, is an exception.

IGUANODONTS AND DUCKBILLS

In comparison to hypsilophodonts, iguanodonts were rather large. During the Late Jurassic and the Early Cretaceous, they reached more than 10 meters in length. Associated with this size increase is the tendency to be bipedal rather than quadrupedal. Iguanodonts exhibit large, toothless, long-snouted skulls with a long row of rather large, tightly arranged, ridged cheek teeth. The immovable first finger of the hand was set at a right angle to the other fingers and ended in a conical nail (a "thumb spike"). Numerous remains of Jurassic iguanodonts are known from America, Europe, and Africa. During the Cretaceous, they spread over South America. Mass burials of more or less complete skeletons have been discovered in Europe.

Hadrosaurs, or "duck-billed" dinosaurs, are the crown of the iguanodont line of ornithopods. They appeared in the Late Cretaceous, lived until the end of this period, and then constituted the most diversified and abundant group of large herbivorous animals in different parts of North America, Asia and Europe. Though less numerous there, they also lived in South America. Some hadrosaur species lived in herds and are known from several dozen specimens, complete skeletons included. Our knowledge of hadrosaurs is relatively complete and includes not only the study of development and skeletal anatomy but also behavior. For example, it is very probable that at least some of the hadrosaurs looked after their young. Hadrosaurs were large (7 to over 10 meters in length) and herbivorous, with long and low skulls, a toothless front of the snout and a complex cheek dentition consisting of complicated dental batteries with hundreds of teeth. They exhibited lightly built hands and massive hindlimbs. Hadrosaurs constitute a group of great diversity. They are basically divided into forms with flat skull roofs and those that carry crests of different shapes above the skull.

THICK-HEADED AND HORNED DINOSAURS

The last major taxon of ornithischian dinosaurs is called the Marginocephalia ("margin-headed" dinosaurs) forming a sister line to the Ornithopoda and including two related subgroups: Pachycephalosauria ("thick-headed" reptiles) and Ceratopsia ("horned" dinosaurs). The unique feature of those two subgroups, which is proof of their close relationship, is the rear edge of the skull roof overhanging the back of the skull as a shelf or margin (that is where the group name comes from).

Both groups first appear in the fossil record from the Early Cretaceous. The only example of the earliest pachycephalosaurian comes from the British Isles. It was a small animal, less than one meter long. There are some more advanced forms, rather rare but more widespread, known from the Upper Cretaceous sediments of North America, Asia, and Madagascar, which reached about 8 meters in length. These bipedal dinosaurs had very short forelimbs, but their unique feature was the unusual thickness of their skull roofs, which in several Late Cretaceous forms are fused into a single massive element forming a high dome.

Horned dinosaurs, well known to everybody, form a sister group to pachycephalosaurs. The features common to all members of the Ceratopsia include the presence of an additional bony, unpaired element (called a rostral bone) at the anterior end of the snout; the triangular shape of the skull in top view; and a bony frill formed from the bones of the back part of the skull roof overhanging the occiput and neck to a greater or lesser extent. The oldest ceratopsians, known from the late Early Cretaceous, came exclusively from Asia and are the psittacosaurs ("parrotlike" dinosaurs). They lived for only a short time, since in sediments of the Upper Cretaceous we do not find their remains. The psittacosaurs' remains are very numerous, and knowledge of some species is based on hundreds of specimens. They were small dinosaurs (about 2 meters in length) with short faces and nostrils positioned very high on the snout. Currently the psittacosaurs are recognized as the primitive sister group to the remaining ceratopsians.

All other Late Cretaceous ceratopsians are called Neoceratopsia. These include protoceratopsids, small (1 to 2.5 meters in length), more primitive quadrupeds capable of rapid bipedal progression. Also there were medium to large (4 to 8 meters in length), exclusively quadrupedal ceratopsids. Skulls of all neoceratopsians are large in relation to the whole body. They have bony frills above the nose and eyes, horns, and tooth batteries adapted to cutting tough plant food.

Protoceratopsids represented a radiation that started in the middle Late Cretaceous and lasted till the end of the Cretaceous in different areas of North America and Asia. They were especially abundant in Asia. The ceratopsids are known from the Upper Cretaceous sediments mainly from North America. In some localities their remains have been discovered in mass burials. This might indicate a gregarious mode of life. Uncertain reports about isolated remains of ceratopsids come from South America and Asia.

REPTILE-HIPPED DINOSAURS

Having covered the bird-hipped dinosaurs, let us discuss reptile-hipped dinosaurs. The major dividing line between the two saurischian sister lines can be drawn between bipedal, carnivorous theropods ("beast feet") and mainly quadrupedal, herbivorous sauropodomorphs ("reptile type feet"). The latter group contains prosauropods and sauropods. Although the relationship between these two taxa is not completely explained at the moment, such a division is presently accepted.

All representatives of the Sauropodomorpha share such features as a relatively small skull (about 5 percent of body length), lanceolate teeth with serrated crowns, at least 10 very long neck vertebrae forming a long neck, an enormously enlarged claw on the first finger in the hand, and a thigh bone longer than the shank bone.

Prosauropods were the most abundant large or medium-sized (2 to 8 meters in length) bipedal or quadrupedal herbivorous vertebrates living on the earth during the Late Triassic and the Early Jurassic. Their numerous remains can be found, frequently in the form of complete skeletons, in North and South

America, Asia, Africa, and Europe. That they were very numerous is suggested by the fact that in some Late Triassic localities of Germany, for example, the remains of prosauropods (in fact, of only one genus, *Plateosaurus*) constitute 75 percent of all present remains of vertebrates, and in some sites of Early Jurassic in China they represent up to 82 percent. Thus, it is not surprising that prosauropods are considered to represent the first great radiation of herbivorous dinosaurs: the first radiation of early high-browsing dinosaurs, lasting from the Late Triassic to the Early Jurassic.

THE GIANT PLANT EATERS

The Sauropoda, on the other hand, constitute a dinosaur group which proved to be a great success not only due to their differentiation, but also due to their long persistence during Mesozoic time. They appeared in the Early Jurassic and were still present in the Late Cretaceous. However, they reached their peak in the Late Jurassic. They were very large (up to 30 meters in length) quadrupedal animals with long necks and long tails, small skulls, heavy columnar limbs, presacral vertebrae lightened by deep cavities, and a greatly reduced number of phalanges (finger bones). There are two major types of skull structure in sauropods, consistent with their division into two taxa. One of them has a skull with a blunt snout, large nostrils and large, spoon-shaped or spatulate teeth. The second type shows a more elongated skull and slender peglike teeth placed only in the front of the jaws. Sauropods were widespread and their remains are known from Africa, Europe, Asia, and North and South America. However, among some 90 recognized genera, right now we know only 5 with complete skeletons, and only 12 specimens have preserved skulls. Most remains consist just of vertebrae or teeth. Judging from the footprints and trackways of sauropods preserved in

some localities, we can conclude, however, that at least some of them were gregarious.

Before we finish with Sauropodomorpha, I would like to present another group of saurischian dinosaurs with a yet-undetermined position within reptile-hipped dinosaurs, which seems to be most closely related to sauropodomorphs. They are the Segnosauria, exclusively Asian, recognized in the 1970s in the middle Upper Cretaceous sediments of Mongolia and China. So far only a few specimens representing this group have been described. From my Mongolian field experience, I can conclude, however, that in some localities of the middle Upper Cretaceous of Mongolia, this group is represented by great numbers of specimens. These medium- to large-sized dinosaurs with an elongated, rather low skull, a toothless front snout and straight, narrow, somewhat pointed, flattened teeth had a pelvis with the pubic bone directed backward and a front portion of the ilium that flared outward. The trunk of these dinosaurs was bulky and feet were relatively short and broad, which leads us to think that segnosaurs were rather slow-moving plant eaters.

THE PREDATORS

All other saurischian dinosaurs make up the bipedal carnivorous theropods. *Tyrannosaurus* is a widely known member of this group. It is the largest known predator on earth, although the majority of theropods were medium-sized. At least 20 features present in all members are proof of a common origin of all theropods. Most features are linked with the predatory lifestyle of theropods. From among them, I will name only a few obvious ones. They are: the presence of a long row of compressed, pointed, back-curved predatory teeth, large orbits (eye sockets), hands with three or fewer functional fingers ending with recurved claws, and long hindlimbs with a long narrow metatarsus. These features of limb structure in theropods were an adaptation to fast running, and this together with prehensile (grasping) hands and a large skull provided with sharp teeth gives a picture of an agile predator. These features are familiar even in the earliest theropod representatives. The earliest well-known theropod (*Coelophysis*) comes from the earliest Late Triassic of North America. Late Triassic theropods are found anywhere that sediments of that age have been preserved. Their distribution and, at the same time, their already high anatomical specialization prove that their history must have started even earlier. That history is still unknown.

Many theropods living in the Late Triassic and Jurassic are included in the Ceratosauria, which exhibited unique cranial ornamentation in the form of crests on the skull roof; long, pointed, delicately built snouts; powerfully built forelimbs with raptorial hands; and feet with sharp claws. Aside from large forms (about 6 meters in length), there were also smaller ceratosaurs (up to 3 meters). Ceratosaurs are often found in mass burials with hundreds of individuals in one place. According to the latest thought, the Ceratosauria constitute a sister line to all other theropods, which are known under the name of Tetanurae ("stiff tails").

All Tetanurae, which appeared in the Early Jurassic and flourished into the Late Cretaceous, developed independently of Ceratosauria. They share such novelties as a reduction in tooth number, an additional opening in the skull in front of the orbit, and changes in hindlimb structure which allowed them a highly efficient cursorial (running) gait. It was this group of theropod dinosaurs that was best equipped to pursue their prey.

Two phylogenetic lines are distinguished within the Tetanurae: a line of a huge predators named the Carnosauria; and a greatly differentiated line of medium-sized and small predators, the Coelurosauria. The bases for differentiating the Carnosauria are their large bodies, especially their skulls with deep, keyhole-shaped orbits, and a robust postcranial skeleton with shortened trunk portion. And even though the Carnosauria includes *Tyrannosaurus*, which is universally known and stirs up strong emotions, our knowledge of this group is far from satisfactory. This is because from among at least 50 genera of Carnosauria most are represented by fragmentary remains. Only four are known from numerous, well-preserved, complete skeletons. The family Allosauridae, Late Jurassic and Early Cretaceous carnosaurs, were widespread in the areas of Asia, western North America, Africa, and Australia. Tyrannosauridae, characterized by a significant reduction of the forelimbs, are known from Late Cretaceous Asia and North America. The geographical expansion of the carnosaurs proves that they were an important element of the Jurassic and Cretaceous fauna, while the lack of mass accumulations of their remains in one place suggests that these large predators hunted individually and not in large groups.

Recent research has led to new information about the diversity and distribution of the sister group to carnosaurs, the coelurosaurs. Most of them belong to a Late Cretaceous radiation. Within the Coelurosauria, the Ornithomimidae constitute a clearly distinct group from other coelurosaurs. These animals, up to 4 meters long, have toothless, beaklike jaws; three fingers of the hand, equal in length, and slender hindlimbs with an elongated metatarsus. They probably appeared in the Late Jurassic in Africa, but flourished during the Late Cretaceous.

THE MANIRAPTORS

The second line of development within the Coelurosauria constitutes a very interesting and diversified group named the Maniraptora (hand predators), with extremely elongated forelimbs exhibiting long agile hands and many birdlike details. The carpus (wrist) structure, unusual for dinosaurs, allowed the hands to move in different planes in relation to the forearm. The members of this group are known from the Late

Jurassic, but many subgroups only appeared in the Late Cretaceous. Due to the incompleteness of remains, exact relations among particular taxa included here are still difficult to determine.

A very spectacular, exclusively Late Cretaceous representative of maniraptoran theropods is known from very scarce remains from North America, and relatively abundant remains from Mongolia. They are the Oviraptorosauria ("egg thieves"), which grow to 2 meters. Typical for them are the lack of teeth, a very highly modified and pneumatized (air filled) skull, and the presence — in some genera — of high bony crest on the skull. Although the name suggests that they fed on other reptilians' eggs, it is more probable that they were moliluscivorous.

Of a similar time and geographic range was a poorly known and scarce group of small and lightly built predators, the elmisaurids.

Another group of Late Cretaceous maniraptorans is the troodontoids, known from North America, Mongolia, and China. These small predators (2 meters in length) had low skulls with very large eyes that considerably enlarged their range of vision; closely spaced, small teeth; a deep depression in the braincase in the region of the middle ear cavity; and a characteristic, strongly developed, raptorial second toe of the foot that ended in a large claw.

The next group of maniraptoran dinosaurs, dromaeosaurids (which are often grouped with troodontids into the higher rank taxon Deinonychosauria), have a similarly developed second toe in the foot. Dromaeosaurids were small to medium-sized predators (2 to 4 meters in length) that lived during the Early and Late Cretaceous in what is today North America, and additionally in the Late Cretaceous of Asia. They exhibited a relatively short metatarsus, the pubis was directed backward, and they had long processes on the tail vertebrae, which stiffened the back half of the long tail. Judging from many details of anatomy, this group seems to be most closely related to birds, and

all evidence suggests that they constitute a sister group to the birds.

The above is a condensed survey of all major taxa of dinosaurs. As I mentioned in the introduction, it does not reflect the complete picture of dinosaur diversity. Information gaps, particularly concerning the appearance of dinosaurs, and relatively scarce data about Early Cretaceous dinosaurs, are results of geologic conditions unfavorable for preservation of dinosaur remains.

OVERVIEW

While discussing each group of dinosaurs, I specified the time of their occurrence. Let us now try to summarize what we know today. We can certainly conclude that different dinosaur groups appeared at different times, and that their lifespans differed. Aside from those which were numerous and dominant during some periods, there were those which always constituted a small percentage of the dinosaur fauna. One can also observe a replacement of one group by another, more specialized one within groups exhibiting a similar lifestyle. Thus, during the whole time of the dinosaur reign in the Mesozoic Era, we see the appearance and radiation of one group and the extinction of another.

It can be generally said (without going into details of particular groups' lifespans) that in the history of dinosaurs there are three distinct periods of the great radiation.

The first period followed the separation of dinosaurs from their archosaur ancestors, which took place in the Late Triassic, when the earliest herrerasaurids and prosauropods dominated various other herbivorous and carnivorous vertebrates.

The next phase of great radiation and at the same time exchange of dominant dinosaur groups lasted throughout the Middle Jurassic and was marked by great diversity and major expansion of herbivorous sauropods and stegosaurs, the appearance of the first ornithopods replacing the disappearing prosauropods, and a simultaneous great expansion of diversified predators. Triassic and Early Jurassic herrerasaurs and ceratosaurs were replaced by carnosaurian allosaurids and different small coelurosaurian theropods.

The third great radiation took place in the Cretaceous, particularly during the Late Cretaceous. Even though sauropods and stegosaurs still lived at that time, the period of their full bloom had already passed. According to rare finds, in the Early Cretaceous there appeared a series of new dinosaur groups, such as pachycephalosaurs and the first primitive horned dinosaurs. Their flourishing and the appearance of many new groups occurred in the Late Cretaceous. The intensive development of hadrosaurs, replacing the then extinct iguanodonts, the ankylosaurs replacing stegosaurs, and a widespread expansion of horned dinosaurs are just a few examples of the flourishing fauna of herbivorous dinosaurs from the Late Cretaceous. Among predatory dinosaurs of the Late Cretaceous, there occur tyrannosaurids and many diversified but rare small predatory groups such as dromaeosaurids, troodontids, elmisaurids and oviraptorosaurs.

The end of the Cretaceous terminated the reign of the dinosaurs. Many groups widespread in the Late Cretaceous did not first appear until near the end of this geologic period. Some of them — for example, horned and duck-billed dinosaurs — can be seen only in the sediments marking the very end of the Cretaceous.

Since this essay does not describe the causes of dinosaur extinction but their success, I should conclude by summarizing information indicating the reasons for their dominance.

Undoubtedly significant for the first dinosaur radiation was the fact that many groups of land vertebrates that lived on earth before the appearance of dinosaurs died just before their first great radiation. This means that different ecological niches on land were free to be taken over by dinosaurs. Thus their wide distribution did not require fighting for their niche or territory.

The basis of dinosaur success was the fact that among numerous groups of Triassic animals it was the dinosaurs that were able to invade many land niches, thanks to their ability to walk and run very efficiently. The employment of the forelimbs, especially in bipedal forms, for manipulative functions constitutes a further anatomical change favoring their success. The secret of success of herbivorous ornithischians is the constant improvement and specialization of their dental apparatus and snout structure, a selection effected by the changing vegetation.

Geological data indicate that the diversity of Cretaceous herbivorous dinosaurs and their specialization was coincident with and dependent on the origin and diversification of angiosperms (flowering plants) and a simultaneous decline of gymnosperms.

Other factors are related to dinosaurs' physiology and behavior, for example, their metabolism. Their erect limb posture and the ability to run fast at great energetic expense suggest that dinosaurs must have had a metabolism different from that of reptiles. If they were warm-blooded, they may have been able to travel farther and adapt to a wider range of climate than their competitors. Dinosaurs' social behavior, such as parental care, proven for some groups, also influenced their success.

There remains a question, then: Why did these animals, highly adapted to different foods with remarkably large brains, become extinct? One recently popular hypothesis suggests that they have not died out at all. They live among us. Their form, however, is different. Instead of being huge and horrifying, they are brightly feathered and often beautifully singing close relatives of dromaeosaurid dinosaurs: the birds. And if this is really true, at this point we should say the true next great radiation of the dinosaur group is the birds!

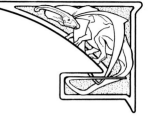

SIREN SONG AT MIDNIGHT

DAVE WOLVERTON

WHEN I WAS A GIRL OF TEN, MY FATHER, STEFÁN ELEGANTE, WORKED AS A PALEOGENETICIST for the Pacific Fisheries Commission, trying to restore extinct tuna and marlin, dolphins and blue squid. He took me to his lab and showed me how he pulled bits of bone from fossils and dyed the DNA so his computers could read it and begin building living replicas of the cells: "See, Josephina!" he said, pointing to remnants of a cell under his microscope, rainbow-hued ropes of DNA. "You see, the fishes are still there! Waiting for us to bring them back to life, and the DNA is a manual to tell us how." His eyes glowed as he spoke, and I didn't understand half of what he said. "This is old DNA. I like the old stuff best. DNA that is a hundred years old is better than that cloned from a living cell, for when a creature is living, so many chemical processes happen from moment to moment that sections of DNA get torn loose and often return into place reversed. But a cell that is a million years old is sometimes in better shape. The cells heal themselves. In old dead cells, the chemical bonds between amino acids are so strong that reversed DNA corrects itself, you see!"

He gazed at me a moment with his solemn brown eyes, saw my confusion. "Don't worry. Someday, you will understand all of this, and more," he said, kissing my forehead. "You know, I sometimes wonder, if we destroy our world, do you think God could take this old DNA and rebuild us?" he asked, sincerely awed by this marvel. I saw his fossils and understood only that, like God, he brought creatures to life from the dust of the Earth. On that day, I decided to become a paleogeneticist.

But somehow his hope died. Just as a wasp will lay its eggs in pear blossoms, corrupting their fruit, so despair corrupted him. Once he dared to dream of a restored world with vast rain forests, alive with the cries of macaws.

Wait. I am confused, exhausted to the bone. I'm not sure what to say. I must turn off the recorder for a moment.

[Two seconds of silence.]

I think I began too early. I know I'll live for only another few minutes, and I must record this while I can. Let me begin with the arrest of my father:

Last September, five plankton-harvesting ships exploded in a single evening. From childhood I've seen these Chinese ships off the Chilean coast — floating ceramic cities whose brilliant halogen lights sputter like fallen stars in the evening out on the horizon. During the attack, I was working at El Instituto Paleobiológico in Cartagena, extracting DNA from fossilized dimetrodons. I heard a distant explosion, almost a popping noise, and ran out into the evening. One plankton-harvesting ship had exploded on the horizon, and where it had floated, a great violet curtain of spray was rising into the night, higher and higher, looking almost like a thunderhead. Beside me, a small boy cried, "What is that!" and his mother, who perhaps wanted to protect him, said, "It is only angels, washing the curtains of heaven in the ocean."

I thought India must have attacked China, that the

Plankton Wars had started again, that they might blow all the ships. But if the Plankton Wars had begun again, they did so with a twist, for that night the Rio Negro dam blew in Brazil, and two million died as black torrents flooded down the Amazon.

A few hours later, the media revealed that the bombers were *chimeras*, genetically-engineered men that General Torres had modified to better adapt to life on other planets. They were an aquatic breed and had lived off the coast of Chile for years. By morning, the streets were ablaze with news of the attack by "Los Sirenos," the Sirens. The detonation of seven bombs was heralded as if it were a major war, and the Alliance of Nations began to hunt the Sirens. The news fascinated me, not because I longed for vengeance against the chimeras, but because the work of the genetic engineers who created these beings was similar to my own, yet a far greater art.

After the attack, the news showed Brazilian mothers mourning for children who had washed out to sea as the Amazon flooded; showed twisted wreckage, tiny orphans desperate for food. One commentator told how it could only have been a few Sirens who were gallantly bidding for control of Earth's waterways, trying to stop the plankton harvesters that continually stole food from their mouths. But his voice was drowned by others who decried the Sirens' "crime against humanity." Experts paraded through the media, telling how destruction along the Rio Negro was only the beginning. They said millions in China and India would starve without the plankton harvesters, and they hinted hunger would strike in South America because of the loss of our fisheries.

My father had risen to become Director for the Pacific Fisheries Commission, so I called him on commlink to ask if these reports were accurate. He weighed each word, saying, "The Chinese pay so little for fishing rights, we won't miss it. In three months,

they'll be harvesting like always." He sounded harried, tired, and I imagined he was under great pressure.

For a couple of days my friend Rosalinda recorded news holos about the chimeras. We planned to watch the holos for entertainment, but as the holos displayed, I was horrified. Our Marines hooked electronic sniffers to stunners that looked like torpedoes; with these they hunted the Sirens by scent. When they scored a hit, they dragged the stunned Siren from the water, shrieking and flapping its tail. The sirens had pale blue scales covering their bodies, the color of the summer sky on the horizon, and icy green eyes and hair the silver of mountain water. Their women were delicate, with an unearthly beauty, and their cries as they were dragged from the waters sounded like the song of dolphins mingled with a human scream.

Most captured Sirens were women and children who could not swim fast enough to evade the stunners, and the powerful chemical jolt of the stunners was too much for them. Many women and children died. As we watched the children cling to dead mothers wrapped in seaweed, and as we listened to the wails of pain and grief, the horror struck in a way we would not have understood if we had seen the single broadcast of each capture as it happened. We lost our innocence, and Rosalinda ended up hugging me, offering me comfort late into the night. After that, I had no stomach for news. I avoided listening to it, did not think about it. I tried to put it out of mind.

Then, my world changed. On September 15 as I worked in my lab, a man crept in — a pale man with an effeminate face, dressed in putrid-smelling street clothes, carrying a metal bar. His hand bled as if he'd cut it while prying the back door open. He stalked toward me nervously, sweat glistening on his brow, swinging the bar into his palm, watching side hallways for signs of others. My coworkers had gone home an hour before. We were alone. The way he looked, I thought I would be lucky if he only raped me.

"Josephina," he said quickly. "Josephina Elegante? Daughter to Stefán?" I nodded dumbly, backed away. He lurched toward me. "Here, get these to your father! It is *mem-set!*" He held out two small gelatin capsules the color of urine.

"What?" I asked, so frightened I did not know what to do.

He looked at me strangely, smeared the blood from his hand across his shirt. "Mem-set — a mind-wiping drug. It keeps one's memories from being scanned. You must give it to your father, for he has secrets that he wants to keep concealed, even beyond the grave."

"What? Are you crazy?" I asked, backing away. And I worried, for it seemed obvious he was crazy.

His eyes suddenly widened. "You do not know?" he asked. "Your father has been arrested for giving explosives to the Sirens. It is on the news even as we speak! He has been charged with high treason and murder. He will surely be executed. As his only relative, you will be allowed to attend the execution. You must give these to him before he dies!" He held out the drugs, watching the halls as if he believed the secret police would burst into the room.

"Wait," I said. I thumbed the subdural pressure switch behind my right ear and jacked into a simulcast news holo, keeping it on multitask so I could watch the stranger at the same time. My father, Stefán Elegante, was shown huddling among what must have been twenty Allied Marine troops, all of them in their space-blue armor. They rushed through the streets of Cartagena in a block, and peasants tossed bricks and burning sacks, shouting "Murderer!" The peasants looked confused. They did not know my father's crime and functioned only as a mob. The narrator said, "Now we see Stefán Elegante, alleged traitor to his species, rushing for cover." I stood in shock, as my father boarded a military transport. I jacked out of the newscast,

thumbed my commlink again and read in my father's code, but he did not answer the call. I jacked back into the newscast: it showed my father on a small boat offshore from our beach home in Concepción, unloading boxes into the waiting arms of the Sirens. The reporter said the boxes held explosives.

I jacked out in shock, for I knew that this was all some magnificent lie, knew my father was innocent despite the holos. What was their evidence? Pictures of boxes?

"Please," the stranger said. "I'm a friend. I'm only one of dozens who helped give your father weapons for the Sirens. Many others like me still hope for a restored world. Yet your father knows who we are. His memories will convict us. Alliance laws forbid the police from scanning the memories of criminals while they live, but once your father is executed, then his right to privacy dies with him, and Alliance surgeons will slice away his cerebral tissue so they can scan his memories at leisure. He knows this. He promised to take the mem-set. We all promised to take mem-set if we were caught. When you go to the execution, hold the capsules between your cheek and teeth until you get them to Stefán, then have him bite them. This is a powerful dose — enough for a dozen people, but you must get it to him at least two minutes before the execution. Once he breaks the capsules, the mem-set will form restriction enzymes. The membranes of his neural cells will harden, and the DNA in his brain will be chopped into pieces, destroying all his memories. Understand?"

The stranger wrapped my fingers around the capsules. "If any of us could hope to get past security to your father, we would gladly take this task upon ourselves. Please, save us! We are desperate!" he said, then he turned and ran.

I stood for a long time, holding the capsules, wondering what to do. I could not believe this stranger, and I wondered if it were some plot to discredit my father. That evening, I began trying to obtain permission to see my father —

[Two seconds of silence.]

I'm sorry. I had to turn the recorder off. I can't think. This day has exhausted me. I am so angry that they call my father a "traitor to his species." He loved every species. Perhaps he loved them too much. As I record these words I am sitting in my terrarium at El Instituto Paleobiológico de Colombia — the institute my father funded — feeding my pet Euparkeria *from a bag of eggs. The* Euparkeria *are a small dinosaur from the Early Mesozoic, the earliest age of dinosaurs, and they are a branch of thecodonts. the first true dinosaurs. They are the size of geese, with long graceful necks as delicate as a pianist's fingers, tiny front legs, and forest-green skin. On their backs are yellow-white speckles, the color that the primeval sun must have cast as it burned through fern jungles. One* Euparkeria *licks at an egg with a long olive-green tongue, cleaning the egg yolk from inside a shell, looking for all the world like a small, wingless dragon.*

My father used to say that Euparkeria *are an important link in the chain of life. From them sprang many species — birds and pterosaurs, meat-eating carnosaurs, saurischian dinosaurs like the* Brontosaurus *and* Supersaurus, *and ornithischians, such as the* Triceratops *and* Ankylosaurtus. *If each higher animal species were a branch on a tree, the* Euparkeria *would be close to the tree's root. They are one great main trunk from which higher animals evolved, while at the top of the tree would be an insignificant twig, a bud without fruit: mankind.*

My father was not a traitor to our species. He only realized that we look on ourselves and think that instead of a twig, we are the whole tree, that we are the crown of creation instead of only another stem.

Anyway, my father was a military prisoner, and despite my pleas I was forbidden to speak to him before the trial.

My friends disappeared, pretended not to know me. Even Rosalinda, a girl I've known since childhood, closed the door when I tried to speak to her. She shouted at me through the door, told me to go away, and she was crying, saying that the secret police had come to question her. At first I was angry and hurt, but her family had no political connections, and I knew it was better to keep my distance from her.

I accomplished nothing at work, did not eat. I could not ignore the instinct that drove me to believe in my father's innocence. I'd spoken to him at least three times a week for years — knew him better than anyone, and I knew he was incapable of murder. I searched his office, looking for proof of his innocence. His appointment books were gone, and only his computer logs were on-line. I sat late into the night, reading notes about the various genomes of extinct fishes, trying to extract some clue to prove his innocence.

I imagined that my father had been lured into this. Could it have been that he thought he was giving food to the Sirens? I wondered. That would be like him. He could have handed out boxes, unaware that weapons were stored in them, and now that he'd been caught, he would nobly protect the others with his life, even though they betrayed him.

I so wanted this scenario to be true that I looked for evidence to support it. I read until my eyes burned from viewing every computer log, until perspiration trickled down my back. Late that night, an orderly came to the office, Mavro Hidalgo, an old man who had worked for my father since before I was born.

"Josephina, what are you doing here?" he asked.

"Looking for something," I said. "I don't know what — anything to prove my father's innocence."

Señor Hidalgo shook his head sadly. "I've already

been through all those records," he said. "I've already thought about it. You want proof that Don Stefán is innocent, but you won't find the proof in scraps of paper."

I looked at old Señor Hidalgo, and my eyes became wet, and I blurted, "Are you saying he is guilty? You believe these lies?"

But Señor Hidalgo shook his head. "You don't need papers. The truth of his innocence is in your heart." He sat next to me, smelling of sweat and beans. He placed his leathery hand on my shoulder. "You know, your father has been sick for many years, suffering from depression." I nodded, for I'd known this. "When he was young, he was worse. For days at a time he would laugh and his eyes would glow, and he would come to work practically walking on the ceiling! Oh, he was so happy, he did not need wings to fly.

"But then, the smile would fade and he'd come to work and you would see him drag, as if wrapped in chains, and he'd sit for days and do nothing. We were all afraid for him, thinking he might kill himself, so one day I asked, 'Don Stefán, why put yourself through this? You could cure this malady with a pill! Then, why do you suffer?' and do you know what he said?"

"No," I answered.

"Your father told me that the time he spent flying through the air more than rewarded him for the time he spent in the abyss. He said, 'Mavro, I know you worry for me, and I know I could take the cure. But I love my illness. You people — how can you appreciate life as I do? How can you live even one moment with passion? It is all so grand, so beautiful. Even when I am lost in the blackest well of midnight, *life* tastes so sweet to me! Life is so sweet!'"

Señor Hidalgo patted my shoulder, told me to go home, then began to straighten the office. I knew he was right. I didn't need more proof of my father's

innocence than the life he'd led. My father could not have given explosives to the Sirens. I'd seen his innocence in the tender way he fed his fish by hand at the aquariums, in the way he kissed the pain away from my childhood injuries, in the way he relished to draw a breath. Life, all life, was too precious to be wasted.

That night, I drove to Concepción, to the sea house, and arrived at dawn. The police had scavenged the house until it was in ruins. I cleaned the mess, walked the beaches in the mornings. I kept the mem-set hidden in my room, and twice the police came to question me, always asking names of my father's friends, of those I'd seen him with. I answered by declaring his innocence.

The details of my father's trial were never publicized. I learned through the news that my father was convicted of treason and accused of stealing a vast fortune through graft. He was found guilty of complicity in the murder of two million Brazilians and was sentenced to die. I find it ironic that they convicted him in a secret trial, yet respected his right to privacy so much that they refused to pry his memories from him. Perhaps for them it was just a waiting game, and they believed they would get his accomplices in time.

After that, I learned that a news special would be broadcast by a famous reporter, a gringo cyborg named Todd Bennett who promised to have an "Interview with a Madman." The interview was advertised for days, and I could not sleep because I wanted so badly to see my father, to hear his voice. I watched the holo at home, enlarging the image so it filled the entire living room.

When the interview started, they showed Señor Bennett wearing a smooth white tungsten half-face with six glittering eyes that recorded all he saw in different spectra. The bottom half of his face was still human. He wore a glorious multicolored cape of light, which contrasted with my father's drab attire of prison blue, and it struck me that Señor Bennett knew the effect that his dress would have, for he looked as if he were a beautiful angel of light sent down to torture some damned soul in a tired hell.

"Can I begin by asking a few questions?" Señor Bennett said in flawless Spanish, using over-precise inflections common to those who speak with the aid of a translation chip.

My father wiped sweat from his face, pulled his long hair back over his shoulder, and looked out the window of a small cell. "You can ask," he said.

"Fine," Señor Bennett said. "Then let's establish your guilt. Records show that for months you fed the Sirens. In itself, that was admirable. But what caused you to commit the sin, this crime against humanity, of shipping them explosives?"

My father looked at the cyborg and said, "I am a fantasist, a dreamer. That is my only sin: to dream and hope."

The cyborg smiled placatingly. "Hope is no sin. It's one of the three great abiding virtues. When we die, we take it with us to heaven." I laughed, for I was correct in my assessment of the cyborg. He did want to disguise himself as an angel, and he was too stupid to be subtle about it.

"Hope has done me no good," my father said. "You want to establish my guilt. It has been established in court. I masterminded the War of the Sirens — if you can call it a war. I gave them explosives. It was not a sin."

"Surely," Bennett countered, "you do not expect us to believe that you acted alone in this act of terrorism? You have no expertise in explosives. You could not have trained the Sirens."

"Believe what you will. If I had accomplices, I will die before I reveal their names. I will die!"

"You can't protect them forever," the cyborg af-firmed. My father shrugged. Bennett asked, "Tell us why you aided the murder of over two million people?"

"When I was appointed as Director of Pacific Fisheries, I hoped to save the world," my father said. "Ever since we first raped the Sea of Cortés and destroyed the world's richest oyster beds, we Latin Americans have sold the spoils of our oceans to the highest bidder. First the oysters, then the sailfish and tuna, dolphin and manta — till we were left with nothing but algae and plankton."

"One moment," Señor Bennett asked. "These animals you mention, are they food animals that became extinct?"

"Yes," my father said, *"temporarily* extinct food animals."

Señor Bennett smiled, "I don't eat flesh, myself."

My father roared, "You eat your own children!" Señor Bennett lurched back as if my father would strike him. My father stood and began pacing the cell. "When I was appointed director, I thought, 'Here I am at last: a man who can't be corrupted by graft! I can restore the ancient fisheries, rebuild seabeds laid waste by centuries of pollution.' Today, because of continual algae harvests, our atmosphere has seventeen percent less oxygen than when I was born. You worry about the poor who have no food — what will you say to those poor in a generation, when the seas are dead and they have no air to breathe?

"When I took office, even the trash fish that used to eat our turds had become extinct." My father paced the floor, moving so fast, speaking so fast, he almost gibbered, "So I committed the sin of hope. As Director of Pacific Fisheries, I sought funds to resurrect extinct fishes and phytozoa, give the oceans time to rebuild. But I received only promises of money. I tried to reduce the amount of plankton the Chinese could harvest, but Director Nestor de Ia Luz told me to keep silent. He said the Chinese paid too well and that we would have to let the harvests continue for another year. We were rebuilding after the war with the Socialistas, and he said we needed money for the reconstruction, so money never came to me. It took months and years before I realized I was only paid to be a figurehead — no one really wanted me to restore the fisheries."

"Is that why you betrayed your species?" Señor Bennett asked in a cutting voice. "Because you were frustrated in your efforts to reduce the harvest? Because you wanted to be more than a figurehead?" He was baiting my father, and I hated him for it.

"No!" my father said. "Emotions had nothing to do with it. For years I enforced the quotas as best I could, but when Nestor died and I took his place, I found that fisheries money hadn't been siphoned off for reconstruction: it had been going into Nestor's pockets all along! He'd stolen from us! And at the same time, I learned that for years Torres' chimeras had begged us to halt the plankton harvests. The Sirens were starving. Nestor had kept their pleas hidden — fearing that if people knew the truth, they might protect the fisheries here, and it would cut into the income he earned from graft.

"But I knew that no one would care. We wouldn't stop the harvests, so I took the bribes from the Chinese, just as all my predecessors had done, but instead of pocketing the money, I bought explosives!"

My father's eyes became wild. I wondered if he'd been drugged for benefit of the viewers. He sat down and then stood up again immediately and paced the room, back and forth, quicker than you would believe possible.

"Truly, I hoped to wake you all, but the explosions only dull your ears! You kill your own children. I pity the poor who will not be able to eat or breathe or escape this planet. Someday they will remember me as a hero for trying to stop this madness while we yet had something to save! We are a diseased branch on the tree of life, and because of us, the whole tree will fall into ruin. I commit the sin of hope no more!" My father began raving, and a curious light shone from his eyes. I don't think he saw the reporter any longer, saw nothing but his own death, for he cursed the world.

Despite his confession, I did not believe he was guilty. I was angry with his accomplices and wondered why the truly guilty party, the person who had trained the Sirens to use explosives, did not step forward.

All that night, I remembered my father's words, "I will die before I reveal their names. I will die!" Was that a plea? I wondered: Did he really want the memset so badly that he would almost announce it to the world? I sat in my room, replayed the interview. The man in the holo, the convict, did not look like my father. He did not look like some gentleman, nobly protecting men more wicked than himself. He looked like a killer, eaten by guilt and rage, unrepentant for his murders, and as I watched him again and again, pacing his cell like a leopard, I began to consider: My father's illness had made him passionate, a man quickly moved by both joy and despair. He spent so much time walking in that dark abyss that I wondered: Could some Siren's song at midnight, sung while my father was deep in despair and at his most vulnerable, have drawn him to his destruction? If, at just the right moment, the Sirens pleaded for weapons instead of food, would my father have succumbed?

As I record this, I've been remembering how when my father put me in charge of El Instituto Paleobiológico, he said, "Once you show people that we paleogeneticists can recreate life from the Mesozoic, they will see that there are no limits to what we can do. The concept of extinction will fall away, and we will be free to rebuild this world, turn it into a Garden of Eden."

Such was my father's hope. But six years ago I

recreated the Euparkeria *and the world has regarded my work with meager curiosity and some fear. It was then that I first realized that my father's assessment of the world was wrong. He wanted to recreate rain forests, restore oceans to their pristine conditions; but once people saw my dinosaurs, they did not unite with our cause. In government hearings, bureaucrats decried the cost of such an effort. They said it would take generations to rebuild this world, that such an effort was impractical and would bankrupt nations. My father told them that an effort that took five generations would repay itself for a hundred thousand generations to come. Yet his talk was all for nothing. People eyed my father with the same curiosity and fear that they showed my dinosaurs.*

Curiosity and fear. Here in Cartagena, we have a great zoo where they have begun to exhibit some dinosaurs, especially the fierce flesh-eaters of the Jurassic. Many peasants fear I will create such monsters, and that they will stalk the ghettos and eat their children. Ah well, it is shortly past noon. My father has been dead for more than two hours. I feel tired, and my tongue and mouth are going numb, so I must hurry and record these words:

After the newscast, I pressed the small yellow capsules of mem-set between my fingers, wondering how much pressure it would take to release the liquid inside. I worried that the poisons might escape if the capsules came in contact with my saliva, so I spat on them, then watched to make sure that the capsules not disintegrate. I remembered a story of an old Socialista general who was captured in Argentina, and he'd poisoned himself with mem-set. I jacked into the computer network and called up the story, learned how he had taken the mem-set and lain paralyzed in his cell. Despite all his captors could do, he died within hours. The article noted that mem-set, because it is catalyzed by uric acid which is a natural byproduct of dying cells, is perhaps the only drug that is more effective in a deceased person than in a living being. Yet it is also deadly—for uric acid is present in small amounts in every human.

In the early morning, I walked the beach and looked out to sea, and among the ghost crabs that scuttied across the beach like something from a dream I saw a dozen gulls flapping above a heap that looked like a corpse. I ran to it and found a child, a Siren of palest blue, wrapped in red kelp, drowning in the open air. She was gasping, and her eyes were rolled back. I dragged her back to the water and held her under the waves. I watched up and down the beach, afraid someone would see what I was doing, and a moment later a female Siren swam at my ankles in the foam and thrust her head out.

"Thank you," the Siren sang, and I looked into her deep green eyes and saw gratitude burning there. For days I'd been depressed and frightened, but I looked in her eyes and felt only warmth and peace. The gentleness in that creature's eyes was so convincing, so alien, that I could not imagine the Sirens killing humans. I wondered, when the Sirens blew the dam on the Rio Negro, could they have been aware that so many humans would die? Could creatures of the sea conceive how vulnerable we humans would be in their element? Later that day I saw the Allied Marines in the bay with their black gunships, dropping torpedoes into the water, hunting for the mother and her child.

After less than two months, the authorities declared the War of the Sirens to be over. The Marines imprisoned six hundred of them in secure holding tanks in Jamaica. I suppose the rest of them died. The Alliance slated my father's execution date, making him a single sacrificial lamb. I found nothing to prove either his innocence or guilt.

[Two seconds of silence.]

The Alliance did not reveal my father's location before his execution. All last night I paced my room, waiting for them to call to tell me where the execution would be held. At dawn, commlink tones sounded in my head. A woman told me to come to Camp Bolívar, outside Cartagena. I rode to the Marine camp in a taxi, too nervous to drive, and I found a military shuttle armed with neutron cannons warming its engines just inside the gates. Two police scanned me for weapons and ushered me into the shuttle with a dozen guards. I knew even before we left the coast that we were heading for the desert — the soldiers in the shuttle were adjusting the color settings on their body armor so that it turned an ivory shade, the color of alkali soil. The sun shining through the shuttle windows reflected from their visors as if each helmet were a single white star opal.

We thundered south for fifteen minutes, plummeted into a desert ghost town high in the Andes. The portals to the shuttle slid open and my guards scurried like sow bugs from beneath the shadow of an overturned rock. They dropped to the ground and covered the old limestone buildings with their pulse rifles. The cold mountain air hit me, and a cloud of smoky-gray dust and chaff swirled up from the shuttle's landing skids. I stepped out and surveyed the town: the morning sun cast long blue shadows across each fold of the mountains, across each jutting stone. The light was so intense that my eyes could not focus on objects in the shadows. Everything was either black or white in this hard land; there was no room for grays.

From the door of one stone building a dark little mestizo squinted at the bright sunlight. He wore the space-blue uniform of the Alliance Marines and smoked a thin cigar. He straightened his back, tossed his cigar to the dirt, and ground it under his heel as if it were a locust. "Señorita Elegante," he said, "I am Major Gutierrez. The press will be here shortly, and you will not have much time to spend alone with your father before the…ceremony."

"Fine," I said, shaking. I held the capsules behind my teeth, hoping he would not search me. He ushered me to the tiny stone building, and my hope rose. The facility was a prison, hundreds of years old with antiquated steel cages for the criminals, though all the cells were empty. I thought that if my father were kept in such a facility, it would be easy to pass the mem-set to him.

We walked down a long corridor to a darkened cell, and I saw my father huddled in a corner, sobbing. He was sweating profusely, as if he had labored in the hot sun, so that his hair hung to the side of his head like a damp black rag, and his jaw was set with fear. A soft orange glow in the air around his cell showed that a repulsion field had been hastily installed. Two armored guards and a priest stood outside the cell. I would not be able to get the mem-set to him.

"Can I go into the cell?" I asked Major Gutierrez.

"I am sorry," the major answered, "but, no."

"Can I speak with him alone?"

"No," the major answered, but he ordered a guard to follow him as he left, affording a little more privacy. The priest would have left also, but my father beckoned, "No, stay! Please. I want you to hear my confession."

"Father," I said, "I'd have come sooner, but no one would tell me where you were."

"What does it matter?" he said, and he stood and looked out a small window. He placed his palms on the stone wall. His hands shook.

"It matters to me," I answered. "It matters very much. It matters to your friends." My father seemed so despondent, that I wanted to see the hopeful fire that had once burned in his eyes, so I said, "I saw a Siren three days ago, a child. She washed up near the beach house. I noticed her only because a flock of gulls had gathered, waiting for her to die. Her skin was purpled, and her gills and fins were chafed. I pulled her to the shallows and held her underwater to breathe. After a moment, her mother swam up and took the child out to sea. The mother thanked me. If she were here, perhaps she would thank you, too."

I do not know why I told my father this in public. Perhaps I was angry with the Alliance, and wanted the guards to arrest me—helping the Siren had been an act of treason. I felt that the government was corrupt, and I wanted the guards to prove to me how evil they had become.

"It was the pollution," my father said, as if he were lecturing one of his classes in paleogenetic engineering. "The acidic water makes their gills itch, so the Sirens come to the beach to let the sand wash through their gills and scratch them. Sometimes their gills fill with silt, and as they strangle they pass out and wash to shore." He fell silent a moment, his voice changed, filling with despair. "You should have let the gulls have that child! You should have let her die! She will starve if the pollution doesn't get her first. Better to let the child die!"

"How can you say that?" I asked. His dark eyes held no hope or solemnity, only crazed despair. He got up and paced across his cell, back and forth, full of frantic energy, and I wondered what had happened to him during the Alliance interrogations, wondered if he were sane. I wanted to ask if he were guilty of treason to his species. I wanted to ask if he had really given the Sirens weapons, just as I had wanted to ask for weeks, but at that moment I was suddenly too afraid to ask.

"Father," I said, "I love you."

He nodded, bobbing his chin with a lunatic grin. *"Por supuesto.* Of course, of course," he said, as if my love were a given. He was shaking, and he began to

cry, then suddenly burst into a fit of laughter. "How is your work? How are the *Euparkeria*?" he asked, not even looking at me, pacing.

"They are fine," I lied. I couldn't tell him that the government had seized our bank accounts. They claimed that, like his little private war, my father had funded my research with graft. I did not have enough money to feed my dinosaurs for another week, so I made arrangements for the zoo to take them.

He continued pacing across the room, licking his lips, caught in the web of his thoughts. I spoke his name twice, but he did not answer. He swore softly. I'd never seen him like this, never in such despair.

I so wanted him to be happy. I tried to touch him through the repulsion field, and said, "Father, even now, doesn't your life taste sweet?"

My father gazed at me, as if trying to pierce my thoughts, then spat on the floor. I stepped away, and in that moment I realized that he rejected life. Despite my childish faith, my father was guilty of murder.

Gutierrez came to escort me from the room, back down the corridors of the old prison to a walled court. In the courtyard stood a dozen dignitaries, as many reporters, and six Alliance Marines with projectile rifles. My father walked into the bright sunlight in company with the priest. My father's hands and feet were shackled, so he took tiny, clumsy steps, pulling at his chains.

A hawk was soaring on the thermal updrafts, and my father stopped to watch it sail over a ridge. "My God," my father said, "what does it find to eat here?" He looked across the desert toward the plains, and said to the priest, "Beyond those valleys, there were once rain forests. Great, endless forests."

One Marine fidgeted with his rifle. Until that moment, I do not think I believed the execution would take place. I somehow hoped that others would recognize my father's innocence, that the great wise leaders of Earth would stoop to save him. I looked at the rifles, and a thin scream issued from my lips, and I bit it back, tried to control myself. The major escorted my father to a wall and stood with him a moment. Everything was so quiet.

The major said, "Señor, do you want a blindfold?"

My father looked at the ground and shook his head and sighed. Inside his cell he had been sweating, depressed, but the cool morning air dried his sweat, and I imagined that he was almost glad to finally finish it.

"It is traditional to offer a cigar," the major said. My father shook his head, still staring at the ground. "Any last words, Señor Elegante? Last requests?" My father only shook his head. One reporter coughed.

"I have a last request!" I shouted, and the major looked up at me. "Can I speak to my father alone, only for a moment, to say good-bye?"

"I am sorry," the major said, "but no."

"A kiss? Can I kiss my father good-bye?"

The major looked up at me, sighed. "If you wish."

I ran to my father. Everyone was watching, and there was no way to pass the mem-set to him. I was afraid he might swallow the capsules instead of break them, and I had no way to tell him how to use the drug, so I burst the capsules between my teeth, hard. The mem-set tasted bitter, slightly of anise, and I thought I might gag, but I held it on my tongue. And as we kissed, I spat the poison into his mouth, rubbed it onto his lips.

My father lurched backward a step and his eyes widened in horror. "Josephina!" he said, crying out as if begging to know what I had done.

"I don't want to live without you!" I said. "All our work is destroyed. I will always love you! God knows how to read the manuals of our lives. He will put everything back together. For a while — only for a

while — the restoration will continue without us!"

My father threw his arms around me and wept. "No, Josephina," he cried. "I did not want this to touch you. I did not want to hurt you."

Major Gutierrez pulled at my shoulders. "Do you think you could die, and I would not be hurt by it?" I asked my father. I grabbed him and held, and Gutierrez let me hug him for a full minute, weeping, then the major spoke to me softly and escorted me back in line with the reporters. My father watched, his eyes riveted on me. He wept as Major Gutierrez read the list of charges and called his troops to ready their arms.

My father shouted. "Someday, we will rebuild this world! The time will come when your children will play in rain forests, and canaries and hummingbirds will fill the skies! Every beast of the field will be reborn!"

The troops raised their rifles. "Fishes will swim in your rivers!"

"Aim!" Gutierrez ordered.

"Crickets will make music in your pastures, and whales will sing love songs in the seas!" my father cried. "You watch! It will happen!"

"Fire!" Gutierrez shouted, and the rifles spat their bullets, filling the bright courtyard with smoke.

My father staggered back, red holes gaping in his shirt. He stared up in the air, beyond the heads of those in the firing squad, and his eyes filled with light, as if he saw salvation hurtling through the sky. The look on his face was so filled with awe, so compelling, that everyone suddenly turned and gazed into the sky also, and then I heard him cry "God," and he spun and staggered against the stone wall, smearing blood on the ash-gray stones.

I sit here in my terrarium and look at my little Euparkeria and stroke his neck. I'm out of eggs to feed him, yet my wingless dragon stands on his back legs, tenderly searching the folds of my dress, expecting an egg to magically appear. It has been nearly three hours since I broke the mem-set between my teeth. Opalescent clouds seem to be forming at the edge of my vision, and everything looks as if it is covered with gauze or silken threads. My feet and fingers are so numb I do not feel them, yet my mouth burns as if it is on fire. I believe the mem-set has begun attacking my DNA, chopping it in pieces so fine that in a million years, even God may not be able to put me back together. I cannot talk into this microphone much longer.

On my way home. I jacked into a news broadcast.

The reporter says that the Alliance of Earth Nations is considering plans to exile the Sirens to Darius Four, a water planet without human occupants. So, the pollution will continue unabated. I could not help thinking that though the Sirens lost their brief battle, they have won themselves a world, while day by day we are losing ours.

Also on the news, I heard a reporter say that as my father died, he shouted "*¡Vivan los Sirenos!* Long live the Sirens!"

But that is not true. I was there. He shouted only one word, crying with a thrill of hope in his voice: "*¡Vivamos!*" Let us live!

[Uninterrupted silence to end of tape.]

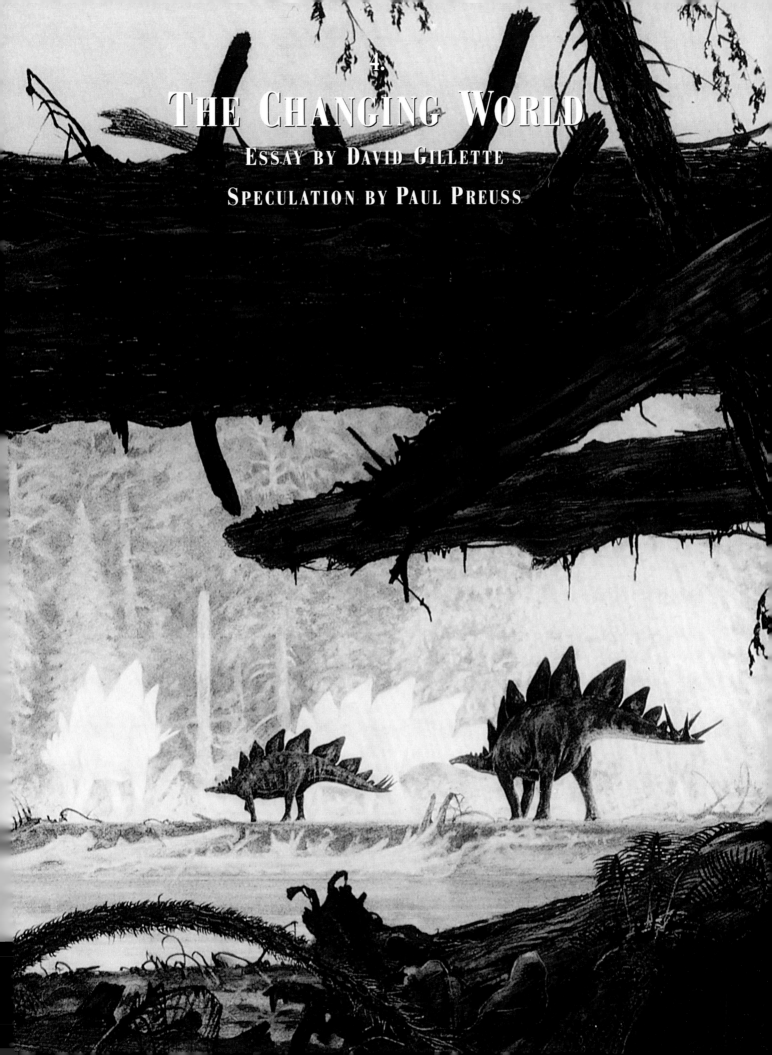

4.
THE CHANGING WORLD
ESSAY BY DAVID GILLETTE
SPECULATION BY PAUL PREUSS

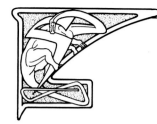
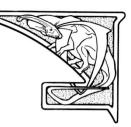

THE JURASSIC PERIOD:
A TIME OF GREAT CHANGE

DAVID D. GILLETTE

THE TRIASSIC CALM THAT FOLLOWED THE GREAT BIOLOGICAL CALAMITIES OF THE PERMIAN EXTINCTION episode was abruptly interrupted with volcanic activity in Pangaea. In North America from modern Canada to the Carolinas an immense trough developed in the Late Triassic, anticipating the opening of a great ocean basin. Lava and ash poured out in a long succession of volcanic episodes that continued into Jurassic times. The Jurassic began about 210 million years ago and came to a close 145 million years ago, during which time

the backbone of the giant supercontinent weakened. Great internal forces were soon to reorganize the entire surface of the earth.

In early Mesozoic time, the globe had been lopsided. Pangaea was isolated on one side, extending uninterrupted from pole to pole. Occupying the remaining 75 percent of the global surface, the World Ocean was likewise continuous and uninterrupted. This universal ocean delivered predictable and monotonous weather patterns to the continents. Warm equatorial waters circulated directly to the poles without deflection by land masses. The climate everywhere on land favored broad expanses of forests, ranging from luxuriant tropical forests in low latitudes to temperate forests near the poles. There were no glaciers, no frozen ocean at the North Pole; snow and ice were probably rare even at the poles. Animals and plants were free to expand their populations without interference from major geographic obstacles or climatic barriers.

This tranquillity was shattered in the Early Jurassic when the land was largely submerged and most landscapes were wet. The disturbance of Pangaea intensified. The great north-south belt of volcanoes through the backbone of Pangaea gave way to a much more profound event. The Atlantic Ocean was about to open, as eastern and western portions of the great

land mass were cleaved by plate tectonics. The great plates carrying fragments of Pangaea began to move at the expense of the margins of the World Ocean. The disarray was global. As the Atlantic Ocean opened in the middle of Pangaea, the ancestral Pacific Ocean basin began to shrink: continents converged on the Pacific as they spread apart with the opening of the Atlantic.

Pangaea broke into four parts, each moving in different directions. The ancient northern landmass Laurasia finally separated from Gondwanaland (the southern mass) along the old Tethys seaway. But neither Laurasia nor Gondwanaland remained intact. The opening of the northern Atlantic Ocean basin in the Middle Jurassic divided forever the plate that had united Laurasia. Modern Europe and Asia moved eastward and slightly northward from the Mid-Atlantic Rift; North America rotated westward and slowly to the north.

Gondwanaland disintegrated. Modern South America and Africa began to separate late in Jurassic time, extending the Atlantic Ocean basin to the Southern Hemisphere. South America rotated clockwise and Africa counterclockwise, and both moved southward as the ancient Tethys sea was lost to the growing Atlantic Ocean. The ancient land masses that were to become Antarctica, India, and

Australia remained attached to the southern tip of Africa, and peninsular connections to South America for a while prevented the total disintegration of the old giant southern land mass.

The geologic monotony on the continents and ocean basins was broken. Broadly continuous habitats were interrupted. No longer spanning tens of thousands of miles on land, populations of plants and animals became segregated and isolated. Broad expanses of ocean separated Early and Middle Jurassic land masses, creating barriers to dispersal.

In addition, oceanic circulation was interrupted. In the newly opened bays and inlets new habitats appeared in the marine world, where fauna and flora could exist as populations protected from competitors whose larvae and spores circulated in the World Ocean. Isolation of seas and gulfs increasingly intensified the climatic effects of local geographic conditions on land. The consequences were pronounced and irreversible. Moving with a velocity about the same as the rate of growth of a person's fingernail, continents and the old ocean floor were on a collision course.

Today as in the Jurassic, the forces generated by these tectonic movements, compounded over millennia, are relieved by earthquakes and volcanoes, and ultimately have the capacity to wholly fracture and isolate tectonic plates or destroy ocean basins. Indeed, no ocean basin today contains rocks older than Jurassic. This seemingly trivial observation has profound implications to paleontologists: during the last 4 percent of earth history all preexisting ocean basins disappeared and new ones took their place. Three-fourths of the earth's surface (the ocean basins) has originated in the past 200 million years. The resulting new habitats became the proving grounds for new forms of life in the seas, and to a lesser extent on the land. This colossal reorganization, driven by plate tectonics, continues today with unrelenting force.

Primitive diapsid reptiles and the therapsids were gone. Other surviving reptiles, including the dinosaurs, and the animals and plants with which they lived, were being tested.

MOUNTAIN BUILDING

Horizontal movements of tectonic plates caused friction and compression along plate boundaries. Plates carrying continental land masses pushed over the oceanic rocks which in turn were pushed downward toward the mantle. The World Ocean was being reconstituted as the ancestral Pacific Ocean, with active tectonism, including major faults and massive volcanoes, on all its margins.

The ancestral Rocky Mountains in North America and the ancestral Andes in South America originated as these plates thickened on their leading edges. Thousands of feet of lava was brought from deep within the earth's crust and upper mantle to the surface, as rock recycled from the margins of vanished ocean basins. With the rise of mountain chains came dramatic climatic effects. They cast rain shadows which generated arid landscapes where forests once grew. Aridity was so pronounced in many places in the Jurassic that immense dune fields, spanning thousands of miles, blocked dispersal as effectively as oceanic barriers. By some calculations, these dune fields were the largest in the history of the earth.

Thickening of the western edges of the American continents hastened erosion of landscapes due to increased stream gradient. Habitats were divided into a patchwork of isolated pockets that no longer extended over thousands of miles. Mountains and deserts interrupted the continuity of habitats, isolating even large animals. The setting was perfect for one of Nature's grandest experiments: the rise of the dinosaurs in the Jurassic.

Preceding page: Two large, herbivorous ankylosaurs, Edmontonia, *square off in a Cretaceous jungle. By Brian Franczak.*

GLOBAL WARMING: JURASSIC DESERTS IN NORTH AMERICA

In the interior of North America, for example, a vast area covering tens of thousands of square miles (an area almost as great as the sand seas of today's Arabian peninsula) became a biological wasteland. The Wingate, Navajo, and Entrada sandstones are petrified sand dunes that were once hundreds of feet high. Oases in these dune fields were the only refuge for animals and plants. Recent discoveries of dinosaur tracks in oases preserved in the Navajo Sandstone, complete with large petrified logs, testify to arid adaptations among the reptiles of the Jurassic. These great deserts of the American West became barriers to dispersal, isolating populations of plants and animals at their periphery.

The net result of this increasing aridity in the Jurassic might have been global warming, accompanied by new temperature extremes and pronounced north-south temperature gradients. In many places on the newly fragmented continents temperature and moisture limited population growth. Few dinosaurs could tolerate persistently hot and arid conditions, because they were large and continually active and required abundant food and water. Under severely arid conditions, small dinosaurs and other reptiles could live in oases. But limited food and water probably excluded large dinosaurs from occupying desert habitats.

Early and Middle Jurassic dinosaurs were widespread, but their remains generally occur as isolated skeletons rather than in concentrations in deposits where analysis of habitat and rock deposition can be combined for paleoecologic interpretations. New discoveries in Asia promise to fill in these gaps in our understanding of these dinosaurs and how they lived.

Nevertheless, dinosaurs invaded even the deserts in the Early and Middle Jurassic, albeit in limited numbers and diversity. Dinosaurs living in the oases now preserved in the Navajo Sandstone were generally small, bipedal desert specialists. Lizards and other reptiles probably lived in the vegetation around the oases; early birds (relatives of *Archaeopteryx*), if they lived in this part of North America, and pterosaurs may have found shelter and food there beside the dinosaurs.

JURASSIC SEAS

In western North America shallow seas invaded the continent several times in the Early and Middle Jurassic, repeatedly separating dinosaur populations on land. There, in some places giant dune fields still predominated. Dinosaur populations were isolated and their diversity restricted by the severe conditions. Elsewhere, climatic conditions were probably less severe, but the geologic record of Middle Jurassic sediments containing dinosaurs is too scanty for reliable interpretation.

The shallow seas in equatorial North America were highly saline, due to increased washdown from rapid erosion, and apparently too salty for abundant sea life. Diversity of fishes and invertebrates was low, and populations were small. For example, only three species of fish occupied the seas that deposited the nearly barren gypsum and limestone sediments of the Todilto Formation of the Colorado Plateau. These fish were small, reaching lengths no greater than 30 centimeters, and their remains are to be found in only a few restricted localities. For a pterosaur lost at sea, or a dinosaur wandering the shores in search of food, the future would have been gloomy indeed.

However, reptiles flourished in the Jurassic open oceans and seas, where ichthyosaurs, plesiosaurs, and sharks were abundant. These active, sometimes gigantic predators are never found together with dinosaurs. There is no evidence of any marine dinosaurs, although many that lived in coastal habitats may have ventured occasionally into shallow waters. In a few instances, dinosaur skeletons have been found in marine sediments. Rather than indicating that they occupied marine habitats, this situation has generally been interpreted as due to transport of a carcass down a river to its mouth, where it might settle and become buried.

In the Late Jurassic of southern England and the European mainland, great deposits of lime muds accumulated in quiet, protected lagoons where the marine reptiles found shelter and food. These were warm, tropical seas; fish were abundant, as the principal food for plesiosaurs, ichthyosaurs, and the occasional marine crocodile that ventured into the open sea. Fine-grained limestones, preserving in spectacular detail the anatomy of the inhabitants of these seas, have been mined for centuries. The limestones of Solnhofen and Eichstatt of southern Germany preserved even the traces of feathers in the rare specimens of *Archaeopteryx* and the impressions of membranes on the wings of pterosaurs such as *Rhamphorhynchus*.

Mollusks were abundant in the same seas. Clams and oysters lived in shallow waters in mud or on harder substrates. Ammonoids, free-swimming relatives of squids and the modern pearly nautilus, grew in great abundance. Their complex and durable shells are common in nearly all marine sedimentary layers of Jurassic age. Because they evolved rapidly, had worldwide distribution by virtue of their open-water habitats, and species are readily distinguished, ammonoids are index fossils for the Jurassic. Jurassic marine strata are often correlated worldwide with great precision and confidence by recognition of a regular succession of ammonoid fauna that occurs in the same sequence wherever marine sediments of suitable age are preserved.

JURASSIC STREAMS AND LAKES

Lakes and streams were rare in North America in the Early and Middle Jurassic, but by the Late Jurassic, bodies of fresh water were common. These sources of drinking water greatly expanded the range of habitats that Late Jurassic dinosaurs could exploit. Most were probably affected by seasonal extremes of precipitation and heat. Life cycles of small animals and plants were closely linked to the alternating cycles of wet and dry seasons.

Although not frequently encountered in the dinosaur-bearing sediments of the Jurassic Period, turtles were probably abundant and were much like modern turtles. Crocodiles were widespread and abundant in lakes, streams, and estuaries, lurking in the water or stalking prey along the shore. Indeed, these were probably among the principal competitors of the predatory dinosaurs, and a frequent menace to the plant-eaters. Fish, sharks, coelacanths, a few squirrel-sized mammals, and lungfish were also common in freshwater terrestrial habitats, especially in the Late Jurassic when the effects of aridity were ameliorated.

These lakes and streams were frequented by dinosaurs for drinking water, and probably occasionally for refuge from predators and as shelter from summer's sun. Predatory and scavenging dinosaurs may have found good hunting for fish or amphibians in streams and lakes, and for small prey on the shores.

JURASSIC FLORA

There were no flowers in the Jurassic — no fruits, no grasses, no nuts, no great abundance of pollen or nectar, no bees, no butterflies, no songbirds. The angiosperms had not yet taken over the landscape.

In broad aspect, three plant groups prevailed, each contributing to the structure of the habitat and

The Dilophosaur *was the earliest of the large carnosaurs and lived in the Early Jurassic. By Brian Franczak.*

providing food and shelter to dinosaurs and other occupants of the Jurassic landscape. The largest were the gymnosperms, growing as trees and shrubs; the cycadophytes and tree ferns, which were mainly shrubs; and the smallest, the ground-dwelling ferns, horsetails, and lycopods.

Gymnosperms, largely holdovers from the Triassic, were the dominant trees and shrubs where sufficient moisture was available. These are the "naked seed" trees, today represented by two major groups, the conifers and the cycads. Pine trees, familiar to people who live in temperate latitudes, were not present in the Jurassic Period. Instead, primitive relatives of the pines such as the ginkgo and various species related to the modern Norfolk Island "pine" (the plant family Araucariaceae) were the dominant trees. Although the remnants of this group survive today in specialized habitats, these Mesozoic flora are poorly known. Their ecological setting in the Jurassic is even more conjectural; presumably the Araucariaceae and ginkgos formed the climax forests, controlling the development of canopies where high-reaching sauropod dinosaurs may have grazed.

If plant-eating dinosaurs depended on gymnosperms for their nutrition, the effects on the landscape must have been devastating. With relatively slow growth and a lack of vegetative reproduction, gymnosperms do not recover easily from disturbances. A herd of browsing sauropods, taking leaves and branches by the ton, would have opened broad tracts of open landscape where once the tall trees prevailed. An important benefit to the forests to be derived from such ravages would have been the persistence of a mosaic of habitats, promoting diversity and protection from disease and fire.

Cycads and cycadeoids, collectively known as the cycadophytes, grew as shrubs and small trees, some occupying the undergrowth in the conifer forests, and others living in the open under drier conditions. Both had vegetative reproduction that would have allowed for rapid recovery after an attack by plant-eating giants of the Jurassic.

Ferns and tree ferns also grew in the shadows of the tall trees, probably forming the dominant ground cover everywhere. These were abundant especially where moisture was plentiful, and may have been an important food source for herbivores. Their ability to regenerate through vegetative reproduction encouraged rapid regrowth, even when they were cropped close to the ground. Lycopods and horsetails were probably abundant as well, especially near permanent bodies of water.

In oases of the Early and Middle Jurassic, all three of these groups of plants may have been present, occupying distinctive vegetation zones determined by moisture, shade, and exposure to high temperatures.

AERIAL HABITATS

Pterosaurs and birds originated in the Jurassic, attaining for the first time among vertebrates the capacity for sustained flight. Arguments concerning the habitat requirements for these airborne vertebrates are legion. Their motives for flight could have been the search for food or shelter, for escape from predators, for display or mating, or merely for getting from one

place to another. In any case, flight demanded suitable habitats for safe takeoff and landing. Their specific habitats may have been restricted, for neither of these airborne groups is abundant in the Jurassic.

LATE JURASSIC DINOSAURS

The richest bounty of Jurassic dinosaurs, including the well-known genera *Stegosaurus* (ornithischian), *Apatosaurus* (= *Brontosaurus*), *Diplodocus*, and *Brachiosaurus* (sauropods), and the theropods *Allosaurus* and *Ceratosaurus*, all came from deposits of Late Jurassic age in North America and eastern Africa. These two areas have several dinosaurs in common, despite their substantial geographic separation spanning at least 90° longitude. There must have been at least a narrow land corridor connecting these two areas, if not wholly continuous habitat. Desert conditions no longer isolated dinosaur populations on the land.

The aridity that dominated the Early and Middle parts of the Jurassic Period had slowly given over to landscapes with free-flowing rivers. The fresh water in these rivers, even where they passed through deserts, greatly expanded the habitat available for dinosaurs. Conditions may have crudely resembled the semi-arid and arid plateaus of the American West today. The Late Jurassic dinosaurs of North America and Tanzania lived near rivers and lakes that were sometimes salty, and even occasionally dried up.

Such bodies of water today in the American West are called playa lakes: in the spring and summer these depressions fill with water from thunderstorms. Life briefly flourishes in this sudden flush of fresh water, with phenomenal growth of algae, salamanders, toads, frogs, aquatic insects, and predators from surrounding areas. Then in the heat of summer, the shallow waters are overcome by evaporation. The playa lakes turn salty and soon the shallow lake dries up, leaving salt deposits that glimmer in the summer sun. Life seems to vanish, until the next season, when the cycle is repeated. Large animals take full advantage of the all-too-brief surfeit of water, fattening quickly while the plants are green and the food supplies are plentiful.

Similar playa conditions prevailed over much of the late Jurassic landscape frequented by dinosaurs. The plants were different from those we find today, and there were no mammals like the ungulates of today's grasslands. Indeed, grasses had not yet evolved, nor had broad-leafed trees and the multitude of flowering plants that add brilliant displays of color to today's habitats everywhere. The Late Jurassic dinosaurs saw shades of brown and green and gray, but splashes of yellow and orange and red were not to be found.

TENDAGURU

Late Jurassic dinosaurs in eastern Africa lived in a lowland coastal setting. South of the Jurassic equator near the village of Tendaguru in modern Tanzania, *Brachiosaurus* and other giants browsed high in the trees, reaching 40 feet above ground level. The Tendaguru dinosaurs were similar to those of the Morrison Formation in North America on the other side of the equator and fossils are abundant in both locations. Evidently the dinosaur populations of the Late Jurassic spanned the great distances separating these two regions, across landscapes now lost to the forces of geologic recycling propelled by plate tectonics.

The dinosaur giants of Tendaguru ambled along the shorelines, perhaps taking occasional forays into the warm equatorial waters. Most of their time was probably spent in the coastal forests, continually feeding on plant matter that grew in luxuriant forests. Rivers emptied into the Jurassic sea on the east coast of the African mainland. Bone-laden river deposits

alternated with shallow marine sediments, laid down during brief submergence of the coastline. The marine shorelines were sufficiently stable to support populations of shell-bearing animals such as clams and snails. But the dinosaur bones are clearly contained within the beds laid down by rivers. Perhaps the dinosaurs ventured into the open along the seacoast, to cool off in the marine waters or to seek food in the protected lagoons. Sauropod dinosaur trackways in Lower Cretaceous limestones of Texas and Arkansas occur in a similar geological setting, with alternating levels of marine and terrestrial sediments.

Whether the climatic conditions were arid or semi-arid like that found in the Morrison Formation is uncertain. Quite likely, the habitats occupied by Late Jurassic dinosaurs of North America and eastern Afrirca were remarkably similar, dominated by annual wet and dry seasons, without extremes of heat or cold. In modern Tanzania, the climate may have been ameliorated somewhat by the influence of oceanic waters, perhaps minimizing extremes of aridity that characterized habitats in the Morrison Formation.

MORRISON DINOSAURS

North American dinosaur populations extended far inland in the Late Jurassic, through the modern Colorado Plateau and Rocky Mountain states and beyond: parts of Oklahoma, New Mexico, Arizona, Utah, Colorado, Montana, Wyoming, and South Dakota. The stable American craton lay to the east and south. Subduction of the Pacific Plate at the leading edge of the American Plate produced immense volcanoes in a broad north-south arc. By the Late Jurassic, when the sediments constituting the Morrison Formation were being deposited, the interior seas had retreated, leaving behind a broad, undulating landscape dominated by meandering rivers. Severe arid conditions gave way to climates somewhat more moderate. Dinosaurs and associated populations like tiny mammals were no longer restricted by hypersaline seas or vast dune fields.

The Morrison Formation is a succession of shales and sandstones deposited over an area covering more than a million square kilometers, the product of widespread deposition of muds and sands by rivers and temporary lakes. In some places volcanic ash accumulated in basins in considerable thickness, originating from volcanoes in the emerging American Cordillera. Although some have suggested that volcanic catastrophes may have been responsible for the death of many of the Morrison dinosaurs, no direct link has been established. Instead, this greatest of all Jurassic bounties of dinosaurs probably accumulated as the ordinary action of rivers and lakes.

Some concentrations are clearly mass mortalities. For example, more than 10,000 bones of dinosaurs have been recovered from the Cleveland – Lloyd Dinosaur Quarry in eastern Utah; about half are from the carnivore *Allosaurus*, evidently trapped as they sought easy prey which had been mired in mud. The attraction that brought herbivores to the trap may have been deceptively alluring fresh water. As giants such as *Stegosaurus* and *Camarasaurus* struggled to escape, opportunistic predators probably lay in waiting on water's edge, only to become mired in turn when they moved in to claim their meal.

Typically, skeletons in the Morrison Formation were disarticulated by stream action and scavengers. Eventually, stream velocity diminished and the carrying capacity of the flowing water was insufficient to push dinosaur bones along the stream beds. Bones collected where streams slowed and dropped their loads, often on the inside of bends in the rivers where point bars accumulated as sands finally settled. Such is the case at Dinosaur National Monument in Utah, where skeletons of several dozen dinosaurs are scattered over a large point bar in a thick accumulation of sand.

In other cases, flood waters spread over the vast floodplains adjacent to the rivers, floating carcasses until they became mired in the mud as water level receded. Dinosaur bones in the Morrison seem to be more frequently encountered in mudstones rather than sandstones, perhaps reflecting the dinosaurs' preference for the flat floodplains and adjoining lowlands.

Streams were widespread, penetrating into the semi-arid landscape and providing fresh water for the rapidly expanding populations of large dinosaurs and small mammals. Plants must have been more abundant, too, for these immense dinosaurs required vast quantities of food. Geological evidence points to semi-arid conditions, whereas the demands for nutrition argue for luxuriant forests. Perhaps both conditions prevailed — semi-arid landscapes with through-flowing rivers and adjoining lowland forests.

In some places the Morrison Formation includes limestones, deposited as freshwater carbonates in alkaline lakes and playas that periodically dried up. There are few genuine lake deposits with the fossil remains of aquatic animals such as fish and amphibians, indicating perhaps that lakes were temporary and subject to marked seasonal change in water quality. Frogs, salamanders, turtles, and small mammals occur in some sites, however, indicating permanent water and luxuriant vegetation. Pterosaurs occupied some areas, too. Their feeding habits probably demanded continual availability of prey without seasonal interruptions. Thus, in some regions of the Morrison depositional area seasonal extremes of aridity must have been moderate rather than severe.

Windblown sand accumulations occur in a few places in the Morrison Formation, but dune fields must have been restricted and constituted a relatively minor aspect of the physiography in the Late Jurassic. Coal beds and plant fossils are rare in the Morrison, not because plant life was rare but because oxidation and destruction of the plant matter must have been rapid and complete in this region of seasonal aridity.

Dinosaur skulls in the Morrison Formation are rare. Bones of the skull were among the smallest of the body, and the neck and head muscles would have been easy targets for scavengers. Because the heads of sauropod dinosaurs in particular were small and the first cervical vertebra also small and the cranio-cervical joint relatively weak, disarticulation by current action and scavengers was common. Thus it is no surprise that skulls are separated from the skeletons.

On the other hand, skulls are relatively common in a few sites, especially where mass mortality is evident. Where dinosaurs were mired and their carcasses not easily reached by scavengers, scattering was minimal. For example, the Cleveland – Lloyd Quarry in Utah contains dozens of skeletons of the predator-scavenger *Allosaurus*. Although the skeletons are disarticulated and hopelessly mixed, probably from trampling by newly mired individuals struggling to escape, skull parts are as frequent as other elements of the skeleton. Neither scavengers (perhaps *Allosaurus* itself) nor stream action affected this mass accumulation of whole skeletons.

Other natural traps in the Morrison sediments are recorded at the Howe Quarry and Quarry 13, both in Wyoming, where sauropod skeletons are abundant. Leg and foot bones for some are articulated and upright, while the upper parts of the skeletons are disarticulated and scattered. Apparently some individuals became mired in mud, their legs sinking beneath the depth where the feet could be extracted, in the manner of cows around watering holes today. After death, the buried legs and feet remained buried, while the vertebrae and ribs scattered on the surface as easy meals for smaller scavengers that could manage the mud without becoming trapped.

Dinosaur bones occur throughout the geographic extent of the Morrison Formation. Skeletons are often isolated, and may be located far from permanent bodies of water. Moreover, the giant plant-eating dinosaurs such as *Diplodocus* and *Camarasaurus* must have exacted a heavy toll on the plant community. These herbivores were probably on the move continuously, slowly wandering in search of food. There is no paleoecologic evidence that any of the Morrison dinosaurs spent appreciable time in water. Instead, they evidently moved freely from aquatic habitats through shorelines and floodplains, to dry landscapes. Indeed, they may have been migratory, moving with the seasons to new habitats for feeding and reproduction.

CONCLUSION

The age of dominance of the giant sauropods, described above, drew to a close near the end of the Jurassic, for reasons unknown. Dinosaurs still dominated the land, but they were of other types. The Jurassic was also the time of the rise of other saurischians, one class of which made meals of many sauropods. These canivores were the theropods, the most famous being *Tyrannosaurus rex*, which evolved in the Late Cretaceous. The subject of the predaceous dinosaurs is taken up in the sixth chapter.

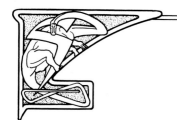

RHEA'S TIME

PAUL PREUSS

The execution was set for March 29th, at 9:00 A.M. This delay (whose importance the reader will grasp later) was owing to the desire on the authorities' part to proceed impersonally and slowly, after the manner of vegetables and plants.
— *Jorge Luis Borges,* The Secret Miracle

RHEA K. (A PSEUDONYM) IS A GEOLOGIST IN HER EARLY THIRTIES WITH A FIRM REPUTATION IN biostratigraphy, which I gather is a field of study that tries to impose order upon the chaos of the Earth's jumbled rocks by examining the remains of life, if any, that can be detected in them. Her photographs reveal an attractive woman — striking, really — with blue eyes, reddish blond hair in loose curls, a sunburned, lightly freckled complexion; of medium height, slender of build but strongly muscled. In this shot she's wearing lederhosen, a white cotton sleeveless undershirt with no bra, and clumpy boots, and there are some rather frightening mountain peaks in the background, which I suppose she has just climbed or is about to.

Her problems began in what appeared to be a straightforward way. With hindsight, of course, we note that matters were not as simple as they seemed. Her case has come to me because...

You're too tired to be precious, Rowan; just write the truth and clean it up later.

DECEMBER 17, 10:30 P.M.

The end of a typically foul New England winter's day, and my distinguished colleague, formerly professor and hetman of neurology, has at last made his getaway — well tanked on very fine old sherry, with handshakes and relieved smiles all around — to that renowned research institution in Manhattan of which he is to be the next president. Rhea was his patient, so—called. After so many months and so little change in her condition, her care has become a matter of rote — if not a silent reproach.

He dumped her on me. He did not fail to let me know, as he left, that he would understand completely if I recommended that she be transferred to custodial care. Free up needed space in the neurology wing, old boy; or in other words, old boy, the record will show that I tried, you failed.

So now the party's over and I've just spent an hour reviewing her medical history. More hole than doughnut.

Patient involved in skiing accident near Geneva, December 29th of last year. No immediate symptoms. Two days later, at New Year's Eve party, patient complained of severe headache, soon lost consciousness. On arrival at ER, patient was in coma; blood pressure and heart rate low, respiration rate low, and (odd note) body temperature elevated to forty degrees C (104°F).

CAT scan, NMR, spinal tap, the full menu. Contusion above left eye, subdural hematoma of minor extent over the right visual cortex, but other than presumed blow to the head, no sign of injury. Brain structure normal. Blood chemistry normal. No tumor. No infection. Neurosurgeon decided against intervention (correctly, for within a few days the hematoma was reabsorbed).

Only the EEG admitted a problem: the electrical activity of her left hemisphere was essentially flat, while that of the right hemisphere was chaotic. I have

the plots in front of me now; I can call up the whole eleven-plus months on disk. Never seen anything like it.

Patient remained in coma. After two months, transferred at husband's request. . . .

Thus Rhea was installed in our wing, where she still remains and where I noticed her for the first time, a rag doll of a young woman in a thin hospital gown, whose faintly yellow skin, even though inflated by intravenous fluids, could not disguise her loss of muscle tone. She did not react to light, sound, or touch. She lay in whatever position her nurses arranged her — if they opened her eyes, her eyes remained open and unblinking; if they closed them, they remained closed. I had seen many like her, usually the victims of trauma or drug overdose. I remember glancing at the record: blow to the head . . . cerebral hemorrhage . . . coma. Simple. She was not my patient.

It was mid-March then — springtime, which means nothing, or rather the opposite of what one might think, for like most large buildings on this coast of America, our hospital is a furnace during the cool half of the year, a freezer during the warm half. (The microorganisms love us for it.) Rhea was generally covered only with a sheet, with a light blanket kept folded at the bottom of the bed; on successive mornings the nurse noticed the blanket pulled neatly up to Rhea's chin. Nurse would fold it and return it to the bottom of the bed. After a week of this she thought to ask the night nurse why it was necessary to cover Rhea every night, and learned that the night nurse had not been doing so.

One has to skim the videotape they made that night; it moves like an Andy Warhol film of the Empire State Building. The fluorescent light in Rhea's windowless room is that of a morgue. Her left hand moves at a speed of inches per hour toward the foot of the bed, until her body is bent almost at right angles. She grasps the hem of the blanket and begins pulling it up at the same rate, straightening herself by millimeters,

and now using her creeping right hand to smooth the blanket across her chest. Her hands, moving at the speed of glaciers, resume their former position at her sides. This takes eight hours. No one glancing briefly at the monitor or into her room from the hall could have known that she was moving at all.

Against this date I can barely decipher the abbreviated jargon of our former neurological mikado ordering up a new round of tests which, however, reveal no quantifiable change.

Thereafter Rhea is observed shifting the bed clothes constantly, around the clock. Pulls up her blanket, pushes it down again, pushes away her sheet, pulls up her gown, exposing her naked self. At this hint of sex, the local pack of witch doctors becomes highly aroused.

She reverses the process: down with the gown, up with the sheet, up with the blanket, down again. The cycle takes days, and repeats. She's always in motion, the same slow motion, almost too slow to catch. A nurse tries to stop her from pulling up her gown — nurse records astonishment at the juggernaut strength of the wasted woman. The nurses grow impatient with Rhea's immodesty and untidiness and strap her wrists to the bed rail, but so persistently does Rhea strain against the bonds that she is in danger of dislocating a joint. Our maharaja orders her untied — man's been around, he can handle the sight of rumpled bedclothes.

In May, Rhea begins to hum. Or growl, or groan. At any rate, she makes tuneless rumblings deep in her throat, occasionally punctuated by quiet little yelps and gasps. Somebody notices that the EEG has changed: right hemisphere still a chaotic jumble, but the left hemisphere has perked up considerably. It occurs to me — it would not have occurred to them — that the new pattern on this side could be almost normal, for someone in deep hypnosis.

Boards and committees, meetings and consultations. The shamans are given their way with her. Interventions with various psychoactive drugs have no effect except to precipitate one life-threatening crisis. Husband (wisely, in my opinion) refuses permission for electro-stimulus of his wife's brain, despite assurances that "the procedure would serve to, if not normalize, at least *regularize* her brain wave patterns." Rhea still hums, growls, mutters meaninglessly to herself, still incessantly crumples and stretches, twists and smooths her sheets and blankets and gown. Bursts of fever still bloom on her skin without warning. . . .

Six months of this bring us to the present.

DECEMBER 18, 11:00 A.M.

I've just come from my first interview with Rhea.

Before coming in this morning I called in orders that she was to be helped out of bed and into her clothes. I don't approve of the American custom of coddling patients like infants, and Rhea has been doing isometric exercises for months — no fear of her collapsing on me. I wanted to see her sitting up.

Fuss and mutter, but when I arrived I found it done. Rhea was sitting bolt upright in a steel armchair, looking toward me with wide bright eyes that saw I knew not what. They had dressed her in a plaid wool skirt, a high-collared white blouse, a light wool cardigan, white socks and loafers — done their best to make her look like a schoolgirl, in other words. But her chapped hands were destroying their work, millimeter by millimeter; her skirt was on its way to her waist, and one side of her blouse was already out of the waistband.

"Rhea, can you hear me?"

No answer, of course. I did the usual examination, peering into her eyes, testing her strength and reflexes. Discounting her complete lack of awareness of me, or at any rate her total disregard, she was physically normal.

Next I put the cassette player on the tray table where she could hear it and started a Bach flute sonata. I studied her face, but her expression did not seem to change. "Rhea, I think you can hear me. I think that at some level my words are making sense to you — but that you can't, mm, put together an answer."

I paused to see if this elicited any response, meanwhile working my grandfather's fat old gold watch free from its waistcoat pocket, where the pressure of my belly secured it. "I'm going to try to help you by hypnotizing you."

My fondness for hypnotism was one of the reasons our once-upon-a-time generalissimo of neurology had liked to call me "old boy," and certainly one of the reasons I was regarded askance by staff, but it had stood me in good stead over the years — even if neither I nor anyone could explain why it worked, any better than my grandfather could. Normally one required an alert and cooperative subject, but I was privately convinced that at least half of Rhea's brain was — for want of a better term — already hypnotized. I hoped merely to introduce specific suggestions.

I let the watch swing before her eyes while I muttered the usual soothing incantations. I kept this up for several minutes, far longer than usual. I thought perhaps Rhea's pupils flickered ever so slightly from side to side, but that may have been wishful thinking.

I put the watch away and introduced myself again, as if I had just walked into the room. "Hello, Rhea. I'm Doctor Rowan. You are able to hear and understand me — and speak whenever you want." So I hoped. "May I ask you some questions?"

"Yes."

Fireworks. Church bells. Nobel prizes in physiology or medicine. "Good. That's very good." I took a long breath to calm myself. "Now first of all would you mind telling me, what is your name?"

She answered correctly. "And today 's date?"

"We don't know." Her voice was dry, toneless, but strong and clear. Her eyes were focused somewhere behind me. Before I could ask the next question, she continued, "The time is approximately one hundred and sixty-nine million, nine hundred and eleven thousand, three hundred years before the present."

A weirdly paradoxical response — she claimed to experience a time she *knew* to be before the present? Certainly odd enough to make me abandon my script. "What do you mean by the present?"

"The time here."

"And that is different from some other time?"

"From my time."

Her left brain was formulating these answers, I reminded myself, acting as a sort of translator for the outside world of language. Apparently "her time" was what she experienced in the inarticulate right brain.

"What is your time...like?" Stupidly put; I knew so even as I asked it.

"Inside time, time is time."

Indeed. What did I really want to know? I watched her hands, which had never ceased their hauling and pushing. "What is happening — where you are?"

"Mountains rise and fall. Rivers flow. I am alive everywhere."

"What time is it now?"

"Approximately one hundred and sixty-nine million, nine hundred and one thousand, nine hundred years before the present."

In the minute or so since I'd asked her before, almost nine thousand years had passed in "her time."

"Can you see yourself?"

"I see and feel myself."

"What do you see?"

"The land of me is all in front. The water of me is everywhere else. The molten stuff of me pours out in seams, and the land of me has begun to split apart."

The most extraordinary delusion! Did she believe this, or was she, as her use of the words "here" and "we" suggested, aware of her dreaming half, somehow aware that part of her was consciously creating a

fantastic global metaphor? The map of the body can be drawn and redrawn by many agents, of course, and sophisticated self-knowledge is no defense against illusion. Even such a renowned neurologist as Professor Sacks was capable of seeing his own nerve-damaged leg as a chalky white cylinder, now short and fat, now "a thousand feet long and two millimeters in diameter," changing size and shape and position many times each second, "a thousandfold switch between successive 'frames,'" as he put it in one of those popular bestsellers of his.

"Do you know what will happen to you next?"

"No. Here we know it, but I live there."

Something in me recoiled then, and I said, rather sharply, "Rhea, wake up."

But she did not wake up.

SAME DATE, 7:30 P.M., IN THE MEDICAL SCHOOL LIBRARY.

Time seems to be one of those topics that once generated great philosophical enthusiasm among physiologists but has withered for want of a means of extracting relevant human results from the overwhelming experimental mass. The more recent the work, the less ambitious it is — viz., "Hypothalamic control of circadian rhythms in the hamster," etc.

Going back a few years one finds Fischer, Cohen, et al. recording that hypnosis, some forms of psychosis, hallucinogenic intoxication, paresis, all give rise to distorted time sense, i.e., scrambled sequence, sense of simultaneity, or overestimate of chronological time. And Pieron, Arrhenius, Hoagland, et al. correlated body temperature with the internal metabolic clock, e.g., elevated temperature corresponds to faster oxidative metabolism, thus a faster internal clock, thus the sensation that (external) time is slowing down; charts were given for increase in alpha wave frequency with increasing body temperature. (But even at 104°F the increase, not much more than one Hertz, could hardly contribute to the persistent chaos in Rhea's right-brain pattern. If pattern is the word.)

(Perhaps pattern *is* the word.) There may be a possibility here that no one would have entertained as worthy of investigation even if it had occurred to them. Even I. The notion is absurd on its face.

Back to the bibliographies, on a different tack. Goldberger, Rigney, and West, nonlinear dynamics in physiology: heart rate exhibits self-similarity at different time scales. No such data on brain waves; given specific input, however — Rhea's chart — it is the sort of question even a precomputer-era fossil like me can pose to an expert system.

Off to my shared office in Neurology to retrieve the disks from the drawer I call my own. I log on to the local network and tap furiously. I get a cheerful display: "Welcome to BIOMATH HELPER. This software system is down until further notice."

DECEMBER 19, 3:30 P.M.

Another extraordinary conversation with Rhea. After the lightest brush of suggestion she talked readily; yet when I left she was as deep in trance as ever. Questioning her, I became entranced myself; so relentless was the flow of dates that, almost, I was the one hypnotized.

So precise were her descriptions that I sent myself back to the library and dug up stacks of illustrated articles, some technical, some popular — God knows there is no shortage of them — which picture the wanderings of the continents for the past 200 million years or more. It seems we live near the end of only the most recent spreading of the seafloors, which have expanded and recontracted many times before; the Earth might be taken for a thing that breathes. In the course of her career Rhea has mastered these coordinates and timetables, which to the uninitiated seem so many unrelated numbers, and she now regurgitates them obsessively.

DECEMBER 20, MIDDAY.

It's time to have a talk with Rhea's husband (I'll call him Arthur), and since my rooms are in one of the new colleges, a short walk from Science Hill, I decide to beard him in his den.

I am told that the university's accelerator laboratory is small as such places go, but it has a certain futuristic dignity all its own. Outside, it's a block-long Neolithic burial mound, geometrically precise, carpeted with clipped green grass; inside, it's a concrete vault, which houses a stainless steel machine as big as a U-boat.

They find Arthur for me and take me to him, down on the floor beside a nest of metal boxes garlanded with black rubberized cables, rooting like a scavenger in a basket of computer printout. He's a compact fellow, mid-forties, his face almost completely obscured by a brushy blond beard, with bristling blond brows and stiff blond hair going to gray. When he finally looks up, dark brown eyes stare out of the thicket through rimless plus-three diopters, giving him the look of a pugnacious sea otter.

I ask him about the ski accident and the New Year's Eve party. He adds a few details to the record — talking a mile a minute in the pained manner of someone explaining the obvious to an idiot. They took their holidays in the mountains near Geneva — the Juras, not the Alps, the Alpine resorts being too expensive and crowded — because he was working for six months at the big European physics laboratory near there. The New Year's party was at the apartment of Arthur's team leader, a Professor Kertesz. When Rhea complained of a blinding headache, nobody did anything at first because they thought she'd simply drunk too much. The ambulance was an hour late because of the holiday mob.

I want to know something about Arthur personally, about his work. He blinks rapidly and tells me he's a theorist; apparently this means his interest in machines is confined to the graphs they excrete. The one nearby is a sort of electromagnetic cannon that pushes the nuclei of large atoms to some significant fraction of the speed of light, thus allowing him to study their interactions.

Mm, I nod sagely. Interactions.

Like these, he says, and shows me a graph which could well be a pen and ink sketch of the Dolomites. He mumbles about the contraction of the t coordinate and shows me another, even more jagged.

The contraction of what?

"Picture a Minkowski diagram in which…"

— but he sees that I fail the Snow test and could not distinguish the second law of thermodynamics from the dust of Alexander stopping a bunghole. (Or do they amount to the same thing?) With an elaborate sigh — which leads me to suspect he has often rehearsed what is about to come, doubtless on sophomores in those obligatory Science for Poets classes — Arthur fetches me over to the coffee setup on a table against one chilly concrete wall.

He plops a filter cone into the top of the pot (a Chemex, what else?) and produces an unnaturally sharp pencil from the handkerchief pocket of his tweed jacket, which he stands in the cone, eraser down, point up.

"This is a Minkowski diagram. The t coord… uh, *time* is vertical, space is horizontal. The pencil is a worldline, pointing in the direction of increasing time. Right now it's standing straight up — which means the particle it represents is going nowhere in space; it's just sitting still, getting older. Light paths lie on the surface of the cone. … Uh, you know that nothing travels faster than light?"

"So I have heard." Really, Arthur.

"All right then, as I tilt the worldline — the pencil — away from the vertical, what does that say about the speed of the particle it represents?"

"Increases. Approaches the speed of light," I croak.

Should I not rejoice in the opportunity to learn something new? Why do I want to scream?

He grunts — "I will omit the subtleties" — and returns the pencil to the vertical. "What, in your experience, is the subjective feeling of the passage of time if one is sitting still, going nowhere, doing nothing?"

"In my experience it passes very slowly indeed, Arthur."

He lets the pencil fall against the cone. "What do you suppose would be the experience of a photon, moving at the speed limit of the universe?"

This question gives me pause. I'm sure I've heard or read it before, and it seems there is a trick answer — no doubt I could find it in that yellowing copy of Hawking's *A Brief History of Time*, which lies unread on my sitting room table.

But I have become intrigued in spite of myself, and actually try to think this out. If nothing travels faster than light, how could a particle of light get news from other parts of the universe? It doesn't seem that it could — it could only experience the universe as it participated in events along its own… worldline, as Arthur calls it. Between events, nothing. Therefore everything would seem to happen at once; therefore…

"No time," I venture. "It seems there would be no experience of time."

Arthur's eyes gleam hugely behind his glasses, and he nods; I realize that this is as near to congratulations as he is likely to come. How many sophomores get that question right? I wonder, flattering myself.

He moves the pencil back and forth in the coffee filter like an upside-down pendulum. "From our point of view as observers, we simply see something speeding up, slowing down. We can't experience *its* time; certainly our own experience is unaffected. A material object can never actually reach the speed of light." He waves at the great stainless steel machine. "We observe this every day in our accelerators, we are forced to take this into account in our calculations: nuclei grow ever more massive, require ever greater inputs of energy to increase their velocities by ever smaller degrees. I am certain, however, that if such a nucleus were conscious, it would notice nothing unusual about its own state. It would look out at us observers and think how odd that *our* lives were passing so quickly."

Arthur repockets his pencil, and we stare at each other. His bright black button eyes gleam at me out of his grizzled fur.

"You've written rather extensively on the subject of time, have you?" I ask.

He seems genuinely surprised. "I have?"

"I ran down your bibliography on the library computer. 'Quantum Gravity and Space-time,' several titles of that sort."

"Oh. Every physicist wrestles with time. It's nothing, just mathematics." A distracted look has come into Arthur's bespectacled eyes.

Another tack. One learns not even to wonder what people see in each other — in the case of Rhea and Arthur I can't imagine — but I want to know how they met. They'd been married less than two years before her accident.

"In Vermont, on a mountaineering club outing," he says. "We were both rock climbers. We took an interest in each other's work. She had a good understanding of what I have just been telling you."

Better than I do, he does not need to add. "What was of particular interest to you in her work?"

After a moment spent brooding on the question he replies, "Whereas I am concerned with objects with typical half-lives of a few milliseconds up to a few seconds, the shortest time scales of interest to her were a few thousand years; more typically a million years, or a dozen million, or a couple of hundred million."

Though I persist a few minutes longer, Arthur has by now left for some other mental universe and gives me nothing more.

● ● ●

Leaving the accelerator center I notice the natural history museum standing on the flank of Science Hill to the east, almost diffident in its too-appropriate apposition to the nuclear accelerator. It is a miniature Gothic castle of flaking orange sandstone, once the stronghold of our university's famous nineteenth-century robber-baron paleontologist.

I remember my first and only visit to the building, not long after receiving my appointment here — seeing with an *aha!* of delight the murals high up on the walls of the tiny central hall (most of which is taken up by the bones of some long-necked, long-tailed dinosaur, a brontosaurus I suppose, although I'm told there's no such beast anymore; taxonomy marches on). These murals are the originals of the illustrations that entranced me when I saw them in an American picture magazine as a child: toothed, clawed, bone-and-leather-armored monsters (actually rather roly-poly in depiction, if the truth be told) plodding through the mud among thickets of exotic palms and cycads; distant silhouettes of nightmare flying things; lurid volcanoes turning the horizon red with fire, black with smoke; finally the blooming of lush magnolias and rhododendrons — and on the opposite wall, the improbable woolly giants of a later age, rambling across endless grassy plains, nonchalantly fleeing the ice.

The artist had arranged what Arthur would call the *t* coordinate to unscroll continuously from left to right; it was all there at once, as fast as the beam of the eye could flicker across the epochs, dozens of millions of years at next to the speed of light.

DECEMBER 21, A SATURDAY MORNING.

A nagging question remains from my talk with Arthur. With some effort I reach him on the phone. "Arthur, these relativistic atomic nuclei of yours — what exactly makes them . . . interact?"

"Well, uh . . . they smash."

"What?"

"Some calculable proportion of beam nuclei collide with target nuclei. Metal, plastic. Depends on the experiment. We look at what flies out."

"What if you didn't put anything—a target—in their way?"

"Why wouldn't...?" I can almost hear his shrug. "They'd smash anyway. Into the wall, the ground."

"So from our point of view these nuclei appear to live longer the faster they move. But not from theirs. Then they smash."

He pauses—debating whether to go all technical, I think—but evidently deciding against. "Yes, essentially. Something like that."

SAME DATE, EVENING.

Our expert system has come back on-line. I load my precious data and ask for analysis. The program probes with a few pertinent questions; luckily I can now specify the key factor with some precision. The machine runs swiftly and gives me... nothing. A set of absolutely flat curves, rows of parallel lines of Euclidean perfection. Instead of the structure within chaos I had led myself to expect, I get the encephalogram of a dead woman.

I'm hardly superstitious, but before quitting for the day I decide to look in on Rhea. The floor at night has its customary air of busy quiet, that of an air-raid watch, abuzz with stifled jokes and whispered confessions in anticipation of the crises that come at dawn. Even the blinking red and yellow and blue bulbs on the floor's solitary, wobbly Christmas tree have the look of warning lights.

With half its overhead fluorescent lamps off, Rhea's room is only symbolically dim, far from dark. I step to within a foot of her bedside. She is on her left side, back arched, right arm cocked, pushing the sheet slowly down over her breast toward the blanket-clutching left

hand that moves up from her ribs. Her eyes are closed. Her tongue clicks and her cheeks suck into hollows. Her breathing is long and deep, the air sighing in and out of her like the wind of a thousand winters.

Closer. Her right ear is feverishly suffused with blood, glowing like a red neon sign. I am a few inches from her side, watching the blanket collide with the sheet under the inexorable force of her shifting hands, the sheet sliding under the more pliable, less dense blanket, a ridge of olive-drab material rising and crumpling upon itself—one fold, then another, a range of parallel folds.

In the rustle of cloth I hear grinding cataclysms.

SAME DATE.

Almost midnight now, in my rooms—a fragrant oak fire in the grate, a balloon of old French brandy in my hand, and beneath the casement, undergraduate males howling at a winter moon. I have just realized that at normal amplitudes the energy required to produce the EEG frequencies I have been toying with wouldn't have simply elevated Rhea's temperature, it would have exploded her head.

No wonder the curves were flat. But in fact there may be a signal there. Are the EEG machine's skin contacts sensitive enough to detect as weak a signal as the one I suspect?

DECEMBER 22.

"Good morning, Rhea. Can you hear me?"

"Yes."

"I would like to perform some simple tests. They shouldn't take long. And a little Mozart on the cassette player. I'll try to make sure you aren't uncomfortable."

She said nothing.

"Is that all right with you?"

"Yes."

I personally inplanted the sheathed-needle contacts in her scalp while a techinician looked on, disapproving — nothing wrong with my technique, but I certainly was not putting them where he would have. Half an hour later I came away with a scroll of paper in one hand — five minutes of Rhea's actual right-brain encephalogram — and a fan of computer printout the size of a telephone book in the other, showing the same data reworked by multiplying the amplitude and dividing the frequency by a factor of 4.5×10^9. The approximate age of the Earth in years.

The book-sized printout looked like an encephalogram all right. Not a mere five minutes' worth, though. It might just as easily have been taken for a forty-five thousand-year-long seismogram.

DECEMBER 23.

I convinced Arthur to take an hour and visit his wife; he'd got out of the habit in recent months. He remembered to bring a Christmas present; from the shape of the box I guessed it was a nightgown. (It was, floor-length flannel with pink ribbons.) I walked with him to her room, trying to prepare him for what he would see.

He listened to me distractedly. "She was obsessed with gaining a feeling for the eons she dealt with," he said when I paused. "We were talking about it the day we...we went skiing. She seemed very unhappy with the old calendar cliché — you know, compressing Earth's geological record into a single year. 'If the Earth formed a second after midnight on the first of January...'" Arthur stopped, his open mouth forming a hole in his fur. "Oh dear," he said. "Is that...?"

"Mm," I grunted. "Why did she seem unhappy with the calendar metaphor?" An odd thing to get upset about.

"She said it was hard enough to remember one time scale; having to convert it to another was a waste of mental energy," he murmured, distracted. "You know, the dinosaurs evolved in the Triassic — or was it in November? That sort of thing."

Rhea sat upright in her chair, dressed in a long cotton print dress buttoned down the front. Her hands threatened to tear it open over her abdomen, but the process would require hours.

Arthur sat close in front of her. Where I was standing I could not see his face, but he was quiet for an unusually long time. Finally he put out his hand and laid it cautiously over one of hers. While a Bach canon unrolled endlessly on the cassette player, her hand moved, undeterred, beneath his.

I cleared my throat and said, in a loud, formal voice, "What time is it, Rhea?"

"One hundred and seven million, two hundred and seventy-one thousand, six hundred years before the present."

"And what do you see?" I was like a trainer putting a tame animal through its paces, but I told myself it was necessary for Arthur to understand the whole truth.

"Laurasia has rotated about its center and the western part is high above my equator. What we call the North Atlantic has opened to the west, by an average of twenty degrees of latitude. The Tethys Sea is narrow and closing. Gondwanaland is split by the rift that will become the South Atlantic. To the east, the India plate..."

"I don't want you to tell me about all of you," I said, interrupting the detailed recitation. "Go closer to the surface. I want you tell me about what is happening in the center — in the center of you."

Arthur jerked his bushy head around and looked at me with a frightening gleam in his eye. I wondered what I had said. His burning gaze rested on me a moment longer before he turned back to Rhea and leaned close to her. "Where we might stand and watch together," he said.

"I glisten under the moon and sun. The shallow water comes and goes over me."

"Do you remember when we went skiing in the Juras last year?" he demanded.

"No."

"Do you remember going to Professor Kertesz's apartment on New Year's Eve?"

"No."

"What do you remember about last year in the... in the center of you?"

"In the shallow waters that come and go, the myriad creatures are born and die."

With effort, I kept my mouth shut. There were more basic questions I thought Arthur ought to be asking her, but I was loath to interfere.

He thought of one of them on his own. "Do you know who I am, Rhea?"

"Here you are our husband."

"Here." He nodded. "Can you take me *there*?"

"You cannot go there."

"I mean, can you tell me about it? Tell me about one single minute, one single hour?"

"No. The years flow like water. The sun and moon spiral and spin in the sky — the stars and the blue sky follow one upon the other, so quickly that they are one. In my clear shallow waters the uncountable microscopic creatures of me die and sink and turn swiftly to smooth layered rock. Here in this place my clear waters recede; my silver rivers braid themselves across the featureless plain of silt. The land of me tries to rise. Before our eyes the twisting rivers grind down the folded schist, smooth and flat. Still the deep rock strains toward the sky, riding up over diving Africa. The roots of my mountains sink and their roofs rise and are stripped bare almost as fast as they rise, but still they rise, and all the clay and sand that wash down

from them are spread smooth upon my fine mud, and soon there are layers upon layers of fine mud, which press themselves together and make the fine stone of me, press themselves upon the beaks and bones and scales and footprints and feathers of my myriad creatures. Still the granite and the dolomite are forced up out of me and rise, faster than they can be planed away. My waters recede farther. Black earth covers me, and green plants grow thick over me, and blue ice collects on my high glittering rock...."

Arthur seems willing to let this go on forever, but I can take it no longer. "Rhea, wake up!"

She stops talking, but she does not wake up.

DECEMBER 29.

I don't know why Arthur is so fascinated by these obsessively detailed products of Rhea's unconscious imagination. Having learned to ask the triggering questions, he listens to her recite for hours at a time. I could restrict him to visiting hours, but what would anyone gain by it?

Arthur pulled strings with the computing center and got me help in analyzing the year's worth of her EEG, a process which has taken most of the week. The evidence is conclusive, enough to persuade even my most unimaginative colleagues; her case, when it appears in the journals, will make me famous for a week, perhaps for several months. For in Rhea's encephalogram can be read the rift of the Earth's crust, the outpouring of magma, the spread of sea floors, the drift of continents, the rise of mountain ranges — correlated absolutely with the best geological evidence, a topic Rhea had not only mastered but to which she herself had contributed significantly. When she is asked to speak, her running narrative tells the details — at any desired spatial scale, as if her perspective were that of a powerful spy satellite. Her coordinate system is apparently centered on a spot that today is in the Jura mountains northwest of Geneva, the place of her accident.

But her relative time scales are fixed. Therein resides the unanswerable question.

DECEMBER 31.

Within the last half hour, genus Homo has taken to its collective feet, chipped its stone tools, painted the caves of the Pyrenees. Asia and North America have parted and come together again on opposite shores, and humans spill into new continents, extinguishing Quaternary fauna as they go. In a few seconds the Parthenon will be erected, Constantine will see a sign in the sky, Gabriel will speak to Mohammed in the desert, the Americas will be discovered once or twice again, we shall have invented modern warfare, and midnight will be upon us.

From somewhere outside comes the muffled distant noise of car horns and firecrackers. Arthur looks at me, full of apprehension. When my watch chimes softly, I push the key on the cassette player and freeze Bach in the midst of a cantata.

"Rhea, wake up."

Her suddenly limp hands fall like dead birds to lie motionless in her lap. When she lifts her weary head to look at Arthur, I imagine the hint of a twinkle in her eye.

POSTSCRIPT

Since a more literate version of this account was first published *(The New York Review of Books*, August 199__), Rhea has continued her slow recovery. I persist in thinking of her year-long enchantment as a form of self-hypnosis, triggered by physical circumstances but making use of the emotional and intellectual content of whatever was between her and Arthur, who after all do seem to be following rather different worldlines. She retains a vivid memory of her experience and says she can no longer look at a landscape without imagining it flowing and bending like soft ice cream. She reports that at times in her dreams she finds herself in long-vanished places — on a placid shore under a humid gray sky, perhaps, with dragonflies the size of condors buzzing among the horsetails, and scaly things rippling the oily waters — and she wonders if she will ever waken. Curiously, this prospect, which to me would be a nightmare, bothers her not at all.

She is pregnant and obviously pleased about it. Arthur is pleased too, engagingly so. Rhea — to my mild surprise, given how verbal she could be in trance — has turned out to be a woman of few words; when I asked her how she felt about the prospect of having a baby, she said simply, "I feel confident."

There is much Rhea has not told me, perhaps having to do with what really happened on that ski trip — and why it took so long for someone to call an ambulance on New Year's Eve. What transpired in the sixty hours between the accident and her collapse? I can't help but wonder if this *is* her first pregnancy — if some disappointment or tragedy in that line had previously robbed her of the confidence she now expresses so firmly. Whatever may have happened before that fateful New Year's Eve, however, in the twelve months that followed Rhea was granted a profound vision, unique in the long history of the Earth.

5.
THE AGE OF GIANTS
ESSAY BY ANTHONY FIORILLO
SPECULATION BY GREGORY BENFORD

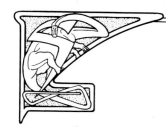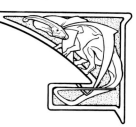

THE AGE OF GIANTS
ANTHONY R. FIORILLO

THE JURASSIC PERIOD REPRESENTS THE FIRST TIME THAT VERY LARGE-BODIED ANIMALS, SUCH AS SAUROPODS and stegosaurs, were a major influence in the terrestrial environment. The presence of these huge animals put new pressures on the terrestrial ecosystem. For example, in North America the Jurassic environment was humid to semi-arid. In the regions with a semi-arid climate, the presence of large, possibly gregarious, herbivores must have threatened the existing stands of vegetation with overgrazing. In order to avoid this problem, it seems likely that at least one group of dinosaurs, the sauropods, migrated great distances. Perhaps these animals followed a "green wave" of blooming vegetation across the countryside much the same way some of the grazing ungulates of the East African savanna do today. If these animals did migrate, this may be the first time that long-distance migrations were incorporated into the behavior of terrestrial herbivores. There is no evidence yet about the migration of other herbivores, the ornithopods. We might guess that at least some theropods also migrated, to keep up with their prey.

THE SAUROPODS AND STEGOSAURS

By the end of the Jurassic, sauropods, the grandest of all the dinosaur groups, were, in terms of abundance, the most significant vertebrates within these terrestrial ecosystems. They must have dominated the Jurassic landscape by both their sheer size and numbers. By the Early Cretaceous, however, their abundance had been greatly reduced, and sauropods played a more subordinate role in terrestrial ecosystems.

These dinosaurs were gigantic four-footed, plant-eating animals which represent perhaps the epitome of most people's perception of dinosaurs. Certainly the appeal of sauropods stems in part from their immense size. Some sauropods achieved lengths up to 30 meters and weights of 80,000 kilograms, making them the largest animals ever to walk the earth. Contributing to, and perhaps helping to sustain this popular image, has been such characterizations of sauropods as Dino the dinosaur from *The Flintstones* cartoons and the logo for the Sinclair Oil Company.

Sauropods can be described as having a simple body plan which varied only slightly throughout the group. They had very long necks and tails, relatively small skulls and brains, and erect limbs reminiscent of elephants. In addition, the nostrils of these animals, rather than being located at the end of their snout like so many other animals, were located high up on the skulls. In fact, in some examples these nostril openings were so far up the skull that they are located in the vicinity of the eye openings. Still another unusual feature which appeared in some of the later sauropods was rudimentary body armor.

Geographically, these animals were widespread, with remains, in the form of bones or footprints, having been found on all of the continents except Antarctica. In addition to their wide geographic distribution, sauropods are also one of the most long-lived groups of dinosaurs, spanning some 100 or so million years, from the Lower Jurassic to the Upper Cretaceous.

Sauropods were certainly not the only dinosaurs

inhabiting the terrestrial realm during the Jurassic. Contemporary with these animals were other groups of herbivorous dinosaurs, such as the armored and the unarmored ornithischians, or bird-hipped dinosaurs. The armored ornithischians, or thyreophorans, include animals such as *Scutellosaurus*, *Scelidosaurus*, and the stegosaurs. These first two dinosaurs probably represent the primitive stock from which animals like the stegosaurs were derived. In addition to these herbivores, there were also numerous groups of meat-eating, or theropod, dinosaurs in the Jurassic such as the large allosaurs (perhaps the most abundant of the predators), the medium-sized ornithomimids, and the rather small coelurosaurs.

The stegosaurs are known to have had incredibly small brains. In some species like *Stegosaurus* itself, the brain may have approximated the size of a walnut. Also contributing to the image of this group is the unusual array of spikes and plates that adorn the backs and tails of these animals. The former protected against predators, while the latter feature seems to have been instrumental in regulation of body temperature.

Remains of stegosaurs are quite often found associated with the remains of the sauropods. Although they are a common element to many Jurassic dinosaur assemblages, stegosaurs were geographically and temporally more restricted than their sauropod contemporaries. Stegosaurs are known from Africa, Asia, Europe and North America, and temporally from the Middle Jurassic to the Upper Cretaceous, although the later record of this group is decidedly fragmentary. Based on recent work, it appears that China was the center of stegosaur diversity and evolution.

SAUROPOD ANATOMY

Since sauropods were such a major component of Jurassic terrestrial ecosystems, it is worth discussing some of the specifics of this group. In general, sauropods can be characterized as being quadrupedal and having very large body size, long tails, long necks, and relatively small heads. The skulls of these animals are unusual since they all have the nares (nasal openings) located dorsally. In the case of the diplodocids, this opening is in fact between the eyes. Some people have speculated that due to the position of the nares on these animals, at least some sauropods had trunks similar to those seen on elephants and tapirs. A comparison of the skulls of these three groups of animals shows, however, that although the nasal openings may be similarly situated, the elephant and tapir skulls have further modifications which are not present in the sauropod skull. For example, the nasal bone in the skull of the tapir is highly reduced and in the elephant skull it is virtually nonexistent. This feature allows these animals to have a high degree of flexibility with their respective trunks. Associated with this reduction of the nasal bone is a deep incision beneath the bone, which is particularly noticeable in a tapir skull. These features are not present in the skulls of sauropods, making a tapirlike or elephantlike trunk for these animals seem unlikely.

Sauropod teeth are generally simple, ranging from more robust, spoon-shaped teeth as in *Camarasaurus* and *Barapasaurus* to thin, pencil-like teeth as in *Diplodocus*. In *Diplodocus* and closely related sauropods such as *Apatosaurus*, these teeth are restricted to the front of the mouth corresponding loosely to mammalian incisors. Teeth of all sauropods show wear which is probably attributable to cropping of vegetation rather than prolonged chewing of vegetation since the teeth lack the grinding and shearing surfaces found on the teeth of many ornithischians. In addition, sauropod teeth are arranged differently than those of ornithischians by being along the margins of the palate and jaw. This suggests that sauropods did not have a muscular cheek, which would have helped

Above: The Seismosaur, *a recently discovered sauropod of the Late Jurassic. With a length of 140 feet,
it was perhaps the longest beast that ever lived.*

By Brian Franczak. Preceding spread: Titanosaurs
*from the Late Cretaceous, herding at a waterfall.
By William G. Stout.*

retain food in the mouth during chewing. Because of
these simple teeth and the lack of cheeks, food was
probably processed with the aid of some other digestive feature, like a gizzard as in birds, or it may have
occurred within the digestive tract with the aid of
symbiotic microorganisms.

The necks of sauropods contain 12 to 19 vertebrae,
as compared to most mammals which only have 7 cervical vertebrae. The number of tail vertebrae was
highly variable, ranging from 34 to more than 80
vertebrae. Evolution increased the strength of the
vertebrae, and reduced the amount of weight of the
skeleton as sauropod vertebrae have a number of

cavities and vertebral connections were reduced to
slender rods and struts.

SAUROPOD SYSTEMATICS

Most sauropods are known only from fragmentary
fossil material. The most diagnostic parts of the sauropod skeleton are the skulls and the feet, which are
rarely both preserved. However, specializations of the
vertebrae for weight reduction due to the immense
size of these individuals, have provided some means
for taxonomic identification. Based on vertebral
characters, approximately 90 different genera and

150 species of sauropods have been identified. Of these sauropods, most have been identified on fragmentary material which makes comparison between different sauropods difficult, if not impossible, because the animals have been defined on different skeletal elements.

In fact, complete or nearly complete skeletal material is known from only five genera of sauropods. Additionally, only about a dozen sauropods are known from good skeletal materials, while another dozen are known from reasonably complete skeletons. Of this group of approximately two dozen sauropods, skulls are only known from approximately one dozen. This collection of largely incomplete material serves as the basis for radical differences between various workers' schemes of relationships of various sauropods. Based on the better-known sauropods, a five-fold division of sauropod families can be erected which includes the following families: the Cetiosauridae, the Camarasauridae, the Diplodocidae, the Brachiosauridae, and the Titanosauridae. In addition to these five families, a sixth, lesser-known family, the Vulcanodontidae, is also included here because of its potential significance to sauropod origins.

The origin of sauropods has remained controversial. This controversy stems from the presence of a significant gap in the fossil record, which occurs in the earliest part of the Jurassic and covers some 30 million years. This was a critical time in the history of dinosaurs, since after the gap a whole new set of dinosaurs, which included the sauropods, appear. New discoveries of sauropod materials, however, have helped fill in this hole in the fossil record. These new fossils have provided further support of the idea that sauropods were derived from a group of dinosaurs called the prosauropods, a group well known from strata below the gap in the fossil record. This hypothesis had also been put forth based on the trend in prosauropods toward quadrupedality and larger size.

The first prosauropods may have had adaptations for a carnivorous diet, while some of the later prosauropods developed herbivorous adaptations which seemed likely to continue along a progression toward the sauropods. These newly discovered early sauropods show many of the skeletal features which are associated with the later sauropods, while retaining many of the prosauropod characters.

One of the problems preventing the full acceptance of this ancestry, however, is in a comparison of the hind feet of prosauropods and sauropods. All prosauropods have a reduced fifth toe, a feature which is not reduced in the later sauropods. This may not seem, at first, to be significant. However, in the evolutionary development of most animals, once an anatomical feature is lost or reduced during the course of the history of that group of animals, the feature is not redeveloped at some later point. Additionally, there are aspects of the sauropod ankle which suggest to some workers that sauropods evolved independently of the prosauropods.

In general, with the discovery of new sauropod material from the Early Jurassic, many dinosaur workers concur that sauropods arose from prosauropod stock. These new sauropod materials form the basis of the family of sauropods called the Vulcanodontidae.

FAMILY VULCANODONTIDAE

This family is based on the skeletal material of two different sauropods, *Vulcanodon* and *Barapasaurus*. The former sauropod is known from a headless skeleton from the Lower Jurassic of northern Zimbabwe, while the latter animal is known from partially associated skeletal material and isolated bones from the Lower Jurassic of central India. Another possible member of this family is *Ohmdenosaurus*, an incomplete animal from the Lower Jurassic of Europe. No skull material is as yet known for this family except for isolated teeth attributed to *Barapasaurus*. These teeth resemble those of the later camarasaurids by being spoon-shaped, but the vulcanodontid teeth differ by having denticles, or bumps, which run along the front and back margins of the teeth. As well as skull material, neck and dorsal vertebrae are also unknown for this group.

Many of the skeletal characters of this family clearly show the transition from the ancestral prosauropods to the later groups of sauropods. In particular, aspects of the pelvis and the feet show clear affinities to the prosauropods. Also, the known vertebrae of this family are not cavernous as in the later sauropods, but they do show marked depressions within the vertebrae that indicate a change from the earlier prosauropods. So transitional is the nature of this family that *Vulcanodon* was initially described as a prosauropod. What separates *Vulcanodon* from the prosauropods, however, is the presence of a well-developed fifth toe, like that observed in the later sauropods. The hind feet of *Barapasaurus* are unfortunately not well known. Both *Vulcanodon* and *Barapasaurus* differ from the other sauropod groups by having a particularly narrow pelvic region. In addition, the limbs of these animals tend to be more slender than those of the other sauropods.

FAMILY CETIOSAURIDAE

Remains of *Cetiosaurus*, a member of this family, were first described in 1841 by Sir Richard Owen, making this family one of the first groups of dinosaurs to have been documented. In addition to the historic interest that this family holds, it is also the family that represents the most generalized body plan for all sauropods. The vertebrae of this group contain simple cavities, while the length of the upper arm bones of these animals approaches that of the thigh bones. In addition, the neural spines of the neck vertebrae of these animals are not split, as in some of the more evolved sauropods. Although some members of this family, such as *Zizhongosaurus*, were present in the Early Jurassic of China, the heyday for this family was in the Middle Jurassic. Representatives of the cetiosauridae, such as *Omeisaurus* and *Haplocanthosaurus*, existed into the Late Jurassic of China and North America, respectively.

Shunosaurus, dating from the Middle Jurrasic, has only recently been discovered and described from nearly complete skeletons. This animal is only the second sauropod to be known from a complete skeleton. In contrast to the primitive nature of most of its skeleton, the spines of the tail vertebrae of *Shunosaurus*, particularly those toward the end, developed into a clubshape. This would have given *Shunosaurus* an almost clublike tail.

One feature of the anatomy of the cetiosaurs that breaks from the simple or generalized body plan of sauropods is the large cavities located on the neural spines. These are typically considered to be derived features. Based largely on these cavities, some workers feel that the cetiosaurs may have been ancestral to the diplodocids, the camarasaurids, and the brachiosaurids. Additionally, the dentition of the Middle Jurassic sauropod, *Shunosaurus*, shows features which may be ancestral to both the camarasaurids and the diplodocids.

FAMILY CAMARASAURIDAE

This group of sauropods represents the most common sauropod of the Upper Jurassic of North America. This family is unknown anywhere else in the world except for materials found in the Upper Cretaceous of Asia. *Camarasaurus*, the most common representative of this family, is one of the few sauropods in which virtually all of the skeleton is known. These animals are characterized as having short, sturdy skulls with large, spoon-shaped teeth. The nasal opening is not as high up on the skull as it is in *Diplo-*

docus, but is instead slightly forward of the eyes. Many of the vertebrae have well-developed cavities. The length of the upper arm bones compared to the thigh bones of camarasaurs is longer than that of the diplodocids, but less than that of the brachiosaurs and the cetiosaurs. In general, many of the limb and pelvic elements of the camarasaurs are more robust than their counterparts in the other Late Jurassic sauropods.

FAMILY DIPLODOCIDAE

Unlike the short, robust skull of the camarasaurs, the diplodocid skull is elongated and much thinner, more gracile, and almost horselike in appearance. The nasal opening of the diplodocid skull is located much more dorsally than in the camarasaurid skull. The teeth of these animals are also quite different than the previously discussed sauropod families in that they are thin and pencil-like. Whereas camarasaurs have teeth throughout the entire jaw margin, the diplodocid teeth are restricted to just the front of the mouth. The forelimbs of the diplodocids are much shorter compared to their hindlimbs than in other sauropods.

The cavities of the vertebrae of these animals are complex and very well developed, making the vertebrae appear to consist of a series of struts and rods. A dominant character that distinguishes this family is the development of a set of forked bones located beneath the middle tail vertebrae. These bones, called chevrons, are present in most dinosaurs, but they usually occur as straight bones descending vertically from the tail vertebrae.

The ends of the tails of the diplodocids are not usually complete, due in part to their great length. Of those tails found, some appear to be very long and whiplike, which may have been for defense, like those seen in some modern-day reptiles.

This family was very common in the Upper Jurassic and includes *Seismosaurus, Diplodocus, Apatosaurus,*

Barosaurus, Supersaurus (all from North America), *Cetiosauriscus* from Europe, *Mamenchisaurus* from Asia, and *Dicraeosaurus* from Africa. The youngest diplodocids are known from the Late Cretaceous of Asia and include *Nemegtosaurus* and *Quaesitosaurus*.

FAMILY BRACHIOSAURIDAE

Brachiosaurus, the sauropod that typifies this family, is perhaps best known as the heaviest of all the dinosaurs, with weights of up to 80 tons. The skulls of brachiosaurs are intermediate in length between the diplodocids and the camarasaurs; the nasal openings of these animals are greatly expanded and higher on the skull. The teeth of these animals resemble the spoon-like teeth of the camarasaurs. Unlike the diplodocids, brachiosaurs had rather short tails. All the other sauropods had a sauropod "normal" stance, with the shoulders lower than the hips, but due to the longer arms of brachiosaurs, they had a "reversed" stance with the shoulders higher than the hips.

The brachiosaurs first appear in the Middle Jurassic of Europe in the form of *Bothriospondylus* and in the Middle Jurassic of China with *Bellusaurus*. The fossil record of this family extends through the Upper Cretaceous. This family is rare in the Upper Jurassic of North America and is represented only by *Brachiosaurus* and *Ultrasaurus*. In contrast, *Brachiosaurus* is quite common in the Upper Jurassic of Africa.

FAMILY TITANOSAURIDAE

Although present by the Late Jurassic, the titanosaurs did not achieve dominance among the sauropods until the Late Cretaceous. Remains of these animals have been found on most continents, but this family was particularly abundant in South America and perhaps India. This family of sauropods is decidedly rare in North America.

Titanosaurs are unusual among the sauropods in that they had developed large dermal bones which presumably served as body armor. The cavities of some of the body vertebrae were irregular, while the spines of the backbone were tilted backwards. The length of the forelimb compared to the hindlimb in these animals is particularly disproportionate, favoring the hindlimb. Unfortunately critical pieces of the skeleton of these animals, such as the skulls, remain poorly known, making the identification of these animals and their relationship to other sauropods difficult.

The oldest titanosaur known is *Tornieria*, from the Upper Jurassic of Africa, and it is associated with several other sauropods including *Brachiosaurus*. Although based on very incomplete remains, *Tornieria* has been tentatively assigned to the titanosaurs because of the unusual nature of its vertebrae.

SAUROPOD PALEOECOLOGY

The natural history of sauropods has always been controversial. In what types of environments did sauropods live? How were they able to sustain their immense size? Were sauropods gregarious or solitary? Did sauropods give birth to live young? These and many more questions are still open.

Typically, these animals have been pictured wading in swamps and lakes, a restoration that has lost favor among paleontologists today. This picture originated with the idea that these animals were too large to have lived on dry land, and that they needed water to help buoy up their weight. More recently, however, it has been recognized that the structure of the limbs and feet of sauropods provided them with a graviportal posture that resembles that of elephants. Additionally, sauropod remains have been found in a variety of deposits that range from river channel deposits to floodplain deposits. These data suggest that, although sauropods did perhaps wander through streams and swamps, they were well adapted for life on dry land.

In contrast to their immense body size, the mouths of these animals are ridiculously small. The diplodocids make this contrast even more extreme given the smaller number of teeth in their jaws. This apparent lack of appropriate tools for harvesting the needed vegetation to achieve the large sizes of the sauropods has stimulated much speculation. To account for this paradox, some scientists speculate that these animals had gizzards to assist in the assimilation of food, much the way birds do today. Unfortunately, the evidence from the fossil record to support this notion is incomplete.

The reproductive behavior of these animals is even more speculative. There has been only one report of eggs attributed to sauropods *(Hypselosaurus)*, from the Late Cretaceous of France. These eggs were not found in direct association with sauropods, but based on their size (the largest known dinosaur eggs) and the occurrence of sauropods of the appropriate age found in the same beds, the consensus is that they are probably sauropod eggs. Others have argued that sauropods gave birth to live young. This claim has been made based, in part, on the interpretation of sauropod pelvic anatomy, and in part on the lack of direct association of eggs with sauropods. This lack should not suggest to anyone that all of the remaining dinosaurs gave birth to their young live. Instead it should be realized that eggs are particularly fragile and need special conditions in order to be preserved. To emphasize this point, consider that the eggs of Mesozoic birds are even more rare than those of the dinosaurs. If one were tempted to use the above negative reasoning for the issue of dinosaur births, one would also have to consider the unrealistic idea of live birth for Mesozoic birds. Also, the pelvic anatomy of sauropods better supports egg birth.

What other aspects of sauropod life history can be deduced based on the data from the Late Cretaceous? For example, what about egg mass or clutch size? It has sometimes been argued that the putative sauropod eggs from France, although quite large, are of too small a mass to have been sauropod eggs. However, the value of the ratio of the mass of a clutch of these eggs compared to the mass of a female *Hypselosaurus* falls within the range of values established for the other three dinosaurs for which this information is known. Therefore, it seems reasonable to accept the designation that these eggs are those of *Hypselosaurus*, and that the clutch sizes reported of fifteen to a hundred eggs are applicable to sauropods.

At what age did sauropods first reproduce? Larger animals tend to take longer to achieve the age of sexual maturity than do smaller animals. Estimates for sauropods have been as high as sixty years. However, for sauropods to have taken this long to reach sexual maturity, they would have had to have juvenile survival rates that were higher than any observed among animals today. It is more likely that sauropods reached sexual maturity at about twenty years.

Questions concerning the social behavior of dinosaurs are even more speculative than questions concerning their life history. Based on the available information on sauropods, however, speculation on a few aspects of their behavior is reasonable. For example, did sauropods live in herds or were they solitary individuals? A number of bone beds of Late Jurassic age contain numerous individual sauropods, such as the Carnegie Quarry in Dinosaur National Monument in Utah, and it may be tempting to use these as evidence. Closer examination of these bone beds reveals that in all cases they are the result of individual deaths independent of the social dynamics of sauropods. The way to answer this question lies not in these bone beds but instead with footprints.

In the Lower Cretaceous rocks of Texas and Arkansas, and the Upper Jurassic of Colorado, there are a number of dinosaur trackways preserved. Among these trackways are several containing sauropod tracks. These tracks are all arranged in a near parallel direction, indicating movement by a large group of sauropods in one direction. If the tracks were put down at the same time, this would certainly suggest that a herd of sauropods made this trackway. Some workers have even argued that close examination of one of these trackways reveals that prints of juvenile sauropods are confined to the central part of the trackway. In turn they interpret this distribution of tracks as evidence of true herd behavior by the sauropods, with the adults surrounding the juveniles. This last point is highly speculative and is by no means fully accepted.

STEGOSAURS

Another group of herbivorous dinosaurs that was exceedingly abundant during the later Jurassic was the stegosaurs. Unlike the sauropods, which are saurischian, or reptile-hipped dinosaurs, stegosaurs were ornithischian, or bird-hipped dinosaurs.

Complete skulls belonging to stegosaurs are, as with sauropods, very rare. In fact good skulls for this group are known only from *Stegosaurus* and *Huayangosaurus*. Teeth of the stegosaurs are very small and simple; some scientists speculate by the same lines of reasoning as those applied to sauropods, that these animals, too, may have possessed gizzards. Based on the rest of the skeleton, stegosaurs can be characterized as four-footed animals with plates along their backs. The shape and arrangement of these plates in *Stegosaurus*, found in skeletons in Europe, seem to have been perfectly designed for radiation of body heat. In addition, several of the vertebrae along the back have elongated spines. The feet of stegosaurs have lost the inside toe, and unlike other groups of ornithischian dinosaurs, stegosaurs lack ossified tendons along the backbone.

Known from the Middle Jurassic of China, *Huayangosaurus* has shed light on the probable origins of the stegosaurs. Clearly this stegosaur represents a primitive state compared to later stegosaurs, having a tall snout and a relatively unfused skeleton.

OTHER ORNITHISCHIAN DINOSAURS OF THE JURASSIC

The beginning of the Jurassic marked the beginning of the most common group of dinosaurs, the ornithischians. The most primitive member of this group is a small dinosaur from the Lower Jurassic of South Africa, *Lesothosaurus*. The later ornithischians are distinct from this dinosaur since they have developed cheeks, rounded chins, and more elaborate articulation of the lower jaw with the rest of the skull.

Heterodontosaurus was a primitive, small ornithischian known from only a few high-quality skeletons from the Lower Jurassic of southern Africa. By far the most interesting aspects of this animal are in the mouth. Along the tooth row, for example, the bone flares out, perhaps indicating the presence of a cheek, which would have aided in chewing by keeping food in the mouth cavity. In addition to this adaptation, the teeth of this animal are quite complex and specialized, including incisorlike, caninelike, and molarlike teeth. These teeth suggest that this animal chewed its food as mammals do.

Whereas these first two dinosaurs are ornithischians, they are quite primitive in nature. These two animals, combined with the stegosaurs, are excluded from a more advanced group, called the ornithopods, which includes *Yandusaurus, Hypsilophodon, Dryosaurus,* and *Camptosaurus*. These ornithopods outline a progression from the more primitive hypsilophodontids to a more advanced state epitomized by the Cretaceous hadrosaurs. This progression led to an eventual dominance within the terrestrial ecosystem by the duckbills.

Yandusaurus, found in China, is a member of a group of ornithopods called the hypsilophodontids, which can be characterized by *Hypsilophodon*, found in England. The hypsilophodonts, it is generally believed, led to the more advanced iguanodonts and hadrosaurs. *Hypsilophodon* was fairly small, of light build, and two-legged. In addition, this animal had a more efficient tooth replacement pattern than other more primitive reptiles.

Dryosaurus was an ornithopod, known from the Late Jurassic Morrison Formation of North America, which was more closely related to the iguanodonts and hadrosaurs than to the hypsilophodonts. As such, this animal represents a transitional phase along this progression. This phase is represented by a reduction in the number of teeth in the front of the mouth, and the reduction of the third finger of the hand.

Camptosaurus is a true iguanodont. One of the features of these dinosaurs is the initiation of the development of a true tooth battery rather than isolated teeth. *Camptosaurus* is well known from reasonably good and fairly common skeletal material. It was a moderate-sized animal with an elongated snout, and stout limbs, feet, and hands. Although *Camptosaurus* is a reasonably common animal from the Jurassic, it is a puzzle of sorts, since it had no obvious defenses against predators.

CONCLUSION

Though the dinosaurs established themselves in a uniform world, the fossil record we have discussed shows they continued to evolve, and came to dominate the land in an era when the supercontinent split, mountains were built, and varied habitats came into being. The evidence shows that they found niches in almost every type of land environment, at one time or another. They adapted to the new conditions of the Jurassic and set the stage for their survival and continued evolution into the Cretaceous.

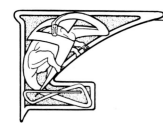

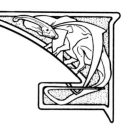

SHAKERS OF THE EARTH

GREGORY BENFORD

1988

SQUINTING AGAINST THE SLICING SUNLIGHT, DWIGHT RASER SHOUTED, "LIFT!"

The excavation crew leaned heavily on crowbars. The heavy-duty winch roared, chains clinked and tightened, dust stirred in the desert breeze — and nothing happened. The crew was already tired from a half day of laborious picking away at the dinosaur vertebrae. They grunted and thrust down harder to free the enormous chunk of pale, sandy fossil.

"Careful!" Mito could not help herself crying out. She reached over and touched Dwight's arm, alarm widening her eyes.

Dwight glanced at her, seeming to be more surprised at this touch from a woman who was normally reserved, compact. "That sucker's heavy, but don't you worry. We'll get it — "

Something broke free at the base of the vertebrae and the winch growled louder. It was mounted on the back of a grimy flatbed truck. Mito watched the big black tires fatten as they took the weight.

Dwight had estimated over three thousand pounds. Why did Americans persist in that antiquated system of units? Mito watched the mass lift with excruciating slowness and translated into kilos. Almost fifteen hundred! How could the winch —

It couldn't. A thick steel-blue bar supporting the chains bent abruptly. The crew scattered — except for one young woman, who held on to her crowbar.

Something snapped. The stony vertebrae lurched, dropped. The woman screamed.

Dust settled as she lay sprawled.

The next few minutes were a fevered blur. Shouts. Attempts to free the woman's leg from under the mass. Recriminations. Angry denials. Sweaty tugs at the crowbars.

Dwight said nothing, just walked around the tilted chunk that had come down to them out of a hundred and fifty million years of pressing silence, and thought. Mito watched him closely, and not merely to distract herself from the contorted face of the woman.

Three young men began digging at the hard-packed soil around her calf, but Dwight stopped them. Instead he told the crew to realign the chains. An angle here, oblique tension there, forces vectoring away from the crushed leg — Mito gained fresh respect for the man's quick competence. She was more at home in cool laboratories and had always felt awe for the rough-and-ready elements in science, the rub of the real.

As the crew got ready their faces were drawn, eyes hollow. If the chunk of massive vertebrae slipped again, it could roll.

The woman lay staring blankly up into the piercing winter sun, shock numbing her. She mumbled incoherently. Mito wondered if it was a prayer.

The crew set themselves, digging in. Mito could see wary flickers in their faces as they calculated where they would flee if something went wrong. Following Dwight's gesture, Mito took hold of one of the woman's shoulders and set her feet to pull. Two men also held the woman. They all looked at each other, nodded, said nothing.

"Lift!" Dwight called again.

This time the massive bulk tilted, escorted by crowbars. The grinding labor of the winch swallowed a chorus of grunts.

The sandy chunk rose a centimeter, two, three — Mito pulled. The woman slid free. They dragged her several meters away and she began yelping with pain.

After a jeep had taken the woman away for a long, jouncing journey into San Ysidro, she stood with Dwight and watched the crew beef up the hoist assembly. Nobody suggested knocking off for the day.

"Damn stupid, that," Dwight said. "Some kinda introduction for you, eh?"

"You said yourself that it is not easy to estimate the weight of such segments," Mito said.

"Well, I screwed that one up pretty bad." He scuffed at the dust. "This baby's sure bigger than that 'Ulltrasaurus' Jim Jensen's been talking about. He found a spine of one a few years ago. They didn't get anybody hurt, though."

The skeleton was mostly uncovered now. The deep trench curved along the brow of a worn sandstone bluff. Dwight's terse report had said it was 140 feet long, bigger than *Diplodocus*, bigger even then the largest of the plant-eaters, *Brachiosaurus*.

Mito said, "A set of vertebrae so massive can easily — "

"Two-inch cold rolled steel, too; just gave way."

"Do not blame yourself. That woman was slow." Her voice must have given away the depth of her feeling, for Dwight turned and looked at her with surprise, something fresh coming into his face.

"Thanks for sayin' so," he said quietly. "But it's my fault."

She saw then that beneath the gruff manner he was tired and sad and yet undaunted. "My dad, he used to say being fast on your feet was one talent nobody could teach you. Maybe so."

A moment passed between them which she was to remember to the end. A crinkling of his eyes, a wryly sour smile tugging at the corners of his mouth. Brooding, assessing blue eyes. She breathed shallowly, as if not to disturb the currents that brushed between them. She had found Americans confusing, but this man held a kind of limpid mystery.

She had always been drawn to puzzles, and a man like this was doubly odd. A westerner in both senses of the word, cowboy/scientist, walnut-brown from years of scouring the rocky wastes, yet also known for his precise, meticulous excavations of great fossils.

He had made this remarkable find by dragging an 8-gauge shotgun through these ranges on a wheeled cart. It fired a slug of soft metal into the ground. The slug flattened and sent out a pulse of sound waves. An array of microphones lowered down a drilled hole picked up the waves. A computer unfurled their signals into a three-dimensional picture of the sandstone beneath. Sound sped through bone faster than through stone, and the difference in arrival time cast a sharp sound-shadow. Oak Ridge had developed the shotgun technique to find old sites where drums of radioactive waste had been buried. Dinosaur bones were about the same size, and paleontologists had seized upon this happy accident to extend their grasp.

"This sucker's gotta be ten EEU's, easy," he said.

"Uh...EEU?"

"Oh, sorry. Field jargon. Equivalent Elephant Units, a little joke. Elephants weigh about seven and a half tons. This guy's gotta be ten EEU's — that's twice the mass of a *Brontosaurus*."

"What will you name it?"

"Well..." He seemed a bit embarrassed. "I figure the ground shook when it came by. How 'bout *Seismosaurus*?"

She allowed herself an amused smile. Her hair was pulled back in a severe black bun held with a blue clasp, and she wore a tan field jumper. Dealing with men in such delicate professional matters had never been her strong point, and it was best to not give any unwanted signals.

He led her to the tail dig. They climbed down through nearly three meters of sandstone into the cool trench. The beast had apparently died beside a river and had been quickly buried by drifting sand, she remembered from his report. That kept predators from rending and scattering the bones.

This was a wonderful discovery site, deep inside a federal wilderness area, easy to hide and defend from tourist-vandals. Dirt bikers didn't like the rippling rock formations. This was an upthrust of the Morrison Formation, which stretched across the American west. It held the great herbivores, a massive sheet of rock entombing the classic era of giants. They had found early human fossils here within the first few days of scraping, mere minor newcomers on the scale of deep time.

She sneezed from the dust and knelt to follow his description. He had launched into lecture mode, probably to put her at ease, letting her lapse back into her usual air of formality.

"These're Jurassic rocks, laid down in a river channel that sliced into older basalt. It's fine-grained sandstone and gray shales with lacings of reddish brown and tan-yellow. Material was mostly unconsolidated, which accounts for the undisturbed fossil."

It was a beautiful job, stripping away the rock at an inch a day to reveal the smoothly curving, colossal spine.

"These projections, big fat chevrons, see? I figure they helped adjust the weight. Beast like this, carryin' the load's a big problem."

"Thus the hollow bones," she said.

"Huh? How'd you know that?" A sudden scowl.

"Do not patronize me, my colleague." She enjoyed the consternation that flitted across his face.

"Okay, let's cut the socializing. I hoped you Los Alamos types could tell me what I've got here."

"Indeed, I can." Her visiting two-year appointment under the US-Japan exchange program gave her freedom to pursue eccentric ideas. On impulse she had volunteered for Dr. Raser's curiously worded request. He had refused to give away any information about the fossil material he had brought to the Laboratory — including the fact that some of it was not fossil at all.

She had prepared her conclusions for a more formal presentation, but somehow, standing here in a shaded trench amid the hammer and clang of the continuing work, sweaty even in the winter sun, skin plated with tangy dust — it all felt sharper, pungent, more earthily real, than her antiseptic life amid Pyrex precisions.

"I respect your intentions," she said, wishing her tone was not naturally so stiff; a liability of her strict Japanese upbringing, perhaps. "Still, I would have appreciated knowing exactly what I was given to analyze."

He chuckled. "I wanted straight scoop, no preconceptions."

"I knew the scrapings had to be old, of course. Very old."

"How?" His bristly eyebrows knitted together with suspicion. "Somebody leak it?"

"I ran isotope tests. There is a high concentration of uranium."

"Um. Guess it maybe could've concentrated in the bones. . . ."

"Not 'maybe' — it did. Scintillation counters do not lie."

"Uh huh." Noncommittal, eyes giving nothing away.

"You gave me some standard fossil material, yes?"

He grinned. "Sure. Know which ones?"

"Samples 3, 7, and 11 through 16."

"Bingo." His grin broadened.

"The signatures were clear. Silica, pyrite, calcite —

they had intruded into the bone, replacing the organic matter."

"Standard fossil process, right. I took those samples from the outer segments of the sacrum, pelvis, ribs."

"And the others?"

He smiled slyly. "Not so fast. What'd you find?"

"Very well. Collagen."

She could have laughed at the blank expression on his face. "What's that?" he asked.

"A protein."

"Um." He peered up at the rectangle of blank blue sky, then gave her a guarded look. "What else?"

"No, it is your turn. I suspect you merely gave me fossil samples which had been contaminated — correct?"

"Huh? Contaminated how?"

"By your assistants' handling. Flecks of skin. Human dander."

He shook his head strongly. "Nossir. We took pelvis bones, femur, some spine. Real careful."

"Hollow bones, all?"

"Right. Drilled 'em in vacuum. You got the samples straight from the vac box, believe me."

She felt a strange prickly sensation rush across her skin. A chilly breeze? Here? "How . . . how did you pick the sites for drilling?"

"Most of this fossil was formed by the usual process. Organic molecules were leached out by ground water, then the interstices filled — with quartz, mostly. But the biggest dinosaurs evolved hollow bones to help 'em keep their weight down." He gave her a look of respect. "You looked that up, right?"

"Of course. I became suspicious."

Look, I'll come clean. It looked to me like the quartz intrusions had sealed up the pores and connections in some of the bones. There was stuff inside — hard but lighter."

"Those were the other samples."

"Right. I figured maybe the solids had trapped some bone in there, preserving it. Real bone, not stuff replaced by minerals. The bones didn't crack, see, so the inside might still be chemically intact. Hell, maybe there's even marrow."

His face had a pensive, almost shy quality. His eyes seemed to plead with her. She had enjoyed playing this game with him, but now there was a tingling in her, a shortness of breath, and she could constrain it no longer.

"I found collagen, yes. Then I performed a thirty-element analysis. Twenty-eight of the elemental abundances matched modern bone to within five percent."

"Ah. Close."

"Very."

His mouth twisted in sudden speculation. "So if bone hasn't evolved a whole lot since the Jurassic."

"There is more. I found twelve other proteins. Clear signatures."

He blinked. His mouth made an o of surprise, then closed.

In the long silence that hung between them she heard, as though coming hollowly down a distant tunnel, the clatter and muted mutterings of the restless human energies around them, delving deeply and with patient persistence, seeking.

"You thinking what I am?" he asked, eyes glinting. "I believe so. The protein will be broken, of course, by thermal damage."

She was surprised at her voice, still restrained and professional and not giving away a hint of the quickening in her body, of her attraction to this man mingled with the suddenly apparent idea he had begun. He must be thinking along the same lines, or he would not have asked for so specific a series of tests."

The air held a savor of tingling possibility.

"We'll want to be careful."

"Indeed."

"People'll say it's sensationalistic."

"I expect so."

"But we don't want to get scooped, right? Got to be fast on our feet, like my dad said."

She stepped nearer him and caught a heady scent, a sweaty musk that hung in the dry air. Looking up at him, she knew exactly what he was thinking behind his shy smile. His head blotted out the sun. She said quietly, "We can try."

2050

Sixty-two years, she thought. Sixty-two years of trying, of steadily carrying forward their dream. Did they guess then how far it could go? Mists shrouded the decades...she couldn't remember.

"Dr. Nakawa?" a young man asked at her elbow. She recognized him: Flores, the microtech specialist. He had made some of the first DNA reconstructions that proved out. That had been a decade ago at least — yet his face was still unlined. Molecular tinkering nowadays corrected many of nature's flaws.

"I was just resting." The pain had passed.

"Your husband is already out in the canyon. He said —"

"I know — hurry up." She made a fierce, comic frown. "He's been pacing around since dawn."

She let the man lead her through the hushed carpeting of the executive offices, past labs and workshops and big work bays. The place had a spruced-up sharpness, part of the half-century observance. She recognized some of the equipment, vastly better than the bulky stuff they had used decades ago to do the first detailed protein chain readings.

The sign over an impressive entrance said HELICAL LIBRARY — a bit of romantic dash, unusual for the bureaucracy-heavy Park Service. She reminded herself that after today she would take some time to browse in there. The flood of new data and ideas made research resemble trying to take a drink from a fire hose, but she was damned if she wouldn't try.

That had been the analogy she and Dwight first used in their grant proposals: the DNA library. For the

Seismosaurus they had millions of copies of the same book — DNA segments — but each copy had only a page or two left in it. Worse, the pages weren't numbered. The blind rub of millennia had ripped out all but a few of the *Seismosaurus* genetic plans.

The trick lay in realizing that each fragment of DNA they found was a book with different pages left. Find enough books, compare the pages, stitch and splice and edit...and they could eventually patch together a complete book.

As Dwight often said, after all the talk about molecular groups and amino acids, the library analogy *felt* right. Even a congressman could grasp it.

The young man opened a door — and the fragrance and noise and buzz of the crowd hit her. She blinked at the sudden sun glare. Here were familiar faces, grins, hands to shake, 3D cams doing zoom-shots. She made perfunctory greetings, smiled a lot. Then they fell away from her as the officials performed their best function, brushing people off. She walked a bit unsteadily through a stand of gum trees, shielding her eyes against the slanting morning light.

"Mito!" Dwight called. He was with a small group of technical people, all carrying field equipment and communicators. She waved and hurried to his side.

"It's almost here," he said. "Ready?"

Then the tech types were talking, checking, reassuring, and she never answered. They all fell silent.

Through the moist air they could hear now the snapping of small trees. A strange, hollow bellowing. And the steps. Long, heavy blows, like a boulder bounding endlessly down a mountainside. Regular, stolid, remorseless.

She had never quite become accustomed to the sight. It was more like a moving jade-green hill, not a living thing at all. Human intuitions of size failed in the face of the great muscle slabs, the smoothly sliding hummocks of fat.

But the hammer blows of its broad, clawed feet

belied its grace. The bountiful tail held over eighty vertebrae, tapering to a long, slender whiplash. The beast did not drag such mass, though. The tail arched smoothly upward, pert and buoyant. This weight balanced precisely the pipeline neck which swiveled with lazy grandeur, carrying the head aloft to browse among the tallest palms.

The improbability of the sight always struck her first. This most massive of land creatures moved with measured, easy elegance. A great deal of its brain dealt with balance and movement because it did not need the sharpened senses and low cunning of the hunters.

They all stepped back involuntarily as it approached. A technician whispered to her, "Don't worry, ma'm, we've done this a thousand times. It'll stop right over there."

Of course, Mito thought, of course. But if everybody's so sure, why are they whispering?

She stepped back anyway, taking Dwight's arm.

The lumbering immensity halted exactly at the right spot. Then a crane lifted the two of them to the prepared chairs perched securely on the broad, leathery back. As all this happened it was as though Mito was two persons, one experiencing the heady swirl of smells and sounds, the other abstractly recalling the many hard struggles and failures they had seen through decades past.

From the proteins in its bone marrow, long before they knew its DNA, she and Dwight had shown that the *Seismosaurus* was a milk-maker. She turned and watched this mother's brood ambling along nearby, munching small saplings. They were a mere two meters high, tails pointed nearly straight up, perky and alert. One cooed for its mother. Mito knew that today the moving mountain under them would not pause to give suck, however. The control relay rode like a silvery helmet atop the square head, giving carefully programmed orders.

The cheering from below fell away and behind them. Walking was a slow, grave rhythm. The young ones skipped ahead, calling to each other. They were moving appetites, stripping leaves and bark from the copse of gum trees. These babies grew quickly, evolution's best way to offset against predators, but there were none such here.

"You okay?" Ralph asked, concern deepening the furrows in his face.

"I am indulging in memories." She smiled at the passing broad expanse of the canyon as it opened toward the Kansas plain.

"Remember the first ones?"

She laughed. "I thought we would never get one to survive."

"It was you who saw what they needed."

"No, I merely carried it out."

"Nonsense. They had milk but no mothering. And you were the only one on the whole team who had the guts to mother something like a calf with claws."

She beamed. "All that would have amounted to nothing if you had not suggested feeding them stones."

He shrugged. "*That* didn't take guts."

Even the babies needed stomach stones to crush tough leaves and pine needles, a staple of their diet after the first month. In their antiseptic cages the babies had no way to find any pebbles. Such simple points had eluded the brainy genetic engineers.

Park Service HQ helicopters hissed overhead, but their directives, relayed through the silvery helmet, did not completely offset all natural impulses. Feeding had to be constant, automatic. The beaked jaw was so powerful it could bite into a fat redwood and mash it to pulp in a sawmill of blade-sharp teeth. To work the vast jaws and support the massive skull, thick slabs of muscle worked over an arc of bone back down the thick neck. The cheeks bunched and flowed, chewing perpetually below eyes protected by horned ridges. It fed quickly, not even breaking stride. Its life was a perpetual odyssey, browsing four hundred kilos of leaf and needle a day.

Dwight pointed. "River comin' up."

Her composure slipped along with her smile. "Are you —"

"Just watch. This doll knows her limits."

One of the freshly carved rivers that had remade Kansas rushed and frothed at its banks. The *Seismosaurus* slowed, apparently working through its slow calculations. Then it waddled into the water. The pipeline neck rose in lofty disregard of the torrent. Currents lapped and swirled higher, higher — and held a meter below their carriage chairs.

"See?"

Dwight always had more confidence in physical matters than she did. "*Her* head is up there. What does she care if her back gets wet?"

"Ummm. Rest easy. Feelin' okay?"

Though the pains had returned to her lower abdomen she gave him what she hoped was a sunny smile. "Wonderful."

The beast showed no concern for the churning river. The sauropods were proving to be astonishingly versatile. They were true land animals, not the pond-loungers envisioned earlier. In the nineteenth century the first discoverers of the huge fossils had thought they were an extinct variety of whale-like reptiles. Bulk was their best defense. Challenged, they could deliver a massive, rib-crushing blow with the strong hind legs or tail.

The young ones crossed the river at a shallows farther down, then raced to join their mother. Swaying, Mito let the summer heat claim her. They worked their way into some undulating hills crowded with the new fast-growth olive trees, which their mount gulped down with gravelly grunts of relish.

They met a *Brachiosaurus*, russet-red among the shifting silver-greens of the olives. It thudded around a rocky ledge, surprising the humans, but provoking no reaction from the *Seismosaurus*.

Neither beast displayed hiding behavior, Mito noted abstractly. Only once had any of the sauropods shown a fighting stance, when surprised by a holo-projection of a model *Tyrannosaurus*. It had reared onto hind legs like an elephant, claws extended.

The *Brachiosaurus* was like a smaller edition of their mount, with folds of fat and ribbed colorings of pink and blue. Over the last half-century fossil-hunters had found organic traces of nearly fifty species, and a dozen now walked the earth. The most startling differences among them were the vibrant splashes of oranges, burnt-yellows, milky blues and rich browns that each species displayed as soon as they were weaned, as their reproductive patterns took hold. Mito watched the *Brachiosaurus* approach, appreciating the contrast of colors, when suddenly a powerful explosion jarred her.

"What — " Dwight jerked around, alarmed.

The great tail curled high above them. Fierce bellows boomed. The tail descended, a blur that abruptly sent forth a hammer-hard crack.

The *Brachiosaurus* jerked, daunted. Its massive feet pounded as it turned, a sight which brought laughter from them, and then it beat a hasty retreat.

"Protecting its grazing rights," Mito said.

"And here I always thought it used that tail as a weapon."

"The best weapon is one you do not have to use."

Dwight blinked as their mount gave a loud parting shot. "Damn impressive."

"You see what this means? We humans thought we were the first creatures to break the sound barrier. But a great whip like this — it must, yes?"

He thought a moment. "Suppose so. The dinos beat us to it by 150 million years."

What she most loved about her life was the way surprises abounded. To bring true a deep human dream, to conjure forth the great lizards again, would have been quite enough, even without the cornucopia of amazements that followed.

Who would have guessed, she thought, that the sauropods' pursuit of mass as a defense against the meat-eaters would in the fullness of time give them immortality? The quest for sheer weight had led them to the efficiencies of hollow bones. Cradled in those chambers, the dinosaur genetic heritage slumbered for over a million centuries...while the solid-boned meat-eaters' legacy trickled away, the helical chains besieged by the salts of ground water. Finally, the meek did inherit the earth.

The stabbing pain returned, catching at her breath.

They rose over the last line of slumped hills and there before them spread the center of the park. The fresh, glittering river rapids lay like a string of white-water jewels in a verdant setting. Dinosaurs grazed all along the broad, lush plain, their splashes of color like gaudy ornaments. Amid the fields of tan wheat and stretching orchards were discreetly positioned cameras, observers, elite guests. Even the grandest class of all dinosaurs could spook and run, given provocation, as more than one trampled specialist had learned.

As they descended along a slow-sloping hillside, something strong and dark welled up in her. Perhaps it was the ancient sway of the great beast, or her mounting suspicions about the pain that had ebbed and returned in her now for days. Medicine had prolonged life in the best possible way: lengthening the robust days, then ending them with a sudden, sure collapse. There was little to do at the end, which was a final kindness. And if she kept her serene outer glaze, Dwight would not guess and worry until the last possible moment.

So long as it fell after *this* day, she reminded herself. A happy accident, that the Park could open at the half-century mark, and that they had both labored into this era. They could have been caught beneath the blundering incoherence of one of the first rebirths, crushed by the malformed beasts made in the first few years of experiments. Several of the unwary had been.

But no. Now the immense mass beneath them had been harnessed with skill and love.

As they descended a cheer rose all down the ample plain, thousands of voices giving them greeting. The sky itself swarmed and lit with the new electro-display she had heard about but never witnessed.

KANSAS SAUROPOD PARK
OPENING CEREMONIES DEDICATED TO
MITO NAKAWA AND DWIGHT RASER
THEY OPENED OUR PAST

It was a dazzling irridescent display. The letters loomed across the pewter sky bowl, yellow cascading into orange.

"Y'know, I still wish we'd patented the *Seismosaurus* DNA," Dwight said.

She laughed; he could always make her do that.

With a sudden swelling of emotion, she felt herself let go of all her concerns. This might be the last of days but it would certainly be one of the greatest. Her heart thumped with love of the man next to her, and with love for the rough beast beneath them, slouching into their strange world.

As she made ready to depart, it was arriving, brought forth from the pressing solemn silence of a million centuries, into a territory free of the predators its kind had borne for so long. Humans might tinker all they would, but they could not with any genetic certainty reconstruct the great *Tyrannosaurus*, or any of the rest of that blood-drenched legion which had bedeviled these vast, simple creatures.

She grasped Dwight's hand and drew in a breath containing scents unsensed for longer than humans had walked the world.

They would evolve, of course. But this time they would have a shepherd.

6.
DINOSAUR PREDATORS

ESSAY BY HALSZKA OSMOLSKA

SPECULATION BY ROBERT SILVERBERG

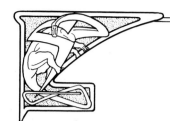

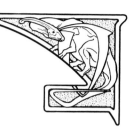

DINOSAUR PREDATORS

HALSZKA OSMÓLSKA

ALL CARNIVOROUS DINOSAURS, EXCEPT FOR THOSE LIVING AT THE VERY BEGINNING OF THE DINOSAUR era, may be assigned to a group called the Theropoda, all of whose members are closely related. The early non-theropod predators, the South American *Staurikosaurus* and *Herrerasaurus* (from the Late Triassic, about 225 mybp) preceded theropods by only a short time, and for a while the two groups were contemporaneous. Yet, soon theropods alone became the most prominent carnivores and for more than 150 million years remained the fiercest and the most nimble terrestrial vertebrate predators. They certainly knew how to take advantage of the common inherited, dinosaurian features, among which were light, hollow leg-bones, the erect posture of their limbs, bipedality, and the elongate neck vertebrae.

The usual tendency to picture all predatory dinosaurs as gigantic monsters is misleading, for not all of them were giants. In fact, those of medium size were at least as numerous and of an even greater diversity. What's more, it was a theropod, *Compsognathus* ("pretty jaw"), a turkey-sized animal, which was the smallest dinosaur known. Throughout the entire dinosaur history, those smaller predators lived side by side with their gigantic cousins. Ultimately, they were the ones that were able to survive the Great Extinction and are now living among us, though we call them birds.

PREDATOR ANATOMY

Many theropod anatomical features are associated with a carnivorous diet and a body adapted for running swiftly. It seems that theropods were perfectly designed for an active, predatory lifestyle. They had sharp, compressed, and recurved teeth, the edges of which were serrated. Their large eye sockets are proof of large eyes, which provided them with good vision. A highly movable joint between the skull and the neck afforded their heads great mobility. The long and flexible neck allowed them to hold the head high above the shoulder in order to scan the landscape and quickly locate a victim or avoid a larger, or speedier, predator. The front legs of theropods are, with rare exceptions, less than half the length of the back legs, and the hand has, instead of five, only three functioning fingers, which terminate in compressed, recurved claws. These claws helped to subdue and dismember the prey. It was not the kind of hand that could serve for locomotion.

Considering the shortness of the front legs, it becomes clear that theropods were obligatory bipeds. Their hind limbs and vertebral column were appropriately modified to carry the entire weight of the animal and to undertake the complete task of locomotion. Each foot had only four toes, all of them clawed, but the first one did not reach the ground, being shorter than the rest. Theropods, like other dinosaurs, were digitigrade animals, which means that the cannon bones (metatarsals) of the three supporting toes were vertical. The entire back leg was elongated. As a result, theropods' stride was long, and the animals were able

to cover distances quickly without expending much energy. An almost identical architecture of the back leg is noted in birds.

Some experts believe the deep, powerful tails of some theropods may have been used for swimming. Therefore, a suggestion has been made that these animals as a rule pursued their prey in the water. However, nothing in the anatomy of most theropods suggests they were predominantly water dwellers. On the contrary, the speedy character of their long back legs and rather narrow feet supports the general opinion that they lived and hunted on land. Nevertheless, there probably existed some wading theropods that could catch their food in water. Some are even suspected of being fish eaters, gaffing fish out of the water in a grizzly bear's manner.

THE OLDEST THEROPODS

The oldest theropod known, *Coelophysis* ("hollow form"), lived at the beginning of the Late Triassic (about 225 mybp). The theropod ancestor, however, might have appeared some 10 million years earlier, during the middle part of the Triassic epoch.

Coelophysis represents a theropod group called Ceratosauria ("horned reptiles"). Their most striking feature is a pair of crests, made of a paper-thin bone, along the preorbital portion of the skull roof in some species, or hornlike processes on nasal bones and above the eyes in others. *Coelophysis* is the only one which lacks them. The ceratosaurian cranial outgrowths were once thought to be used in combat. Due to their fragility, however, it is more likely that they served for visual recognition among the members of the same species. The ceratosaurian hand preserved the fourth digit (or sometimes its remnant), which is evidence for derivation from a four-fingered ancestor.

Coelophysis is the best-known ceratosaurian. It has been estimated that a fully-grown adult might have

weighed less than 30 kilograms, which was small for a dinosaur. Its skull was long because of a long snout. Some bones around the mouth were loosely joined and that probably allowed the animal to stretch the snout around a large chunk of prey. The sharp upper teeth are rather loosely spaced. Light body, long neck, slender hind legs, rather long front legs, and strong, grasping hands all present evidence that *Coelophysis* and its kin were efficient hunters of their times. They preyed upon everything that moved, including their own offspring, as examination of the ribcage contents of some individuals suggests.

At least several hundred skeletons of *Coelophysis* (some people say even a thousand) have been found in the celebrated Ghost Ranch site in New Mexico, while other vertebrates proved to be rare in that place. Many of these skeletons belong to juveniles (not to hatchlings, though). Adults are represented by two forms: the robust ones are probably males, and the more fragile ones, females. This mass burial seems to favor the hypothesis that *Coelophysis* was gregarious and hunted in packs. However, accumulated skeletons in the Ghost Ranch quarry are too numerous to believe that all were members of the same pack. Thus, it is not excluded that this accumulation may be due to some other reason.

Although most ceratosaurians were small dinosaurs, the Late Jurassic *Ceratosaurus* (living about 150 mybp) reached a large size — almost 6 meters in length — and was heavily built. *Ceratosaurus* was also a fierce predator. Because of its size, it presumably would have been less agile than *Coelophysis* but could kill a much larger prey. It had a rather thin nasal horn and a hornlike process above each eye. The skull was lightly built, but the teeth were enormous. Its hand was provided with four fingers, but only three of them bore claws.

Ceratosaurian species so far described have been based on the skeletons coming from the Late Triassic

Preceding page: The agile predator Velociraptor *contemplates a Cretaceous sunset. By Wayne D. Barlowe.*

and the Jurassic (between about 225 and 145 mybp) sediments in North America and Europe, as well as from the Jurassic strata of South Africa and Asia. Most species lived during the Late Triassic and Early Jurassic, and they were then the predominant dinosaur predators. One of the Early Jurassic genera, *Syntarsus* ("fused ankle"), is known from excavations in both Africa and North America.

CARNOSAURS

Because of its huge size, *Ceratosaurus* was once assigned to a group of theropods, called Carnosauria ("flesh reptiles"), in which all gigantic dinosaur carnivores are usually included. However, it is now known that in genetically different vertebrates, large size and weight may often result in a strikingly similar response of the skeletal anatomy. This may obscure other features that are inherited from different ancestors. Thus, the weight-dependent features may not indicate a close relationship. And this is the case for carnosaurs. Out of about 50 valid "carnosaur" genera so far described (many of those descriptions based on a few bones or teeth—at times even just one), only about 15 are undoubtedly related. Others are probably related, and the rest should be classified elsewhere. Differences in paleontologists' opinions as to what a true carnosaur is present an additional complication.

Theropods considered members of the Carnosauria have robust skeletons, exceptionally large skulls, and powerful necks. The trunk is short and the vertebrae have somewhat enlarged processes for the attachment of strong ligaments and muscles which once held the backbone tight. The back legs are robust, with the thigh longer than the shank (the opposite is true in most other theropods). All these attributes are certainly size-related and may also be noticed in other large dinosaurs.

Only some of these large "carnosaurs" addition-

ally display derived characters inherited from a common ancestor. Their skulls often exhibit a roughly keyhole-shaped eye socket with the eyeball occupying only the upper half. Bones that roof the braincase are very short and narrow. The mandible, close to its joint with the skull, bears a browlike ridge to which was attached a powerful, mouth-closing muscle. As a rule, the front legs are feeble and constitute at the most a third of the length of the back legs. The third finger in the hand is thinner than the other two, or it is entirely missing in the most derived carnosaurs.

Evidence of the first carnosaurs comes from the Middle Jurassic (about 170 mybp), but these early forms are rather poorly known. By the Late Jurassic (about 160 to 145 mybp), carnosaurs were already well established on the North American, Asian and African continents. In Early Cretaceous deposits (about 100 mybp), their remains are extremely rare, although some have been found in North America, China, and northern Africa. On the contrary, during the very latest Cretaceous (75 to 65 mybp) carnosaurs were quite common, but mostly in the Northern Hemisphere.

Our knowledge of carnosaurs is largely based on the studies of two North American genera: the Late Jurassic *Allosaurus* ("other reptile") and the Late Cretaceous *Tyrannosaurus* ("tyrant reptile").

The length of *Allosaurus* reached 12 meters and the weight about 2 tons. As in other carnosaurs, its skull is large (60 to 90 cm long) though relatively lightly constructed. The teeth are daggerlike and compressed, with both edges serrated. The neck is relatively short and must have been very muscular. The trunk is short, well balanced over the hips by the heavy tail. The front legs are about a third of the length of the back legs. The strong, three-fingered hands are provided with large claws.

Tyrannosaurus, the most popular of all dinosaurs, is the most derived carnosaur. It seems that almost everything is "the most" in its description. It was the largest (up to 14 meters long) and the heaviest (up to 7 tons) terrestrial predator that has ever lived on our planet. Its head was the longest (up to 1.5 meters) and the most massive among theropods. Thus, it is no wonder that the neck carrying such a large skull had to be short and powerful. The teeth, though stronger and larger than in other theropods, were of generally the same daggerlike shape.

The only things that are "the least" in this animal are its front legs: they are extremely feeble, with only two fingers, and so short (arm, forearm, and hand together were less than a quarter the length of the back leg) that they could not reach the mouth. What they could serve for remains unknown. It was suggested that these "good-for-nothing" limbs were used as props, helping the animal lying prone to stand up.

The dynamic look of carnosaurs, their long, powerful back legs, and the body well balanced by a tail held clear off the ground — all these features convince us that they were active predators. Yet, carnosaurs were heavy animals and capable of running at a high speed only over a short distance. Footprints and trackways left by an unknown, large carnosaur in Early Cretaceous deposits of Australia allowed researchers to estimate its walking speed at about 7 kilometers per hour, but occasionally carnosaurs could certainly run faster. It is probable that carnosaurs stalked their prey and attacked from ambush. It was suggested that, after inflicting a deep bite, carnosaurs waited for weakening of the prey from the loss of blood. It is clear that allosaurs and tyrannosaurs must have had different ways of hunting and feeding. Allosaurs could certainly use front limbs in seizing, holding, and dismembering the prey, while a tyrannosaur had to rely solely on its heavy skull and huge bite to bring its victim down.

ABELISAURS

Some Cretaceous genera of large theropods, recently discovered and described in South America and assigned to the family Abelisauridae, deserve mention here, even though few dinosaur specialists would agree that they belong to "true" carnosaurs. The Early Cretaceous *Carnotaurus* ("flesh bull") from Patagonia is the best-known abelisaurid. In some of its features it resembles the most derived carnosaurs of the Northern Hemisphere: it is gigantic, and has keyhole-shaped eye sockets and extremely short front legs. However, the differences between *Carnotaurus* and the northern carnosaurs are significant. The skull of *Carnotaurus*, short and high, with a pair of prominent frontal horns, is small in relation to the body. The front legs of *Carnotaurus* are more derived in the process of reduction than they are in *Tyrannosaurus*, although the latter is stratigraphically younger by 40 milion years! It is evident that abelisaurids were theropod giants that evolved parallel to carnosaurs after the Gondwanan and Laurasian supercontinents separated some 190 mybp. Abelisaurids and tyrannosaurids clearly played the same ecological role in their respective habitats.

SMALLER CARNIVORES

Carnivores were remarkably diversified and numerous during the Cretaceous, especially its late part. They included many smaller, lightly built and agile predators. The ancestry of the majority of these dinosaurs is unknown. Nevertheless, it has been deduced that some Late Jurassic forms of uncertain affinities — the African *Elaphrosaurus* ("light reptile"), North American *Ornitholestes* ("bird robber") and several other poorly-known ones — may be close to it. It is worth mentioning here that the remains of small theropods are rarely reported from the Southern Hemisphere.

The only "southerner" (unfortunately very incom-

A late Cretaceous scene: Tyrannosaurus *attacks the hadrosaur* Maiasaura, *the "good mother lizard." By Brian Franczak.*

pletely preserved) whose affinity seems to be known, is *Elaphrosaurus,* considered the oldest and the most primitive member of Ornithomimosauria ("bird-mimicking reptiles"). Ornithomimosaurs had skeletons that were remarkably similar to those of modern ground-dwelling birds, such as the ostrich. They were the least fierce and combative of all theropods. Instead, they were the speediest ones, and this is understandable as they evidently didn't possess any means of defense except their fleet legs. Judging from the preserved trackways, the most long-legged ornithomimosaurs might have run at a speed close to 60 kilometers an hour!

Ornithomimosaurs were lightly built, but rather large theropods (up to 5 meters long). They had long, swanlike necks that carried their heads high above their shoulders. The tail was long and its end stiff. The skull was small with a long, low snout and large eye sockets. The long, toothless jaws were once covered by a horny beak. They could be opened wide and quickly closed. Their bite, however, was weak, because they were operated by weak muscles. Judging by the braincase size, the brain was large: about as large as that of the ostrich. As for theropods, the front legs were relatively long: about half the length of the back legs. The hand with three equally long fingers was slender. The claws of the hand were usually only weakly curved or even straight and not very raptorial-looking. Back legs were long due to the long shank and a very long, compact metatarsus (part of foot between ankle and toes). Toes terminated in hooflike unguals. Unlike all other theropods, the first toe was entirely lost in most ornithomimosaurs.

Ornithomimosaurs' food, and how they got it, remain open questions. Some paleontologists believe that they were carnivorous animals, preying chiefly on small and medium-sized vertebrates, swallowed whole. Others would rather think of them as browsing herbivores, which used their long front legs to grab and bend down branches, and their beaks to bite off succulent shoots and buds. But while these latter feeding habits are acceptable for some ornithomimosaurs, namely those rare ones that have recurved claws in the hand, they are not adequate for those which have straight, flat claws. On balance, I believe that ornithomimosaurs were carnivores.

The two Late Cretaceous genera, the North American *Struthiomimus* ("ostrich mimick") and the Asian *Gallimimus* ("chicken mimick"), are the best-known ornithomimosaurs. They differ mainly in the snout shape and the hand size. From this we may conclude that they had somewhat distinctive feeding habits.

Older, Early Cretaceous and early Late Cretaceous Asian members of this group are *Harpymimus* and *Garudimimus* ("mimicking Harpya and Garuda," the mythic Mongolian birds). They show some primitive features. For example, the first one has a few teeth along the front of the jaws, while the second still has the first toe in its foot. Both have hind legs relatively shorter than their more advanced, Late Cretaceous cousins; thus both were probably only moderately fast runners.

In the Late Cretaceous sediments of Mongolia, a specimen, consisting exclusively of a huge shoulder girdle and 2.5-meters-long front limbs, was found and

was given the name *Deinocheirus* ("terrible hand"). It is usually considered an ornithomimosaur. However, its arms are very strong and the claws of the hand are recurved and raptorial-looking, quite unlike those in ornithomimosaurs. If the proportions of this creature were the same as in ornithomimosaurs — which is hardly probable — its back legs would have been 5 meters long and the animal would have been larger than *Tyrannosaurus* itself.

OVIRAPTORS

Another group of toothless theropods, known so far only from the Late Cretaceous of Asia and North America, has been distinguished under the name of Oviraptorosauria. Their first found specimen, a strange-looking *Oviraptor* ("egg thief"), was preserved lying on a nest of eggs of an herbivorous dinosaur, *Protoceratops* ("first horned face"), and it is by this fact that *Oviraptor* has been named. The skull of this theropod is very strange indeed. It is unusually short, has large holes for eyes and muscles and a cassowary-like crest above the nose. Later, when new and better fossils of oviraptorosaurs were found, still other features, unusual for theropods, were revealed. It turned out that many bones of the skull were spongy, the braincase was very large, the upper jaws formed a short, wide beak and, on the palate, there was a pair of downward-projecting, toothlike outgrowths.

Closed jaws of *Oviraptor* leave a gap in front, between the upper and lower jaw. Most probably, the horny beak, which once covered the jaws, was very thick at the front. In spite of the visible lightness of the skull, the mandible was powerful, and it was evidently moved by moderately strong muscles. Therefore, *Oviraptor*'s bite was extremely strong. If the jaw construction can be compared to anything, it is a nutcracker. This casts doubt upon the first interpretation of *Oviraptor* as an egg-eating dinosaur. Its food was certainly much tougher than eggs. It has recently been suggested that oviraptorosaurs might have fed on clams.

If this was the case, one would expect some adaptations in oviraptorosaur skeletons to water-dwelling habits. However, the skeleton seems basically similar to that of most other small, running theropods. The neck is slender and moderately long. The back legs are quite long and the front legs, with a raptorial, clawed hand, are half as long as the back legs (or even shorter). The wrist, however, differs from that of the other theropods. The normal theropod hand could only be either flexed or extended at the wrist joint. Oviraptorosaurs' hands (as well as their cousins, which will be considered below) could also move sideways; thus, their range of movements was much larger. The shoulder girdle of oviraptorosaurs is very peculiar: it is braced across the chest by fused collarbones (resembling the wishbones of birds). Below the collarbones, there is a pair of large breastbones strengthening the chest. In birds, the presence of fused collarbones and enlarged breastbones is connected with flying. But the short front limbs of oviraptorosaurs are not wings, and they must have been used differently. But how? Why were the two halves of the shoulder girdle so tightly tied to each other by the wishbone? We can only guess.

Another open question concerns the role of the crest on *Oviraptor*'s skull. Its similarity with the cassowary's crest may suggest a similar role. However, we don't exactly know what the cassowary's crest serves for!

THE SPEEDY PREDATORS

Two groups of the Cretaceous theropods seem to be closely related to oviraptorosaurs, as suggested by the identical structure of their wrists. These groups are Dromaeosauria ("running reptiles") and Troodontids

("wounding teeth"). Both have feet with sickle-like claws on second toes. Their feet distinguish them from all other predatory dinosaurs. It does not seem likely that such a peculiar feature could appear separately in only distantly related groups. Thus, dromaeosaurs and troodontids must be close cousins. Nevertheless, they differ from each other in many respects. Each of these theropod groups includes only a few genera and both are known only from the Cretaceous deposits of Asia and North America.

Of the dromaeosaurs, the best known are *Velociraptor* ("speedy predator") from Mongolia and *Deinonychus* ("terrible claw") from the United States. They are so similar that some people believe they in fact may represent only two different species of the same genus.

Dromaeosaur skulls were light and had a long, depressed snout. Some bones of the snout and mandible were loosely joined. The slender front portion of the mandible could be slightly rotated in relation to the back portion, due to a movable joint between the two. Such an arrangement could have helped to disengage the teeth from the prey's flesh and prevent an eventual dislocation at the joint between the skull and the mandible. Large teeth, loosely spaced in the jaws, are a distinctive feature of dromaeosaurs. The usual serration is finer along the front than the back edge of each tooth, while in other theropods it is equal along both edges.

Dromaeosaur necks were slender and flexible, the trunk short and narrow, but deep, and the tails were entirely stiffened by bundles of long thin bony rods that stretched along the vertebrae. The tail could only be bent to the sides at its base, just behind the hips.

The hip was distinctive in dromaeosaurs, because the pubic bone was oriented backward, as in birds, and not forward, as was typical not only for theropods but also for all reptiles except the bird-hipped (ornithischian) dinosaurs. In adequately studied dromaeosaurs, one notices that front limbs were remarkably long (about three-quarters of the back limbs), because the three-fingered, slender hands were exceptionally long. The second toe on the hind leg bore a large, strongly curved and sharply tipped sickle-like claw. The horny talon (which once covered all the claws in theropods) made it still larger. The joints within the second toe allowed the claw to be strongly flexed when attacking, or extended and held clear off the ground when running or walking.

The *Velociraptor* specimen engaged in a mortal duel with the herbivorous *Protoceratops* shows how the front and back legs were used in offense. This particular fossil evidence was found in the Gobi Desert. *Velociraptor*'s long hands embrace the large skull of its victim, while one of its back legs is plunged into *Protoceratops*' belly. The prey was evidently killed by disemboweling, but the way it was brought down can only be guessed. It is not improbable that dromaeosaurs attacked with both feet at once, jumping on their victim's back. This required excellent leaping and balancing abilities. The stiff tail, which moved as a unit, probably was an efficient balance device. Surely, dromaeosaurs must have been highly active predators and true killing-machines. Even so, by dinosaur standards, they were animals of modest size and unable to kill a large prey alone. That they might have hunted in packs is suggested by a finding from the Early Cretaceous of Montana. Remains of several *Deinonychus* individuals surround a skeleton of a large herbivorous dinosaur, *Tenontosaurus* ("sinew reptile").

In comparison with dromaeosaurs, troodontids were certainly much less ferocious predators. First of all, their jaws were endowed with rather small, but numerous and densely spaced, triangular teeth, quite unlike the dromaeosaurs'. Troodontids are known for their large brains, comparable in size to those of birds. The eyes pointed partly forward, not only to the sides as in most other theropods, and afforded them binocu-

lar vision. It was probably important for detecting and seizing small and agile prey. These dinosaurs could also hear well, as is evidenced by the enlarged middle ear cavity.

Our knowledge of troodontids is limited due to the fragile nature of their thin-walled bones. There were no bony rods in the tail, and the pelvis followed the normal theropod pattern. The proportion of the front legs to the back ones is not known in these dinosaurs. The hand structure, however, is basically the same as that of oviraptorosaurs and dromaeosaurs. But in spite of the similar sickle-like claw on the second toe of the foot, hind limbs are slender and long, different from dromaeosaurs'. Especially long and slender is the metatarsus, built of loosely attached cannon bones.

Since their back legs are similar to dromaeosaurs', troodontids, it appears, might have used them the same way. This, however, seems unlikely, because in the troodontids the second toe is associated with a totally different metatarsus design. The hindlimb was probably not capable of the strong kicks executed by dromaeosaurs. The claw was also much smaller in troodontids and sometimes even straight instead of sickle-shaped.

The best known troodontid genera are the Late Cretaceous *Troodon* from North America and *Saurornithoides* ("birdlike reptile") from Asia. They are similar and some paleontologists consider them the same.

THE FIRST BIRDS

Now, let me bring to your attention another celebrated theropod, the Late Jurassic *Archaeopteryx* ("ancient wings"). However, almost everybody knows that *Archaeopteryx* was feathered, had wings and thus, in spite of its toothed jaws, should be considered the earliest-known bird, not a dinosaur. Nevertheless *Archaeopteryx* is not only the first bird but also a direct theropod descendant.

The skeletal anatomies of *Archaeopteryx* and theropod dinosaurs are so much alike that were feathers not found with the skeleton of *Archaeopteryx*, it would be considered a very small (pigeon-sized) dromaeosaur. Its front limb, although unusually long, has the three-fingered, clawed hand with the peculiar wrist, identical to that of dromaeosaurs, troodontids, and oviraptorosaurs. The wishbone, a feature typical of birds, is similarly shaped in *Archaeopteryx* and oviraptorosaurs, and it is not known in that form in any other tetrapod. The pubic bone of *Archaeopteryx*, directed partly backward and resembling that of birds, also characterizes the hip of dromaeosaurs. The structure of the hindlimb of *Archaeopteryx* is much like that of many running theropods, except that the short first toe opposes the other three (as it does in all birds, but not in theropods).

The skull, built of fragile bones, is the least known part of this oldest bird. However, we know much already: there were conical teeth, and the large braincase was birdlike in structure.

Since the time of its first discovery in the second part of last century, *Archaeopteryx* has been a controversial creature. Its origins, its systematic assignment, and its flight abilities are a subject of much debate. Most paleontologists agree now that *Archaeopteryx* was a true though primitive bird which was still learning to fly, but, in many respects, it was still extremely close to its dinosaur sisters.

THE BLOOD OF DINOSAURS

There arises another problem which is, to some degree, connected with bird origins. It has to do with the physiology and, more precisely, with the metabolic levels of the protobirds and other theropods (as well as of other dinosaurs). Extant birds, as well as mammals, are "warm-blooded," or endothermic, animals, meaning that they are able to produce internally all the energy that allows them to sustain high activity independent of the surrounding temperature. A flying animal cannot risk being dependent on a changeable outside temperature. Living reptiles, which are "cold-blooded," or ectothermic, move awkwardly, or become entirely inactive, if the temperature falls below a certain optimum.

The assumption that *Archaeopteryx* was endothermic seems reasonable. But was endothermy a novelty, which appeared exclusively in *Archaeopteryx*, or was it already present in the non-avian theropods, or, perhaps in all dinosaurs? We will never know for sure, but many dinosaur researchers agree that it is very probable that at least some small dinosaurs — theropods in the first place — might have had some means to keep the temperature of their bodies relatively high and stable. Thus, they might have been capable of sustained activity, not necessarily dependent on the outside temperature. Although it is not an incontrovertible argument, theropods are evidently designed anatomically for highly active performance and thus fit much better as endotherms or at least incipiently endothermic animals. None of the arguments quoted in favor of the dinosaur endothermy are flawless, but then, nothing speaks definitively against it.

So far, nearly 100 genera of predatory dinosaurs, living over a period of 160 million years, have been described. Certainly, many other dinosaur carnivores still remain unknown. Shortly before the close of the Mesozoic Era, predatory dinosaurs, especially the smaller ones, were a strongly diversified, flourishing group. Yet, only those among them that had learned to fly, and thus were able to explore new habitats, survived into the Cenozoic. It was certainly not a shortage of prey on the land which was the reason for theropods' demise. What happened, then? Maybe predatory mammals became the competitors which could not be surpassed on the land. This remains another mystery in the history of dinosaurs.

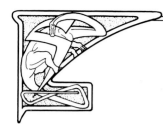
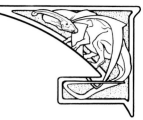

HUNTERS IN THE FOREST

ROBERT SILVERBERG

TWENTY MINUTES INTO THE VOYAGE NOTHING MORE STARTLING THAN A DRAGONFLY THE size of a hawk has come into view, fluttering for an eyeblink moment in front of the timemobile window and darting away, and Mallory decides it's time to exercise Option Two: abandon the secure cozy comforts of the timemobile capsule, take his chances on foot out there in the steamy mists, a futuristic pygmy roaming virtually unprotected among the dinosaurs of this fragrant Late Cretaceous forest. That has been his plan all along — to offer himself up to the available dangers of this place, to experience the thrill of the hunt without ever quite being sure whether he was the hunter or the hunted.

Option One is to sit tight inside the timemobile capsule for the full duration of the trip — he has signed up for twelve hours — and watch the passing show, if any, through the invulnerable window. Very safe, yes. But self-defeating, also, if you have come here for the sake of tasting a little excitement for once in your life. Option Three, the one nobody ever talks about except in whispers and which perhaps despite all rumors to the contrary no one has actually ever elected, is self-defeating in a different way: simply walk off into the forest and never look back. After a prearranged period, usually twelve hours, never more than twenty-four, the capsule will return to its starting point in the twenty-third century whether or not you're aboard. But Mallory isn't out to do himself in, not really. All he wants is a little endocrine action, a hit of adrenaline to rev things up, the unfamiliar sensation of honest fear contracting his auricles and chilling his bowels: all that good old chancy stuff, damned well unattainable down the line in the modern era where risk is just about extinct. Back here in the Mesozoic, risk aplenty is available enough for those who can put up the price of admission. All he has to do is go outside and look for it. And so it's Option Two for him, then, a lively little walkabout, and then back to the capsule in plenty of time for the return trip.

With him he carries a laser rifle, a backpack medical kit, and lunch. He jacks a thinko into his waistband and clips a drinko to his shoulder. But no helmet, no potted air supply. He'll boldly expose his naked nostrils to the Cretaceous atmosphere. Nor does he avail himself of the one-size-fits-all body armor that the capsule is willing to provide. That's the true spirit of Option Two, all right: go forth unshielded into the Mesozoic dawn.

Open the hatch, now. Down the steps, hop skip jump. Booted feet bouncing on the spongy primordial forest floor.

There's a hovering dankness but a surprisingly pleasant breeze is blowing. Things feel tropical but not uncomfortably torrid. The air has an unusual smell. The mix of nitrogen and carbon dioxide is different from what he's accustomed to, he suspects, and certainly none of the impurities that six centuries of industrial development have poured into the atmosphere are present. There's something else, too, a strange subtext of an odor that seems both sweet and pungent: it must be the aroma of dinosaur farts, Mallory decides.

Genzo.

Uncountable hordes of stupendous beasts simultaneously releasing vast roaring boomers for a hundred million years surely will have filled the prehistoric air with complex hydrocarbons that won't break down until the Oligocene at the earliest.

Scaly treetrunks thick as the columns of the Parthenon shoot heavenward all around him. At their summits, far overhead, whorls of stiff long leaves jut tensely outward. Smaller trees that look like palms, but probably aren't, fill in the spaces between them, and at ground level there are dense growths of awkward angular bushes. Some of them are in bloom, small furry pale-yellowish blossoms, very diffident-looking, as though they were so newly evolved that they were embarrassed to find themselves on display like this. All the vegetation big and little has a battered, shopworn look, trunks leaning this way and that, huge leaf-stalks bent and dangling, gnawed boughs hanging like broken arms. It is as though an army of enormous tanks passes through this forest every few days. In fact that isn't far from the truth, Mallory realizes.

But where are they? Twenty-five minutes gone already and he still hasn't seen a single dinosaur, and he's ready for some.

"All right," Mallory calls out. "Where are you, you big dopes?"

As though on cue the forest hurls a symphony of sounds back at him: strident honks and rumbling snorts and a myriad blatting snuffling wheezing skreeing noises. It's like a chorus of crocodiles getting warmed up for Handel's *Messiah*.

Mallory laughs. "Yes, I hear you, I hear you!"

He cocks his laser rifle. Steps forward, looking eagerly to right and left. This period is supposed to be the golden age of dinosaurs, the grand tumultuous climactic epoch just before the end, when bizarre new species popped out constantly with glorious evolutionary profligacy, and all manner of grotesque goliaths

roamed the earth. The thinko has shown him pictures of them, spectacularly decadent in size and appearance, long-snouted duck-billed monsters as big as a house and huge lumbering ceratopsians with frilly baroque bony crests and toothy things with knobby horns on their elongated skulls and others with rows of bristling spikes along their high-ridged backs. He aches to see them. He wants them to scare him practically to death. Let them loom; let them glower; let their great jaws yawn. Through all his untroubled days in the orderly and carefully regulated world of the twenty-third century Mallory has never shivered with fear as much as once, never known a moment of terror or even real uneasiness, is not even sure he understands the concept; and he has paid a small fortune for the privilege of experiencing it now.

Forward. Forward.

Come on, you oversized bastards, get your asses out of the swamp and show yourselves!

There. Oh, yes, yes, *there!*

He sees the little spheroid of a head first, rising above the treetops like a grinning football attached to a long thick hose. Behind it is an enormous humped back, unthinkably high. He hears the piledriver sound of the behemoth's footfall and the crackle of huge treetrunks breaking as it smashes its way serenely toward him.

He doesn't need the murmured prompting of his thinko to know that this is a giant sauropod making its majestic passage through the forest — "one of the titanosaurs or perhaps an ultrasaur," the quiet voice says, admitting with just a hint of chagrin in its tone that it can't identify the particular species — but Mallory isn't really concerned with detail on that level. He is after the thrill of size. And he's getting size, all right. The thing is implausibly colossal. It emerges into the clearing where he stands and he is given the full view, and gasps. He can't even guess how big it is.

Twenty meters high? Thirty? Its ponderous corrugated legs are thick as sequoias. Giraffes on tiptoe could go skittering between them without grazing the underside of its massive belly. Elephants would look like housecats beside it. Its tail, held out stiffly to the rear, decapitates sturdy trees with its slow steady lashing. A hundred million years of saurian evolution have produced this thing, Darwinianism gone crazy, excess building remorselessly on excess, irrepressible chromosomes gleefully reprogramming themselves through the millennia to engender thicker bones, longer legs, ever bulkier bodies, and the end result is this walking mountain, this absurdly overstated monument to reptilian hyperbole.

"Hey!" Mallory cries. "Look here! Can you see this far down? There's a human down here. *Homo sapiens.* I'm a mammal. Do you know what a mammal is? Do you know what my ancestors are going to do to your descendants?" He is practically alongside it, no more than a hundred meters away. Its musky stink makes him choke and cough. Its ancient leathery brown hide, as rigid as cast iron, is pocked with parasitic growths, scarlet and yellow and ultramarine, and crisscrossed with the gulleys and ravines of century-old wounds deep enough for him to hide in. With each step it takes Mallory feels an earthquake. He is nothing next to it, a flea, a gnat. It could crush him with a casual stride and never even know.

And yet he feels no fear. The sauropod is so big he can't make sense out of it, let alone be threatened by it.

Can you fear the Amazon River? The planet Jupiter? The pyramid of Cheops?

No, what he feels is anger, not terror. The sheer preposterous bulk of the monster infuriates him. The pointless superabundance of it inspires him with wrath.

"My name is Mallory," he yells. "I've come from the twenty-third century to bring you your doom, you

great stupid mass of meat. I'm personally going to make you extinct, do you hear me?"

He raises the laser rifle and centers its sight on the distant tiny head. The rifle hums its computations and modifications and the rainbow beam jumps skyward. For an instant the sauropod's head is engulfed in a dazzling fluorescent nimbus. Then the light dies away, and the animal moves on as though nothing has happened.

No brain up there? Mallory wonders.

Too dumb to die?

He moves up closer and fires again, carving a bright track along one hypertrophied haunch. Again, no effect. The sauropod moves along untroubled, munching on treetops as it goes. A third shot, too hasty, goes astray and cuts off the crown of a tree in the forest canopy. A fourth zings into the sauropod's gut but the dinosaur doesn't seem to care. Mallory is furious now at the unkillability of the thing. His thinko quietly reminds him that these giants supposedly had had their main nerve-centers at the base of their spines. Mallory runs around behind the creature and stares up at the galactic expanse of its rump, wondering where best to place his shot. Just then the great tail swings upward and to the left and a torrent of immense steaming green turds as big as boulders comes cascading down, striking the ground all around Mallory with thunderous impact. He leaps out of the way barely in time to keep from being entombed, and goes scrambling frantically away to avoid the choking fetor that rises from the sauropod's vast mound of excreta. In his haste he stumbles over a vine, loses his footing in the slippery mud, falls to hands and knees. Something that looks like a small blue dog with a scaly skin and a ring of sharp spines around its neck jumps up out of the muck, bouncing up and down and hissing and screeching and snapping at him. Its teeth are deadly-looking yellow fangs. There isn't room to fire the laser rifle. Mallory desperately rolls to one side and bashes the thing with the butt instead, hard, and it runs away growling. When he has a chance finally to catch his breath and look up again, he sees the great sauropod vanishing in the distance.

He gets up and takes a few limping steps farther away from the reeking pile of ordure.

He has learned at last what it's like to have a brush with death. Two brushes, in fact, within the span of ten seconds. But where's the vaunted thrill of danger narrowly averted, the hot satisfaction of the *frisson*? He feels no pleasure, none of the hoped-for rush of keen endocrine delight.

Of course not. A pile of falling turds, a yapping little lizard with big teeth: what humiliating perils! During the frantic moments when he was defending himself against them he was too busy to notice what he was feeling, and now, muddy all over, his knee aching, his dignity dented, he is left merely with a residue of annoyance, frustration, and perhaps a little ironic self-deprecation, when what he had wanted was the white ecstasy of genuine terror followed by the post-orgasmic delight of successful escape recollected in tranquillity.

Well, he still has plenty of time. He goes onward, deeper into the forest.

Now he is no longer able to see the timemobile capsule. That feels good, that sudden new sense of being cut off from the one zone of safety he has in this fierce environment. He tries to divert himself with fantasies of jeopardy. It isn't easy. His mind doesn't work that way; nobody's does, really, in the nice, tidy, menace-free society he lives in. But he works at it. Suppose, he thinks, I lose my way in the forest and can't get back to — no, no hope of that, the capsule sends out constant directional pulses that his thinko picks up by microwave transmission. What if the thinko breaks down, then? But they never do. If I take it off and toss it into a swamp? That's Option Three, though, self-

damaging behavior designed to maroon him here. He doesn't do such things. He can barely even fantasize them.

Well, then, the sauropod comes back and steps on the capsule, crushing it beyond use —

Impossible. The capsule is strong enough to withstand submersion to thirty-atmosphere pressures.

The sauropod pushes it into quicksand, and it sinks out of sight?

Mallory is pleased with himself for coming up with that one. It's good for a moment or two of interesting uneasiness. He imagines himself standing at the edge of some swamp, staring down forlornly as the final minutes tick away and the timemobile, functional as ever even though it's fifty fathoms down in gunk, sets out for home without him. But no, no good: the capsule moves just as effectively through space as through time, and it would simply activate its powerful engine and climb up onto terra firma again in plenty of time for his return trip.

What if, he thinks, a band of malevolent *intelligent* dinosaurs appears on the scene and forcibly prevents me from getting back into the capsule?

That's more like it. A little shiver that time. Good! Cut off, stranded in the Mesozoic! Living by his wits, eating God knows what, exposing himself to extinct bacteria. Getting sick, blazing with fever, groaning in unfamiliar pain. Yes! Yes! He piles it on. It becomes easier as he gets into the swing of it. He will lead a life of constant menace. He imagines himself taking out his own appendix. Setting a broken leg. And the unending hazards, day and night. Toothy enemies lurking behind every bush. Baleful eyes glowing in the darkness. A life spent forever on the run, never a moment's ease. Cowering under fern-fronds as the giant carnivores go lalloping by. Scorpions, snakes, gigantic venomous toads. Insects that sting. Everything that has been eliminated from life in the civilized world pursuing him here: and he flitting from one transitory hiding place to another, haggard, unshaven, bloodshot, brow shining with sweat, struggling unceasingly to survive, living a gallant life of desperate heroism in this nightmare world —

"Hello," he says suddenly. "Who the hell are you?"

In the midst of his imaginings a genuine horror has presented itself, emerging suddenly out of a grove of tree ferns. It is a towering bipedal creature with the powerful thighs and small dangling forearms of the familiar *Tyrannosaurus*, but this one has an enormous bony crest like a warrior's helmet rising from its skull, with five diabolical horns radiating outward behind it and two horrendous incisors as long as tusks jutting from its cavernous mouth, and its huge lashing tail is equipped with a set of great spikes at the tip. Its mottled and furrowed skin is a bilious yellow and the huge crest on its head is fiery scarlet. It is everybody's bad dream of the reptilian killer-monster of the primeval dawn, the ghastly overspecialized end-product of the long saurian reign, shouting its own lethality from every bony excrescence, every razor-keen weapon on its long body.

The thinko scans it and tells him that it is a representative of an unknown species belonging to the saurischian order and it is almost certainly predatory.

"Thank you very much," Mallory replies.

He is astonished to discover that even now, facing this embodiment of death, he is not at all afraid. Fascinated, yes, by the sheer deadliness of the creature, by its excessive horrificality. Amused, almost, by its grotesqueries of form. And coolly aware that in three bounds and a swipe of its little dangling paw it could end his life, depriving him of the sure century of minimum expectancy that remains to him. Despite that threat he remains calm. If he dies, he dies; but he can't actually bring himself to believe that he will. He is beginning to see that the capacity for fear, for any sort

of significant psychological distress, has been bred out of him. He is simply too stable. It is an unexpected drawback of the perfection of human society.

The saurischian predator of unknown species slavers and roars and glares. Its narrow yellow eyes are like beacons. Mallory unslings his laser rifle and gets into firing position. Perhaps this one will be easier to kill than the colossal sauropod.

Then a woman walks out of the jungle behind it and says, "You aren't going to try to shoot it, are you?"

Mallory stares at her. She is young, only fifty or so unless she's on her second or third retread, attractive, smiling. Long sleek legs, a fluffy burst of golden hair. She wears a stylish hunting outfit of black sprayon and carries no rifle, only a tiny laser pistol. A space of no more than a dozen meters separates her from the dinosaur's spiked tail, but that doesn't seem to trouble her.

He gestures with the rifle. "Step out of the way, will you?"

She doesn't move. "Shooting it isn't a smart idea."

"We're here to do a little hunting, aren't we?"

"Be sensible," she says. "This one's a real son of a bitch. You'll only annoy it if you try anything, and then we'll both be in a mess." She walks casually around the monster, which is standing quite still, studying them both in an odd perplexed way as though it actually wonders what they might be. Mallory has aimed the rifle now at the thing's left eye, but the woman coolly puts her hand to the barrel and pushes it aside.

"Let it be," she says. "It's just had its meal and now it's sleepy. I watched it gobble up something the size of a hippopotamus and then eat half of another one for dessert. You start sticking it with your little laser and you'll wake it up, and then it'll get nasty again. Mean-looking bastard, isn't it?" she says admiringly.

"Who are you?" Mallory asks in wonder. "What are you doing here?"

"Same thing as you, I figure. Cretaceous Tours?"

"Yes. They said I wouldn't run into any other — "

"They told me that too. Well, it sometimes happens. Jayne Hyland. New Chicago, 2281."

"Tom Mallory. New Chicago also. And also 2281."

"Small geological epoch, isn't it? What month did you leave from?"

"August."

"I'm September."

"Imagine that."

The dinosaur, far above them, utters a soft snorting sound and begins to drift away.

"We're boring it," she says.

"And it's boring us, too. Isn't that the truth? These enormous terrifying monsters crashing through the forest all around us and we're as blasé as if we're home watching the whole thing on the polyvid." Mallory raises his rifle again. The scarlet-frilled killer is almost out of sight. "I'm tempted to take a shot at it just to get some excitement going."

"Don't," she says. "Unless you're feeling suicidal. Are you?"

"Not at all."

"Then don't annoy it, okay? — I know where there's a bunch of ankylosaurs wallowing around. That's one really weird critter, believe me. Are you interested in having a peek?"

"Sure," says Mallory.

He finds himself very much taken by her brisk no-nonsense manner, her confident air. When we get back to New Chicago, he thinks, maybe I'll look her up. The September tour, she said. So he'll have to wait a while after his own return. I'll give her a call around the end of the month, he tells himself.

She leads the way unhesitatingly, through the tree-fern grove and around a stand of giant horsetails and across a swampy meadow of small plastic-looking plants with ugly little mud-colored daisyish flowers. On the far side they zig around a great pile of bloodied bones and zag around a treacherous bog with a sinisterly quivering surface. A couple of giant dragonflies whiz by, droning like airborne missiles. A crimson frog as big as a rabbit grins at them from a pond. They have been walking for close to an hour now and Mallory no longer has any idea where he is in relation to his time-mobile capsule. But the thinko will find the way back for him eventually, he assumes.

"The ankylosaurs are only about a hundred meters further on," she says, as if reading his mind. She looks back and gives him a bright smile. "I saw a pack of troodons the day before yesterday out this way. You know what they are? Little agile guys, no bigger than you or me, smart as whips. Teeth like sawblades, funny knobs on their heads. I thought for a minute they were going to attack, but I stood my ground and finally they backed off. You want to shoot something, shoot one of those."

"The day before yesterday?" Mallory asks, after a moment. "How long have you been here?"

"About a week. Maybe two. I've lost count, really. Look, there are those ankylosaurs I was telling you about."

He ignores her pointing hand. "Wait a second. The longest available time tour lasts only —"

"I'm Option Three," she says.

He gapes at her as though she has just sprouted a scarlet bony crest with five spikes behind it.

"Are you serious?" he asks.

"As serious as anybody you ever met in the middle of the Cretaceous forest. I'm here for keeps, friend. I stood right next to my capsule when the twelve hours were up and watched it go sailing off into the ineffable future. And I've been having the time of my life ever since."

A tingle of awe spreads through him. It is the strongest emotion he has ever felt, he realizes.

She is actually living that gallant life of desperate heroism that he had fantasized. Avoiding the myriad menaces of this incomprehensible place for a whole week or possibly even two, managing to stay fed and healthy, in fact looking as trim and elegant as if she had just stepped out of her capsule a couple of hours ago. And never to go back to the nice safe orderly world of 2281. Never. Never. She will remain here until she dies — a month from now, a year, five years, whenever. Must remain. Must. By her own choice. An incredible adventure.

Her face is very close to his. Her breath is sweet and warm. Her eyes are bright, penetrating, ferocious. "I was sick of it all," she tells him. "Weren't you? The perfection of everything. The absolute predictability. You can't even stub your toe because there's some clever sensor watching out for you. The biomonitors. The automedics. The guides and proctors. I hated it."

"Yes. Of course."

Her intensity is frightening. For one foolish moment, Mallory realizes, he was actually thinking of offering to *rescue* her from the consequences of her rashness. Inviting her to come back with him in his own capsule when his twelve hours are up. They could probably both fit inside, if they stand very close to each other. A reprieve from Option Three, a new lease on life for her. But that isn't really possible, he knows. The mass has to balance in both directions of the trip within a very narrow tolerance; they are warned not to bring back even a twig, even a pebble, nothing aboard the capsule that wasn't aboard it before. And in any case being rescued is surely the last thing she wants. She'll simply laugh at him. Nothing could make her go back. She loves it here. She feels truly alive for the first time in her life. In a universe of security-craving dullards she's a woman running wild. And her wildness is con-

tagious. Mallory trembles with sudden new excitement at the sheer proximity of her.

She sees it too. Her glowing eyes flash with invitation.

"Stay here with me!" she says. "Let your capsule go home without you, the way I did."

"But the dangers — " he hears himself blurting inanely.

"Don't worry about them. I'm doing all right so far, aren't I? We can manage. We'll build a cabin. Plant fruits and vegetables. Catch lizards in traps. Hunt the dinos. They're so dumb they just stand there and let you shoot them. The laser charges won't ever run out. You and me, me and you, all alone in the Mesozoic! Like Adam and Eve, we'll be. The Adam and Eve of the Late Cretaceous. And they can all go to hell back there in 2281."

His fingers are tingling. His throat is dry. His cheeks blaze with savage adrenal fires. His breath is coming in ragged gasps. He has never felt anything like this before in his life.

He moistens his lips.

"Well —"

She smiles gently. The pressure eases. "It's a big decision, I know. Think about it," she says. Her voice is soft now. The wild zeal of a moment before is gone from it. "How soon before your capsule leaves?"

He glances at his wrist. "Eight, nine more hours."

"Plenty of time to make up your mind."

"Yes. Yes."

Relief washes over him. She has dizzied him with the overpowering force of her revelation and the passionate frenzy of her invitation to join her in her escape from the world they have left behind. He isn't used to such things. He needs time now, time to absorb, to digest, to ponder. To decide. That he would even consider such a thing astonishes him. He has known her how long — an hour, an hour and a half? — and here

he is thinking of giving up everything for her. Unbelievable. Unbelievable.

Shakily he turns away from her and stares at the
ankylosaurs wallowing in the mudhole just in front
of them.

Strange, strange, strange. Gigantic low-slung tubby
things, squat as tanks, covered everywhere by armor.
Vaguely triangular, expanding vastly toward the rear,
terminating in armored tails with massive bony excre-
scences at the tips, like deadly clubs. Slowly snuffling
forward in the muck, tiny heads down, busily grub-
bing away at soft green weeds. Jayne jumps down
among them and dances across their armored backs,
leaping from one to another. They don't even seem to
notice. She laughs and calls to him. "Come on," she says,
prancing like a she-devil.

They dance among the ankylosaurs until the game
grows stale. Then she takes him by the hand and they
run onward, through a field of scarlet mosses, down
to a small clear lake fed by a swift-flowing stream.
They strip and plunge in, heedless of risk. Afterward
they embrace on the grassy bank. Some vast creature
passes by, momentarily darkening the sky. Mallory
doesn't bother even to look up.

Then it is on, on to spy on something with a long
neck and a comic knobby head, and then to watch a
pair of angry ceratopsians butting heads in slow motion, and then to applaud the elegant migration of a
herd of towering duckbills across the horizon. There
are dinosaurs everywhere, everywhere, everywhere, an
astounding zoo of them. And the time ticks away.

It's fantastic beyond all comprehension. But even
so —

Give up everything for this? he wonders.

The chalet in Gstaad, the weekend retreat aboard
the L5 satellite, the hunting lodge in the veldt? The
island home in the Seychelles, the plantation in New
Caledonia, the pied-à-terre in the shadow of the
Eiffel Tower?

For this? For a forest full of nightmare monsters,
and a life of daily peril?

Yes. Yes. Yes. Yes.

He glances toward her. She knows what's on his
mind, and she gives him a sizzling look. *Come live
with me and be my love, and we will all the pleasures
prove.* Yes. Yes. Yes. Yes.

A beeper goes off on his wrist and his thinko says,
"It is time to return to the capsule. Shall I guide you?"

And suddenly it all collapses into a pile of ashes,
the whole shimmering fantasy perishing in an instant.

"Where are you going?" she calls.

"Back," he says. He whispers the word hoarsely —
croaks it, in fact.

"Tom!"

"Please. Please."

He can't bear to look at her. His defeat is total; his
shame is cosmic. But he isn't going to stay here. He isn't.
He isn't. He simply isn't. He slinks away, feeling her
burning contemptuous glare drilling holes in his
shoulderblades. The quiet voice of the thinko steadily
instructs him, leading him around pitfalls and obstacles. After a time he looks back and can no longer
see her.

On the way back to the capsule he passes a pair of
sauropods mating, a tyrannosaur in full slather, another
thing with talons like scythes, and half a dozen others.
The thinko obligingly provides him with their names,
but Mallory doesn't even give them a glance. The bru-
tal fact of his own inescapable cowardice is the only
thing that occupies his mind. *She* has had the courage
to turn her back on the stagnant overperfect world
where they live, regardless of all danger, whereas he
— he —

"There is the capsule, sir," the thinko says
triumphantly.

Last chance, Mallory.

No. No. No. He can't do it.

He climbs in. Waits. Something ghastly appears

outside, all teeths and claws, and peers balefully at him through the window. Mallory peers back at it, nose to nose, hardly caring what happens to him now. The creature takes an experimental nibble at the capsule. The impervious metal resists. The dinosaur shrugs and waddles away.

A chime goes off. The Late Cretaceous turns blurry and disappears.

In mid-October, seven weeks after his return, he is telling the somewhat edited version of his adventure at a party for the fifteenth time that month when a woman to his left says, "There's someone in the other room who's just came back from the dinosaur tour too."

"Really," says Mallory, without enthusiasm.

"You and she would love to compare notes, I'll bet. Wait, and I'll get her. Jayne! Jayne, come in here for a moment!"

Mallory gasps. Color floods his face. His mind swirls in bewilderment and chagrin. Her eyes are as sparkling and alert as ever, her hair is a golden cloud.

"But you told me—"

"Yes," she says. "I did, didn't I?"

"Your capsule — you said it had gone back—"

"It was just on the far side of the ankylosaurs, behind the horsetails. I got to the Cretaceous about eight hours before you did. I had signed up for a twenty-four-hour tour."

"And you let me believe—"

"Yes. So I did." She grins at him and says softly, "It was a lovely fantasy, don't you think?"

He comes close to her and gives her a cold, hard stare. "What would you have done if I had let my capsule go back without me and stranded myself there for the sake of your lovely fantasy? Or didn't you stop to think about that?"

"I don't know," she tells him. "I just don't know." And she laughs.

7.
CRETACEOUS DINOSAURS

ESSAY BY DON LESSEM

SPECULATION BY CONNIE WILLIS

SPECULATION BY BARRY MALZBERG

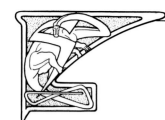

THE CRETACEOUS DINOSAURS
DON LESSEM

THE CRETACEOUS PERIOD, 145 MILLION TO 65 MILLION YEARS AGO, BEGINS IN MYSTERY AND ENDS IN extinction for the dinosaurs. And for some 20 million years before the end, the last of the Cretaceous is a golden age for dinosaurs and our understanding of them — home to the most intelligent, the most loving, the most terrifying dinosaurs, and simply *most* of all dinosaurs we know.

But if the Cretaceous ends as a big-screen spectacular with a cast of thousands and a bang of a finish, it begins as a small and murky drama. The Early Cretaceous (145 to 100 million years ago) is one of the dinosaur times least well represented in the fossil record, a "Twilight Zone" in the words of Yale University paleontologist John Ostrom.

We do know enough of this "Twilight Zone" series to understand that it was syndicated around the world — not as reruns of earlier dinosaur episodes but as new shows with a familiar plot line and cast of characters. Some were about to be spun off into new dramas. And for other groups of dinosaurs then appearing worldwide, the Early Cretaceous was cancellation time.

EARLY CRETACEOUS DISCOVERIES

Dinosaurs that had once expanded their ranges without significant barriers on a single Jurassic land mass were now faced with seaway barriers, with isolated continents moving toward the cool, dark poles of the earth. Northern and southern super continents had broken contact, and Africa and South America were beginning to drift apart. And, with an invasion of new vegetation, dominated by flowering plants, new feeding strategies were called for on the part of those who would browse.

For the two dinosaur families whose members are best known from the Early Cretaceous, the hypsilophodontids and the iguanodontids, the Early Cretaceous was at once the best of times and the worst of times. Both of these groups of plant-eaters evolved sometime in the Middle to Late Jurassic. They likely found their way in those times to most every corner of a then-united world, for both are known from widely separated chunks of Early Cretaceous terrain, Australia included. One was to go on to Late Cretaceous appearances, the other soon to quietly quit the Twilight Zone set.

If the Early Cretaceous remains a limbo land, it is not for want of scientific effort. Early Cretaceous dinosaurs, in Europe, were among the first dinosaurs ever identified. Dinosaur-rich rock exposures dating to Early Cretaceous times have been harder to come by in North America, but that is changing fast.

The quest for North American Early Cretaceous dinosaurs dates back nearly 100 years, when the famed American Museum paleontologist Barnum Brown was exploring the Lower Cretaceous of the American West. Since then, Lower Cretaceous dinosaurs have been dug up along the Peace River in Alberta, in Utah, in South Dakota and, in bits and pieces, in Arkansas and Maryland.

The best new finds from the American Early

Cretaceous are two excavated from Texas. Neither is attributable to a professional paleontologist. In August of 1988, Thad Williams of Mill Sap, Texas, all of eight years old, was walking along a creek bed at the ranch his family had leased, when he chanced upon the skull of a large dinosaur. Paleontologists Dale Winkler and Louis Jacobs of Southern Methodist University in Dallas supervised the dig, excavating most of three dinosaurs much like *Tenontosaurus* ("sinew lizard").

Tenontosaurus is widely known from the American West, yet it is a puzzling animal. It's been called an iguanodontid, and at more than 15 feet long and 1000 pounds in weight, it rivaled some smaller Iguanodontids in size, and like them probably moved on four legs as well as two. But it had a peculiarly long and thick tail, and its teeth and feet more closely resemble smaller dinosaur herbivores, the hypsilophodontids.

Hypsilophodontids are distinguished by their overlapping teeth, which create a long cutting surface. Sturdy jaws and powerful jaw muscles and cheeks allowed these animals to grind up tough forage. This dentition represents a major advance over earlier small herbivores such as the fabrosaurs. Fabrosaurs had simpler teeth, evenly spaced as if in an orthodontist's dream. With narrow jaws, they were far less suited to grinding coarse food than swallowing tender shoots whole. The obvious, but unsubstantiated, conclusion to be drawn from the disappearance of the fabrosaurids and the triumph of the hypsilophodontids in the Cretaceous is that the hypsilophodontids' chewing abilities made them better suited to survival in a changing Lower Cretaceous plant world.

Just what those environments were that favored hypsilophodontid survival is not easily determined. Certainly they were varied. Young Thad's site was clearly an ocean shore environment in *Tenontosaurus*

times — Winkler found oyster shells right on the dinosaur's bones.

We are only beginning to get insights into the life of the hypsilophodontids; this though we've known of *Hypsilophodon*, an animal six feet long that skittered about, perhaps using its long, stiff tail for balance, since a British discovery in 1849. The long-toed and -fingered dinosaur was thought, until well into this century, to be tree-dwelling, a proposition now thoroughly refuted by paleontologist Peter Galton. Hypsilophodonts are relatively uncommon from the Lower Cretaceous in North America. Not, however, in a new-found site at Proctor Lake in Texas. In one little depression, a dozen articulated and nearly complete skeletons of adolescent hypsilophodonts were found. Perhaps Proctor Lake was a breeding site, revisited year after year by hypsilophodont families. According to Jacobs, adults and young appear to have inhabited the site for hundreds or thousands of years.

Proctor Lake may be similar in age, nearly 130 million years, to the Wealden Formation of southeastern England, where *Hypsilophodon*, the animal closest in appearance to the Texas dinosaur, was first found. From that formation, as elsewhere since, came the first iguanodons.

Iguanodon was the first properly documented dinosaur find of all, unearthed in 1822. The Wealden Formation, from which it came, appears to have been dominated by a vast flood plain, extending into France and Belgium, and bordered by mountains that stood where London does today. Vegetation conformed to the classic dinosaurian setting, one loosely compared by paleobotanists to modern South Florida — low, flooded marshes, and fern savannas, broken by patches of more diversely vegetated forest on higher ground. The plants were horsetails and

Preceding page: A Nodosaur, one of the types of armored ankylosaurs with no tail club, browses at a Cretaceous stream in Antarctica. By William G. Stout. *Opposite:* Iguanodons, *bird-hipped herbivorous dinosaurs of the Early Cretaceous. By John Sibbick.*

There was a manila envelope from the State Department of Education, a letter from the Campus Parking Authority marked "Third Notice: Pay Your Outstanding Tickets Immediately," and a formal-looking square envelope from the dean's office, none of which she wanted to open.

She had no outstanding parking tickets, the legislature was going to cut state funding of universities by another eighteen percent, and the letter from the dean was probably notifying her that the entire amount was going to come out of Paleontology's hide.

There was also a stapled brochure from a flight school she had written to during spring break after she had graded one hundred forty-three papers, none of which had gotten off the ground. The brochure had an eagle, some clouds, and the header, "Do you ever just want to get away from it all?"

She pried the staple free and opened it. "Do you ever get sick of your job and want to get away?" it read. "Do you ever feel like you just want to bag everything and do something really neat instead?"

It went on in this vein — which reminded her of her students' papers — for several illustrated paragraphs before it got down to hard facts, which were that the Lindbergh Flight Academy charged three thousand dollars for their course, "including private, commercial, instrument, CFI, CFII, written tests, and flight tests. Lodging extra. Not responsible for injuries, fatalities, or other accidents."

She wondered if the "other accidents" covered budget cuts from the legislature.

Her T.A., Chuck, came in, eating a Twinkie and waving a formal-looking square envelope. "Did you get one of these?" he asked.

"Yes," Sarah said, picking up hers. "I was just going to open it. What is it, an invitation to a slaughter?"

"No, a reception for some guy. The dean's having it this afternoon. In the Faculty Library."

Sarah looked at the invitation suspiciously. "I thought the dean was at an educational conference."

"She's back."

Sarah tore open the envelope and pulled out the invitation. "The dean cordially invites you to a reception for Dr. Jerry King," she muttered. "Dr. Jerry King?" She opened the manila envelope and scanned through the legislature report, looking for his name. "Who is he, do you know?"

"Nope."

At least he wasn't one of the budget-cut supporters. His name wasn't on the list. "Did the rest of the department get these?"

"I don't know. Othniel got one. I saw it in his box," Chuck said. "I don't think he can reach it. His box is on the top row."

Dr. Robert Walker came in, waving a piece of paper. "Look at this! Another ticket for not having a parking sticker! I have a parking sticker! I have two parking stickers! One on the bumper and one on the windshield. Why can't they see them?"

"Did you get one of these, Robert?" Sarah asked, showing him the invitation. "The dean's having a reception this afternoon. Is it about the funding cuts?"

"I don't know," Robert said. "They're right there in plain sight. I even drew an arrow in Magic Marker to the one on the bumper."

"The legislature's cut our funding again," Sarah said. "I'll bet you anything the dean's going to eliminate a position. She was over here last week looking at our enrollment figures."

"The whole university's enrollment is down," Robert said, going over to the window and looking out. "Nobody can afford to go to college anymore, especially when it costs eighty dollars a semester for a parking sticker. Not that the stickers do any good. You still get parking tickets."

"We've got to fight this," Sarah said. "If she eliminates one of our positions, we'll be the smallest department on campus, and the next thing you know, we'll have been merged with Geology. We've got to organize the department and put up a fight. Do you have any ideas, Robert?"

"You know," Robert said, still looking out the window, "maybe if I posted someone out by my car — "

"Your car?"

"Yeah. I could hire a student to sit on the back bumper, and when the Parking Authority comes by, he could point to the sticker. It would cost a lot, but — Stop that!" he shouted suddenly. He wrenched the window open and leaned out. "You can't give me a parking ticket!" he shouted down at the parking lot. "I have two stickers! What are you, blind?" He pulled his head in and bolted out of the office and down the stairs, yelling, "They just gave me another ticket! Can you believe that?"

"No," Sarah said. She picked up the flight school brochure and looked longingly at the picture of the eagle.

"Do you think they'll have food?" Chuck said. He was looking at the dean's invitation.

"I hope not," Sarah said.

"Why not?"

"Grazing," she said. "The big predators always attacked when the hadrosaurs were grazing."

"If they do have food, what kind do you think they'll have?" Chuck asked wistfully.

"It depends," Sarah said, turning the brochure over. "Tea and cookies, usually."

"Homemade?"

"Not unless there's bad news. Cheese and crackers means somebody's getting the ax. Liver pâté means a

budget cut. Of course, if the budget cut's big enough, there won't be any money for refreshments."

On the back of the brochure it said in italics, *Become Upwardly Mobile*, and underneath, in boldface:

FAA-APPROVED
TUITION WAIVERS AVAILABLE
FREE PARKING

"There have been radical changes in our knowledge of the dinosaurs over the past few years," Dr. Albertson said, holding the micropaleontology textbook up, "so radical that what came before is obsolete." He opened the book to the front. "Turn to the introduction."

His students opened their books, which had cost $64.95.

"Have you all turned to the introduction?" Dr. Albertson asked, taking hold of the top corner of the first page. "Good. Now tear it out." He ripped out the page. "It's useless, completely archaic."

Actually, although there had been some recent revisions in theories regarding dinosaur behavior and physiology, particularly the larger predators, there hadn't been any at all at the microscopic level. But Dr. Albertson had seen Robin Williams do this in a movie and been very impressed.

His students, who had been hoping to sell them back to the university bookstore for $32.47, were less so. One of them asked hopefully, "Can't we just promise not to read it?"

"Absolutely not," Dr. Albertson said, yanking out a handful of pages. "Come on. Tear them out."

He threw the pages in a metal wastebasket and held the wastebasket out to a marketing minor who was quietly tucking the torn-out pages into the back of the book with an eye to selling it as a pre-edited version. "That's right, all of them," Dr. Albertson said. "Every outdated, old-fashioned page."

Someone knocked on the door. He handed the wastebasket to the marketing minor and left the slaughter to open it. It was Sarah Wright with a squarish envelope.

"There's a reception for the dean this afternoon," she said. "We need the whole department there."

"Do we have to tear out the title page, too?" a psychology minor asked.

"The legislature's just cut funding another eighteen percent, and I'm afraid they're going to try to eliminate one of our positions."

"You can count on my support one hundred percent," he said.

"Good," Sarah said, sighing with relief. "As long as we stick together we've got a chance."

Dr. Albertson shut the door behind her, glancing at his watch. He had planned to stand on his desk before the end of class, but now there wouldn't be time. He had to settle for the inspirational coda.

"Ostracods, diatoms, fusilinids, these are what we stay alive for," he said. *"Carpe diem!* Seize the day!"

The psych minor raised his hand. "Can I borrow your Scotch tape?" he asked. "I accidentally tore out Chapters One and Two."

There was Brie at the reception. And sherry and spinach puffs and a tray of strawberries with cellophane-flagged toothpicks stuck like daggers into them. Sarah took a strawberry and a rapid headcount of the department. Everyone else seemed to be there except Robert, who was probably parking his car, and Dr. Othniel.

"Did you make sure Dr. Othniel saw his invitation?" she asked her T.A., who was eating spinach puffs two at a time.

"Yeah," Chuck said with his mouth full. "He's here." He gestured with his plate toward a high-backed wing chair by the fire.

Sarah went over and checked. Dr. Othniel was asleep. She went back over to the table and had another strawberry. She wondered which one was Dr. King. There were only three men she didn't recognize. Two of them were obviously Physics Department — they were making a fusion reactor out of a Styrofoam cup and several of the fancy toothpicks. The third looked likely. He was tall and distinguished, and was wearing a tweed jacket with patches on the elbows, but after a few minutes he disappeared into the kitchen and came back with a tray of liver paté and crackers.

Robert came in, carrying his suit jacket and looking out of breath. "You will *not* believe what happened to me," he said.

"You got a parking ticket," Sarah said. "Were you able to find out anything about this Dr. King?"

"He's an educational consultant," Robert said. "What *is* the point of spending eighty dollars a semester for a parking sticker when there are never any places to park in the permit lots? You know where I had to park? Behind the football stadium! That's five blocks further away than my house!"

"An educational consultant?" Sarah said. "What's he up to?" She stared thoughtfully at her strawberry. "An educational consultant — "

"Author of *What's Wrong with Our Entire Educational System,*" Dr. Albertson said. He took a plate and put a spinach puff on it. "He's an expert on restructionary implementation."

"What's that?" Chuck said, making a sandwich out of the liver paté and two spinach puffs.

Dr. Albertson looked superior. "Surely they teach you graduate assistants about restructionary implementation," he said, which meant he didn't know either.

He took a bite of spinach puff. "You should try these," he said. "I was just talking to the dean. She told me she made them herself."

"We're dead," Sarah said.

"There's Dr. King now," Dr. Albertson said, pointing to a lumbering man wearing a polo shirt and Sans-a-belt slacks.

The dean went over to greet him, clasping his hands in hers. "Sorry I'm late," he boomed out. "I couldn't find a parking place. I parked out in front."

Dr. Othniel suddenly emerged from the wing chair, looking wildly around. Sarah beckoned to him with her toothpick and he stooped his way over to them, sat down next to the Brie and went back to sleep.

The dean moved to the center of the room and clapped her hands for attention. Dr. Othniel jerked at the sound. "I don't want to interrupt the fun," the dean said, "and *please*, do go on eating and drinking, but I just wanted you all to meet Dr. Jerry King. Dr. King will be working with the paleontology department on something I'm sure you'll all find terribly exciting. Dr. King, would you like to say a few words?"

Dr. King smiled, a large friendly grin that reminded Sarah of the practice jaw in Field Techniques. "We all know the tremendous impactization technology has had on our modern society," he said.

"Impactization?" Chuck said, eating a lemon tart the distinguished looking gentleman had just brought out from the kitchen. "I thought *impact* was a verb."

"It is," Sarah said. "And once, back in the Late Cretaceous, it was a noun."

"Shh," Dr. Albertson said, looking disapproving.

"As we move into the twenty-first century, our society is transformizing radically, but is education? No. We are still teaching the same old subjects in the same old ways." He smiled at the dean. "Until today. Today marks the beginning of a wonderful innovationary

experiment in education, a whole new instructional dynamic in teaching paleontology. I'll be thinktanking with you dinosaur guys and gals next week, but until then I want you to think about one word."

"Extinction," Sarah murmured.

"That word is *relevance*. Is paleontology relevant to our modern society? How can we *make* it relevant? Think about it. Relevance."

There was a spattering of applause from the departments Dr. King would not be thinktanking with. Robert poured a large glass of sherry and drank it down. "It's not fair," he said. "First the Parking Authority and now this."

"Pilots make a lot of money," Sarah said. "And the only word they have to think about is *crash*."

Dr. Albertson raised his hand.

"Yes?" the dean asked.

"I just wanted Dr. King to know," he said, "that he can count on my support one hundred percent."

"Are you supposed to eat this white crust thing on the cheese?" Chuck asked.

Dr. King put a memo in the Paleontology Department's boxes the next day. It read, "Group ideating session next Mon. Dr. Wright's office. 2 P.M. J. King. P.S. I will be doing observational datatizing this Tues. and Thurs."

"We'll all do some observational datatizing," Sarah said, even more alarmed by Dr. King's preempting her office without asking her than by the Brie.

She went to find her T.A., who was in her office eating a Snickers. "I want you to go find out about Dr. King's background," she told him.

"Why?"

"Because he used to be a junior high girls' basketball coach. Maybe we can get some dirt on one of his seventh grade forwards and him."

"How do you know he used to be a junior high coach?"

"All educational consultants used to be junior high coaches. Or social studies teachers." She looked at the memo disgustedly. "What do you suppose observational datatizing consists of?"

Observational datatizing consisted of wandering around the halls of the Earth Sciences building with a clipboard listening to Dr. Albertson.

"Okay, how much you got?" Dr. Albertson was saying to his class. He was wearing a butcher's apron and a paper fast-food hat and was cutting apples into halves, quarters, and thirds with a cleaver, which had nothing to do with depauperate fauna, but which he had seen Edward James Olmos do in *Stand and Deliver*. He had been very impressed.

"Yip, that'll do it," he was saying in an Hispanic accent when Dr. King appeared suddenly at the back of the room with his clipboard.

"But the key question here is *relevance*," Dr. Albertson said hastily. "How do the depauperate fauna affectate on our lives today?"

His students looked wary. One of them crossed his arms protectively over his textbook as though he thought he was going to be asked to tear out more pages.

"Depauperate fauna are *highly relevant* to our modern society," Dr. Albertson said, but Dr. King had wandered back into the hall and into Dr. Othniel's class.

"The usual mode of the *Tyrannosaurus Rex* was to approach a herd of hadrosaurs from cover," Dr. Othniel, who did not see Dr. King because he was writing on the board, said. "He would then attack suddenly and retreat." He wrote, "1. OBSERVE, 2. ATTACK, 3. RETREAT," in a column on the board, the letters of each getting smaller and squinchier as he approached the chalk tray.

His students wrote, "1. Sneak up, 2. Bite ass, 3. Beat it," and "Todd called last night. I told him Traci wasn't there. We talked forever." Dr. King wrote, "RELEVANCE?" in large block letters on his clipboard and wandered out again.

"The jaws and teeth of the *Tyrannosaurus* were capable of inflicting a fatal wound with a single bite. It would then follow at a distance, waiting for its victim to bleed to death," Dr. Othniel said.

Robert was late to the meeting on Monday. "You will not believe what happened to me!" he said. "I had to park in the daily permit lot, and while I was getting the permit out of the machine, they gave me a ticket!"

Dr. King, who was sitting in Sarah's desk wearing a pair of gray sweats, a whistle, and a baseball cap with "Dan Quayle Junior High" on it, said, "I know you're all as excited about this educationing experiment we're about to embarkate on as I am."

"More," Dr. Albertson said.

Sarah glared at him. "Will this experiment involve eliminating positions?"

Dr. King smiled at her. His teeth reminded her of some she'd seen at the Denver Museum of Natural History. "Positions, classes, departments, all those terms are irrelevantatious. We need to reassessmentize our entire concept of education, its relevance to modern society. How many of you are using paradigmic bonding in your classes?"

Dr. Albertson raised his hand.

"Paradigmic bonding, experiential roleplaying, modular cognition. I assessmentized some of your classes last week. I saw no computer-learner linkages, no multimedial instruction, no cognitive tracking. In one class" — Dr. King smiled largely at Dr. Othniel — "I saw a blackboard being used. Methodologies like that are extinct."

"So are dinosaurs," Sarah muttered. "Why don't you say something, Robert?"

"Dr. King," Robert said. "Do you plan to extend this reorganization to other departments?"

Good, Sarah thought, send him over to pester English Lit.

"Yes," Dr. King said, beaming. "Paleontology is only a field-test. Eventually we intend to expand it to encompassate the entire university. Why?"

"There's one department that drastically needs reorganization," Robert said. "I don't know if you're aware of this, but the Parking Authority is completely out of control. The sign distinctly says you're supposed to park your car first and *then* go get the daily permit out of the machine."

"What did you find out about Dr. King?" Sarah asked Chuck Tuesday morning.

"He didn't coach junior high girls' basketball," he said, drinking a lime Slurpee. "It was junior high wrestling."

"Oh," Sarah said. "Then find out where he got his doctorate. Maybe we can get the college to rescind it for using words like *assessmentize*."

"I don't think I'd better," Chuck said. "I mean, I've only got one semester till I graduate. And besides," he said, sucking on the Slurpee, "some of his ideas made sense. I mean, a lot of that stuff we learn in class does seem kind of pointless. I mean, what does the Late Cretaceous have to do with us really? I thought some of those things he talked about sounded rad. Why *don't* we ever roleplay in class?"

"Fine," Sarah said. "Roleplay this. You are a *Corythosaurus*. You're smart and fast, but not fast enough because a *Tyrannosaurus Rex* has just taken a bite out of your flank. What do you do?"

"Gosh, that's a tough one," Chuck said, slurping meditatively. "What would you do?"

"Grow a wishbone."

Tuesday afternoon, as soon as her one o'clock class was over, Sarah went to Robert's office. He wasn't there. She waited outside for half an hour, reading the announcement for a semester at sea, and then went over to the Parking Authority office.

He was standing near the front of a line that wound down the stairs and out the door. It was composed mostly of students, though the person at the head of the line was a frail-looking old man. He was flapping a green slip at the young man behind the counter. The young man had a blond crew cut and looked like an adolescent Himmler.

"... heart attack," the old man was saying. Sarah wondered if he had had one when he got his parking ticket or if he intended to have one now.

Sarah tried to get to Robert, but two students were blocking the door. She recognized one of the freshmen from Dr. Othniel's class. "Oh, Todd," she was saying to a boy in a tank undershirt and jeans, "I knew you'd help me. I tried to get Traci to come with me — I mean, after all, it was her car — but I think she had a date."

"A date?" Todd said.

"Well, I don't know for sure. It's hard to keep track of all her guys. I couldn't do that. I mean," she lowered her eyes demurely, "if you were *my* boyfriend, I'd never even think about other guys."

"Excuse me," Sarah said, "but I need to talk to Dr. Walker."

Todd stepped to one side, and instead of stepping to the other, the freshman from Dr. Othniel's class squeezed over next to him. Sarah slid past, and worked her way up to Robert, ignoring the nasty looks of the other people in line.

"Don't tell me you got a ticket, too," Robert said.

"No," she said. "We have to do something about Dr. King."

"We certainly do," Robert said indignantly.

"Oh, I'm so glad you feel that way. Dr. Othniel's useless. He doesn't even realize what's going on, and Dr. Albertson's giving a lecture on 'The Impactization of Microscopic Fossils on Twentieth Century Society.' "

"Which is what?"

"I have no idea. When I was in there he was showing a videotape of *The Land Before Time.*"

"I had a coronary thrombosis!" the old man shouted.

"Unauthorized vehicles are not allowed in permit lots," the Hitler Youth said. "However, we have initiated a preliminary study of the incident."

"A preliminary study!" the old man said, clutching his left arm. "The last one you did took five years!"

"We need another meeting with Dr. King," Sarah said. "We need to tell him relevance is not the issue, that paleontology is important in and of itself, and not because brontosaurus earrings are trendy. Surely he'll see reason. We have science and logic on our side."

Robert looked at the old man at the counter.

"What is there to study?" he was saying. "You ticketed the ambulance while the paramedics were giving me CPR!"

"I'm not sure reason will work," Robert said doubtfully.

"Well, then, how about a petition? We've got to do something, or we'll all be showing episodes of "The Flintstones". He's a dangerous man!"

"He certainly is," Robert said. "Do you know what I just got? A citation for parking in front of the Faculty Library."

"Will you forget about your stupid parking tickets for a minute?" Sarah said. "You won't have any reason to park unless we get rid of King. I know Albertson's students would all sign a petition. Yesterday he made them cut the illustrations out of their textbooks and make a collage."

"The Parking Authority doesn't acknowledge petitions," Robert said. "You heard what Dr. King told the dean at the reception. He said, 'I'm parked right outside.' He left a note on his windshield that said the Paleontology Department had given him permission to park there." He waved the green paper at her. "Do you know where *I* parked? Fifteen blocks away. And I'm the one who gets a citation for improperly authorizing parking permission!"

"Good-bye, Robert," Sarah said.

"Wait a minute! Where are you going? We haven't figured out a plan of action yet."

Sarah worked her way back through the line. The two students were still blocking the door. "I'm sure Traci will understand," the freshman from Dr. Othniel's class was saying, "I mean, it isn't like you two were *serious* or anything."

"Wait a minute!" Robert shouted from his place in line. "What are you going to do?"

"Evolve," Sarah said.

On Wednesday there was another memo in Paleontology's boxes. It was on green paper, and Robert snatched it up and took off for the Parking Authority office, muttering dark threats. He was already there and standing in line behind a young woman in a wheelchair and two firemen when he finally unfolded it and read it.

"I *know* I was parking in a handicapped spot," the young woman was saying when Robert let out a whoop and ran back to the Earth Sciences building.

Sarah had a one o'clock class, but she wasn't there. Her students, who were spending their time erasing marks in their textbooks so they could resell them at the bookstore, didn't know where she was. Neither did Dr. Albertson, who was making a papier-mâché foraminifer.

Robert went into Dr. Othniel's class. "The prevalence of predators in the Late Cretaceous," Dr. Othniel was saying, "led to severe evolutionary pressures, resulting in aquatic and aeronautical adaptations."

Robert tried to get his attention, but he was writing "BIRDS" in the chalk tray.

He went out in the hall. Sarah's T.A. was standing outside her office, eating a bag of Doritos.

"Have you seen Dr. Wright?" Robert asked.

"She's gone," Chuck said, munching.

"Gone? You mean, resigned?" he said, horrified. "But she doesn't have to." He waved the green paper at Chuck. "Dr. King's going to do a preliminary study, a — what does he call it? — a preinitiatory survey of prevailing paleontological pedagogy. We won't have to worry about him for another five years at least."

"She saw it," Chuck said, pulling a jar of salsa out of his back pocket. "She said it was too late. She'd already paid her tuition." He unscrewed the lid.

"Her tuition?" Robert said. "What are you talking about? Where did she go?"

"She flew the coop." He dug in the bag and pulled out a chip. He dipped it in the sauce. "Oh, and she left something for you." He handed Robert the jar of salsa and the chips and dug in his other back pocket. He handed Robert the flight brochure and a green plastic square.

"It's her parking sticker," Robert said.

"Yeah," Chuck said. "She said she won't be needing it where she's going."

"That's all? She didn't say anything else?"

"Oh, yeah," he said, dipping a chip into the salsa

Robert still held. "She said to watch out for falling rocks."

"The predatory dinosaurs flourished for the entire Late Cretaceous," Dr. Othniel said, "and then, along with their prey, disappeared. Various theories have been advanced for their extinction, none of which has been authoritatively proved."

"I'll bet they couldn't find a parking place," a student who had written one of the letters to the Parking Authority and who had finally given up and traded his Volkswagen in on a skateboard, whispered.

"What?" Dr. Othniel said, looking vaguely around. He turned back to the board. "The diminishing food supply, the rise of mammals, the depredations of smaller predators, all undoubtedly contributed."

He wrote:

    1. FOOD SUPPLY
    2. MAMMALS
    3. COMPETITION

on the bottom one-fifth of the board.

His students wrote, "I thought it was an asteroid," and "My new roommate is trying to steal Todd away from me! Can you believe that?"

"The demise of the dinosaurs — " Dr. Othniel said, and stopped. He straightened slowly, vertebra by vertebra, until he was nearly erect. He lifted his chin, as if he were sniffing the air, and then walked over to the open window, leaned out, and stood there for several minutes, scanning the clear and empty sky.

Major League Triceratops

Barry N. Malzberg

In the Gallery

IN THE DIM CORRIDOR, THE SPACES HUSHED BY FOG, THE DIM AND DAZZLING LIGHTS OF THE exposed diorama playing, the paleontologist stared at the great, shrouded skeletons revolving slowly into the light, the huge and vaulting figures of *Struthiomimus* and *Triceratops* and that flaming tower, the *Tyrannosaurus*, emerging into the strobe. Look at those sons of bitches, the paleontologist said. He was old as new scientists go, a late career change had plummeted him into university at forty, out at fifty with a deep and final understanding of mortality. Ever see anything like that? The woman whose hand he was holding shrugged and shook her head. She had learned the virtues of silence with this man early on. He would not listen.

They were killers, the paleontologist said. One kick, you were gone. But now *they* are gone. What do you think of that?

I don't think, the woman said.

This was close to the truth, near enough to pass, anyway. The tyrannosaur's enormous kneebone, the arch of that bone, loomed before them and she looked up, the line of her gaze passing almost indifferently, casually, over the small skull, half-concealed behind the foot of the larger *Triceratops*. The skull was the size of a man's and flayed to an ardent white.

Take *that* one on the ranch, the paleontologist said. He scratched his nose. Ride 'em cowboy, he said. Take that one down the loop of Montana, what do you say?

I don't say anything, the woman said. You have taught me the crest of silence. She squeezed his hand, curled a finger in his palm. Not even a haiku, she said. Not even five by seven by five.

The paleontologist turned, stared at her with full interest, his gaze caught by the fine cheekbones, the intensity of her gaze, something of the prehistoria herself, he thought, in this odd and twisted light. Her father had been Japanese, the mother pure *Norteamericana*, and the Orient had seemed buried in her face until this angle, this moment, now in the spattered light cast by the dinosaur, in the clutch of her hand she seemed, suddenly, to bear all of the wound and stain of her heritage. Five by seven by five, the paleontologist said. *In the light the bird/Caught in Cretaceous flight as the bone talks to us.* What do you think of that?

I think it is very decadent, she said. *De-ca-dent,* like the time travelers going back to shoot them on their ranches, that is what I think.

But not touching?

It is touching, she said. Everything is touching in the gallery at noon in the dark. She pointed at the small, shattered ridges of teeth. It may talk to you, she said. It doesn't talk to me.

I have nothing to do with the ranches, he said. It is unfair of you to discuss the ranches. I am a scientist.

Yes, she said, you are very scientific. She made him feel the pressure then, putting her knee against his. *De-ca-dent,* she said again. A great horned thing charging toward us in the night, yes.

You are strange, Maria, the paleontologist said. I do not understand you.

8.
DINOSAUR MIGRATIONS

ESSAY BY PHILIP J. CURRIE

SPECULATION BY MICHAEL BISHOP

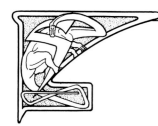

MIGRATING DINOSAURS

PHILIP J. CURRIE

IN RECENT YEARS THERE HAS BEEN A GROWING BODY OF EVIDENCE TO SHOW THAT DINOSAURS, THOSE magnificent creatures that ruled the world for 160 million years,were capable of behavioral responses as complicated as those we normally attribute only to the highest living vertebrates, mammals and birds. One type of behavior that seems to have been widely practiced by dinosaurs is migration.

Many people think of migration as the movement of animals (including humans) between countries or continents. Others conjure up an image of birds flying south for the winter, and returning north each spring. Both views are correct in that the word migration comes from the Latin *migrare,* which simply means "to move from one place to another." We can be more specific by referring to either dispersal (including intercontinental migration), or to annual migration cycles. These two types of migration are not mutually exclusive, and it is not difficult to find modern examples of annual migrations between continents. And, of course, the disruption of a migratory pathway can also lead to dispersal.

INTERCONTINENTAL MIGRATION

There are many examples of intercontinental migration in the fossil record, although analysis of the evidence is much more complicated than simply looking at the distribution of dinosaur fossils. For one thing, our knowledge of dinosaurian history is very sketchy, in part because there are so many gaps in the fossil record. Imagine, if you can, trying to understand the history of humankind if your only source of information was a history book missing most of its pages.

Another consideration is the position of the continents. Continental drift is a phenomenon that is now well understood. The continents are not stable masses of rock. They are in fact constantly moving like flotsam on the surface of an ocean. Measurements made by satellite confirm, for example, that North America is drifting westward at a rate of about two centimeters a year. That may not sound like very much, but when it is extended over periods of millions of years, the distances covered can be quite substantial.

As continents change positions, mountains are built and destroyed, and coastlines change. When dinosaurs ruled the planet, much of the central part of North America was covered by inland seas that at times stretched from the Gulf of Mexico to the Arctic Ocean. And the continental masses are not moving in the same directions or at the same rates, so their present relationships have little meaning for our understanding of animal distribution in the remote past. Little can be said about dinosaur dispersal without referring to geological interpretations of geographical changes through time. For example, the faunal similarities between Upper Jurassic (165 to 145 million years ago) dinosaurs of the western United States and eastern Africa (Tanzania) are striking. *Brachiosaurus, Barosaurus, Elaphrosaurus* and *Dryosaurus* are known from both areas, and there is some fragmentary evidence to suggest that *Allosaurus* and

Ceratosaurus were also present in Africa. Whereas one would initially be tempted to use this as an example of intercontinental migration because of the tremendous separation between Africa and North America today, in fact these continents had direct land connections at that time through Europe and South America, and the Atlantic ocean was just starting to open up.

Better documented examples of intercontinental migrations are to be found in northern hemisphere Cretaceous rocks, which are 145 to 65 million years old. Between 1922 and 1930, the Central Asiatic Expeditions of the American Museum of Natural History sought evidence in the deserts of China and Mongolia to show that Asia was the dispersal center for land-dwelling animals of the northern hemisphere. The expeditions became most famous for their dinosaur discoveries, including the first unquestionable nests of dinosaur eggs. The fossil riches of central Asia subsequently attracted other ambitious international expeditions, right up to the present day. This intensive collecting activity has revealed that almost every family of dinosaurs from North America had representatives in Asia. North America and Asia were separate for a long period of time before the Cretaceous, which allowed the dinosaurs to evolve along different pathways. Sometime during the Early Cretaceous Period (more than 100 million years ago), these two continents contacted each other in the arctic regions and faunal exchange was initiated. The similarity of the dinosaur fauna at the end of their history clearly demonstrates that a land link had been established between the two areas. This allowed Asian dinosaurs to migrate to North America, and vice versa.

Paleontologists, like all scientists, have insatiable curiosities. Once we knew that dinosaurs were migrating between continents, we started to wonder which dinosaurs evolved where, and when the migrations actually took place. But more complicated problems almost always have more complicated solutions, and things are not always what they first seem to be. *Protoceratops* is one of the more celebrated dinosaurs recovered from Mongolia by the Central Asiatic Expeditions. Anatomically, it appeared to be the perfect ancestor for the magnificent horned dinosaurs of North America. Its remains were also found in rocks that are older than any of the known horned dinosaurs. Therefore, it seemed obvious that ceratopsians evolved in Asia and migrated to North America, where they produced the spectacular horned species. Or is it obvious? The Museum of the Rockies in Bozeman, Montana, has now collected protoceratopsians from rocks in Montana that seem to be very close to the same age as those from Mongolia. And modern analysis of the anatomy of protoceratopsians has shown that *Leptoceratops* from Alberta is in fact more primitive than *Protoceratops*!

If dinosaurs were migrating between the continents, then it would be logical to assume that some of the species found on each continent should be identical. This has proven to be difficult to assess, however. There are of course the obvious gaps in the fossil record. And sometimes new species are described without adequate comparison with known species; that is just one of the many reasons why dinosaur names change from time to time. (One of the best examples of changing names is that of one of the most famous dinosaurs, *Brontosaurus*, the "thunder lizard." In this case, two specimens from the same species of animal were given different names, *Apatosaurus* and *Brontosaurus*. When it was discovered that these were in fact the same dinosaur, the correct name became *Apatosaurus*, because it was described first. Nevertheless, the name *"Brontosaurus"* has persisted in the popular literature, even though it is incorrect.) To date, *Saurolophus* is the one of the few dinosaurs that

Preceding page: Iguanodons *migrating up the* *Clayton trackway, on the lookout for predators.* *By Doug Henderson.*

has the same generic name in both North America and Asia. Detailed study may eventually reveal that *Tyrannosaurus* and *Tarbosaurus* are the same animals, and in fact many scientists already believe this. Many other examples could be cited here, but there seem to be at least subtle differences to distinguish the North American and Asian forms at the subspecies or species level.

The differences we see in the species may in part be explained by differences in the ancient environments. Then, as now, animals were specialized for living in certain habitats, and one would not expect to find the remains of a forest-dwelling dinosaur in rocks formed from the sands of a prehistoric desert. Identifying these environments is a major aspect of the work of the Sino-Canadian expeditions going on today. To pursue its objectives, the Dinosaur Project has multidisciplinary teams of scientists and technicians doing fieldwork in China (under the guidance of the Institute of Vertebrate Paleontology and Paleoanthropology, Beijing), the arctic islands of Canada (under the National Museum of Natural Sciences, Ottawa) and in Alberta (under the Tyrrell Museum of Palaeontology, Drumheller). Dr. Tom Jerzykiewicz (Geological Survey of Canada) was a unique addition to the team because he has studied the dinosaur-bearing sediments in both Mongolia (as part of the Polish-Monogolian team of 1965 to 1971) and Alberta. Logistic support from the Ex Terra Foundation (Edmonton) has made it possible to include representatives from all three institutions in the expeditions to all regions.

The environments utilized by dinosaurs also played an important role in the distribution of these animals. Paleontologists have often found it quite remarkable that large horned dinosaurs similar to *Triceratops* did not seem to have dispersed from North America to Asia during the Cretaceous. At least it

seemed that way until 1989 when two Russian scientists described *Turonoceratops tardabilis* from Soviet Central Asia. The absence of horned ceratopsians from most Asian localities can no longer be attributed to geographic separation. The Sino-Canadian expeditions are analyzing the environmental and faunal changes that took place in Asia throughout the Jurassic and the Cretaceous using paleontological and geological evidence. Overall, it appears that the majority of Jurassic and Cretaceous sites were quite dry in Asia, whereas the traditional collecting sites in North America represent relatively wet, well-watered habitats. The absence of horned dinosaurs from traditional collecting sites in Central Asia can be attributed to the fondness of those animals for wetter environments; so understanding the environments of the sites being compared is also critical if we want to understand intercontinental migration patterns.

Bayan Manduhu has proven to be one of the most useful sites in China for comparing Late Cretaceous dinosaur fauna. Literally hundreds of skeletons of dinosaurs (*Protoceratops*, *Pinacosaurus*, *Oviraptor*, *Velociraptor*, and others), lizards, crocodiles, and even mammals were found. Five types of fossilized eggs were identified, and many of them were found in nests. None of the eggs seem to contain embryos, although a skull and partial skeleton of an embryonic *Protoceratops* were found outside of an egg. In spite of the hundreds of specimens recovered, the diversity of this fauna is much lower than that of Dinosaur Provincial Park in Alberta or the Nemegt Basin in Mongolia. The reasons for this were evident from the study of the sediments, which showed that this area was arid during the Cretaceous, just as it is now. And looking across the modern Gobi Desert, one is often surprised by the amount of life that is there, even if it does lack variety. This similarity between past and present environments gives us a unique

The evidence of the tracks in major pathways demonstrates dinosaur herd-ing and migratory behavior, as shown here by a herd of Jurassic Apatosaurs *on the move. By William G. Stout.*

opportunity to make direct comparisons. We were surprised by the number of fossilized burrows made by ancient insects beneath the feet of the dinosaurs. But when we dug into the modern sand dunes, which appeared to be totally sterile on the surface, we found many living invertebrates feeding on layers of wind-blown plant remains that had been buried by the shifting sands.

The framework for the Dinosaur Project is now well established, and future expeditions in China will concentrate on acquiring more detailed information on the timing of intercontinental migration.

EVIDENCE FOR ANNUAL MIGRATION CYCLES

The idea that dinosaurs may have had annual cyclic migratory patterns is not a new one. In 1928, Frederick von Huene speculated that more than 200 million years ago the European prosauropod dinosaur *Plateosaurus* was migrating between regions of winter and summer rainfall. This speculation has often been repeated, usually on the basis of evidence showing that some dinosaurs were gregarious animals that moved in large herds.

I first started thinking about dinosaur migration in the late 1970s when working on dinosaur footprints in the Peace River Canyon of British Columbia. Previously, sites had been reported where there were numerous parallel dinosaur trackways moving in the same direction. However, in the Peace River Canyon, one layer of rock showed a large group of bipedal herbivores moving together in one direction, and changing the trend of direction as they went along. Four trackways were close together, and one can see where one animal slipped and lurched sideways, thereby affecting the path of his neighbor. In turn, this affected (to a lesser degree) the path of the next animal, and

so on. These four trackways show sinuous, S-shaped paths that do not intersect, and the probability is extremely high that the four trackmakers were moving side by side. It is evident from the trackway sites that some of the plant-eating dinosaurs were moving in great herds.

One of the best lines of evidence to show that dinosaurs were gregarious comes from bone beds (extensive, concentrated layers of mixed-up bones from many individuals). Dinosaur bone beds are more common than dinosaur skeletons, and when studied properly can provide information that is not available from any other source. Most bone beds were formed in stream channels, and contain representative bones of all the animals that lived in the area. These animals generally died on land, where their bones were scattered by carnivores and scavengers. As meandering streams cut their banks, the bones would fall into the stream channels and sink to the bottom, where they would be concentrated. Eventually they would be buried by the sand and mud being carried by the water. Occasionally, scientists find bone beds that are dominated by a single species of animal. One such accumulation discovered in Dinosaur Provincial Park (southern Alberta) has been worked for more than ten years by staff of the Tyrrell Museum of Palaeontology. The bone bed is completely dominated by *Centrosaurus apertus*, a horned dinosaur that is distantly related to *Triceratops*. The paleontological and geological evidence suggests that a herd of 400 or more of these 4-ton animals attempted to cross a river in flood. They may have been good swimmers as individuals, but many of them appear to have drowned when they interfered with each other as they tried to swim across as a group. Although this may sound like a rather fantastic explanation, it still happens today with large herds of herbivorous mammals. For example, ten thousand caribou drowned in the Cani-

Sauropod dinosaur tracks — Glen Rose trackway of Jurassic Texas. Photo: American Museum of Natural History.

apiscau River of Quebec in 1984, and there are many examples of mass drowning of wildebeest and bison. As in the modern examples, the carcasses of *Centrosaurus* floated downstream, coming to rest on the banks, point bars, and sand bars of the river. There they were scavenged by large and small carnivorous dinosaurs, who left trampled, tooth-marked bones and the crowns of their loose teeth as evidence of their grisly repast. What was left lay on the surface of the ground until all of the remaining muscles and ligaments had rotted away, at which point the river went into another flood phase and buried the bones in a new layer of sand.

There are other bone beds like that of *Centrosaurus*, which appear to represent catastrophes that befell herds of other horned dinosaurs (including *Anchiceratops*, *Pachyrhinosaurus* and *Styracosaurus*) in different places at other times. Flood waters, drought, forest fires, and disease are just a few of the potential causes for mass mortality, although few of these bone beds have been studied enough to establish the probable causes of death. A tremendous bone bed of the duck-billed dinosaur *Maiasaura* was found near Choteau, Montana, an area that is most famous for its dinosaur egg sites. Preliminary analysis of this site suggests that a herd of ten thousand or more duck-billed dinosaurs may have suffocated in a volcanic ashfall!

In modern mammals, species that live in forests and other closed habitats tend to be relatively smaller, solitary browsers with camouflage coloration and short simple horns. In contrast, open-country species are the most gregarious, are often distinctly marked, tend to be larger with large and/or complex horns, are more mobile, and run away from danger. The most gregarious animals tend to have the highest population densities and are ecologically dominant. Using these as analogies, it seems possible that those relatively large dinosaurs with elaborate horns, frills and crests were animals that lived in open country, may have had distinctive skin markings, and had the most complex social structure. There is at least a good correlation among the horned dinosaurs in that those animals with the most elaborate display structures, such as *Styracosaurus* and *Pachyrhinosaurus*, provide us with some of the best evidence for herding.

The evidence to show that many dinosaurs were herding animals is pretty overwhelming, and is now accepted by most paleontologists who work on these animals. There is not as much agreement on why they might be herding, however. Migration is not an unusual phenomenon in the animal kingdom. Most major groups of mobile animals, including insects, fish, reptiles, birds, and mammals, have examples of species that find migration advantageous. In most cases, migration is linked directly to the search for food and/or water. Among larger animals, there is often a selective advantage in developing a gregarious herd structure as a means of protection from carnivores. However, the collection of groups of large animals is not compatible with remaining in a single area because food sources become depleted, and this in turn gives a selective advantage to large animals that move from region to region. The larger and denser the herd, the more essential it is for it to keep on the move. It is pretty easy to imagine how destructive to the environment a herd of several thousand dinosaurs, each animal weighing as much or more than an elephant, would have been, and how quickly they must have depleted the food supplies. Those animals that develop specific migratory pathways that allow them to be in areas with proven food sources at the right times of the year will of course have a selective advantage over those that wander randomly into regions that may not be able to provide sufficient food.

The study of dinosaur distribution, coupled with the evidence that we have for dinosaur herding behavior, is producing the most compelling evidence for seasonal migration. Although most people seem to believe that dinosaurs lived in tropical areas, the most diverse dinosaur fauna are in fact found at higher latitudes. Dinosaur Provincial Park (in Alberta) and the Nemegt Basin (in the Mongolian People's Republic) have yielded the two richest diversities of fauna, with 35 species of dinosaurs each. During the Cretaceous these animals would have been living at even higher latitudes than they are today. Although sites closer to the equator have produced good dinosaur fossils, the fauna found there are not as varied. This trend suggests that dinosaurs were animals that preferred temperate climates rather than the tropics. From what we now know about dinosaur physiology, it is evident that these generally large animals would have been able to function well in cooler weather, whereas they probably would have had difficulty in discarding excess body heat in the tropics.

Some of the most interesting and promising areas for dinosaur research today are in the polar areas. Work in southern Australia has shown that during the Early Cretaceous, when Australia was much farther south than it is today, several types of small herbivorous and carnivorous dinosaurs were living within the Antarctic Circle. In 1986, an armored dinosaur (ankylosaur) was discovered by an Argentinean party working in Antarctica, and the following year a British party recovered a hypsilophodont there. These south polar dinosaurs are relatively small, and our knowledge of the paleogeography of that time suggests that they may not have been able to migrate great distances to get out of the Antarctic region during the winter months. This shows that dinosaurs must have been capable of surviving adverse polar conditions.

On the other side of the world, however, dinosaurs have been found within the Arctic Circle in Spitzbergen (Lower Cretaceous footprints), the Northwest Territories and Yukon of Canada, and Alaska. Unlike the Antarctic conditions however, the north polar regions were connected by land to more southerly (warmer) areas, and the dinosaurs tend to be larger, more mobile forms.

Plants survive well in the Arctic summers today, in spite of the short growing season and permafrost. With up to twenty-four hours of daily sunshine in the summer, plants are incredibly productive, and even large trees are known to have lived in the Arctic until fairly recently. As these plants also had to deal with up to twenty-four hours of darkness each day in winter, they are all deciduous forms, including "evergreens" like the Dawn Redwood (which even today loses its needles in the winter months). Furthermore, the caloric density of plant tissues is much higher in temperate and arctic regions, and the fiber content is lower. Hence there is a superabundance of forage of a higher quality. In the case of large, modern plant-eating species, this translates into a far greater surplus of energy for fat storage or antler-horn growth than in tropical forms, and this may have been the case with dinosaurs as well.

Dinosaurs were extremely successful throughout their 160 million year history, partially because they were able to adapt and take advantage of a variety of ecosystems. Although it was natural that they would move into the polar regions during summer months to use that high plant productivity, most would not have had enough food during the winter months. The smaller, less mobile species would probably have remained in the north, surviving on seeds and low-grade plant fodder such as bark and dried leaves. Small carnivores could have survived, of course, by eating the plant-eating dinosaurs, plus mammals and any other animals that remained active. Some dinosaurs may even have hibernated as a way of surviving the winter. But the majority of large species had another option. With their long legs and efficient ways of walking, dinosaurs were as capable as modern mammals of moving great distances.

One of the dinosaurs found by the joint University of California (Berkeley)/University of Alaska expedition to the North Slope of Alaska in 1987 was a bizarre dinosaur known as *Pachyrhinosaurus*. This horned dinosaur has been known from southern Alberta for many years. Rather than having three horns on its face like its distant cousin *Triceratops*, *Pachyrhinosaurus* had massive growths of bone over the nose and the eyes. These may have formed a massive battering ram, although their similarity to the base of a rhinoceros horn suggests that the bony bosses may have supported a tough but lightweight horn derived from skin tissues (a rhinoceros horn is actually an agglutinated mass of hair). The frill over the neck was highly ornamented, with huge recurved horns (looking much like those of a Texas longhorn) and a unicorn-like spike rising above the center of the frill. Two bone beds in Alberta have already shown us that *Pachyrhinosaurus* was a herding animal, and with a range of more than 2,000 miles, this animal is one of the best candidates for annual migration.

Two thousand miles may be the known range for *Pachyrhinosaurus*, but it is doubtful that any individual moved the full extent of the species range. For example, North American caribou have a range of more than two thousand miles north to south, but no herd or individual is known to travel more than eight hundred miles in one direction within that range. Even at the maximum known range of *Pachyrhinosaurus*, if an individual moved at five miles an hour (a figure calculated from the trackways of slow-moving dinosaurs in the Peace River Canyon; the record is a

Texas carnivorous dinosaur that moved at 25 miles per hour), it would be able to cover the maximum distance if it walked twelve hours a day for 33 days. Today wildebeest cover up to 50 miles a day, and caribou as much as 100 miles. In all likelihood, however, *Pachyrhinosaurus* herds were moving shorter distances and taking longer periods of time (caribou spend three to four months of the year migrating).

Pachyrhinosaurus is only one of the dinosaurs from Alberta that has been found in Alaska, but less is currently known about the herding behavior and possible movement of other species. Perhaps the greatest promise is shown by a bone bed of duck-billed dinosaurs from Alaska, because analysis of size distribution in the herd and comparison with southern specimens may give us some clues as to where and when these dinosaurs hatched from eggs.

Dinosaur behavior must have been as diverse as the dinosaurs themselves. Not all species would have moved in herds (in Africa today, 41 percent of the 70 antelope and other bovid species south of the Sahara are solitary and 59 percent are gregarious), and of the ones that herded, only some of them may actually have been migrating. The herds themselves are still poorly understood, although we know that they included males, females, juveniles, and babies. Today there are three basic social structures in the cattle (bovid) family: females with or without young (nursery herds), all-male bachelor herds, and solitary adult males. Modern herds are highly variable in organization, and can be composed of a dominant bull with his harem, or of females and their young (but no mature males), or all bachelor males, or almost any other combination you would care to think of. Different species of dinosaurs may well have had different herding strategies. *Pachyrhinosaurus* herds seem to have been simple in organization, composed of almost equal numbers of males and females. As in modern herding animals, migrating herds probably were only together at certain times of the year. They may well have collected into groups at the end of the Arctic summer and moved as a unit south to Alberta and Montana. Here the herds may have dispersed for the winter months, and only gathered together again when they started their migration north into the Arctic in the spring. This model provides an explanation for the rich diversity of plant-eating dinosaurs in places like Dinosaur Provincial Park, because many of them would only have been living there for part of the year.

Seasonal migrations would have provided opportunities for dinosaurs to disperse to other parts of the world. As previously mentioned, we know from studies of the continental positions during the Cretaceous that the connections between Asia and North America lay within the Arctic regions. Those dinosaurs that lived in or migrated to the Arctic would have had the opportunity to move easily between the continents. After all, if you were far enough north and wanted to go south again, turning slightly to the right could take you into Asia, or to the left into North America!

It must have been an amazing sight as ceratopsians and hadrosaurs collected into huge herds in the spring for their migration north. Carnivores large and small would have followed them for at least short distances, picking off the sick, the old or the incautious individuals. And perhaps it was somewhat prophetic that the dinosaurs shared the north with their own descendants, the birds who would one day migrate as much as 10,000 miles a year!

HERDING WITH THE HADROSAURS

MICHAEL BISHOP

IN '08, MY PARENTS — PIERCE AND EULOGY GREGSON OF GIPSY, MISSOURI — RECEIVED PERMISSION to cross the geologic time-slip west of St. Joseph. They left in a wood-paneled New Studebaker wagon, taking provisions for one month, a used 'Zard-Off scent-generator, and, of course, their sons, sixteen-year-old Chad (me) and five-year-old Cleigh, known to all as "Button." Our parents rejected the security of a caravan because Daddy had only contempt for "herders," detested taking orders from external authority, and was sure that when we homesteaded our new Eden beyond the temporal divide, reptile men, claim jumpers, and other scalawags would show up to murder and dispossess us. It struck him as politic to travel alone, even if the evident dangers of the Late Cretaceous led most pioneers to set forth in groups.

That was Pierce Gregson's first, biggest, and, I suppose, last mistake. I was almost a man (just two years away from the vote and only an inch shy of my adult height), and I remember everything. Sometimes, I wish I didn't. The memory of what happened to our folks only two days out from St. Jo, on the cycad-clotted prairie of the old Dakotas, pierces me yet. In fact, this account is a eulogy for our folks and a *cri de coeur* I've been holding back for almost thirty years.

(Sweet Seismicity, let it shake my pain.)

The first things you notice crossing over, when agents of the World Time-Slip Force pass you through the discontinuity locks, are the sharp changes in temperature and humidity. The Late Cretaceous was — in many places, at least — hot and moist. So TSF officials caution against winter, spring, or fall crossings. It's best to set out, they say, in late June, July, or August, when atmospheric conditions in northwestern Missouri are not unlike those that hold, just beyond the Nebraska drop-off, in the Upper Mesozoic.

Ignoring this advice, we left in February. Still, our New Stu wagon (a sort of a cross between a Conestoga wagon and a high-tech *Ankylosaurus*) plunged us into a strength-sapping steam bath. All our first day, we sweated. Even the sight of clown-frilled *Triceratops* browsing among the magnolia shrubs and the palmlike cycads of the flood plains did nothing to cool our bodies or lift our spirits. It was worse than going to a foreign country knowing nothing of its language or mores — it was like crawling the outback of a bizarre alien planet.

Button loved it. Daddy pretended that the heat, the air, the grotesque fauna — all of which he'd tried to get us ready for didn't unsettle him. Like turret-gunners, Mama and I kept our eyes open. We missed no chance to gripe about the heat or our wagon's tendency to lurch, steamroller seedling evergreens, and vibrate our kidneys. Daddy, irked, kept his jaw set and his fist on the rudder knob, as if giving his whole attention to steering would allow him to overcome every obstacle, physical or otherwise.

It didn't. On Day Two, twenty or thirty miles from the eastern shore of the Great Inland Sea, we were bumping along at forty-five or fifty mph when two tyrannosaurs — with thalidamide forelegs dangling like ill-made prosthetic hooks — came shuffle-waddling straight at us out of the north.

Sitting next to Daddy, Button hooted in delight. Behind him, I leaned into my seat belt, gaping at the creatures in awe.

The tyrannosaurs were stop-motion Hollywood mockups — except that, gleaming bronze and cordavan in the ancient sunlight, they weren't. They were alive, and, as we all soon realized, they found our wagon profoundly interesting.

"Isn't that 'Zard-Off thing working?" Mama cried.

Daddy was depressing levers, jiggling toggles. "It's on, it's on!" he said. "They shouldn't be coming!"

The scent generator in our wagon was supposed to aspirate an acrid mist into the air, an odor repugnant to saurians, carnivores and plant-eaters alike.

But these curious T-kings were approaching anyway — proof, Mama and I decided, that our scent-generator, a secondhand model installed only a few hours before our departure, was a dud. And it was just like Daddy, the biggest of scrimps, to have paid bottom dollar for it, his perfectionism in matters not money-grounded now disastrously useless.

"Daddy, turn!" I shouted. "We can outrun them!"

To give him credit, Daddy had already ruddered us to the right and was squeezing F-pulses to the power block with his thumb. The plain was broad and open, but dotted with palmate shrubs, many of which looked like fluted pillars crowned by tattered green umbrella segments; we ran right over one of the larger cycads in our path before we'd gone thirty yards. Our wagon tilted on two side wheels, tried to right itself, and, failing that, crashed down on its passenger box with a drawn-out *KRRRRR-ack!*

Mama screamed, Daddy cursed, Button yowled like a vivisected cat. I was deafened, dangling in an eerie hush from my seat belt. And then Button, upside-down, peered quizzically into my face while mouthing, urgently, a battery of inaudible riddles.

Somehow, we wriggled out. So far as that goes, so did Daddy and Mama, although it would have been better for them — for all of us — if we had just played turtle.

In fact, our folks undoubtedly struggled free of the capsized wagon to *look for* Button and me. What Button and I saw, huddled behind an umbrella shrub fifty yards away, was that awkward but disjointedly agile pair of T-kings. They darted at Mama and Daddy and seized them like rag dolls in their stinking jaws, one stunned parent to each tyrannosaur.

Then the T-kings — lofty, land-going piranhas — shook our folks unconscious, dropped them to the ground, crouched on their mutilated bodies with crippled-looking foreclaws, and vigorously tore into them with six-inch fangs.

At intervals, they'd lift their huge skulls and work their lizardly nostrils as if trying to catch wind of something tastier. Button and I, clutching each other, would glance away. Through it all, I cupped my hand over Button's mouth to keep him from crying out. By the time the T-kings had finished their meal and tottered off, my palm was lacerated from the helpless gnashing of Button's teeth.

And there we were, two scared human orphans in the problematic Late Cretaceous.

Every year since recrossing the time-slip, I see a report that I was a feral child, the only human being in history to have been raised by a nonmammalian species. In legend and literature, apes, wolves, and lions sometimes get credit for nurturing lost children, but no one is idiot enough to believe that an alligator or a Komodo dragon would put up with a human child any longer than it takes to catch, chew, and ingest it. No one should.

On the other hand, although I, Chad Gregson, was too old to be a feral child, having absorbed sixteen years of human values at the time of our accident, my little brother Cleigh, or Button, wasn't. And, indeed, it would probably not be wrong to say that, in quite a compelling sense, he was raised by hadrosaurs.

I did all I could to pick up where our folks had left off, but the extended tribe of duckbills — *Corytho-saurus* — with whom we eventually joined also involved themselves in Button's parenting, and I remain grateful to them. But I jump ahead of myself. What happened in the immediate aftermath of our accident?

Button and I lay low. A herd of *Triceratops* came snuffling through the underbrush, grunting and browsing. Overhead, throwing weird shadows on the plains, six or seven pterosaurs — probably vulturelike *Quetzal-coatli* — circled our wagon's wreck on thermal updrafts, weighing the advisability of dropping down to pick clean the bones of Pierce and Eulogy Gregson. They stayed aloft, for the departed T-kings may have still been fairly near, so Button and I likewise stayed aloof.

Until evening, that is. Then we crept to the wagon — I held on to Button to keep him from trying to view the scattered, collopy bones of our folks — and unloaded as much gear as we could carry: T-rations, two wooden harmonicas, some extra all-cotton clothing, a sack of seed, etc. TSF officials allowed no synthetic items (even 'Zard-Off was an organic repellent, made from a Venezuelan herb) to cross a time-slip, for after an early period of supply-dependency, every pioneer was expected to "live off the land."

A wind blew down from the north. Suddenly, surprisingly, the air was no longer hot and moist; instead, it was warm and arid. We were on a Dead Sea margin rather than in a slash-and-burn Amazonian clearing. Our sweat dried. Hickories, oaks, and conifers grew among the horsetails along the meander of a river by the Great Inland Sea. Button and I crept through the glowing pastels of an archaic sunset, looking for fresh water (other than that sloshing in our leather botas) and shelter.

Which is how, not that night but the following dawn, we bumped into the hadrosaurs that became our new family: a lambeosaurine tribe, each creature bearing on its ducklike head a hallow crest, like the brush on a Roman centurion's helmet.

Becoming family took a while, though, and that night, our first beyond the divide without our parents, Button snuggled into my lap in a stand of cone-bearing evergreens, whimpering in his dreams and sometimes crying out. Small furry creatures moved about in the dark, trotting or waddling as their unfamiliar bodies made them — but, bent on finding food appropriate to their size, leaving us blessedly alone. Some of these nocturnal varmints, I understood, would bring forth descendants that would evolve into hominids that would evolve into men. As creepy as they were, I was glad to have them around — they clearly knew when it was safe for mammals to forage. Q.E.D.: Button and I had to be semisafe, too. "Where are we?" Button asked when he awoke.

"When are we?" or *"Why are we here?"* would have been better questions, but I told Button that we were hiding from the giant piranha lizards that had killed Daddy and Mama. Now, though, we had to get on with our lives.

About then, we looked up and spotted a huge camouflage-striped *Corythosaurus* — green, brown, burnt yellow — standing on its hind legs, embracing a nearby fir with its almost graceful arms. With its goosy beak, it was shredding needles, grinding them into meal between the back teeth of both jaws. Behind and beyond it foraged more *Corythosauri*, the adults nearly thirty feet tall, the kids anywhere from my height to that of small-town lampposts. Some in the hadrosaur herd locomoted like bent-over kangaroos; others had taken the posture of the upright colossus before us.

Button began screaming. When I tried to cover his mouth, he bit me. *"They wanna eat us!"* he shrieked even louder. *"Chad — please, Chad! — don't let them eat me!"*

I stuffed the hem of a cotton tunic into Button's

mouth and pinned him down with an elbow the way the T-kings, yesterday, had grounded our folks' corpses with their claws. I, too, thought we were going to be eaten, even though the creature terrifying Button had to be a vegetarian. It and its cohorts stopped feeding. In chaotic unison, they jogged off through the grove on their back legs, their fat, sturdy, conical tails counterbalancing the weight of their crested skulls.

"They're gone," I told Button. "I promise you, they're gone. Here — eat this."

I snapped a box of instant rice open under his nose, poured some water into it, and heated the whole shebang with a boil pellet. Sniffling, Button ate. So did I. Thinking, "safety in numbers," and setting aside the fact that T-kings probably ate duckbills when they couldn't find people, I pulled Button up and made him trot along behind me after the *Corythosauri*.

In a way, it was a relief to be free of the twenty-second century. (And, God forgive me, it was something of a relief to be free of our parents. I *hurt* for them. I *missed* them. But the possibilities inherent in the Late Cretaceous, not to mention its dangers, pitfalls, and terrors, seemed crisper and brighter in our folks' sudden absence.)

The asteroid that hit the Indian Ocean in '04, gullywashing the Asian subcontinent, Madagascar, and much of East Africa, triggered the tidal waves that drowned so many coastal cities worldwide. It also caused the apocalyptic series of earthquakes that sundered North America along a jagged north-south axis stretching all the way from eastern Louisiana to central Manitoba.

These catastrophic seismic disturbances apparently produced the geologic divide, the Mississippi Valley Time-Slip, fracturing our continent into the ruined Here-and-Now of the eastern seaboard and the anachronistic There-and-Then of western North America.

Never mind that the West beyond this discontinuity only existed in fact over sixty-five million years ago. Or that you can no longer visit modern California because California — along with twenty-one other western states and all or most of six western Canadian provinces — has vanished.

It's crazy, the loss of half a modern continent and of every person living there before the asteroid impact and the earthquakes, but you can't take a step beyond the divide without employing a discontinuity lock. And when you do cross, what you see is fossils sprung to life, the offspring of a different geologic period. In Europe, Asia, Africa, South America, Australia, Antarctica, it's much the same — except that the time-slips in those places debouch on other geologic time divisions: the Pleistocene, the Paleocene, the Jurassic, the Silurian, etc.

We're beginning to find that many parts of the world we used to live in are, temporally speaking, vast subterranean galleries in which our ancestors, or our descendants, stride like kings and we are unwelcome strangers. I survived my time in one such roofless cavern, but even if it meant losing Button to the Late Cretaceous forever, I'd be delighted to see all our world's cataclysm-spawned discontinuities melt back into normalcy tomorrow....

The *Corythosauri* were herding. The tribe we'd just met flowed into several other tribes, all moving at a stately clip up through Saskatchewan, Alberta, and the northeastern corner of old British Columbia. Button and I stayed with them because, in our first days beyond the divide, we saw no other human pioneers and believed it would be more fun to travel with some easygoing nonhuman natives than to lay claim to the first plot of likely-looking ground we stumbled across.

Besides, I didn't want to begin farming yet, and the pace set by the duckbills was by no stretch burdensome — fifteen to twenty miles a day, depending on the vegetation available and the foraging styles of the lead males.

It was several weeks before we realized that the *Corythosauri*, along with six or seven other species of duckbill and a few distant groups of horned dinosaurs, ware migrating. We supposed — well, *I* supposed, Button being little more than a dumbstruck set of eyes, ears, and boyish tropisms — only that they were eating their way through the evergreens, magnolias, and cycad shrubs along routes well-worn by earlier foragers.

Where, I wondered, were our human predecessors? The time-slip locks at St. Joseph and other sites along the divide had been open two full years, ever since Tharpleton and Sykora's development of cost-effective discontinuity gates. To date, over 100,000 people had reputedly used them. So where was everyone? A few, like our parents, had met untimely deaths. Others had made the crossing elsewhere. Still others had headed straight for the Great Inland Sea — to trap pelicanlike pterosaurs, train them on leads, and send them out over the waters as captive fishers. It beat farming, said some returning pioneers, and the westerly salt breezes were always lovely. In any event, Button and I trailed our duckbills a month before happening upon another human being.

How did we become members of the *Corythosaurus* family? Well, we stayed on the lumbering creatures' trail every day and bedded down near them every night. At first, sighting us, the largest males like four-legged, thirty-foot-tall woodwinds — would blow panicky bassoon notes through the tubes winding from their nostrils through the mazelike hollows in their mohawk crests. These musical alarms echoed back and forth among the tribe, alerting not only our family but every other nearby clan of hadrosaurs to a possible danger. At first, this was flattering, but, later, simply frustrating.

Button got tired of dogging the *Corythosauri*. They stank, he said, "like the snake house in the St. Louis Zoo." He griped about all the mushy green hadrosaur patties along our route. He said that the insects bumbling in clouds around the duckbills — gnats, flies, a few waspish pollinators — were better at "poking our hides than theirs." He whined that we couldn't "become duckbills because we don't eat what they eat." And he was right. We were living on T-rations, tiny rodentlike mammals that I caught when they were most sluggish, and the pulpy berries of strange shrubs. We often had tight stomachs, loose bowels, borderline dehydration.

But I kept Button going by ignoring his gripes, by seeing to it that he ate, and by carrying him on my shoulders. Weirdly, it was after hoisting him onto my shoulders that the duckbills stopped running from us at first sight. By that trick, we ceased being two bipedal strangers and became a single honorary hadrosaur.

When he sat on my shoulders, Button's dilapidated St. Louis Cardinals baseball cap gave us both the crest and the bill we needed to pass as one of their youngsters. Then, in fact, the *Corythosauri* let us travel at the heart of their group, with all the other juveniles. There, we were relatively secure from the flesh-eaters — *T. rex*, *Daspletosaurus*, and *Albertosaurus* — that would track us through the Dakota flood plains or try to intercept us in the lush Canadian woods.

The *Corythosauri* did a lot of noisy bassooning. They did it to warn of predators, to let the members of other duckbill clans — *Parasaurolophus*, *Hypacrosaurus*, *Maiasaura*,etc. — know of their nearness (probably to keep them from trespassing on their foraging grounds), and to chase off rival duckbills or timid carnivores.

Button and I took part in some of these performances with our wooden harmonicas. I'd sound a few notes, echoing the call of an upright male in a register too high to make the imitation precisely accurate, and Button would blow an impromptu score of discordant notes that, totally silencing our duckbill kin, would drift across the landscape like the piping of a drunken demigod.

Anyway, by the time we had hiked almost five hundred miles, we were adopted members of the family. Or, rather, one adopted member when Button rode my shoulders, but tolerated hangers-on when he didn't. Trapping small mammals, picking berries, and digging up tubers that we could clean and eat (our T-rations ran out on the twenty-seventh day), we scurried about under the duckbills' feet, but made ourselves such fixtures in their lives that none of the creatures had any apparent wish to run us off.

Thus, we came to recognize individuals, and Button — when I asked him to name the creatures — gave most of them the names of his favorite anserine or ducky characters: Daffy, Mother Goose, Howard, Donald, Daisy, Huey, Dewey, Louie, Scrooge McDuckbill. Adult females, because of their bulk, got monikers like Bertha, Mama Mountain, Beverly Big, Hulga, and Quaker Queen. (I helped with some of these.) We spent the better parts of three days baptizing our *Corythosauri*. Button had such a good time that he wanted me to help him come up with last names, too. I protested that we'd never be able to remember them all. When Button began to sulk, I told him to do the stupid naming himself.

Anyway, we wound up with three McDuckbills, some O'Mallards, a Gooseley, and a covy of Smiths: Daffy Smith, Mama Mountain Smith, Hulga Smith, etc. If, that is, I remember the baptisms correctly. On the other hand, how could I forget any aspect of the most vivid period of my life?

About a month into our trek, we ran into Duckbill Jay McInturff and Bonehead Brett Easley, self-proclaimed "dinosaur men," hunters who traded "lizard beef" and "'gator skins" — welcome supplements to a marine-based economy — to the people in the fishing villages along the northern coastal arc of the Great Inland Sea.

We ran into them because they leapt from the forest through which we were hiking and filled Dewey O'Mallard, a lissome juvenile, with handmade arrows. They shot their arrows, fletched with *Hesperornis* feathers, from polished bows fashioned from *Centrosaurus* ribs and strung with rodent gut. The other duckbills yodeled in dismay, reared, thrashed their tails, and trotted off bipedally in twelve different directions at once. I'd been walking four or five animals behind Dewey, with Button on my shoulders, and when Dewey trumpeted and fell, causing general panic, I simply froze.

The dinosaur men emerged from their natural blinds to butcher Dewey. When they saw Button and me, they started. Then they began asking questions. I took Button, now crying hysterically, from my shoulders. He spat at the men and ran off into the woods. I would have chased him, but the shorter of the two men caught my arm and squeezed it threateningly.

I spent that night with the two dinosaur men. They made camp near Dewey's corpse, tying me to a cycad with a rope of hand-woven horsetail fibers. Why were they tying me? Why weren't they helping me find Button? As they field-dressed Dewey, I shouted, "*Button, come back!*" realizing, even as I yelled, that it would be stupid for him to return to the uncertain situation he had instinctively fled. I shut up.

McInturff and Easley, who had politely introduced themselves, built a fire and roasted over it a white-skinned portion of their kill. They tried to get me to eat with them, but I refused, not because I wasn't hungry or despised dinosaur flesh, but because Button and I had *named* Dewey. How could I turn cannibal?

Despite their Wild West nicknames, Duckbill Jay and Bonehead Brett weren't uneducated yahoos. (To receive permission to use a discontinuity lock, you couldn't be.) But they had separated themselves from other pioneers, dressed up in spiked *Nodosaurus*-hide vests, duckbill-skin leggings, and opossum-belly moccasins, and begun a two-man trading company inspired by North America's rugged trappers of the early 1800's. Playing these parts, they had come to believe that a selfish lawlessness was their birthright.

Unable to coax me to eat, McInturff, a slender, sandy-haired man with a splotchy beard, and Easley, a simian gnome with a high, domed forehead, tried to talk me into joining them. They could use another set of hands, and I'd learn to make arrows, shoot a bow, skin *Parkosauri* butcher duckbills, and sew "fine lizardly duds" — if I let them teach me. They'd also help me find Button so that he, too, could benefit from their woodsy self-improvement program.

I talked to the hunters, without agreeing to this proposal. So they began to ignore me. Easley left the clearing and returned a little later with a half-grown panoplosaur to which was rigged a travois. On this sled, they piled the hide, bones, and butchered flesh of Dewey, after conscientiously treating the meat with sea salt. Then they ambled over to the cycad to which I was bound.

"Any idea where those flute-crests of yours happen to be going, Master Gregson?" McInturff said.

"No, sir."

"Four months from now, the middle of June, they'll hit the Arctic rim, the shore of what Holocene-huggers used to call the Beaufort Sea."

"Holocene-huggers?"

"Stay-at-homes," Easley said. "Baseline-Lubbers."

"You want to traipse eighteen hundred more miles, kid? That's whats in store for you."

"Why?" I said. "Why do they go there?"

"It's a duckbill rookery," McInturff said. "A breeding site. Quite a ways to go to watch a bunch of lizards screw."

"Or," Easley said, "you could link up with some boneheads in the Yukon and tail them across the land bridge into Old Mongolia."

"Where are we now?" I asked.

"Montana," McInturff said. "If Montana existed."

"Its relative vicinity," Easley said. "Given tectonic drift, beaucoups of climatic changes, and the passage of several million years."

I had no idea what to reply. The dinosaur men put out their fire, lay down under the chaotically arrayed stars, drifted off to sleep. Or so I thought. For, shortly after lying down, McInturff and Easley arose again, walked over, unbound my hands, and, in the alien woods, far from any human settlement, took turns poking my backside. I repeatedly cried out, but my tormentors only laughed. When dawn came, they debated whether to kill me or leave me tied up for a passing carnivore. They decided that the second option would free them of guilt and give a human-size predator — a dromaeosaur or a stenonychosaur — several hours of amusing exercise.

"Wish you'd change our mind," Bonehead Brett Easley said. He prodded the sleepy panoplosaur out of its doze.

"Yeah, Master Gregson," Duckbill Jay McInturff said. "We could make good use of you."

Guffawing, they left. The woods moved with a hundred balmy winds. A half hour after the dinosaur men had vanished, Button came running into the clearing to untie me.

It took us most of the day, but using the telltale spoors of shredded vegetation and sour-smelling *Corythosaurus* patties, we tracked our family — Scrooge McDuckbill, Mama Mountain Smith, etc. — to a clearing in the Montana forest. There we tried to rejoin them. But our arrival spooked them, and it was two more days, Button on my shoulders like a tiny maharajah, before we could catch up again, reconvince the duckbills of our harmlessness, and resume our communal trek northwestward.

Long-distance dinosaurs, I reflected. We're going to walk all the way to the Arctic rim with them. Why?

Because the Gregsons had always been loners, because I had good reason not to trust any of the human beings over here, and because we had already forged a workable bond with our "flute crests." Besides, I didn't want to homestead, and there was no one around — close to hand, anyway — to tell us we couldn't attempt anything we damned well pleased.

So Button and I traveled on foot all the way to a beautiful peninsula on the Beaufort Sea, where we heard the duckbills bassoon their melancholy lovesongs and watched hundreds of giant lizards of several different species languidly screw. The males' upright bodies struggled athwart the females' crouching forms, while the tribes' befuddled juveniles looked on almost as gaped-beaked as Button and I. The skies were bluer than blue, the breezes were softer than mammal fur, and the orgasmic bleats of some of the lovesick duckbills were like thunder claps.

Button was dumbstruck, fascinated.

"Sex education," I told him. "Pay attention. Better this way than a few others I can think of."

The males in the mild Arctic forests blew rousing solos and showed off their crests. Those with the deepest voices and the most elaborate skull ornaments were the busiest, reproductively speaking, but there were so many dinosaurs in the rim woods, foraging and colliding, that in less than a month Button and I could see through the shredded gaps as if a defoliant had been applied. We saw boneheads — macho pachycephalosaurs half the size of our duckbills banging their helmeted-looking skulls in forest sections already wholly stripped of undergrowth. The clangor was spooky, as were the combatants' strategic bellows.

Button and I stayed out of the way, fishing off the

coast, gathering berries, trapping muskratlike creatures on the banks of muddy inlets, and keeping a lookout for the human hunters that prowled the edges of the herbivore breeding grounds. We did well staying clear of godzillas like *T. rex* and the *Daspletosaurs*, but, more than once, we narrowly avoided being kicked to tatters by an eleven-foot-tall midnight skulker called — I've since learned — *Dromiceiomimus*. Resembling a cross between an ostrich and a chameleon, this beast could run like the anchor on a relay team. And so Button and I began weaving tree platforms and shinnying upstairs to sleep out of harm's way.

Sexed out and hungry for fresh vegetation, our *Corythosaurus* clan stayed in its breeding haunts only until late July, at which time Scrooge McDuckbill, Daffy Smith, and Donald Gooseley led the group southeastward. Button and I, more comfortable with these lummoxy herbivores than apart from them, tagged along again.

In October, catching the placental odor of the Great Inland Sea, the gravid females (including Quaker Queen, Beverly Big, Mama Mountain, Hulga, Bertha, and several demure ladies from clans that had joined us after our run-in with McInturff and Easley) split off from the unperturbed males and led their youngsters into a coastal region of northern Montana. We went with the females rather than with the males because the females, seeing Button and me as one more gawky kid, matter-of-factly mother-henned us on this journey. Their bodies gave us protection, while their clarinet squeaks and oboe moans offered frankly unambiguous advice.

Then, at an ancestral hatching ground, they dug out mud-banked nests that had fallen in, or fashioned new nests near the old ones. Working hard, the ladies built these nests at least a body-length apart; each nest was about eight feet in diameter and four feet deep at the center of its bowl. When the nests were complete, the female duckbills squatted above the bowls and carefully deposited their eggs (as few as few as twelve, as many is twenty-four) in concentric rings inside the drying pits. Then they left, cropped ferns and other plant materials, waddled back, and conscientiously covered their tough-skinned eggs.

Although I tried to discourage him, warning that he could get trampled or sat upon, Button got involved. He carried dripping loads of vegetation back to the hatching grounds to help Beverly Big and Quaker Queen incubate their lizardings. And when their eggs broke open and baby hadrosaurs poked their beaked noggins out, Button not only helped the mama duckbills feed them, but sometimes crawled into the muck-filled nests and hunkered among the squeaking youngsters. No mother seemed to resent his presence, but what *almost* cured Button of this behavior was having Quaker Queen drop a bolus of well-chewed fruit on him. Even that accident didn't keep him from stalking the mud bridges between nests, though, watching and waiting as our dinosaur siblings rapidly grew.

Button and I stayed with our *Corythosauri* for more than three years (if "years" beyond a discontinuity divide have any meaning). We migrated seasonally with our duckbill family, going from south to north in the "winter" and from north to south toward the end of "summer." We saw the hadrosaurs mate in their breeding grounds, and, after the females had laid their eggs, we stayed in the muddy hatching grounds like bumbling midwives-in-training.

On each seasonal trek, we saw animals for whom we had developed great affection — Daffy, Bertha, a host of nameless youngsters — run down and murdered by the T-kings and the *Albertosauri* that opportunistically dogged our marches. During our third year with the duckbills, in fact, I figured out that only sixty-four of over eight hundred hatchlings made it out of the nest and less than half the survivors reached the Arctic breeding grounds with their adult relatives. Agility, stealth, and even simple puniness often saved Button and me, but the hadrosaurs weren't so lucky. Many of those that didn't fall to predators succumbed to parasites, accidents, or mysterious diseases. The forests and uplands of the Late Cretaceous could be beautiful, but life there wasn't always pretty. (Maybe our folks, escaping it so soon, had known true mercy.)

As for human pioneers from the blasted twenty-second century, A.D., Button and I had no desire to consort with them. At times, we saw smoke from their villages; and, on each of our migrations, bands of human nomads, archers in lizard-skin clothing, helped the T-kings cull the weakest members of the herds, whether duckbills, boneheads, fleet-footed hypsilophodonts, or horned dinosaurs. In large bands, though, the archers sometimes risked everything and went after a *Tyrannosaurus*. Once, from a mountainside in eastern Alberta, Button and I watched a dozen Lilliputian archers surround and kill an enraged Gulliver of a T-king. Neither of us was sorry, but it isn't always true that the killer of your greatest enemy is automatically your friend.

McInturff and Easley came into our lives again the year that Button — who had long ago given up talking in favor of playing duckbill calls on his harmonica — turned eight. Along with nine or ten other raiders, they targeted the duckbills' Montana hatching grounds, shooed off as many of the mothers as possible, and killed all those inclined to defend their nests. The men were egg gathering, for reasons I never fully understood — restocking the fishing villages' larders, providing a caulking substance for boats — and Button and I escaped only because the men came into the nesting grounds shouting, banging bones together, and blowing *Triceratops* trumpets. There was no need for stealth; they *wanted* the females to flee. So Button and I hurried out of there along with the more timid hadrosaur mothers.

The next day, I crept back to the area to see what was going on. On a wooded hillside above the main nesting floor, I found an egg that had long ago petrified, hefted it as if it were an ancient cannonball, and duck-walked with it to an overlook where the activity of the nest raiders was all too visible. Easley, his bald pate gleaming like a bleached pachycephalosaur skull, was urging his men to gather eggs more quickly, wrap them in ferns, and stack them gently in their sharkskin sacks.

The sight of Easley's head was an insupportable annoyance. I raised myself to a crouch, took aim, and catapulted my petrified egg straight at his head. The egg dropped like a stone, smashing his skull and knocking him into one of the hollowed-out nests. He died instantly. All his underlings began to shout and scan the hillside. I made no effort to elude discovery. Three or four of them scrambled up the overlook's slope, wrestled me down, secured my hands with horsetail fibers, and frog-marched me back down to the hatching site to meet Duckbill Jay McInturff.

"I remember you," McInturff said. "Brett and I had a chance to kill you once. I'll bet Brett's sorry we didn't do it."

It seemed likely that McInturff would order me killed on the spot, but maybe the presence of so many other men, not all of them as indifferent to judicial process as he, kept him from it. After finishing their egg collecting, they tied my hands at the small of my back, guyed my head erect with a lizard-skin cord knotted to my bindings, and made me walk drag behind an ankylosaur travois loaded with egg sacks and another hammocking Easley's corpse.

At a village on the Great Inland Sea, I was locked for at least a week in a tool shed with a dirt floor.

Through the holes in its roof, I could sometimes see gulls and pteranodons wheeling.

I had lost my parents, I had lost Button, I had lost our family of hadrosaurs. It seemed clear that McInturff and his egg-hunting cohorts would either hang me from a willow tree or paddle me out to sea and toss me overboard to the archaic fishes or ichthyosaurs that yet remained. I was almost resigned to dying, but I missed Button and feared that, only eight years old, he wouldn't last too long among the harried duckbills.

The last night I spent in the tool shed, I heard a harmonica playing at some distance inland and knew that Button was trying to tell me hello, or good-bye, or possibly "It's all right, brother, I'm still alive." The music ceased quickly, making me doubt I'd really heard it, then played again a little nearer, reconvincing me of Button's well-being, and stopped forever a moment or so later. Button himself made no appearance, but I was glad of that because the villagers would have captured him and sent him back through a discontinuity lock to the Here-and-Now.

That, you see, is what they did to me. The sheriff of Glasgow, the fishing settlement where I was confined, knew a disaffected family who had applied for repatriation. He shipped me with them, trussed like a slave, when they made their journey back toward the Mississippi Valley Time-Slip, just across from St. Jo, Missouri, and the unappealing year known as 2111 A.D. Actually, because of a fast-forward screw-up of some esoteric sort, we recrossed in 2114. Once back, I was tried for Easley's murder in Springfield, found guilty of it on the basis of affidavits from McInturff and several upright egg raiders, and sentenced to twenty-five years in prison. I have just finished serving that sentence.

From the few accounts that sometimes slip back through, Button grew up with the *Corythosauri*. Over there, he's still with them, living off the land and avoiding human contact. It's rumored that, at nineteen, he managed to kill Duckbill Jay McInturff and to catch in deadfalls some of McInturff's idiot henchmen. (God forgive me, I hope he did.)

Because of my murder conviction, I'm ineligible to recross, but more and more people in our desolate century use the locks every year, whether a gate to the Late Cretaceous or a portal on another continent to a wholly different geologic or historical time. This tropism to presumably greener stomping grounds reminds me of the herding and migrating instincts of the dinosaurs with whom Button and I lived so many "years" ago. And with whom Button, of course, is probably living yet.

One gate, I'm told, a discontinuity lock in Siberia, debouches on an epoch in which humanity has been extinct for several million years. I'd like to use that lock and see the curious species that have either outlived us or evolved in our absence. Maybe I will. A document given me on leaving prison notes that this Siberian lock is the only one I am now eligible to use. Tomorrow, then, I intend to put in an application.

9.

Dinosaur Behavior

Essay by Ralph Molnar

Speculation by Ray Bradbury

THE BEHAVIOR OF PREDATORY DINOSAURS

RALPH MOLNAR

"One can well imagine the singular effect which these huge gregarious reptiles would produce, standing motionless, goblin-like, on a horizon lit by a full moon; or lying with outstretched neck and ponderous haunches basking in the noonday sun."

— *Edward Drinker Cope, 1868*

ONE HUNDRED FIFTY MILLION YEARS AGO THE WORLD WAS DIFFERENT, A FABULOUS PLACE FULL OF fantastic beasts. This was near the middle of the Mesozoic Era, when dinosaurs still lived. Not only were the beasts fabulous, but some were frightful — more so than any land animal now alive. These were the great predatory dinosaurs, the theropods, including such famous creatures as *Tyrannosaurus rex*. These animals are no longer the obscure domain of paleontologists, for nearly all school children and thus their parents know of them.

Jacques Gauthier recently established a classification of theropod dinosaurs into six groups: ceratosaurs, carnosaurs, ornithomimosaurs, oviraptorosaurs, troodontids and dromaeosaurs.

THE DESCENT OF BIRDS

Amazingly, near relatives of these beasts are still with us. They are the birds. We might ask if bird behavior is any clue to theropod behavior, and of course whether we can deduce bird evolution and behavior from the theropod fossil record.

The question is from just which theropods birds are descended. In some features, such as the attachment of the vertebral column to the pelvis, the small theropods differ more from birds than large theropods such as *Allosaurus* and *Megalosaurus* do. The Mongolian *Avimimus*, a small animal possibly related to oviraptorosaurs, showed remarkable similarities to birds — but, as we shall see, this is not helpful. It had enlarged cerebral and cerebellar regions of the brain like those of modern birds. The hind limb was sim-

ilar to a bird's, particularly at the knee, and there is evidence that the wrist bones were fused to form a single element known as a carpometacarpus, otherwise found only in birds. Most intriguing, however, is a mechanism of the forearm that links movement at the elbow to rotation of the forearm. In birds this mechanism spreads the feathers when the wing is spread and tucks them away when it is folded. What this did for *Avimimus*, unless it also had feathers, is incomprehensible. In detail, however, this mechanism is different from that in birds, so *Avimimus* could not have been their ancestor, or even closely related.

Other theropods were also similar to birds. For example, the skull and feet of ornithomimosaurs were like those of birds. Dromaeosaurs had a similar configuration of certain wrist bones and generally similar proportions of the forelimb and pelvis, including a backward-directed pubis. Troodonts were similar in certain details of skull structure. Oviraptorosaurs also had birdlike skulls and seem to have had a furcula (wishbone). Nonetheless, there is no one group of theropods that is now generally accepted as including the ancestors of the birds.

If birds are descendants of theropod dinosaurs, then presumably birds learned to fly from the ground up, so to speak. John Ostrom has proposed that feathers evolved to aid in snaring fast-moving insects with the forelimbs. Jacques Gauthier and Kevin Padian carried this further, suggesting that small theropods habitually folded their forelimbs. In capturing prey these were unfolded and swung forward and upwards and this movement formed the basis for the wingbeat.

Maybe — but not everyone agrees, and not all the evidence supports this view. There is some evidence (not generally accepted) for feathers or similar structures in animals much older than *Archaeopteryx*. One early relative of the dinosaurs, *Megalancosaurus*, had many birdlike features in the skull, forelimb and pelvis, but is much older than theropods and not closely related. And recent detailed studies of how bird flight originated suggest that birds learned to fly by gliding from trees or rocks, and not from the ground up. Still, most evidence at present suggests that this group of frightful "killing machines," the theropods, probably was responsible for bringing into the world the bright colors, beautiful songs and cheerful (if sometimes inane) behavior of today's birds.

Unlike some other dinosaurs, theropods have been found just about everywhere that dinosaurs have been sought. Their fossils are known from North and South America, Europe, Asia, Africa, Australia, and probably New Zealand; only Antarctica has no theropods. But only two Antarctic dinosaurs are known to date — sooner or later theropod fossils will be found there as well. Theropods are probably the longest-lived of any dinosaur group. They appeared in Late Triassic times (around 230 million years ago) and lasted until the end of the Cretaceous (65 million years ago), thriving for longer than 150 million years — almost twice as long as any living groups of mammals or birds.

THE BITE OF THE DINOSAUR

So what was it that gave these great carnivores their impressive success in staying alive? Perhaps the most significant thing about the great predators is just that — they were predators. The efficient killing and eating of other large animals dictated many features of theropod anatomy. It led to the possession of large heads with large mouths (the better to bite with) often lined by large, backward-curved teeth. These flattened, recurved, saberlike teeth easily penetrated the skin of the prey, because the force of closing the mouth was concentrated directly through the sharp tips of the teeth. Backward-curved teeth also keep prey (which quite naturally object to being prey) from escaping the grip of the predator — it is easier to slide toward the throat, along the curve of the tooth, than to get out again.

The edges of the teeth were lined with small denticles, that gave a steak-knife-like serration. Like steak-knives, these easily sliced skin and muscle. The more advanced theropods, such as *Allosaurus*, *Tyrannosaurus* and *Ornitholestes*, had more or less straight, peglike teeth at the front of the mouth for holding or gripping the flesh sliced by teeth along the cheeks.

It has been argued that the largest of theropods, creatures such as *Allosaurus*, *Spinosaurus*, *Tarbosaurus*, and *Tyrannosaurus*, were not active predators, just scavengers. Yet these arguments seem to mean more to the people involved in them than to the animals themselves. Most modern predators also scavenge (e.g., lions), and many scavengers (e.g., Tasmanian devils) also sometimes kill prey. Certainly crocodilians do both. The important thing to the animal, after all, is simply to eat. Disregarding the emotional overtones of whether an animal is a predator or a scavenger, a more useful division of carnivorous feeding habits

Above: The forest shook when the fearsome giant carnivores of the Late Cretaceous walked by. Here a tyrannosaurid, the Albertosaur, *sniffs for prey. By Brian Franczak. Preceding spread:* Deinonychus *were swift, clever hunters, as shown in this scene of a hunting party stalking across a Middle Cretaceous swamp. By Doug Henderson.*

seems to be between those animals that can crush bones (like hyenas or Tasmanian devils) versus those that cut flesh. Crushing bones requires strong muscles and robust teeth — the large predatory dinosaurs, especially *Tyrannosaurus*, clearly met these requirements. But this doesn't imply that they avoided killing live prey.

Certainly the skulls of some theropods are constructed to produce a very strong bite. Without knowledge of the details of their jaw muscles, we cannot estimate just how strong they were, but the jaw musculature of *Tyrannosaurus* was approximately 15 centimeters in diameter on each side, so its bite must have been impressive! In *Tyrannosaurus* and *Nanotyrannus* the chambers housing the jaw muscles were enlarged compared to those of other large theropods, such as *Allosaurus*. Presumably the bite was stronger than in *Allosaurus*. Although theropods usually had rather long snouts, some, such as *Carnotaurus*, had very short snouts that brought the teeth nearer the point of attachment of the jaw muscles. This increased the leverage, and hence the force, applied to the food. In general it seems that the large theropods could bite hard enough to tear apart their prey, and probably crush the bones. Their eating abilities were enhanced by joints within the jaws, roughly like those found in pythons, that allowed the mouth to open more widely, and the teeth to be positioned more effectively. *Allosaurus* even had joints within the skull that raised the snout, enabling it to engulf large pieces of meat.

THEROPODS' FOOD AND HOW THEY HUNTED FOR IT

What theropods ate, however, is a trickier question. Both *Coelophysis* and *Compsognathus* fossils have, within their ribcages, skeletons that testify respectively to the "cannibalism" and agility of these dinosaurs. Specimens of *Coelophysis* have been found at Ghost Ranch (unintentionally aptly named), New Mexico, with skeletons of young *Coelophysis* within. Eating one's offspring is a quick road to extinction, and as *Coelophysis* did not become extinct that quickly, we may assume that the adults were not eating their

own offspring. The first specimen (of the only two) of *Compsognathus* had fed upon a small lizard, *Bavarisaurus* by name. We would expect Late Jurassic small lizards to have been just as agile and swift-running as their modern descendants, and for a *Compsognathus* to have caught one requires quite respectable agility and swiftness of foot. The big theropods have left no such informative fossils; however, some fossils of sauropods retain marks of teeth, probably of *Allosaurus*. So this theropod fed, or at least scavenged, on some very large prey indeed.

Ornithomimosaurs and oviraptorosaurs (both toothless), may have been herbivores and egg-eaters respectively. We now think ornithomimosaurs fed on small animals that they raked out of the forest litter with their long, grasping hands. The absence of teeth would have bothered them no more than it does modern secretary birds. Oviraptorosaurs seem to have been shore- and bank-dwellers, crushing bivalves between their short, stout jaws. The other small theropods — dromaeosaurs, *Coelurus*, and the like — seem to have been predators like their large relatives.

For the large theropods, size alone was a potent determinant of their structure. The vertebral column had to be strong to support the weight of the body (and of the tail in the other direction) and transmit it to the limb bones. Having vertebrae as light as possible, for their strength, would be advantageous, and this was achieved by cavities in the vertebrae. The hind limb bones supported the body, and during walking each had to support the entire body weight, so these bones were robust. The hollow construction of the vertebrae may have been a factor in allowing some theropod dinosaurs to grow to their great size. Even small theropods, such as *Coelurus*, had remarkably hollow vertebrae. This seems to be a case of a structure that served some unknown purpose (perhaps related to breathing?) in small theropods, also allowing them to evolve to great size without becoming overly heavy.

Another interesting instance of this tendency to low density skeletons involves the skulls of theropods, especially the larger kinds such as *Allosaurus* (although not the tyrannosaurs). In these the skull is actually more lightly built than in small forms. Great apertures, the fenestrae, occur in the cheek region of the skull, behind the eyes, and also along the sides of the snout. These fenestrae are characteristic of all theropods, and indeed of all primitive dinosaurs, but in allosaurs and abelisaurs they were relatively larger than in others. In addition to these fenestrae, which lightened the skull by converting it essentially into a framework of rods and bars, the skulls of carnivorous dinosaurs (including the tyrannosaurs) had an impressive system of cavities in the snout, jaws, and particularly in the bone surrounding the brain.

Next to eating, getting around is important to an animal. Carnivorous dinosaurs — with the exception of the seemingly quadrupedal Chinese *Xuanhanosaurus* — got around on two legs, rather than four as in mammalian carnivores. This is not because two legs are inherently more (or less) efficient, but because it appears to have been the result of dinosaurian history. The eary thecodontian ancestors of dinosaurs had relatively short forelimbs. It is not clear why, but may have been related to their ability to swim. Runing requires long steps, and long hindlimbs tend to collide with forelimbs, so it is easier, and more efficient, to get the forelimbs out of the way by raising them off the ground altogether.

But, as young children show, in using two legs — as opposed to four — standing comes before walking. Standing on two legs implies a certain minimum ability to balance. After all, if its balance was not good, the beast would soon be on all fours. Standing on two legs requires constant use of the limb muscles to keep

from toppling over. The long tails of the theropods certainly helped maintain their balance, but even so strong hind-limb muscles would have been necessary to keep the dinosaur upright.

Like other dinosaurs, theropods held the limbs under the body, and probably ran much like modern flightless birds. Their limb joints were basically hinges, like our knees, but in theropods not only the knees, but also the hip and ankle joints were hinge joints. It is useful for large animals to keep their feet placed as nearly under their center of gravity as they can, and so it comes as no surprise that fossil theropod tracks overlap, indicating that their feet were held close together. That theropods walked is clear enough, but how fast they could move and whether they ran is still far from clear. Different paleontologists have different interpretations. Robert Bakker and Gregory Paul contend that tyrannosaurs could run at up to about 70 kilometers per hour; others say this is "preposterous." There is some evidence from trackways that large theropods could run at up to about 40 kilometers per hour, and it is generally accepted that ornithomimosaurs could probably run at least 50 kilometers per hour.

In addition to running, or at least walking, there is good evidence that theropods could swim. Certain tracks of large (and small) theropods from the Connecticut Valley and Colorado show that they were swimming, and just barely touching bottom with their hind claws. This seems not to have been unusual behavior. A group of tracks from Brazil represents about 40 individuals (perhaps abelisaurs) swimming.

Of what use were the small forelimbs? Certainly this would depend upon which theropod one had in mind. Although the forelimbs are smaller than the rear ones, the hand is quite large in comparison with the rest of the forelimb. In ornithomimosaurs and dromaeosaurs the forelimbs were used in gathering food. But what about the very small forelimbs of the tyrannosaurs? Henry Fairfield Osborn thought they were used during mating, and Barney Newman suggested they might have been used to assist the beast in arising from lying down, a more prosaic, but no less necessary function. Most likely they served several functions.

And speaking of mating, little is known about the reproduction of carnivorous dinosaurs. Presumably they laid eggs, as did other dinosaurs, but theropod eggs have not yet been recognized.

THEROPOD ANATOMY AND PACK BEHAVIOR

The brains of carnivorous dinosaurs, as of dinosaurs in general, were smaller relative to the size of the bodies than in most living mammals and birds. On the other hand the old chestnut about the brain being the size of a walnut is simply wrong. In size the brain was quite large, and in relation to body size, it was as large as would be expected from living reptiles. However, it is not the size, or even the relative size, of a brain that counts in staying alive but the sophistication of the "wiring patterns"; that is, how well the brain provides for behavior that keeps the beast well fed, out of danger and attractive to the opposite sex. This has no obvious relationship to the size of the brain and can be deduced only, if at all, from fossils that preserve effects of the creature's behavior. Still, it is clear that dinosaurs, and especially the carnivorous dinosaurs, were not the stupid creatures of cartoons and the popular imagination. Dinosaur brains, of course, have not been preserved, and we must deduce their form and size from that of the brain cavity of the skull. The brain cavity of carnivorous dinosaurs is known for only a few kinds, including *Allosaurus, Ceratosaurus, Dromaeosaurus, Tarbosaurus, Troodon* and *Tyrannosaurus*. In all of these, it indicates a brain

of basically the same form: the great development of cerebral hemispheres, found in mammals, is absent. Instead the forebrain lies horizontally, as does the hindbrain, and these are connected by an inclined midbrain. The forebrain seems only slightly expanded in the large theropods, but is substantially enlarged in small forms. In fact, theropods were the dinosaurs that had, relatively speaking, the largest brains, or at least, the largest brain cavities. *Allosaurus* and *Ceratosaurus* reportedly had unusually large brain cavities (for their sizes), although troodonts and ornithomimosaurs probably had relatively the largest brains of any dinosaurs. They were comparable to those of modern birds and some mammals.

The large orbits (eyesockets) suggest that theropods possessed acute vision, and the large size of the olfactory tracts leading to the brain likewise suggests acute smell. The stapes (the bone that transmitted sound to the inner ear in dinosaurs) is known only in *Dromaeosaurus*. It suggests that the hearing was acute. There is even evidence that some carnivorous dinosaurs (such as *Tyrannosaurus, Carnotaurus,* and *Troodon*) had stereoscopic vision. In these animals the orbits are oriented so there was considerable overlap of the fields of vision as in cats or humans. However, simply having forward-facing eyes does not guarantee stereoscopic vision. All it guarantees is not being able to see in back of one's head. Oilbirds have forward-facing eyes but lack stereoscopic vision. However, the small theropod *Troodon* not only had forward-facing orbits, but also forelimbs suited for grasping. Though the evidence for stereoscopic vision in theropods is inconclusive, the occurrence of both forward-directed eyes and grasping forelimbs together in the same animal suggests that stereoscopic vision was present. *Troodon* probably used its forelimbs to capture prey.

Many theropod dinosaurs (among them *Allosaurus, Albertosaurus, Alioramus, Carnotaurus, Cerato-*

saurus, Dilophosaurus, Oviraptor, and *Procerato- saurus*) had crests or horns on the skull, either on the snout or over the eyes. Such structures were not useful for catching prey or, at least in some instances, for fighting among themselves. In modern-day animals, mountain sheep for example, horns are often symbols of status in the social hierarchy. This in turn suggests that there were a social hierarchy and social interactions among the carnivorous dinosaurs. Modern mammalian carnivores and crocodiles do not have horns, antlers and such, and this suggests that in some ways the lives of theropods must have differed from those of modern large meat-eaters. The modern animals that do have horns and antlers are the herbivorous mammals, such as deer, antelope, and the like. These are, by and large, animals that hold territories, which suggests that perhaps the prey of the theropod dinosaurs was sufficiently abundant that they also could afford to hold territories. Holding territories in turn suggests fighting over them. There are some injuries to the bones of *Allosaurus* and *Tyrannosaurus* that seem to have been made by biting. So perhaps such fighting did occur between these animals.

Although some theropods probably hunted individually, there is evidence for hunting in packs as well. Fossils of several theropods, especially ceratosaurs such as *Coelophysis, Dilophosaurus,* and *Syntarsus,* have been found in groups, of from 3 to several hundred individuals. And there are tracks that indicate several individuals traveled and hunted together at the same time (as for the swimming Brazilian theropods mentioned above).

Were Dinosaurs Warm-Blooded?

These considerations have led some paleontologists to believe that dinosaurs were warm-blooded. However, whether the blood is warm or cool is not really important; after all, a "cold-blooded" lizard basking on a rock in the Andes can have a higher body temperature than a "warm-blooded" echidna in Australia. What is important is the source of the heat. Thus physiologists speak of "endothermic" and "ectothermic" animals, rather than "warm-blooded" and "cold-blooded" ones. Ectothermic animals are those that derive most of their heat directly from the sun — solar-heated animals, so to speak — and endothermic animals are those that generate their own heat internally. But why be endothermic? What are the advantages? Chiefly, that by generating your own energy you, the animal, have a higher rate of metabolism and so can be more active for longer periods than ectothermic animals, which need prolonged periods of warming up in the sun. Endothermic animals are able to get out and about on cloudy or chilly days, and even at night. The drawback is that having a higher metabolic rate is not exactly cost-effective: you need to eat about ten times as much food per day as an ectothermic animal of the same size. Another disadvantage of ectothermy is that, if there are any endothermic predators around, you, the ectotherm, will become cost-effective food: the endotherms will be out and about and eating before you are warmed up enough to get away. The potential benefits of endothermy to predators are obvious, and mammals may well have perfected endothermy, because the early types were predators.

Unfortunately one cannot simply go out and offer a thermometer to a dinosaur (even if they were still alive), so various indirect methods of finding the body temperatures of dinosaurs have been tried. These include comparison with modern animals, inferences from their anatomic structures, and computer modeling of their thermal behavor.

Just as large objects heat up and cool off slowly, so did large dinosaurs. Therefore, if a theropod were large enough and able to bask in the sun long enough to thoroughly heat up, it could maintain this temperature through short cold spells. This effect of size is known as gigantothermy. How large did the theropod need to be? Well, *Allosaurus*, *Ceratosaurus*, and the tyrannosaurs were big enough to be gigantotherms.

Another factor related to body temperature is the level of activity of the animal, which can be inferred from the form of the joints. Theropod joints are like those of birds, with smooth surfaces and clear, distinct forms — not like the rather rough cartilage-covered joints of lizards and turtles. Such smoothly surfaced joints suggest that theropods were active beasts. And in addition there is *Deinonychus* with its slashing claw on the second toe of each foot and its semi-rigid balancing pole of a tail. If the slashing claw was used for anything, that animal must have been both agile and active — you can't just wait for your prey to crawl underfoot in order to slash at it. *Deinonychus* must have been able to strike with one foot while balancing on the other, and since prey animals usually don't stand still for this kind of treatment, this was probably carried out on the run, or at least on the jog. This implies the kind of prolonged activity seen in endothermic mammals and birds, rather than ectothermic lizards and turtles. On the other hand *Deinonychus* may have slashed with both feet together while jumping, but this also implies a level of activity comparable to those of endothermic beasts.

The elongate spines of the vertebral column of *Spinosaurus* are also interesting in this context, although their implications are not so clear. No matter what their primary function (which may have been social display),they must also have affected the blood temperature of the animal, if only because they presented so large a surface to the air (and sunlight). They would have functioned as a radiator, to absorb solar heat when cool, and radiate heat when the

spinosaur was warm. This doesn't indicate that spinosaurs were endothermic, but it does imply a capacity for more sophisticated control of body temperature than in living ectotherms.

The microstructure of theropod bones has also been used to argue that they were endothermic animals. In mammals certain portions of the bone are absorbed during growth, and then redeposited. This results in a characteristic microstructure known as Haversian systems. Such structures have also been found in theropod (and other dinosaurian) bones. The problem here is that the Haversian systems are not directly related to body temperature, and may in fact reflect only the large size of the dinosaurs, rather than their metabolic rates. They have also been reported in large non-dinosaurian reptiles.

Because endothermic predators must eat about ten times as much food per week as ectothermic predators of the same size, a given population of prey animals will support different numbers of endothermic than of ectothermic carnivores. While one pig might support a crocodile for a month, a tiger of the same weight would need ten. So if it were possible to count up the potential prey-dinosaurs in a given region, and the theropods, one could determine if the theropods were endothermic or ectothermic — couldn't one? Well, yes, but only if one were prepared to make some rather unlikely assumptions about the theropods. These include assuming that almost all the theropods and their prey not only became fossilized at the same rate, but also were found by paleontologists in those proportions. It would also require assuming that the theropods ate only these prey animals, and never wandered off over the river to try something different for a change. However, even making these assumptions, the story is not clear: Robert Bakker and James Farlow, working from the same data on Late Cretaceous theropods and their prey, from

Alberta, came to diametrically opposing conclusions. Bakker claimed the data showed theropods were endothermic, while Farlow concluded the data more convincingly showed they weren't. The whole question is far from settled, but if birds are descendants of theropods, as many now believe, then at least one line of small theropods very likely was endothermic.

The carnivorous dinosaurs are all extinct, the last of them dead for 65 million years. But it is fun, and sometimes instructive, to ask what would have happened if events had not gone as they did. What if theropods had not become extinct? One paleontologist, Dale Russell, has suggested that if troodonts continued to evolve in the same fashion as they had — a rather big if — they might have developed into intelligent, social, cultural creatures much like us. Maybe the greatest influence of theropods on the modern world was not what they did, but what they didn't. They didn't survive — if they had, maybe you and I would both be troodonts reading here about our own distant ancestry.

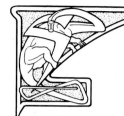

Besides a Dinosaur, Whatta Ya Wanna Be When You Grow Up?

Ray Bradbury

ASK ME A QUESTION, OKAY?"

Benjamin Spaulding, aged twelve, had spoken. The boys, strewn on the summer lawn around him, didn't so much as blink an eye or wag a tail. The dogs, strewn with them, did just about the same. One yawned.

"Go on," said Bejamin. "Someone ask."

Maybe it was staring at the sky that made him say it. Up there were great shapes, strange beasts traveling who-knows-where out of who-knew-when. Maybe it was a growl of thunder beyond the horizon, a storm making up its mind to arrive. Or maybe this made him remember the shadows in the Field Museum where Old Time stirred like those other shadows seen last Saturday matinee when they reran *The Lost World* and monsters fell off cliffs and the boys stopped running up and down the aisles and yelled with terror and delight. Maybe —

"Okay," said one of the boys, eyes shut, so far deep in boredom he couldn't even yawn. "Like — whatta you wanna be when you grow up?"

"A dinosaur," said Benjamin Spaulding.

As if on cue, thunder sounded on the horizon.

The boys opened their eyes.

"A *what*?!!"

"Yeah, but *besides* a dinosaur — ?"

"No," said Benjamin. "No other job worth having."

He eyed those clouds which moved in titanic shapes to eat each other away. Great legs of lightning strode over the land.

"Dinosaur — " whispered Benjamin.

"Let's get *outa* here!"

One dog led the way, the boys followed, snorting. "Dinosaurs? Ha! Dinosaurs!"

Benjamin jumped up and shook his fist. "You be what *you* wanna be, I'll be *mine!*"

But they were gone. Only one dog stayed, and he looked nervous and miserable.

"Heck with them. Come on, Rex. Let's eat!"

But just then the rain arrived. Rex ran. Benjamin stayed, looked proudly this way or that, head high, not minding the drench. Then, with miniature majesty, alone but wet and wondrous, he stalked across the lawn.

Thunder opened the front door for him. Thunder slammed it tight.

Self-made described Grandpa. Trouble was, he often said, shoveling in the chicken and spading in the apple pie to tamp it down, he had never decided what to make of himself.

So he had kind of run up a ramshackle life out of one-part railroad engineer, retired early to become town librarian, retired early to run for Mayor, retired early from that without ever starting. At present he was fulltime operator of a Print Shop downtown and a dandelion wine press in the anti-Prohibition cellar of Grandma's boarding house. Between shop and cellar, he prowled his vast library which spilled over into dining room, halls, closets, and all bedrooms adjoining, up or down. His multitudinous hobbies included

MEAKER

collecting butterflies trapped and kept on auto radiator screens, flower intimidation in a garden which refused his thumb, and grandson watching.

Right now, said watching was like buying a ticket for a volcano.

The volcano was inactive, seated at the noon table. Grandpa, sensing some hidden eruption, napkined his mouth and said:

"What's new out in that great world today? Fallen out of any flora lately? Some fauna, mad bees that is, chase you home?"

Benjamin hesitated. Boarders were arriving like cannibals and leaving like Christians. He waited for some new cannibals to start chewing, and then said:

"Found a lifetime job for myself."

Grandpa whistled softly. "Name the occupation!"

Benjamin named it.

"Jehoshaphat." Grandpa, to gain time, cut himself another chunk of pie. "Great you decided so young. But, how you go into training for that?"

"You got books in your library, Gramps."

"Chockful." Grandpa toyed with the crust. "But I don't recall any How To books dating from the Jurassic or the Cretaceous, when killing was the fashion and nobody seemed to mind...."

"You got billions of magazines in the cellar, Grampa, half a zillion in the attic." Benjamin turned his flapjacks like pages, seeing the wonders. "Got to have nine hundred ninety pictures of primeval times and the stuff that lived there!"

Trapped in his awful habit of never throwing anything out, Grandpa could only say, quietly, "Benjamin —"

He lowered his eyes. The boy's parents, when he was ten, had vanished in a storm on the lake. They and their boat were never found. Since that time, various relatives had had to go down to the lake to find Benjamin yelling at the water and shouting, where was

everyone and why didn't they come home? But he was down at the lake less often these days, and more often in the boarding house here. And now — Grandpa frowned — in the library.

"Not just any old dinosaur," Benjamin interrupted. "I'm out to be the best!"

"Brontosaurs?" suggested Grandpa. "They're nice."

"Nope!"

"*Allosaurus*, now, you take *Allosaurus*. Pretty as toe-dancers, the way they kind of *sneak* along —"

"Nope!"

"Pterodactyls?" Grandpa was in fever now, leaning forward. "Fly high, look like those pictures of kite-machines drawn by Leonardo, you know, da Vinci."

"Pterodactyls," Benjamin mused, nodding, "are almost Number One."

"What is, then?"

"Rex," whispered the boy.

Grandpa glanced around. "You call the dog?"

"Rex." Benjamin shut his eyes and called out the full name. "*Tyrannosaurus rex!*"

"Hot diggety," said Grandpa. "There's a name that rings. King of 'em all, eh?"

Benjamin was lost in time, mist, and sump-water trackless bogs.

"King," he whispered, "of 'em all." He blinked his eyes wide, suddenly. "Got any ideas, Gramps?"

The old man flinched under that sunfire stare.

"No. Er — just let me know what you find. In your research...."

"Yay!" Taking this as approval, Benjamin vaulted from his chair, shot toward the door, froze, and turned. "Besides a library, where do you put in for it?"

"Put *in*?"

"Firemen put in at fire stations to train. Locomotive engineers put in at depots to learn. Doctors —"

"Where," said Grandpa. "Where does a boy go to

graduate *summa cum laude* in First Class A-1 Lizard?"

"*All* that!"

"Field Museum, maybe. Full of bones from God's lower attic. Dinosaur college, boy! *Take* you there!"

"Gosh, Gramps, thanks! We'll be so happy, we'll run up and down, yelling!"

And—bang! the front door slammed. The boy was gone.

"I bet we will, Benjamin."

Grandpa poured more syrup in patterns of golden light and peered down into the bright stuff, wondering how to douse a boy so full of fire.

"I bet we will," he said.

A great mad beast arrived, a great wild monster took them away. The train, that is, to Chicago, and Benjamin and Grandpa on it, in the belly of the beast, as 'twere, trading smiles and shouts.

"Chicago!" cried the conductor.

"How come," Benjamin said, frowning, "he didn't mention the Field Museum?!"

"*I'll* mention it," said Grandpa. And, a few minutes later, "Here it *is*!"

Inside they moved under murals of beasts to gape at monsters so dandy it knocked your wind out. Here they marveled at lost flesh, there they gasped at refound-restrung skeletons, hand in hand, wonder in wonder, young joy leading old remembrance of joy.

"Gramps, you ever notice? Look! This whole darn great place, and no guys, no folks from Green Town here!"

"Just you and me, Benjamin."

"Only folks I remember from home being here, a long time ago was"—the boy's voice faded to a whisper—"Mom and Dad...."

To keep the moment from slopping over, Grandpa cut quickly in: "They sure did love it, boy. But now, look! Come on!"

They trotted over to be amazed, stunned, and awed by a pride of nightmares painted by Charles L. Knight.

"Man's a poet with a brush," said Grandpa, teetering on the brink of this Grand Canyon of Time. "Shakespeare on a wall. Now, Benjamin, where's that big dog, Rex, you been hankering on?"

"*That* skyscraper! That's *him!*"

They went to stand under the vast shape, their eyes playing silent tunes on the long xylophone necklace of bones.

"Wish we had a ladder."

"Climb up like mad dentists and tell him to open wide?"

"Ain't that a *grin*, Grandpa?"

"Similar to my mother-in-law at our wedding. You want to perch on my shoulders, Ben?"

"Could I?"

On Grandpa's shoulders, Benjamin, with one wondrous gasp, touched—the ancient Smile.

Then, as if something were wrong, he touched his own lips, his gums, his teeth.

"Stick your head in, boy," said Grandpa. "See if he *bites*!"

Somehow the weeks ran on, the summer slid by, the books piled up, the sketches got laid out in Benjamin's room: blueprints of bones, dental charts from the Jurassic and Cretaceous.

"Also, the My Gracious," mused Grandpa, peeking in. "What's *that*?"

"Sockdolager paintings by Mr. Knight, the man who sees through time, and *paints* it!"

Just then a pebble rapped the upstairs window.

"Hey!" cried some voices down below. "Ben!"

Ben went to the window, raised it, and yelled through the screen. "What do you want?"

It was one of the boys on the lawn below. "Ain't seen you in weeks, Ben. Come on swimming."

"Who cares," said Ben.

"Making ice cream, later, at Jim's."

"Who cares!" Ben slammed the window and turned to find a further aghast grandparent.

"I thought banana ice cream turned you mad with desire," said the old one. "You haven't been out in weeks! Hold'er, Newt." Grandpa delved into his pockets, sorted papers, found an announcement. "I know a way! Read!"

Benjamin grabbed and read:

> SUNDAY SERMON. FIRST BAPTIST.
> 10:00 A.M. *VISITING PREACHER:*
> ELLSWORTH CLUE. SERMON:
> THE YEARS BEFORE ADAM,
> THE TIME BEFORE EVE

"Boy!" cried Benjamin. "This mean what I *think* it means? Can we go?"

"Here's your hat, what's your hurry," said Gramps.

It not being Sunday, there was a long wait. But Sunday morning early, Ben came dragging Grandpa down the street to the First Baptist.

And, sure enough, inside, the Beast Tamer, Reverend Clue, launched behemoths smackdab into his sermon, fished for whales, caught leviathans, shadowed the Deeps, and ended with a thundering herd which, if they were not dinosaurs, were sulphurous bestial first cousins. And all waiting in the fiery pits for Christian boys who might fall through and land in that delightful burning place.

Or so it seemed to Benjamin, who sat upright for the first church hour in his life, his eyes ungummed, his mouth unyawned.

The Reverend Clue, seeing the boy's bright smile and flashing eyes, checked him out from time to time as he raved on through a genealogy of beasts with Lucifer the black goatherd on the swarm.

At noon, the congregation, released from the Bestiary, and smoking from its rollercoaster slide through Hell, staggered out blinking-blind into full sunlight, knowing more about prehistoric butcheries than they had wished to know. All, that is, save Benjamin, who found the Reverend, stunned by his own rhetoric, and yanked his hand like a pumphandle, hoping more miracles of beast might squirt out of the holy man's mouth.

"Gosh, Reverend, that was great! The monsters!"

"Don't hold a candle to monsters like men, however," said the Reverend, trying to keep his sermon on the track.

Benjamin was not to be veered.

"I liked the part about wishing making it so. That true?"

The Reverend almost flinched under the boy's signal-fire blink.

"Why — "

"I mean," said Benjamin, "if someone wishes for something bad enough, it comes true?"

"If," said Grandpa, arriving to save the Reverend from his offspring, "if you give to the poor, say proper prayers, do homework neat, clean up your room...."

Grandpa ran out of gas.

"That's a goshawful lot," said Benjamin, glancing from precipice of Grandpa to high mesa of Reverend Clue. "What do I do first?"

"The Lord wakes us each day to our work, son. Me to mine: reverending. You to yours: being a boy, willing and ready to wish and become!"

"Wish and become!" Benjamin chortled, his face afire. "Wish and become."

"After chores, however, boy, after chores."

But Benjamin, pepped up and vinegary-full, ran, stopped, came back, not hearing.

"Reverend, God invented those beasts, right?"

"Why, bless you, son. He *did.*"

"You ever figure *why?*"

Grandpa put his hand on Benjamin's shoulder, but Ben, he didn't feel it. "I mean, why would God make dinosaurs and then lose them?"

"He works in mysterious ways—"

"Too mysterious for me," said Ben, bluntly. "Wouldn't it be great, if we had our very own dinosaur here in Green Town, Illinois, arrived again, and never lost? The bones are great. But the *real* thing, wouldn't that be *swell*?"

"I have a partiality to the monsters, myself," admitted the Reverend.

"Do you think God will ever invent them again?"

The conversation, the Reverend could see, was headed for the bog. He did not intend to sink there.

"All I know for sure is, if you die and go to Hell, the beasts'll *be* there, or a facsimile, waiting for you."

Benjamin beamed.

"Almost makes dying worthwhile!"

"Son," said the Reverend.

But the boy was gone, running.

Benjamin raced home to cram his stomach and feed his eyes. He laid a dozen books spread-eagled on the floor and laughed quietly, with joy.

There they were, the beasts of all the Bible generations and beyond into the Deeps. That had a fine ring to it. The boy went around saying it from Sunday dinner at two until Sunday naptime at four. Deeps. Deeps. Take a long breath. Breathe it out. Deeps.

And brontosaur begat pteranodon and pteranodon begat tyrannosaur and tyrannosaur begat the great midnight kites—pterodactyls! and...so on and so forth and et cetera.

And as he turned the pages of the great fat family Text there were the leviathans and the creatures of time, and when you moved over into Hell and took a room there, why there was Dante pointing to this terror and that nightmare and this snake and that coiling serpent, all first aunts and dreadful uncles of Lost Time and strange blood and odd flesh. It made your socks crawl up your ankles and your ears drop to see the like! Oh, lost upon the Earth, but try to come again, good pets who once lay by the foot of God and got tossed out for fouling the carpet, sound! Oh, great lap-beasts of rolling mist and boiling fogs, whose voices are the trump of time that cracks the gates and lets the horrors forth, sound! Cry!

Moan from the—Deeps.

His lips moved as he slept and the sun moved shadows across his bed in the late afternoon. Twitch. Murmur. Whisper....

Deeps.

Good old animal Rex had his name changed by Benjamin the next day. From then on he was known as just plain Dog.

About three days after that, whining, Dog limped shivering out of the house, and disappeared.

"Where's Dog?" asked Grandpa, who looked in the cellar, the attic (what would a dog do in an attic? nothing to dig up *there*!), and the front yard. "Dog!" he called. "Dog?" asking a huge question to the clear breeze that crossed the lawn in place of the best friend animal. And at last, "Dog? What you doing there?"

For Dog was across the street, lying in the middle of a field of clover and weeds, an empty lot where no one had ever built or lived.

After about half an hour of calling, Grandpa lit his pipe and strolled over. He stood above Dog looking down. Dog looked up with a dreadful sorrow in his eyes.

"What you doing here, boy?"

Dog, being inarticulate, could not answer, but thumped his tail and lowered his ears and whined. The world was cursed, that was for sure, and he wasn't coming home.

Crossing back over, leaving Dog behind in the safe grass, Grandpa beheld something like the Manatee of an old sailing vessel on the porch. It was of course

Grandma, breasting the noon wind, a spatula in her hand. She waved it at Dog.

"I hope you didn't take him anything to eat!"

"Lands, no," said Grandpa, turning to look back at the dog, who now slunk, quavering, in the clover. "Why?"

"He's been in the icebox."

"How'd a dog do that?"

"The Lord hasn't told me, but there's food all over the floor. Hamburger I had put aside for today, gone. And messes of dropped burger and bone all around."

"Dog wouldn't do that! Let me *see*!"

Grandma gave a final, tart, mean wave of her spatula at the dog across the street, who promptly retreated another ten yards in the grass. Then she went, a parade of one, in and through the house to thrust her spatula at the floor, which was indeed a jigsaw puzzle of strewn food.

"You mean to say that creature knows how to unlock that icebox lever? Don't make sense."

"You think it was some boarder walking in his or her sleep?"

Grandpa crouched and began picking up the bits. "Been chewed all right. No other dog around here I know. Well, now. Well."

"You better have a talk with him. Tell Dog, one more incident like this and its rice-stuffed Dog for dinner Sunday! Outa the way, I've got the mop!"

The mop descended and Grandpa, in retreat, tried one curse or another, of a gentle sort, and went back out to the porch.

"Dog!" he called. "There's lots to discuss!"

But Dog, he lay low.

The list of disasters leaning into cataclysm grew. It seemed as if the Four Horsemen of the Apocalypse were galloping over the roofs, knocking apples to rot off the trees. Grandpa suspicioned that somehow he had been invited to a dark Mardi Gras, the end results of which might be bed-wetting, slammed doors, fallen cakes, and printing errors.

For the facts were these: Dog came back to visit from across the street, but no sooner back, left again, his hair brushed in all directions, his eyes hard-boiled eggs of apprehension. With him went Mr. Wyneski, faithful boarder and all-time town barber. Mr. Wyneski hinted he had had it up to about here, gill-high, with Benjamin grinding his teeth at the table.

Why, he further hinted, didn't Grandpa haul in the town dentist to remove the boy's thrashing-machine bicuspids, or loan the boy out to a wheat mill and let him earn his keep grinding flour!

Mr. Wyneski, in sum, would not be combed smooth. He went early and stayed late at his barber shop, coming back on occasion for his afternoon nap, but turning around and leaving as soon as he saw that Dog was still in the meadow.

Worse, the boarders were busy rocking forty times a minute, as though they were rushing down a road, instead of lolling along at the easy mileage of about once every twenty seconds like they did in the good old days of just last month.

That rocking, and the sight of the cat coming down off the roof, would be Mr. Wyneski's barometer. If he saw them, he'd vault in for some of Grandma's sorely missed noontime shortcake.

Oh, about the cat. Starting about the same time as Dog went to weave clover through his twitching pelt, the cat clawed its way to the roof where it skittered nights, yowling, and making a grand hieroglyph of graffiti on the tarpaper, which Grandpa tried to decipher each morn.

Mr. Wyneski even volunteered to prop a ladder and fetch the cat down so he could sleep nights. This done, the cat, in terror of some invisible force, ran right back up, roof-writing along the way, to jump shivering at any leaf that fell or wind that blew as Benjamin watched from a window in his room....

Grandpa finally settled for putting cream and tuna up in the rain-trough where, starved, the cat shivered down once a day to feed and then panicked back up as far as its sanity allowed.

With the barber hiding out in his shop, Dog in the meadow, cat on roof, Grandpa began to misset type down at his printing palace. Some of the misprints were words he had often heard boilermakers or railroad workmen use, but which had never fired off his own tongue.

On the day when he typeset Hot Dog as Hot Damn, Grandpa tore off his green celluloid visor, crumpled his ink-stained apron and came home early to dandelion wine before, as well as after, dinner.

"It's a crisis for sure."

"Eh?" said Grandma, late on the front porch.

Grandpa hadn't realized he had spilled the beans. He covered his lapse by pouring more wine in his mouth.

"Nothing, nothing," he said.

But it was something. Listening, he thought he heard the source of the Apocalypse upstairs:

Benjamin bicuspiding the silence, grinding the summer to a lurching, locomotive halt. All with his teeth. They were getting sharper. . . .

This was the final night. It had to be, or else, in one more day, the cat would tear itself down the middle of the roof, Dog would bone-rot in the grass, and the boarders be carried off to the nut bin, talking in tongues.

Half in, half out of an irritable sleep, Grandpa awoke and sat bolt upright.

He had *heard* something. *Really* heard it this time.

It was a sound from an old movie, but he couldn't remember where or what, and was forgetful about the when.

But it stirred the fuzz in his ears and raised the hackles of his soul and bumped the flesh along his ankles like a strange new growth of hair.

He saw his toes, down at the far edge of the bed, like small mice peering out at the dreadful night, and pulled them in.

He heard the cat dancing around in hysteria on the high attic roof. Dog, far over in the empty lot meadow, bayed at the moon, but there *was* no moon!

Grandpa held his breath and listened. But there was no further sound, no echo, no ricochet off the soundboard courthouse tower and back.

He turned over and was about to sink back into the black tar for a billion-year snooze when he thought: strange! wait! why tar? why billion years? why snooze!?

That got Grandpa bolt upright, out of bed, into the cellar, clothing himself in bathrobe on the way; clothing himself, in basement, with one sip of dandelion wine, and while he was at it, how about three?

In the library, finishing his libation, he heard a last, smaller sound, and trudged up to Benjamin's room.

Benjamin lay with a fever sweating his brow, resembling nothing more nor less than a lover fresh from a multifaceted encounter with a fine lady off a Greek vase. Grandpa laughed to himself. Come now, old man, he thought, he's only a boy—

He turned and almost stumbled over the litter of books put out on the floor, or laid open for sightseeing, on the shelves.

"Why, Benjamin," he gasped. "I didn't know you had so much, so many! Lord!"

For there in a panoply, a bas-relief, a tapestry, a museum explosion, were half a hundred books, spread-eagled and butterflied, with dinosaurs grinning, lurching, touching primeval mists with fingerprinting claws. While others rode the kite skies with whistle-drumming membrances, or periscoped up with long boa-constrictor necks from smoking bogs, or grasped at the teeming sky as they sank to vanish in tombs of black tar, lost in the billion years that had summoned the old man awake.

"Never seen the like," he whispered.

And he never had.

The faces. The bodies. The great graffiti-etching spider feet, or the ham feet or the ballet feet, take your pick, find your shoe. And the mad scientist-surgeon's claws, scalpeling delicate sandwiches of meat, pâtés, minces from fellow beasts. Here a *Triceratops* raked the jungle sands with his upside-down horny fronds, knocked over and yanked to oblivion by *Tyrannosaurus rex.* There sailed a grand brontosaur, like an arrogant Titanic, headed for unseen collisions with flesh, time, weather, and bergs headed south overland in an Age of Ice. Above all, the stringless kites, the warplane nightmare pterodactyls, scissoring the mists, kettle-drumming the winds, flirting and shuttering like ugly fans, like books of horror, in the always-murdered and so always-drying crimson sky.

"So. . . ."

Grandpa bent to shut the books, firmly, grimly.

He went down the stairs to fetch new books, his own. He brought them back up and opened them and laid them out on the floor, the shelves, the bed.

He stood for a moment in the center of the room and then he heard himself whisper:

"What do you want to be, when you grow up?"

The boy had somehow heard in his fevered sleep. His head thrashed on his pillow. One hand flailed softly, reaching for the dream.

"I —"

The old man waited.

"I," murmured the boy. "I'm . . . growing . . . *now.*"

"What?"

"Now . . . now," whispered Benjamin.

Shadows moved on his lips, his cheeks.

Grandpa bent and stared.

"Why, Ben," he said, hoarsely. "You been grinding your teeth. And —"

A trickle of blood rimmed the edges of the boy's tight mouth. A bright drop fell and dissolved into the pillow case.

"Enough's enough."

Grandpa sat and took Benjamin's restless hands quietly but firmly in his own. He leaned his head forward and began to recommend:

"Sleep, Ben, sleep. Sleep, but . . . *listen here!*"

Benjamin turned his head this way and that, squirming, perspiration flowing down his face, but — listened.

"Now," said Grandpa quietly, "what you're up to, or I think you're up to, won't do. I'm not sure what it is, and I never want to know, but whatever it is must stop."

He paused for a moment, rallied himself, and then went on:

"The magazines get shut, the books go back to the library, the chicken stays whole in the icebox, the dog comes home from across the street, the cat comes down off the roof, Mr. Wyneski rejoins us at table, and the boarders stop stealing my dandelion wine to get them through a night of strange sounds.

"Now listen even closer. No more Field Museums, no more bones, no more dental charts of old smiles, no more shadow-shows on walls of cinema houses with great ghosts of super-primeval times. This is your Grandpa talking and advising and telling you his love, but firmly warning you, for certain-sure: *no more!*

"Otherwise the whole house will fall. The attic will crash down through the bedrooms, through the dining room, the kitchen into the cellar to ruin the summer preserves and Grandma and me and the boarders with it.

"We can't have that, can we? Shall I tell you what we can have? Look *there.*

"In the night, when I'm gone, when you get up to go to the bathroom and see what I've laid out on the floor, all around, open and waiting. There you'll find the beast, the monster, something for you to be part of, something that shouts and roars and runs and eats fire and shortens time.

"A different beast? Yes, but a grand and glorious one you can surely fit and grow into. Listen to me in your sleep, Ben, and during the night before you sleep again, prowl *these* books, these pages, these pictures. Yes?"

The old man turned to look at the books he had brought and laid out like a spell on the bedroom floor.

Pictures of fiery locomotives lay waiting for perusal, belching flames and rushing soots across night country, great animals shot from Hell. And atop the dark beasts, the locomotive engineers leaned out to dog the firewinds, smiling their locomotive-happy smiles.

"There's an engineer's cap here, Benjamin," whispered Grandpa. "Grow your head, grow your brains, but especially, grow your dreams into it. There's enough wildness there for any boy, and a lifetime of travel and glory."

The old man prowled over the flaming machines, envious of their pistoned beauties, imagining the great primeval sounds they made.

"You hear me, Ben? You *listening*?"

The boy stirred, the boy moaned, in his sleep.

Grandpa said, "I dearly hope so, boy."

The bedroom door shut. The old man was gone. The house slept. Far away, a train wailed in the night. Benjamin turned a final time in his sleep, and his fever broke. The perspiration faded on his luminous brow. A quiet wind from the open window ficked the open pages of all the books, revealing iron beast after iron beast after iron....

The next morning, Sunday, Benjamin came late to breakfast. He had slept long and hard and full of dreams, prayers, wishes, bindle sticks of this, old bones of that, flesh and blood of something lost and beyond, vanished pasts, promising futures.

He came slowly down the stairs, looking fresh-washed and brand-new.

The few boarders still at table, when they saw him, got up, napkined their mouths, and left in what they hoped didn't look like a hurry.

Grandpa, at his end of the table, pretended to read the international news on the front page of the newspaper, but all the while his eyes, above the headlines, watched as Benjamin sat down, picked up his knife and fork and waited for Grandma to place his stack of pancakes drowned in liquid sun.

"Morning, Benjamin," said Grandma, sailing back out to her chores.

Benjamin waited, his mouth shut. He seemed to be thinking about something, wondering, pondering, eyes half shut.

"Benjamin," said Grandpa, behind the paper, "good morning."

Benjamin still pondered over his shut and secret mouth.

The silent table waited.

Grandpa could not help leaning forward. He found that his legs were tensed. When the boy's mouth opened, would there be a terrible-ancient cry, a dreadful shriek, announcing the birth of young Benjamin's new career? Would his smile be a fence of daggers and his tongue a field of blood?

Grandpa glanced sidewise.

Dog, home from the meadow, had just trotted into the kitchen to wolf a biscuit. Cat, down from the roof, was slicking its whiskers of cream, leaning against Grandma's right ankle. Mr. Wyneski? Would he soon be trotting up the front steps again?

"Ben," said Grandpa at last. "Besides a dinosaur,

what do you want to be, when you grow up?"

Benjamin raised his head, smiled, and showed plain ordinary nice little corn-kernel teeth. His plain little old tongue moved quietly across his lips. From his lap he raised and put on a striped engineer's cap which, while large, fitted very well.

A train sighed off across the land, running on the rim of morning. Benjamin listened to it, nodded, sighed, perked some of its sound in his throat, and said:

"I think you know, Grandpa. I think you know."

And, not grinding his teeth anymore, he poured breakfast in. Grandpa could not but do likewise. Dog and cat watched from the door.

Grandma, oblivious to it all, trotted in with more hotcakes, trotted out for more syrup.

10.
MONSTERS OF THE SEA AND AIR

ESSAY BY KENNETH CARPENTER
SPECULATION BY POUL ANDERSON

Monsters of the Sea and Air
Kenneth Carpenter

THE MESOZOIC MAY BE REFERRED TO AS THE AGE OF DINOSAURS, BUT MANY OTHER REPTILES ALSO alive at that time were just as spectacular and interesting. In the sea, this included the mosasaurs, plesiosaurs, and ichthyosaurs, and in the air, pterosaurs. These reptiles have frequently and erroneously been called dinosaurs, when, in point of fact, most differ from dinosaurs in many important anatomical details. For example, earlier in this book, it was mentioned that based on the pelvis dinosaurs are subdivided into the bird-hipped ornithischians and the lizard-hipped saurischians. Except for marine crocodiles, no marine reptile has either pelvic type. Furthermore, the limbs of the marine reptiles are frequently modified into flippers. Pterosaurs are not considered dinosaurs either because the forelimbs have been altered into wings.

Sea Life

Today, most reptiles are terrestrial, like lizards and snakes, or semiaquatic, like crocodiles. But during the Mesozoic, several different reptile lineages took to the sea independently, where they adapted so well that life on land was impossible for them. Why did this occur? One clue comes from studies of the energy needs of modern reptiles. These show that a swimming reptile requires only one-fourth the energy it would need for walking on land. This difference is due to the buoyancy of the water: the only energy needed is that required to propel the animal through the water. On land the reptile needs energy to overcome the pull of gravity and to hold the body off the ground, and energy to move the limbs during locomotion.

Another possible clue as to why reptiles adapted to life at sea is the abundance of fish, squid, and belemnite (a squid-like cephalopod) parts found in the stomachs of many marine reptile fossils. This suggests that the Mesozoic seas were an enormous larder of animal protein waiting to be tapped. Ocean productivity is greatest in shallow coastal water, so it is not surprising that marine reptiles evolved in the shallow seas of the Mesozoic.

The buoyancy of sea water also allows an animal to get larger. Today the largest animal is a marine animal: the blue whale. Although none of the marine reptiles got as large, there was a trend toward increased size over time in many of the lineages.

But life at sea has its difficulties too. Prey fish were generally fast swimmers. Successful reptiles adapted by evolving to look more fishlike. That is also why the porpoise, a mammal, has in recent times evolved to be like a fish.

The Family of Fish Lizards

Ichthyosaurs, or "fish lizards," best show this change toward a more fishlike body. An early genus, *Utatsusaurus*, from the Early Triassic (about 245 to 240 million years ago) of Japan, had a lizardlike head, long, slender body, and long tapering tail. The limbs were already modified into flippers, but show none of the specializations seen in later ichthyosaurs. Swimming was achieved with side to side undulations of the tail.

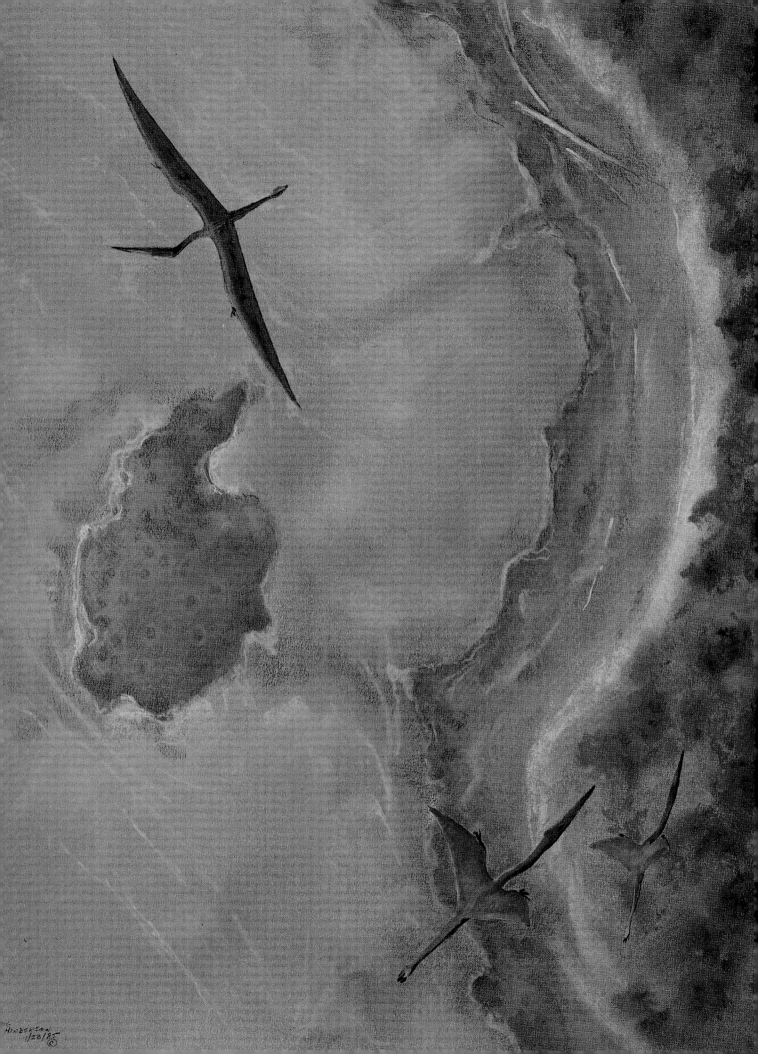

Henderson
1/23/85
©

A much more derived form is *Ichthyosaurus* from the Early Jurassic (208 to 187 mybp) of Germany and England. The head and body were so evolved that the animal looked like a porpoise. The head was short, with a long, toothy snout. The neck was also very short, as were the body and tail. The vertebrae had evolved into simple discs from their more complex ancestral shapes. The flippers were considerably modified from those in the earlier forms, being shorter and with many more rows of finger bones. Even the finger bones themselves were changed into small disks.

Utatsusaurus was small, only 5 feet long. This contrasts with the largest ichthyosaur, *Shonisaurus*, from the Late Triassic (230 to 208 mybp) of Nevada, which was almost 50 feet long. *Shonisaurus* was deep-bodied and had limbs modified into long slender paddles. The end of the tail was bent downward, as in advanced ichthyosaurs, suggesting the presence of a large vertical fluke. The teeth were relatively small and restricted to the front of the mouth. The overall body shape suggests that *Shonisaurus* was a moderately fast swimmer compared to the earlier (Middle Triassic) thirty-foot, long-bodied, long-tailed *Cymbospondylus*.

By the Early Jurassic, the optimal fishlike body was seen in *Ichthyosaurus* and *Eurhinosaurus*, with its long swordfish-like snout. Until their extinction in the early part of the Late Cretaceous, little further change occured in the ichthyosaurs' body shape.

Ichthyosaurs all had a pair of openings in the skull behind the eye socket, a condition referred to as "euryapsid" (the number and position of skull openings is used to classify various reptile groups). These openings were atop the skull and opened into a large chamber on each side of the braincase. These chambers housed powerful muscles for closing the mouth quickly on a meal.

Vision appears to have been acute in ichthyosaurs, as in most predators. The eye socket was typically very large and the eyeball itself was strengthened with thin overlapping plates of bone. These plates may have changed the shape of the eyeball in response to water pressure, allowing the prey to remain in focus as the ichthyosaur chased after it. The toothy snout was greatly elongated, giving it a porpoise-like appearance. And as in porpoises, the teeth were usually long and slender, suggesting a fish diet. Indeed, fossilized stomach contents do indicate a diet of fish and belemnites.

Carbonized skin impressions have been found around the skeletons of ichthyosaurs in the black shales at Holzmaden, Germany. These show that the body had a sharklike fin on the back, and the tail had a whalelike fluke. The orientation of this fluke, however, was vertical, whereas in whales it is horizontal. This unusually fine fossil preservation is probably due to the bottom waters at Holzmaden being inhospitable to life because of the absence of oxygen. Any ichthyosaur dying and sinking to the sea floor would lie undisturbed because of the absence of scavengers (crabs, small fish, etc.) picking the body apart. Fine mud would eventually cover the carcass, recording the delicate skin as a dark silhouette.

Ichthyosaurs swam by a side-to-side motion of the tail which was greatly aided in derived forms by the large vertical fluke. The flippers were used to stabilize the animal as it raced through the water, and may have also aided in steering.

It is also from the Holzmaden specimens that we learn about the reproduction of ichthyosaurs. Since they were aquatic reptiles, it might seem by analogy likely that the females would lay their eggs on a sandy beach much like sea turtles today. However, several specimens of *Stenopterygius* from Holzmaden reveal baby ichthyosaurs within the body of the mother, indicating that the young were born live. One mother apparently died during birth because in her fossil one of the babies is partially out of the body cavity. Like porpoises today, the young were born tail first.

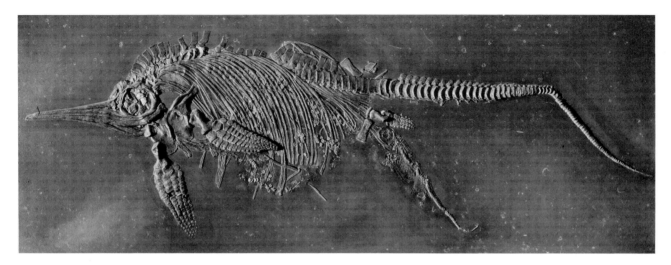

Above: There is direct evidence that some dinosaurs gave birth by laying eggs. But there is equally vivid evidence of live birth among other reptiles, as shown here. A baby Icthyosaur *pops tail-first out of its mother. Photo: the State Museum of Natural History, Stuttgart. Preceding spread: Near the edge of* a shallow lake, pterosaurs (winged reptiles that were not bird ancestors) soar over the water. The small island represents the famous Egg Mountain, site of the Late Cretaceous* Maiasaur *nests. By Doug Henderson.*

NOTHOSAURS

Appearing in the oceans about the same time as the ichthyosaurs were another group of euryapsid reptiles called the nothosaurs. *Pachypleurosaurus* is a typical genus from the Middle Triassic of Switzerland. Growing to a length of three feet, it was characterized by a small, toothy head attached to an elongated neck and body. The tail was long and apparently did not develop a fishlike fin as in the ichthyosaurs. The long body and tail were probably moved from side to side to propel the animal through the water. This mode of swimming is still used today by crocodiles. The limbs were not modified into flippers, but may nevertheless have been used for steering.

Adult nothosaurs ranged in size from the small species of *Neusticosaurus*, about 8 inches long, to large *Nothosaurus* and *Ceresiosaurus*, both about 13 feet long. The smallest known specimen of nothosaur is a 2-inch-long baby *Neusticosaurus peyeri* from Italy. The baby was found in marine deposits, but it is not certain whether the baby hatched on land and died at sea, or if it was born live at sea like an ichthyosaur and then died. The limbs of nothosaurs show none of the modifications seen in ichthyosaurs and they could have supported the adult on land if they came ashore to lay eggs. But whether they did so or not is unknown.

Nothosaurs first appeared during the Early Triassic (245 to 240 million years ago), but were most common during the Middle Triassic (240 to 230 million years ago). Their teeth were long and pointed, indicating a fish diet (based on analogy to today's predators). The bones of the body are especially dense, to keep the animals from bobbing to the surface when they chased after prey. Nothosaurs resemble the long-necked plesiosaurs, so it was natural for paleontologists to suggest that they were Pleisiosaur ancestors. But careful restudy of the structure of the roof of the mouth and of the shoulder bones of these animals indicates that most nothosaurs are too specialized to be plesiosaur ancestors. One possible exception is *Pistosaurus* from the Middle Triassic of Germany. It apparently bridges the gap between the nothosaurs and plesiosaurs in having a nothosaur-like skeleton, but with a more primitive, almost plesiosaur-like skull.

Nothosaurs show clearly how natural variation explains the way some marine reptiles evolved long necks (as in some plesiosaurs) or long bodies (as in some mosasaurs), by increases in the number of vertebrae. Studies based an hundreds of specimens of *Neusticosaurus* from one deposit in Switzerland have shown that the number of bones in the neck and body varied from 33 to 41 vertebrae. In another nearby deposit, a population of the same nothosaur shows a range of 35 to 42 vertebrae. Other reptiles likely evolved in much the same way.

BIZARRE RELATIVES

Two other marine reptiles known from the Middle Triassic of Switzerland are the thalattosaurs and the bizarre tanystropheids. *Askeptosaurus* is the best-known thalattosaur and shows many of the characteristic features of the group. The skull had an elongated muzzle with nostrils set well back from the front of the snout, the lizardlike body was long and broad, and the tail, used for swimming, was deep. The limbs were short, but not modified into paddles. The teeth were long and conical, suggesting a diet of fish.

Tanystropheus is perhaps the most bizarre marine reptile that ever lived. It had a greatly elongated neck, a feature characteristic of the tanystropheids. The neck of *Tanystropheus* was twice as long as its body! The only other marine reptiles with this feature were some of the long-necked plesiosaurs.

However, the plesiosaurs evolved to this by an increase in the number of vertebrae in the neck (up to 76). *Tanystropheus*, on the other hand, had long necks because each of its nine to twelve vertebrae were elongated, some up to a foot long!

A growth series of *Tanystropheus* skeletons shows that the juveniles had more normal vertebrae. Each progressive age group shows that the neck increased in length as the animal matured towards adulthood. This change seems to correspond to changes in behavior. The short-necked juveniles seem to have been more terrestrial and to have crushed small insects and other prey with their multicuspid teeth. The adults, however, appear to have been mostly aquatic, with simple conical teeth and long necks well suited for catching fish.

THE PLESIOSAURS

The plesiosaurs are perhaps the best-known marine reptiles. They are often thought of as having a small, toothy head attached to an elongated neck, and limbs modified into flippers. But in actuality there were two major types of plesiosaurs, the long-necked plesiosauroids, and the short-necked pliosauroids. The limbs of both forms were modified into flippers, while the shoulder and pelvic bones formed broad sheets of bone for the attachment of powerful swimming muscles.

The plesiosauroids can be subdivided into two forms, one of which, the elasmosaurs, had much longer necks than the other, the plesiosaurids. *Elasmosaurus*, from the Late Cretaceous of Kansas, has one of the longest necks in the animal world, with 76 neck vertebrae. The plesiosaurid, *Plesiosaurus*, from the Early Jurassic of England, on the other hand, had only 30 neck vertebrae. This contrasts with the pliosaur *Peloneustus* which had 21 neck vertebrae.

The long, slender teeth and the stomach contents of plesiosauroids show that they mostly fed on small fish. The enormous size of the pliosaur *Kronosaurus*, as well as the stout shape of its teeth, suggest that this

A terrible reptile, but not a dinosaur, this Mosasaur *devours a nautiloid of the Late Cretaceous seas. By William Parsons.*

forty-foot pliosaur may have been a "killer whale" of the Mesozoic, feeding on smaller plesiosaurs and other marine reptiles. Smaller species may have eaten squid-like belemnites.

How *Kronosaurus* and other plesiosaurs may have swum has long been a source of debate. The British paleontologist D.M.S. Watson suggested in 1924 that plesiosaurs might have paddled along like rowboats, using their long necks to grab at passing fish. More recently, analysis of the shoulder and hip joints suggests that locomotion of plesiosaurs was more like that of sea lions, in which the main thrust comes from the down stroke of the flippers. We can imagine a sleek pliosaur, looking like a seal, racing in and out of the kelp as it chases a small school of fish.

Although plesiosaurs did well in the ocean, they became extinct along with the mosasaurs about 65 million years ago. The last occurrences are from the latest Cretaceous of Antarctica and Arctic Canada.

PLESIOSAUR COUSINS

Placodonts were distant cousins of the plesiosaurs and also descendants of the nothosaurs. They are known from the Middle and Late Triassic of central Europe. One of these animals, *Placodus*, looked very much like an overly fat lizard with a short, broad head. The head was unique in having long nipping teeth at the front and large, flat crushing teeth in the cheeks and on the roof of the mouth. The front teeth were probably used to pluck mollusks from the sea floor, while the crushing teeth were used to crack the shells open. The limbs are short and only slightly modified into paddles. *Placodus* swam by sculling its tail back and forth.

Another placodont, *Henodus*, had a turtle-like shell on its back. It may have served as protection against predators, but the fossil record has not provided us a clue as to what that predator might have been.

THE MOSASAURS

About 120 million years after the placodonts became extinct, the giant marine lizards, the mosasaurs, appeared. Descendants of the varanoid lizards (the Komodo dragon is a living relative), the mosasaurs first appeared early in the Late Cretaceous, about 88 million years ago. Mosasaurs are typified by a lizard-like skull, in which there are two openings behind the orbit: a pair on the sides of the skull separated by a pair atop the skull. This condition, called diapsid, occurs in lizards, snakes and dinosaurs. There was a ring of bone within the eyehole, as in the ichthyosaurs, which probably had a similar function.

The body also looked very lizard-like, but the limbs had undergone considerable change. Both the front and hind limbs were short relative to the size of the body, and the hands and feet were modified into paddles. It is doubtful that these were used for swimming. Instead, mosasaurs sculled their tails from side to side and used their paddles to steer with. The wide variety of body and tail shapes indicates that not all mosasaurs swam equally well. Some, such as the long-bodied *Mosasaurus*, must have been slow swimmers, slithering through the kelp after prey. Others, such as the short-bodied, large-paddled *Platecarpus*, must have been considerably faster and more maneuverable. Perhaps it fed on squids the mangled remains of which have been found in the same deposits.

Mosasaur tooth shape and fossilized stomach contents indicate that not all mosasaurs ate the same food, but rather had various specific diets. The stout-toothed, 30-foot *Tylosaurus* was probably the "killer whale" among mosasaurs, because parts of another mosasaur, *Platecarpus*, have been found in the stomachs of some fossils. The smaller *Platecarpus* and *Clidastes* are known to have eaten various fish.

Mosasaurs are known from every continent, including Antarctica. Assuming that mosasaurs were cold-blooded like their living lizard relatives, global temperatures must have been much warmer than today. The distribution of such cold-blooded animals is one way that paleontologists can reconstruct ancient climates.

SEA TURTLES

Another group of important marine reptiles of the Cretaceous was the sea turtles. The best-known is the giant *Archelon*, with a shell almost 8 feet in length. The limbs evolved into flippers by elongation of the fingers. A similar change has occurred in modern sea turtles, and a study of their locomotion shows that the flippers move in a cycle shaped like a figure "8." This motion propels the turtle with both the up and the down strokes.

The skull of *Archelon* is of a type called anapsid, in which there are no openings on top of the skull, nor on its sides. There is, however, a pair of large openings at the back of the skull and in many sea turtles these have moved onto the top rear of the skull.

The earliest sea turtles have been found in coastal and lagoonal sediments from the Upper Jurassic. One of these, *Solnhofia*, is known from the same sediments that produced the first bird, *Archaeopteryx*. It is doubtful that these early sea turtles are ancestral to the later Cretaceous ones, because of certain features in the skull. It appears, in fact, that several turtle lineages adapted to life in the sea independently of one another.

By the Late Cretaceous, sea turtles became very abundant and widespread. This was due, in part, to the spread of shallow inland seas. Some of these turtles show modifications of the typical solid shell into one that has large gaps between ribs. These gaps were probably covered with skin much like those on the leatherback turtle today. *Archelon* was one of these, as was the smaller *Protostega*.

It is not known what these turtles ate because

fossilized stomach contents have not been reported. Based on modern sea turtles, the diet may have been small fish and sea plants.

SEA CROCODILES

One other group of sea reptiles during the time of the dinosaurs was that of the sea crocodiles, the teleosaurids and metriorhynchids. They and all crocodiles have a diapsid skull with a pair of openings on the top and sides of the skull.

The teleosaurids apparently descended from a terrestrial crocodile about 188 million years ago, during the Early Jurassic. Teleosaurids had a worldwide range, as their remains are known from almost all continents except Antarctica. All of them were characterized by vertebrae concave at both ends and a palate modified by the addition of other bones. One of these, *Steneosaurus*, is well known from complete skeletons from Holzmaden, Germany. *Steneosaurus* still retained armor plates on the back and belly, a holdover from its fully terrestrial ancestors. The front limbs were much shorter than the rear ones, but it could probably crawl onto land on occasion. The skull had a long and toothy snout similar to that found in the modern gavial, a freshwater crocodile from India. The gavial diet is almost exclusively fish, and we may assume the same for *Steneosaurus*.

The other major group of marine crocodiles, the metriorhynchids, probably evolved from the teleosaurids during the latter part of the Early Jurassic. A close relationship is inferred from the similarity of the vertebrae and palate. One form, *Geosaurus*, is known from the Late Jurassic of Europe. It shows specialization for life at sea by the loss of the body armor, making the skin smoother and more streamlined. The forelimbs have been converted into flippers, and the end of the tail bent downwards as in ichthyosaurs, suggesting the presence of a fishlike fin. With all of these changes, it is not certain if metriorhynchids could have ventured on land to lay their eggs. It is possible that they had live births in a manner similar to sea snakes today. Metriorhynchids are known mostly from Europe and South America. They became extinct during the Early Cretaceous and were not replaced by other specialized crocodiles.

FLYING REPTILES

The other major group of non-dinosaurian reptiles that lived during the Mesozoic was the pterosaurs, or flying reptiles. These reptiles appeared suddenly in the fossil record about 210 million years ago, along with the first dinosaurs, during the Late Triassic. They evolved very rapidly and became an important part of the Mesozoic communities. But they became extinct, along with all of the marine reptiles and dinosaurs, at the end of the Cretaceous, 65 million years ago.

Pterosaurs appeared fully developed in the Late Triassic. *Eudimorphodon*, from northern Italy, had all of the characteristic features of later pterosaurs, including hollow bones, a head that was large relative to body size, a long neck, short body, long rear legs, small hips, and, of course, the forelimb modified into a wing.

It was this wing that made pterosaurs successful and allowed them to spread to almost every continent. The wing differed from that of birds in that it was featherless. Instead, it was made of a skin membrane similar to that of a bat. But whereas the bat has four fingers to support this membrane, pterosaurs had only one. A common misconception is that birds and bats evolved from pterosaurs, but the differences in the wing show otherwise.

The development of the pterosaur wing required numerous changes to the forelimb. Because of the forces generated in moving the wing up and down against the air, it must have been braced against the body. Therefore, the shoulder bones, the scapula and coracoid, were fused together, and each in turn was braced against the back vertebrae and against a large breastbone, or sternum. To further strengthen the back against the force of the wing, some pterosaurs, notably *Pteranodon*, had the back vertebrae fused into a plate called the notarium.

The wrist bones were small interlocking blocks supporting a spur of bone called the pteroid. The pteroid supports a small membrane of skin connected from the front edge of the wing to the base of the neck. Moving this bone changed the shape of the membrane, allowing the pterosaur to fly at slower speeds without stalling. An analogous feature is seen in the slats on the leading edge of a passenger jet. These slats are lowered when the jet approaches for landing so that it will not stall and crash.

The main part of the pterosaur wing was made of an elongated fourth finger. The finger was longer than the rest of the arm and supported the skin membrane. The membrane was reinforced with numerous thin, closely spaced fibers. The membrane is well known from specimens of *Rhamphorhynchus* and *Pterodactylus* from the Solnhofen limestone of Germany. These are the same deposits that preserved the delicate impressions of feathers in *Archaeopteryx*.

THE EVOLUTION OF FLIGHT

How and why did flight evolve in pterosaurs? To understand this, it is necessary to consider flight in general. We find that it has evolved several times in the animal kingdom in organisms not at all closely related. For example, the dragonfly, bee, bird, and pterosaur have all developed wings. These wings superficially resemble one another, despite the fact that none of the animals are closely related to one another. The fact that flight has evolved independently suggests that there must be strong advantages in doing so. Predator avoid-

ance must be one of these advantages. Another advantage is that it allows the animal to cover a large territory in the quest for food. A good example is a locust swarm that takes to the air once all the food resources in one region are exhausted. When more vegetation is found, the locusts descend.

Thus, pterosaurs evolved flight for more than one reason. What is not yet known is whether flight evolved from a tree-climbing ancestor leaping from branch to branch, or from a ground runner chasing after insects. What this ancestor is we do not yet know. The fact that both pterosaurs and dinosaurs have the same simple, hingelike ankle, suggests that this ancestor was related to both dinosaurs and pterosaurs.

Flight requires a great rate of expenditure of energy, suggesting that pterosaurs might have been warm-blooded. Is there any physical evidence for this? Possibly, because a warm-blooded animal requires insulation to prevent heat loss to the cooler environment. This insulation is provided by feathers on birds and fur on bats. Traces of what may be a dense coat of hair or fur have been found on the body of the pterosaur *Sordes* from the Upper Jurassic of Kazakhstan in Soviet Central Asia. What is not known is how widespread this body covering was among pterosaurs, but it seems reasonable that all of them had hair because all of them flew.

Did pterosaurs fly by flapping of their wings or by soaring? This is still being debated. Certainly none of the pterosaurs had a large keeled breastbone, like a bird's, for the attachment of powerful flight muscles, but then neither does a bat. A way to find the answer is to consider the aerodynamics of wing shape. *Pteranodon*, for example, had a very long, narrow wing, similar to that of an albatross or a man-made glider. The former spends a considerable amount of time soaring over the ocean. Both the albatross and the glider rely on updrafts to stay aloft. *Quetzalcoatlus*, on the other hand, had a short, broad wing resembling

The Early Jurassic pterosaur, Dimorphodon, *eats an early relative of the herring,* Leptolepus. *By Wayne D. Barlowe.*

that of a hawk or a jumbo jet. Such a wing is not suitable for gliding long distances, suggesting that like the hawk, *Quetzalcoatlus* had to flap a lot in order to stay aloft.

Although pterosaurs were well adapted for flight, how did they get around when they were not flying? An early suggestion was that they walked or crawled on hands and feet with the wings folded against the body. Recently, Kevin Padian has noted a similarity between the hind limbs and feet of pterosaurs and dinosaurs, suggesting that they may have been bipedal, walking only on their hind legs. *Rhamphorhynchus* and related forms had long tails and may have used them to counterbalance the body in a manner similar to bipedal dinosaurs. One prehistoric-animal illustrator, Zdenek Burian, thought that perhaps when they weren't flying they hung upside down from tree branches like fruit bats.

Pterosaurs can be subdivided into two major types, the rhamphorhynchoids and the pterodactyloids. The rhamphorhynchoids included the most primitive pterosaurs and were characterized by long tails, relatively short necks, and a long fifth toe. The pterodactyloids had short tails, an elongated neck, and no fifth toe.

Rhamphorhynchoids include the tiny, short-faced *Anurognathus* from the Solnhofen Limestone. It was well suited for eating insects because its peglike teeth and short deep muzzle could crunch the tough chitinous shell of an insect. *Rhamephorhynchus*, also from the Solnhofen Limestone, had a long tail ending in a triangular or diamond-shaped "rudder." The long slender snout bristled with long, needlelike teeth for catching fish. One specimen of *Rhamphorhynchus* shows that they had a pelican-like mouth pouch. Possibly *Rhamphorhynchus* flew just above the water with the tip of the lower jaw skimming through the water. Once a fish was snared it was temporarily stored in the pouch until it could be safely swallowed.

The small, fuzzy *Sordes* mentioned earlier is also a rhamphorhynchoid. We can imagine this small robin-sized pterosaur flitting over a small lake at dusk catching insects.

The other pterosaur group, the pterodactyloids, includes both the smallest and largest pterosaurs. *Pterodactylus elegans*, about the size of a sparrow, is also known from the Solnhofen Limestone. Its teeth were tiny and clustered to the front of the mouth. Because of its small size and high metabolism, *Pterodactylus elegans* probably needed lots of protein, suggesting that it ate insects. The giant *Quetzalcoatlus*, with a 40-foot wingspan, may have been a scavenger feeding off dead dinosaurs. This suggestion is based primarily upon the observation that the largest birds today are scavenging vultures and condors. But another pterodactyloid, *Pteranodon*, also grew to the size of *Quetzalcoatlus*, and stomach contents indicate a diet of marine fish. So perhaps the analogy of vultures with *Quetzalcoatlus* may not be valid.

Pteranodon longiceps, the pterosaur with the largest head, lived in the Late Cretaceous (85 to 80 mybp) of Kansas. In this species, the head was longer than the body because of a 6-foot long bony crest on the skull. The purpose of this crest has been a subject of much debate. Scale models of *Pteranodon* in flight have been analyzed in wind tunnels. These suggest that the crest functioned as a rudder to aid in steering. However, the studies have only used one species of long-crested *Pteranodon*. In fact, crest shape differed among different specimens of *Pteranodon*: some have a short erect crest, and others a long slender crest.

It now seems likely that the aerodynamic studies do not reveal the entire picture. Recent studies by Chris Bennett suggest that crest shape changed as an animal matured. For example, the short-erect-crested forms are juveniles that eventually would have become large-erect-crested adults. It also seems likely that the degree of crest development reflects the sex of the animal, with the males having larger crests for sexual display. This is analogous to the show tailfeathers of the male peacock.

A crest also occured in *Dsungaripterus* from the lower Cretaceous of Wuerho, China. This crest, however, extended along the top of the snout. The oddest pterodactyloid is *Pterodaustro* from the Late Cretaceous of Argentina. This pterosaur had long fibrous structures in the lower jaw analogous to baleen in certain whales. This "baleen" allowed the pterosaur to strain water for plankton.

What caused the pterosaurs and so many of the marine reptiles to become extinct by the end of the Cretaceous is unknown. Many suggestions have been made, including an asteroid impact, draining of the shallow seas from the continents, climatic change, etc. What is puzzling about the extinction, however, is that certain marine reptiles, such as sea turtles, were not greatly affected. No mechanism has been suggested to adequately explain this selective extinction.

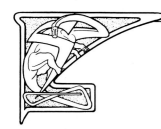
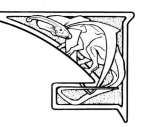

UNNATURAL ENEMY

POUL ANDERSON

CALL HIM HARPOON. AS HE SWAM IN HIS MAJESTY THROUGH THE SEA, HIS HEAD STOOD SHARP at the end of a sinuous shaft of neck, so high that he looked across miles. When a glimpse of dashing argency caught his eye, that head lanced sideward and down. Teeth snapped shut, blood made salt water momentarily savory, the fish still struggled as it went through gullet to belly and that too was good; but Harpoon paid little heed. He was not hunting now, only grabbing whatever food happened along. His onwardness never slackened. He scarcely noticed an isle nearby. What called him was a hazy blue line which had appeared on the horizon, the mainland, and the as yet unseen breeding ground of his kind. Nor did he mark the shadow that moved to meet him.

Alae the pteranodon did, though to him it meant nothing. Himself on the alert for anything he might snatch, he always flew well beyond reach of any large creature in health. A dead one, a hurt one too weak to fight, a hatchling, an egg — those were different, of course. Pteranodons flocked to the elasmosaur rookery in that season when females gathered to lay and males did battle for the right to beget new young.

Riding the wind, Alae would have been a splendid sight had Harpoon glanced up and possessed an understanding. Late afternoon sunlight blazed off wings of a whiteness like the cloud streamers blown above, the foam that swirled below. They rippled the least bit along their trailing edges, those leathery wings; the same shiver passed through their fur in faint iridescences. Beak and crest poised arrogant between them, athwart heaven. At his height he saw vastly, from the forest ashore, out across a green-tawny-violet wrinklescape of ocean, to rain and lightning afar. He saw, without really noting, a darkness in the water, gliding to intercept the gray bulk of the elasmosaur.

Harpoon swam on. Air shrilled around him, cold, briny, warming somewhat as he approached land. The seas filled it with noise, rush, hiss, crash. They raised him up, swept him down, rocked and swung him. Below their throbbing streamed the subtler forces of tide and current. Nonetheless his wake remained straight. Forty feet from snout through broad flat body to the end of the ruddering tail, he was not the fastest of swimmers, but four flippers drove him with a steadiness that might have seemed stolid, had not his neck, half the length of him, kept straining forward ever more eagerly.

Once again the ancient urge was awake. Days grew longer, the sun climbed higher; windborne, seaborne, fainter than mistfall, tastes and odors reached him in his cruising grounds; presently the hunger they roused was all the hunger that mattered, and he followed them toward that sandy peninsula where he had always, exultantly, been victorious.

Never since he got his growth had he needed wariness. For most of the year his kind held many miles apart. At mating time he soon sent any challengers scuttling and bleeding off, while he covered every female he chose. Two-legged predators stayed away from scores of jaws that would have united against

dragged, spumed. Thrice undertow sucked Harpoon back, he wallowed helpless and would have drowned except for that snaky prow of his. Strength drained from him with the blood. Blindly he fought. Somehow he won through, crept onto the beach fronting the island, and sprawled.

Alae swept low. Several other pteranodons had observed his hopefulness and were joining him. The shadows of their wings sickled across the elasmosaur. He raised his weary head and coughed at them. Sunlight gleamed off teeth. The flyers rose, went into hover mode, kept watch for carrion or safe prey. They would wait thus awhile and see what happened.

Vorax had no incentive to do so. When the blood in the water thinned to nothing, likewise did those traces that served him for memory. He too would patrol this new region, but more widely and in his shark fashion. He departed, swimming high for the sake of an overview, his dorsal fin cleaving the wind.

Harpoon lay where he was. Breath went raggedly in and out of him. Tide ebbed, turned, crept back. The sun trudged down the sky. Now and then Alae led an investigative foray; once his beak actually stabbed; but the neck rose and whipped about, jaws clashed, the pteranodons scattered barely in time. At evening they gave up and flapped off, black double crescents against an orange flame of sunset. Otherwise Harpoon rested.

His life was too deeply seated for shock and blood loss to kill him as they would have killed a more developed animal. The stump of his flipper clotted over. Darkness fell, stars glittered multitudinous. His body worked slower as it cooled with the night, and hence required less. After the tide flowed back, he could stretch around and drink; he used salt water readily enough. His injuries pained him, but he had not the brain to dwell upon how much they did. He lay quiet.

The stars wheeled. Wind lulled through leaves inshore. Little hairy creatures scuttled about in search of insects and grubs. Once something screamed.

Dawn turned the east wan. The sun followed, and the sea went molten with light. When warmth returned, it brought quickening. Harpoon knew hunger.

Yet he felt also his weakness, his unfitness for the waves. Besides, he had just sufficient mind that yesterday had not gone from him. The carcharodon might still lurk offshore.

Ebb had left a jellyfish stranded within his reach. It only made him entirely famished. However, instinct is patient. It has its cunning. Harpoon flopped heavily across the beach to a big elm. Shade would be necessary against the heat of midday. He splayed himself around the trunk, coiled his neck twice underneath his head, and slumped corpselike, minimally breathing. Perhaps the pteranodons would come back, and this time get careless.

Hours passed. Did he, in some dim wise, brood on the wrong he had suffered?

His luck suddenly turned. A stir, a rustling in the brush caught his attention. His yellow eyes swiveled in that direction and held fast. A four-foot shape groped out of the undergrowth and waddled over the dunes. Feathered but flightless, web-footed, beak armed with teeth, the diving bird had sat on her nest until she could trust the air to keep her eggs warm while she went after food. They were well hidden. She herself could cope with any of the land animals that had found their way to the island.

Her faith betrayed her. Harpoon's neck uncoiled. His head leaped. She squawked and stumbled, but afoot she was hopelessly awkward.

He finished everything the sand did not blot up. A hot meal like this was to him a rarity. It seemed to fill and restore him better than twice the weight of fish. He gusted a sigh, stared seaward, presently gathered himself and crawled that way. It was his rightful element too.

The tide was again low, the surf mild. Water

caressed him. Enemy or no, he struck out. He went not altogether heedless. Besides possible prey, he kept a new alertness for things from beneath. But he swam on toward his goal. The urge within him was that potent. Had Vorax reappeared, Harpoon would not have fled but fought.

As it happened, he fared in peace, though sluggishly and erratically. He had lost a major part of his propulsion. Unbalanced, he moved inefficiently, slewed off course, wasted his dwindled strength in making recoveries. The churning progress alarmed fish for hundreds of yards around; he caught no more. Frustration, exhaustion, pain brought him to a state you could call sullen anger. Nevertheless, he moved.

Again the stars, and just before dawn a sliver of moon. At midmorning clouds piled over the edge of sight, wind lashed froth off greenish-brown whitecaps, and rain burst loose.

By then Harpoon was almost at journey's end. Through the skirling and torrent boomed hoarse cries, through the salt spray rolled a dizzying smell of lust. With his last force, he rowed.

Storm or no, the trail had become unmistakable, for most of the elasmosaurs went ashore from the same sheltered inlet. It was rank with their musk. Harpoon dragged up through the shallows and flopped on the sand. For a while he merely heaved air into his lungs and out. Shapes moved huge and blurred before him.

One slithered closer. It was a female. Harpoon raised his head. He barked, too low for her to hear against the wind and downpour. His front flippers dug at the ground, hauled him forward. She perceived him, stopped, arched her neck coyly.

A larger form loomed into view behind her. The male saw Harpoon. He elevated his own neck in the zigzag that meant threat. Harpoon's response shaky. The unhurt animal rumbled deep in his chest and hunched toward him. Abruptly the jaws shot forward.

They chattered within inches of Harpoon's throat. The male withdrew them and waited to see whether his rival would yield.

Harpoon had endured too much for that. Raging, he struck. His fangs gouged along the other's ribs. The cuts were slight, but blood oozed forth. Rain turned it pink and sluiced it away. The male, more offended than injured, hooted. He smote once, twice, thrice, slashes that Harpoon was too slow to parry. The female watched with interest.

Harpoon lowered his head and hissed. The rival recognized flagging defiance. He coughed a louder challenge and lurched close in. Harpoon, who had ruled the rookery, drew back. He could not move fast. The rival took it for intransigence and ripped at him, again and again. Were the water's edge farther off, Harpoon would soon have been mortally wounded. He got to it in time and splashed away. The rival croaked triumph. He turned about and sought the female. They entwined necks in courtship.

The storm passed. Sunlight blazed through riven clouds. A rainbow stood above the lovemaking of the elasmosaurs. Harpoon lay offshore and watched.

Alae the pterosaur watched also, from aloft or sometimes from a perch on a rock. An outright death in battle was rare, but now and then a weakened beast succumbed, or weather uncovered a clutch of eggs that had been buried too shallowly. The rest of the eggs would hatch in due course, and many of the young would never make it to the water.

For Harpoon, at least the compulsion that kept him skulking around, thwarted and burning, likewise kept his fellows too busy to hunt. Hence fish were plentiful in the neighborhood. Their young would nourish the elasmosaur hatchlings. Harpoon caught an abundance of adults. Gradually his strength returned.

It was as yet inadequate, though, when the season ended and the sated breeders went their separate ways.

The females that swam past Harpoon had no more lure in them. A sense of loss was beyond his capacity, but unsatisfaction poisoned him. Vicious-tempered, he set homeward.

That became a much longer voyage than erstwhile, and harder. Lying motionless near the peninsula, he could let fish come to his vicinity. This was scarcely possible in open sea. He lacked both stamina and agility for the chase. He might have remained where he was. That would have been ill for the new generation, and instinct forbade — or habit, or what you might call a certain bleak stubbornness. Yonder ocean range was *his*.

He learned, by blind trial and error, failure and pain or success and cessation of pain. Handicapped, he could in some measure compensate. His swimming continued slow but became smoother, more efficient, less apt to scare prey off. He took things he once disdained, fingerlings, tiny squid, crabs around reefs or in patches of floating weed. They kept him fueled in between the occasional real catches.

It was hunger that gave him his most important lesson, which set his destiny. Fortune deserted him, and for days and nights he traveled empty-mouthed. Seas rolled waste, bare of all save wind. He plowed on. Hollowness grew until it was a dull anguish. His regained vitality began to fade anew. At last, soon after nightfall, when stars trembled forth, he raised his head and snapped at them.

Still almost full, the moon rose a while later. A trail of light shimmered and sparked across unrestful jet. Wind had died and the waves gone low, their murmur the only sound in the world.

Abruptly, from its height, Harpoon's vision captured a darkness that broke the moonglade on his starboard quarter. The thing slipped to and fro, not driftwood, awash but alive. He shuddered. His three flippers stroked hard. His tail slanted left, a steering oar, because of what he had lost. A bow wave sheened at his breast, radiance shattered on the wake swirling aft.

When he drew nigh, he laid paddles flat against sides and glided. Now he knew what he saw, a tylosaur. It was casting about for meat. If it noticed him in its turn, it paid scant attention. An adult tylosaur, one of the mosasaur tribe, had some twenty feet of length, half Harpoon's. Stockily built, it was more massive, and its jaws were meant for larger prey than his. Still, the two kinds ordinarily passed each other by. Carnivores avoid game that could inflict serious injuries on them. When they kill, they do it dispassionately. Half-grown, this one was already powerful. Unmaimed, it had been hunting well. What was an elasmosaur to it?

Harpoon was starved, desperate, but thus far little weakened. Moreover, he, the invincible, had suffered mutilation, defeat, ignominy, outcasting. It scarred him inwardly as well as bodily. Say that he had gone daft. He attacked.

He did so, however, with cold, hard-won precision. The tylosaur had twice his bite. Harpoon had incomparably more reach. He used that advantage for all it would give.

From his remove, he struck. His teeth ripped, closed. With a slantwise twist, he flensed a yard-long strip of skin and flesh. Blood gushed, black across moonlight. Astounded, the tylosaur merely gaped. Harpoon tossed his booty in the air, caught it on the way down, and swallowed. Immediately he raked again.

The tylosaur unfroze. It gurgled rage and threshed forward. Gracefully formed, even in his crippled state, Harpoon slipped aside from the ponderous rush. The tylosaur came around quickly, and almost avenged itself. Harpoon dived. The tylosaur pursued. Harpoon brought his muzzle above. Thus free to breathe, he had more energy for dodging about as he felt the oncoming of the foe. When the tylosaur passed, he lowered his head and got a piece out of its after end.

A cornered creature will fight, but the sea has no corners. The tylosaur knew of nothing it could gain except possibly a victory it did not need. It fled. Harpoon followed. Over and over, hour by hour, under the relentless white moon, he tore. Often the victim turned, but always the tormentor escaped, only to come back.

Sunrise threw fresh red across the waters. By then the tylosaur was waning. It swam passive, directionless, spiritless, ever more feebly. Harpoon escorted it, eating at such times as he wished. Dusk had fallen when the tylosaur sank. Harpoon accompanied it as deeply as he could endure, stuffing himself. Afterward he floated on the surface and digested through the next day and night. He had fed amply for the rest of his voyage.

So did he swim home to his kingdom. How he found it, how he knew the bounds of it, is for another language than words — mathematics or music, perhaps. Write equations describing magnetic gradients, Coriolis force, seasonal changes in the arcs drawn by sun, moon, and constellations long since permuted out of existence. Play symphonies metaphorizing currents, temperatures, drowned mountains, breakers on skerries, hues and saltiness eternally shifting but always unique. Consider the versatility of the honeybee in its own multifarious environment. Grant that a highly evolved reptile can be of a complexity sufficient for madness.

Harpoon roved alone. He still took such prey of a size normal for him as happenstance allowed. He still gleaned what formerly for him had been contemptibly small. But sometimes he went after animals he used to shun because they were too dangerous. Though their ranges overlapped his, they seldom competed with him in what they hunted. Now he pursued the great marine crocodile. He quested through labyrinths of coral till he found and grappled with the giant squid in its lair. Twice he slew shorter-necked kin, plesiosaurs. The combats left him with grievous wounds, but also with enough meat to sustain him while they healed. He grew gaunt and scarred and grim; but he survived, he won, and in his darkling awareness he brewed implacability.

Days lengthened, waned, lengthened afresh. Sunlight and storm walked the seas, moon and stars wheeled above. Earth and her sister planets sailed on their immemorial rounds. An asteroid passed too near Mars and was perturbed into a new orbit. Shadows ghosted over its pocked mass as, tumbling, it fell inward.

Springtime blew across ocean. Often those winds howled violent, spume flew in sheets off the manes of waves cresting mountainous above blue-black troughs and thickly flung rain cratered them. Harpoon rocked and pitched, uncoiled his neck and whistled reply. All mighty things had become his foes. When calm returned, the world breathed wholly blue and white. Rivers on land bore blossom odors down to sea, whence currents took them onward. Well-nigh imperceptible they were after hundreds of miles; but there were senses out there to which they whispered.

Blood quickened. Eyes turned toward sunrise. One by one, the saurians embarked on their journey.

That day came likewise for Harpoon. He might have denied it. Males commonly did when they lost hope of gaining a mate. Within his limits, the elasmosaur could learn. Rather than be torn and tantalized, at last fatally hurt, he would linger a few more years by himself surly, forsaken, a rogue. But Harpoon had gone beyond mere beggarly existence. Despite his lameness — or because of it — the terrors of the deep went in fear of him. Why should he not once more dominate his fellows?

He never thought in those terms. That narrow skull carried no means of imagining a future. He did what his urges commanded. Killing was a compulsion like mating, save that it never left him. Was its wellspring that which had happened the year before? Did he wordlessly, dreamlessly seek revenge? Call him obsessed, call him crazy. He set forth.

First he had fed well. Reptile, he could live on it for days. His noisy three-limbed passage continued to drive fish away, and now he took no time to lie in wait for them, so food became very scant while he fared. Bit by bit, hunger grew, and with it his wrath. Woe betide any creature that crossed him.

Waves marched from horizon to horizon, turquoise, emerald, amber, smoke, foam-dappled; sun-blink, star-blink, moon-shimmer, cloud shadow, rain, rainbow; sometimes something sprang in the distance, a brief gleam, but otherwise Harpoon was alone, forever in the middle of immensity. He swam on.

Then at last scraps of weed appeared to him, and then pieces of wood, abob in the water. A vague blue-gray limned the forward rim of the world. It sharpened and enlarged, hour by hour. An island hove in sight, trees swaying under the sea wind, above the combers along a beach. The same whiteness danced over outlying coral reefs and shone off a pair of wings at hover aloft.

To Alae the pteranodon, Harpoon was a fresh element in the scene beneath his gaze. Could a meal result? Effortlessly he waited, like a part of the air that whittered around and ubore him. Sunshine soaked into his membranes.

When he spied a submarine shade, his vigilance focused more closely. Perhaps a fragment of memory flickered, perhaps it was only that anything new might hold promise for him.

Vorax the carcharodon was not actually hunting. He had killed an elasmosaur on her way to rendezvous, just a few days ago. A part of her still stewed in his belly. These had turned into excellent grounds, ripe for his reaping. He moved with lazy tail-flicks because he must, to maintain flotation way and a stream through his gills. Close to the surface, he too drank warmth. The water flowed easily past the tall white blade of his dorsal fin.

Head on high, Harpoon saw. For minutes he lay moveless, adrift, while the impulses warred within him.

Fear he had known when he was small, but he outgrew his enemies and forgot. Whatever seed of it remained, the acid that is in suffering and rancor had eaten away. Hunger had overcome discretion, and recklessness was rewarded. The conflict that seethed here was between his drive to kill and his need to beget. He shuddered with it.

Insanity won. He charged. The sea surged by his prow. Teeth flashed. He hissed his hatred forth into he wind.

Lordly and leisurely, Vorax went unaware until the assault was upon him. As ever, Harpoon struck from yards away. With inborn knowledge, though it clamored against engaging such a foe, he ripped into the vulnerable juncture where fin met armor-tough hide. Blood spurted into his throat, ocean-cold and salt.

Set upon by an unknown out of nowhere, Vorax dived. No fright made him flee, no outrage made him turn. Devoid alike of love and malice, he would simply depart from a place become unpleasant. Water slid around him. Its green duskened.

Mad Harpoon came after.

His neck stretched in front. He tore at the beating flukes. There also he drew blood. It curled aft to mingle with the bubbles that trailed and caught the last light. He overtook and slashed at the wan flank.

Then Vorax must needs come about. Suddenly Harpoon confronted the gates of the gape. He shot his head between them and tore the huge tongue open. But the air in him was gone. He stroked upward to breathe. Vorax followed, a machine now set for slaughter.

From heaven Alae beheld waves roiled and broken apart. He folded his wings to drop closer. Nothing like this had happened before, combat between kelp-necked elasmosaur and grinning shark. Blood shone across the blue-green, itself incandescent crimson. Yes, chunks of loose flesh jumped in the spray.

The carcharodon closed in. His jaws took hold.

When his antagonist bit him no longer, he did not press the battle. He had no more cause to. He withdrew into the deeps, where he could cruise through darkness till his wounds healed.

Harpoon's front flippers churned the water white. It began to swirl about the hulk of him, the blood and entrails. Down and down he went. The sight was too much for Alae. Greed sent him stooping upon the red wealth. Meaning to stay a safe distance from the saurian, he misgauged. The neck flashed forth, the fangs caught a wing. Frantic, he fluttered and shrieked, his beak turned up to heaven. The grip held fast.

The maelstrom collapsed, and the sea rolled on as before.

One night in a later season, a new star shone. Hasty and widdershins, it flitted across the constellations, dim at first but steadily brighter and more near.

11.
THE END OF AN ERA
ESSAY BY WILLIAM GALLAGHER
SPECULATION BY HARRY HARRISON

BECOMING A MODERN WORLD

WILLIAM B. GALLAGHER

BY THE BEGINNING OF THE CRETACEOUS (145 MILLION YEARS AGO), THE CONTINENTS HAD DRIFTED farther toward their present positions as the Atlantic Ocean continued to widen. A great seaway separated the southern continents from the northern landmass; Eurasia was still connected to North America by Greenland. The equatorial sea that today we call the Tethys Sea swept through the strait between North and South America, for Central America did not yet exist. The Tethyan waters poured through the Gibraltar region and submerged the Middle East, creating a globe-girdling tropical oceanic current that helped warm the earth's climate. India, still adjacent to Australia and Antarctica, had yet to begin its long voyage northward to join Asia.

As continents split apart, ocean waters flooded the lower-lying regions of the land. By the middle of the period, the western interior region of North America was inundated by waters creeping up the Mississippi lowlands from Texas and the Gulf of Mexico and coming down across the Canadian Plains from the Arctic Ocean on the north. North America was cut in two by a vast inland sea, sometimes called the Western Interior Seaway. To the east of the inland sea, the old low Appalachian region formed one landmass; worn down by erosion, its low-gradient streams and rivers did not carry much sediment to the eastern part of the seaway. On the west, the rising lands of the Rockies contributed large quantities of sand and mud to the western edge of the interior sea, not to mention tremendous amounts of volcanic ash from great eruptions.

MARINE PLANT COMMUNITIES

Warmed by the equatorial circulation of the Tethyan seaway, tremendous blooms of floating plant plank-ton (phytoplankton) filled the marine waters. The most abundant of these were the Coccolithophoridae (or "coccoliths"), microscopic algae that secreted a limy shell composed of tiny platelets of calcium carbonate. The White Cliffs of Dover in southeastern England are largely composed of chalk made out of these minuscule plates, and chalk of this age is widespread, found from Nebraska to Australia. In fact the name "Cretaceous" is derived from the Latin word for chalk. Other microscopic algae common in the Cretaceous phytoplankton included diatoms (which secrete silicate-rich shells) and dinoflagellates ("terrible whippers"), curious half-plant, half-animal single-celled organisms that can propel themselves by means of a whiplike organ; today, some dinoflagellates are responsible for red tides that poison fish populations in coastal ocean waters.

Subsisting on the plant plankton were zooplankton, microscopic single-celled animals such as foraminiferans (or forams for short) and radiolarians. Forams are essentially amoebas that secrete a calcareous shell, while radiolarians grow glassy shells, often shaped like pincushions. The rapid evolution of forams and their widespread presence in the Cretaceous oceans make them ideal as index fossils, whose specific forms mark certain restricted stratigraphic levels of Cretaceous rock formations.

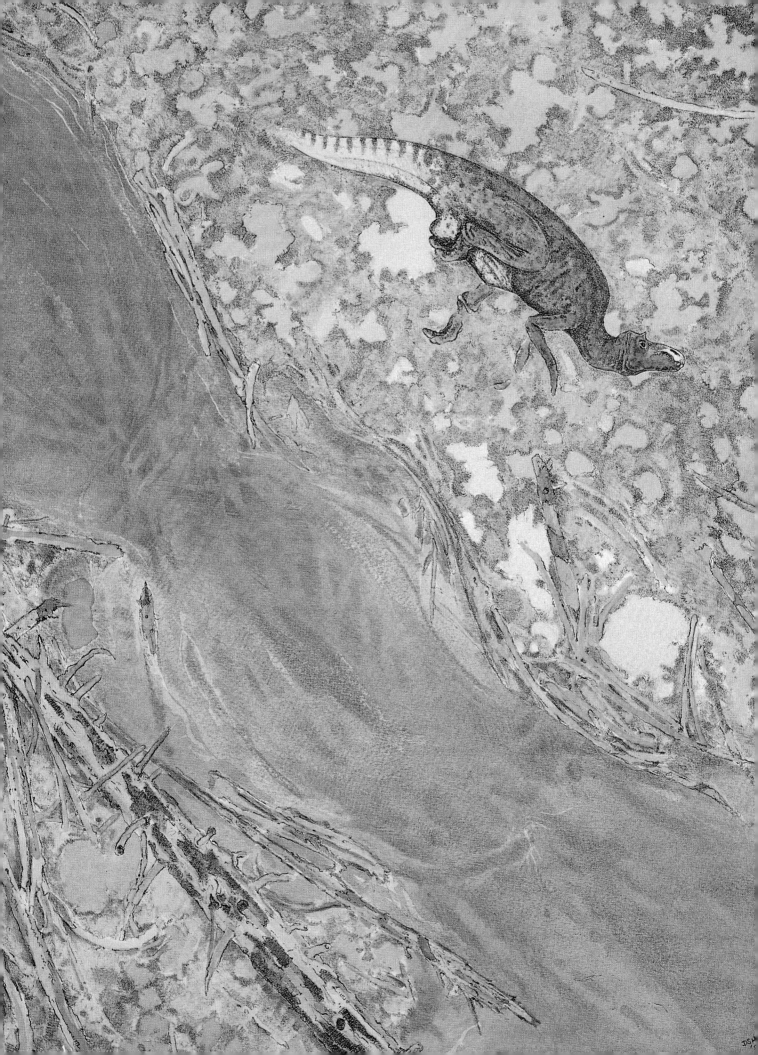

MARINE INVERTEBRATES

Among larger marine invertebrates (animals without backbones), the mollusks were the most important group in the Cretaceous. Some clams, such as inoceramids found in the Niobrara Formation of the American West, grew up to a yard long. In the muddy bottoms, these big shells became stable islands of hard substrate that other shellfish colonized. Prehistoric oysters including *Gryphaea*, *Pycnodonte* and *Exogyra* formed dense shellbank communities that probably provided food resources for many shell-crushing predators. Snails drilled holes into oyster and clam shells, and many different kinds of these gastropods proliferated. Some clams that we call rudists tried to become like corals; growing barrel-like valves that cemented together in colonies, these clams became the dominant reef-building organisms of the warm Cretaceous seas. Today their buried reefs are important petroleum traps in the Middle East and Mexico.

The most spectacular of Cretaceous mollusks were the ammonites, chambered cephalopods related to the modern pearly nautilus and, more distantly, to squid and octopus. These, too, evolved rapidly into a wonderful variety of forms, making them useful as index fossils. While some shells were straight cones (like *Baculites*, a common Cretaceous form) and some were coiled in a plane (like the modern nautilus), there were other ammonites that had spirally coiled shells and recurved shells. The distinguishing characteristic of all ammonites was the complex suture pattern formed by the meeting of the growth chamber walls with the outside shell. This junction produced a complicated pattern of lobes and saddles that is frequently seen in the ammonite fossils found today in Cretaceous marine deposits. In addition, many ammonites were ornamented with regularly placed bumps and nodes. Ammonites swam through the water by jet propulsion, pumping water through a fleshy nozzle by muscle action to provide propulsive power; their chambered shells were gas-filled, and they probably could regulate their buoyancy by controlling the gas in their shells. They had two eyes and a powerful beak, and were predators and scavengers. The largest of these cephalopods was over six feet in diameter.

Closely allied to the ammonites were the belemnites, smaller straight-shelled cephalopods more closely related to modern squid. Unlike modern squid, however, they grew a stout and solid guard shell that preserves very well as a fossil. Considering that in some Cretaceous marine deposits there are vast numbers of these shells, the belemnites must have concentrated together in schools much as do modern squid. Measuring concentrations of oxygen isotopes trapped in belemnite guard shell fossils, scientists have determined that the seas of that time were warmer than today. For instance, from measurements made on belemnite fossils from New Jersey, the ocean temperature in the latter part of the Cretaceous at this latitude seems to have been around 72 degrees Fahrenheit year-round, a warmth comparable to the seas around southern Florida today.

THE FISH AND THEIR PREDATORS

It would seem from the abundance of shark, ray, and swordfish fossils found in freshwater and estuarine deposits that the cartilaginous fish were more common in rivers and brackish-water environments back in the Cretaceous Period than they are today. While many sharks will come into estuaries to breed and feed (especially during a spring tide), this may reflect an an-

Preceding page: After a dinosaur died, if its resting place was undisturbed, it usually was gradually turned to stone by mineral replacement, as is occurring with this Maiasaur. By Doug Henderson.

cient origination for some of these groups in brackish-water, tidally-influenced environments. Many types of cartilaginous fish that are deeper-water inhabitants today are amply represented by fossils (mostly teeth) in near-shore and estuarine beds of the Cretaceous. Primitive bony fish living in freshwater streams and rivers during the latter part of the age of reptiles include gar, bowfin, and sturgeon. It may be that some of the chondrichthyan (or cartilaginous) fish were driven out of their nearshore and estuarine environments and into deeper ocean waters by the appearance and spread of more modern bony fish types.

In the early part of the Cretaceous, the Gulf of Mexico extended clear across Texas, and thick deposits of marine limestone were laid down in the central and western parts of the Lone Star State at this time. Many shellfish lived on the limy sea bottom, and fossils from the Fredricksburg Group of Texas include numerous snails, clams, sea urchins, and ammonites. Various types of shell-crushing skates, rays, and primitive sharks swam in the Early Cretaceous Texan seas, feeding on the marine invertebrates. Pycnodont fish with deep bodies and blunt bean-shaped teeth also fed on shellfish; these primitive bony fish, sometimes called "coral-nibblers," were diverse and widespread at this time. While the first lamnoid sharks of more modern aspect had appeared, there were only a few species of small bony fish of the type that would give rise to herring, tuna, bass, and all the fish that dominate the world oceans today.

Feeding on these fish were large marine reptiles of several types. The ichthyosaurs were fishlike reptiles that gave birth to live young. They had a very streamlined body similar in form to modern dolphins and tuna. *Platypterygius* was the last of the ichthyosaurs in North America. By about the middle of the Cretaceous Period all the ichthyosaurs had disappeared

from this continent, although there are some indications that they may have lasted until near the end of that period in Australia.

Sharing the rule of the Early Cretaceous seaways were the plesiosaurs, long-necked, heavy-bodied sea monsters that have sometimes been invoked as ancestors of the Loch Ness monster. With strong, powerful flippers, these animals propelled themselves through the water, striking out with their serpentine necks at schools of fish. Also present in the marine waters were crocodiles and sea turtles.

By the beginning of the Late Cretaceous, the inland sea was well established, and the limy waters produced chalky sedimentation over a wide area, from Kansas to Saskatchewan and from New Mexico to Minnesota. These widespread chalks of the Niobrara Formation are very fossiliferous in some locales. Also, the fine-grained chalk has preserved skeletons in remarkable detail, saving for us today an ancient aquarium of Cretaceous sea life.

LATER FISH AND TURTLES

By the middle of the Cretaceous, the sharks typical of the later part of the period appeared. These included ancestors of the modern lamnoid shark such as the mackerel shark and great white shark, the bizarre goblin shark which today is only found in deeper open ocean waters, and the characteristically Cretaceous form *Squalicorax*. All that we have of these fish are teeth and vertebrae, since the rest of the skeleton was cartilage. Primitive shell-crushers like *Ptychodus* and pycnodont fish were still present, but the waters seemed to have been filled with more advanced bony fish. There were billfish, gar, bowfin, a kind of sailfish, needlefish, various small sardine-like fish, and a predaceous troutlike fish, *Pachyrhizodus*. One of the more bizarre types was *Enchodus*, a small to medium-sized fish derived from the same lineage as salmon; it possessed a large set of outsized fangs, similar to the large teeth grown during breeding season by migrating salmon. But the biggest fish swimming in the Niobrara sea was *Xiphactinus*, the so-called "bulldog tarpon"; it had the large long body of the tarpon, with a blunt powerful head containing a jaw full of big sharp teeth. Undoubtedly it was the top predator of its day; an exquisitely preserved specimen of 14-foot-long *Xiphactinus* has been found with a 6-foot fish called *Gillicus* inside the ribs in the stomach region, apparently the larger fish's last meal. There were also barracuda surrogates, smaller predators like *Saurodon* and *Saurocephalus* with long lean bodies and underslung jaws filled with small pointed teeth.

Sea turtles oared through the waters, including the largest of their type. The protostegids were the biggest sea turtles ever, reaching their greatest size in the giant *Archelon*, a turtle 12 feet long. Like modern leatherback turtles, *Archelon* had reduced the bone in its shell, perhaps to maintain buoyancy.

PLESIOSAURS OF THE NIOBRARA CHALK

The Niobrara chalk of Kansas has produced some wonderful specimens of plesiosaurs, for which it has been famous for over a century. In fact, the greatest rivalry in American paleontology was initiated by a plesiosaur skeleton. E. D. Cope of Philadelphia and O. C. Marsh of New Haven were the most eminent vertebrate paleontologists of the last half of the nineteenth century. Originally they were friendly colleagues, having met in Europe during the Civil War when both men were traveling and studying at the universities and museums of the Old World. But their relationship degenerated into rivalry, of which an account is given in Chapter 12.

Cope, possibly out of revenge for perceived wrongs at Marsh's hands, decided to go out to Kansas and look for fossils in areas nether he nor Marsh had visited. He hired a local guide, Charles Sternberg, who went on to become one of the greatest fossil collectors in the history of paleontology. One of the fruits of Cope's labors was the vertebral column of large marine reptile, a plesiosaur. Although bits and pieces were known from New Jersey, and complete specimens of smaller species had been found in England and Germany, Cope's find was a giant long-necked form of plesiosaur which he called *Elasmosaurus*.

Plesiosaur remains actually come in two different forms. The long-necked elasmosaurs usually have small heads; their snakelike necks may have as many as 76 vertebrae. The other type are short-necked, large-headed forms variously called pliosaurs or polycotylids. Both types ate cephalopods (such as squid or ammonites) and fish, as evidenced by fossil stomach contents. At least one plesiosaur fossil contained the remains of a flying reptile in its stomach.

While the ichthyosaurs had largely disappeared by the middle of the Cretaceous, another group of reptiles returned to the sea at about this time. The aigialosaurs were large land lizards related to the modern monitors such as the Komodo dragon of Indonesia and the Nile monitor of Africa. Adopting an aquatic way of life, they rapidly gave rise to the marine mosasaurs, giant sea lizards that were the terror of the Late Cretaceous seas. By Niobrara time, the mosasaurs had diversified into a variety of genera and species.

FLYING REPTILES AND BIRDS

The superb preservation of the Niobrara chalk has allowed us to see the rare and fragile skeletons of flying reptiles (discussed in Chapter 10) and birds in exquisite detail. Both groups had slender, hollow bones, an adaptation to life in the air, so their presence is a testament to the remarkable preservative qualities of the Niobrara Formation.

Birds interred on the chalky seafloor belonged to primitive avian groups that still possessed teeth, a vestige of their reptilian ancestry. Two varieties have been preserved in the Niobrara; flightless forms that floated on the sea's surface, probably diving for their fishy food, and winged types that flew. The former, known as hesperornithiforms, were virtually wingless; they had long stout legs for propelling themselves across and under the water. *Hesperornis* is the most commonly found bird in these deposits, although other flightless types include *Parahesperornis* and *Baptornis*. The most common of the winged birds belonged to the genus *Ichthyornis*, shaped somewhat like a sea gull but armed with a jaw containing small pointy teeth.

THE CRETACEOUS INLAND SEA

Why were conditions so favorable for preservation on the Niobrara sea bottom, particularly in Kansas? Outcrops of the Niobrara Formation farther west are not so chalky nor so fossil-rich. In this direction, the rising lands on the western side of the interior sea contributed large quantities of sand and mud; conditions were more turbulent, and bottom waters supported more scavengers and other organisms. On the eastern side of the seaway, the lowlands of the emerged portion of the midwest did not supply much sediment. Along this side of the seaway, chalky deposition was undiluted by mud and sand. The sea bottom here was a soft soupy substrate; only specially adapted animals, such as the giant flat inoceramid clams, could live on it. Oxygen levels were low, also a limiting factor for marine life. So when a carcass sank down from the water column above, it

was immediately entombed in the soft, fine yielding ooze, and there were no scavengers or currents to disarticulate the skeleton and scatter its bones about.

The conditions that led to the abundant production of coccolith chalk in the interior seaway changed about 84 million years ago. Instead, dark oxygen-poor muds and clays accumulated over a wide area of the seaway, forming what geologists today call the Pierre Formation. The black shales of the Pierre contain abundant evidence of Cretaceous sea life; they are now exposed over a wide area of South Dakota, especially around the Black Hills and along the Missouri River.

Inoceramid clams and ammonites are especially common in some layers of the Pierre. The most abundant form is a straight-shelled ammonite called *Baculites*; it is usually found with its mother-of-pearl layer intact, creating an iridescent specimen of striking beauty. Some of the coiled ammonites display holes which appear to be puncture marks; these holes have been matched to the tooth patterns of mosasaurs.

While bottom conditions had changed, apparently life in the water column above it had not been drastically affected. Many of the animals present in the Niobrara sea were also around during Pierre time. Among the fish, large lamnoid sharks were present; judging from the size of their vertebrae found in the shale, they probably grew as large as the modern great white shark. Ichthyodectid fish like the giant *Xiphactinus* were relatively common. Salmon-like fish such as *Enchodus*, *Stratodus*, and *Cimolichthys* were also abundant, as were the saurocephalid fish with their barracuda-like underslung jaws.

More modern types of sea turtles (e.g., *Toxochelys*) plied the Pierre waters, in addition to *Archelon*, also found in the Pierre. Short-necked plesiosaurs were relatively more common than the long-necked *Alzadasaurus*.

Mosasaurs thrived in the Pierre Sea. Smaller forms

such as *Clidastes* were common; an unusual mosasaur with blunt, shell-crushing teeth called *Globidens* appeared in the inland sea. Larger mosasaurs included *Tylosaurus*, *Mosasaurus*, and others. The mosasaurs became masters of the sea in Pierre time. They are the most commonly found and widespread fossils of large marine reptiles not only in the dark shales of the western interior but also in the Upper Cretaceous marine deposits along the Gulf and Atlantic coastal plains. The large mosasaurs were probably ambush predators, lying in wait until their prey approached, then lunging after it. The massive skull was equipped with long jaws lined with large sharp curving teeth; even the back of the roof of the mouth had smaller stout teeth for holding the captured prey. Most unusual was the joint in the middle of the lower jaw; it would appear that mosasaurs could pop open their lower jaw, perhaps in order to bolt down larger food items. In addition to ammonites, preserved stomach contents show that *Tylosaurus* ate sharks, bony fish, the diving bird *Hesperornis*, and even other smaller mosasaurs.

Hesperornis bones are found in the Pierre shale, especially its stout femurs and long leg bones. *Pteranodon* has also been collected from the dark shales. The most common dinosaur types found in marine deposits are fossils of duck-billed hadrosaurs which washed down from rivers.

Volcanic ash beds called bentonites can be traced for long distances within the Pierre Formation. Large and repeated volcanic eruptions in the rising land to the west of the interior sea were the source of these ash beds. About 73 million years ago, the pace of uplift quickened as the Rocky Mountains were born in a mountain-building event geologists have labeled the Laramide Revolution after the Laramie Mountains in southeastern Wyoming. Sheets of sand were swept down off the eroding highlands and transported to the east, where the sediments were deposited as the Fox Hills Formation along the margins of the shallowing and retreating inland sea. *Enchodus*, fresh-water rays, and a very ugly relative of the sharks, the ratfish, have been found along with ammonites and clams in the Fox Hills sandstone. Before the end of the Cretaceous, the inland sea was gone from the western interior, and North America began to look much more like its modern configuration.

While the interior of the continent was flooded, the coastal plain margins on the southern and eastern flanks of North America were also inundated. This flooding of the continental margin alternately shoaled and deepened, like a great tidal cycle, leaving behind a succession of sands, clays, and a peculiar kind of sediment called glauconite, more commonly known as greensand. Perhaps this alternation of shallow-water and deeper-water sediments reflects global changes in sea level, as huge underwater eruptions spewed forth enormous quantities of lava along the volcanic mid-ocean ridges, decreasing the volume of the ocean basins and displacing seawater onto the low-lying areas of the land.

LAND FLORA OF THE CRETACEOUS

At the beginning of the Cretaceous Period, the land was covered by a typically Mesozoic flora of tree ferns, cycads, ginkgos, and conifers. In the Early Cretaceous, a new form of plant appeared and spread rapidly: the flowering plants. They quickly diversified, and by the middle of the period angiosperms of modern aspect had spread all over the planet. Sands and clays deposited in swamps and rivers in Maryland and New Jersey record the early development of flowering plants, as they supplanted the previously abundant pines, ferns, and cycads. Precisely how this happened is still a matter of conjecture; some experts believe

The Late Cretaceous hadrosaur, Parasaurolophus, *walks a riverbank. By Brian Franczak.*

that flowering plants started out colonizing unstable environments such as frequently flooded riverbanks. Other authorities have suggested that the angiosperms originated along estuaries and bays as the ocean waters flooded the continents. Some paleontologists have proposed that the major changeover in land vegetation may have been responsible for the turnover in the dinosaur population from the Late Jurassic Morrison fauna to the more typically Cretaceous dinosaurs such as hadrosaurs, ankylosaurs, and ceratopsians. These low grazers may have found a favorable niche by cropping the fast-growing fodder of the flowering plants and eating their richly nutritious fruits, distributing their seeds in the process.

By the end of the Cretaceous, modern plants such as magnolias, buttonwood trees, and the rose family decorated the landscape. It would appear from the shape of some of these early flowers (preserved as fossils) that quite early on in the evolution of angiosperms an interdependence between flowering plants and insects developed. The flowering plants came to depend upon insects such as bees for pollination, while the insects utilized plants for food resources. Indeed, some of the earliest bee fossils known are preserved in amber found in the same New Jersey Cretaceous beds that contain the leaf impressions of early angiosperms.

LAND ANIMALS OF THE LATE CRETACEOUS

As the sea encroached on land, the river valleys flooded and brackish embayments developed. Soft-shelled turtles, freshwater rays, gar, and sturgeon swam in these estuaries. But the ruler of these tidewater regions was a giant crocodile known to science as *Deinosuchus*. From Montana to Texas, from Georgia to New Jersey, this toothy monster prowled the backwater bays; growing up to 40 feet in length, with a big ugly snout full of stout fangs, this croc was capable of devouring any unwary hadrosaur that may have waded too deeply into the marsh. There were numerous other crocodiles and smaller alligators present along the Cretaceous coast, some of which ventured farther out to sea.

The near-shore sea bottom of the Late Cretaceous coastal plain region supported prodigious oyster banks, where large oysters such as *Exogyra* and *Pycnodonte* crowded together in dense concentrations. These oyster banks supported shell-crushing fish such as hybodont sharks, skates, and bonefish. Larger sharks patrolled the waters, and plesiosaurs and mosasaurs were present. The mosasaurs reached their apex in *Mosasaurus maximus*, which grew to 40 feet long. Probably these later types also depended heavily on shellfish for food: broken and punctured ammonite shells have been found in eastern marine beds also.

On land, the smaller animals looked more like a typically modern fauna. Frogs and salamanders were about, and the great dinosaurs found lizards similar to skinks, iguanas, and geckos underfoot. Snakes, a relatively late development in the evolution of reptiles, were already present; *Paleophis* was a primitive constrictor whose rare remains are found in Western U.S. Cretaceous strata. Among the mammals, pouched marsupials are represented by fossils of *Alphadon*, an opossum-like form. Placental mammals (those mammals with bellybuttons) included the insect-eating shrews. Most other mammals belonged to the primitive group known as multituberculates, small ratlike animals that were probably nocturnal. At the and of the Cretaceous, long-legged shore birds resembling curlews and plovers arrived on the scene, the predecessors of more modern toothless birds.

THE END OF THE ERA

As modern mountain ranges rose and ancient seaways closed the long summer of the Mesozoic came to an end. The retreat of the inland sea from western North America meant that the moderating influence of warm ocean waters was withdrawn from the continental interior. Elsewhere, the drifting of continents cut the

Tethyan Seaway, and the Alps began to rise in a broad arc across southern Europe, cutting off the worldwide tropical circulation of the ocean. Widespread and intense volcanic activity associated with the rise of the Rockies and other newly-forming mountain chains may have affected atmospheric conditions on a global scale. Temperatures fluctuated over wider ranges in these continental regimes, and forms of life long used to stable environmental situations were now faced with extremes of climate such as increasing aridity, cooler climates, and real seasons. It was against this backdrop of changing geographical, oceanographic, and meteorological conditions that one of the great crises in the history of life, the terminal Cretaceous mass extinction event, took place.

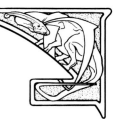

DAWN OF THE ENDLESS NIGHT

HARRY HARRISON

AKOTOLP WAS DEEPLY ASLEEP, IMMERSED IN THE DREAMLESS AND IMMOBILE SLEEP OF THE Yilanè. Then the dawn came and she was instantly awake, instantly aware at the same time that something was very wrong. The light was far too bright for dawn, far brighter even than midday, burning through the gaps between the leaves that walled her sleeping chamber. Her nictitating membranes closed as she pushed aside the vines and stepped out beneath the branches of the city tree.

"It is wrong, all wrong," she said to herself, making the twisting tail movement of intensity magnified. For this dawn that was not dawn was in the west. This could not be, but it certainly was. As a scientist she was forced to accept the evidence of her senses, no matter how unbelievable they were.

The light was fading, slowly becoming dimmer, obscured even more by the figure that stood before her. A fargi; Akotolp waved her aside but she did not move. She spoke instead.

"The Eistaa . . . summons of great urgency."

"Yes, of course — now move out of the way."

Akotolp watched until the last glimmer had faded from sight. The stars reappeared, as well as the almost full moon that spread silver light across the city. The fargi led the way, stumbling and shuffling through the shadows towards the open, central area of the ambesed where the Eistaa waited.

"You saw the light," she said when Akotolp stopped before her.

"I did."

"Explanation-expatiation desired."

"Desire to obey — however insuffiency of knowledge-information."

The Eistaa signed surprise and disillusion. "In a lifetime of acquaintance-friendship I have never heard you admit to any lack of knowledge."

"There is a first time for everything. I am considering this matter slowly and rationally. The cause of this great light is unknown. It is not fire, for I have seen fire."

"What does that term *fire* mean?"

"Explanation time-consuming, unneeded."

"The fargi panic, my scientist knows nothing. It is all very disturbing."

"A strange phenomenon — but it is over."

Akotolp instantly regretted saying this, for no sooner had she spoken than the earth beneath her feet shuddered and a great sound assaulted them. The attendant fargi wailed in fear and clapped their hands over their ear-openings; some even fell to the ground and lay writhing there. The Eistaa was made of sterner stuff and stood stoutly upright, back arched with legs spread wide, toe-claws sunk into the soil to hold her erect. When the noise had sunk to a rumble she signed great disapproval.

"You did say it was over, scientist of great knowledge?"

"Apology for misconception, humble submission."

Akotolp stretched her neck back, exposing her throat in added emphasis. The Eistaa signed acceptance and rejection of death offer.

"Tell me your thoughts, for feeble as they are this night you are still the only one who might possibly explain what happened."

"I cannot explain. Only analyze."

"Then proceed."

"An event of geological magnitude —"

"Definition needed unknown term *geological*."

Akotolp fought not to disclose her agitation at the interruption. She concealed her movements of distaste by turning and kicking aside some fallen leaves, then settling back comfortably on her tail. She used the simplified motions of night-talk, clearly visible in the clear moonlight.

"Geological refers to the earth on which we stand. There are beneath this solid ground great forces at work. I have seen, beyond the jungles of Entoban to the east, a range of high mountains that have burst open and give forth melted rock. I saw fire there as well. An event that can tear open solid mountains and melt solid rock is of geological magnitude."

"Was this a geological event?"

Akotolp sat rigid and unmoving, wrapped in thought. It was some time before she stirred and spoke.

"No, I am certain it was not. It was too sudden. All of the events I watched began slowly, grew and proceeded. This came too quickly. And it was very large, though distant."

"Distant? Explanation needed." The Eistaa, while efficient at ruling and ordering her city, neither knew nor cared about the facts of science. Akotolp forced herself to proceed patiently.

"Distant because of the strong light that awakened us. A Yilanè of science in the city of Yebeisk to the south conducted a series of experiments to discover at what speed light passes through the air. She told me that refine the experiments as she might the speed

always seemed to be close to instantaneous. But the speed of sound is very slow. This is easily demonstrated. Therefore, since the sound of the event came a good time after we saw the light, the conclusion is that what happened was far distant in the ocean. And very large."

The Eistaa made motions of impatience-confusion. "As always I find your explanations impossible to follow. Now you will clarify-simplify."

"Something very large happened far out in the ocean."

"The light flared. Later there was the sound and the ground moved. Why?"

"The ground must have been moved by the movement of the sea —"

Akotolp gasped, her mouth opening wide with shock. She jumped to her feet and turned to look at the smooth water of the bay.

"It will happen!" She signed urgency and fear so strongly that the Eistaa recoiled.

"What is it? What is happening?"

"What will happen. You must order your fargi to go among the sleepers at once. Awaken every Yilanè. Order them inland as quickly as possible, to the hills beyond the fields where the onetsensast graze. Order it, Eista."

"Why?"

"Don't you see? A force so distant that could shake the ground here must be very strong indeed. It will make waves such as we have never seen in the worst storm. Those waves are coming even as we speak."

The Eistaa reached an instant decision. "I will so order —"

It was already too late, far too late.

The waters of the bay were draining away, pouring through the harbor entrance into the sea. And distantly, growing instantly louder, was the crashing rumble of water falling on water, churning and roaring. Drowning out all other sounds.

Striking and drowning the shore, filling the bay in

an instant. Rising in a flood that engulfed the city tree, broke off the limbs, stripped away the smaller growth, hurtled inland.

Akotolp closed mouth, eyes, nostrils, struck out in panic at the salt water that engulfed her. Felt the pressure of the water above her. Swam upwards in the darkness. Was struck a terrible blow in her side that numbed her. Clutched her wounded arm with her other hand, thrust violently with legs and tail.

Burst into foam-filled darkness, gasped in air.

Was struck again in the darkness. Almost unconscious, weakened by pain, she swam on, knowing that this was her only chance of survival. If she sank below the surface again she would never emerge.

An unmeasurable, pain-filled time passed before she felt solidity beneath her feet. Muddy, debris-laden water streamed about her, dropped lower, to her midriff, then to her knees. She staggered and fell heavily, screamed with pain as a greater darkness closed over her.

Akotolp woke slowly to light and agony. A heavy, warm rain was falling. Black rain, streaming filthily across her skin. She blinked with incomprehension, felt the grit in her eyes. Sat up and her vision blurred red with pain. Arms and legs moved, apparently no bones broken. But the immense soreness in her side must surely be more than mere bruising; some ribs might be broken. It hurt to breathe. Alive and injured — but still alive. Only when she was gratefully aware of this did her scientific curiosity return.

She was standing ankle-deep in a plain of mud. Branches, entire uprooted trees were strewn about her. Two dead Yilanè were nearby, broken and unmoving, one of them crushed by the bulk of an armored fish of some kind. Her arms crossed across her ribcage, Akotolp walked slowly and painfully up a rise to the top of a nearby mound, leaned gratefully against the broken trunk of a tree on its summit.

Nothing looked familiar; she was pinned in a night-mare landscape of mud and destruction. Only when she faced inland, blinking through the sheets of rain, did she manage to make out the familiar shapes of the range of hills. They ran down almost to the sea, almost to the outlet of the bay. Using this as a guide, she was horrified to see that the birth beaches were gone, gouged out by the sea and washed away. The far side of the bay was gone as well, the bay and lagoon now joined directly to the ocean.

Then that heap of dark debris must be all that was left of her city tree. She moaned in agony at the sight. If she were weaker she might have died. Yilanè, when deprived of their city did die, she had seen it happen. But she would not. Others might. Not her; she was strong enough to bear the shock. Pushing herself upright, she stumbled toward the remains.

And she was not alone. Others were moving that way as well, fargi who signed respect and gratitude when they identified her. They moved close to draw strength from her presence. One of them, despite the the bruises and filth caked to her skin, she recognized.

"You are Inlenu — she who commands the workers at the fish pens."

Inlenu signed gratefulness for attention. "We have happiness-magnified and greet you, Akotolp. Humbly request explanation of happenings."

"Your knowledge is as great as mine. Something disastrous occurred far out in the ocean. With it was a great light, a great sound. This something caused the earth to move, the sea to rise. What you see around you is the result."

"The city, everything is destroyed. What will become of us?"

"We will live. The waters will not have covered all of Entoban. There will be food, in the forests and in the sea."

"But our city —"

"Will be regrown. Until that time we will sleep on the ground under the stars, as countless others have done before us. Do not despair, strong Inlenu, we need your strength."

"As we need yours." She signed respect-admiration, a movement that was echoed by all the fargi watching and listening. They would survive now.

Surely they would — for when they were closer they saw that hidden behind the rubble was the sturdy trunk of the city-tree, some of its thick branches still intact.

And — wonder of wonders! — standing at its base was the solid form of the Eistaa. The fargi hurried forward, bodies and limbs writhing with pleasure and great awe at her presence. They signed gratitude and happiness as well. Pushed close, then moved back when she signed them this order, parted to let Akotolp through join her.

"You have survived, Eistaa, and therefore the city shall survive as well."

"There has been great damage, many deaths." She signed the fargi away so that they could speak without being heard.

"Two out of three, possibly more, are dead. Others badly injured will die as well." With quieter words and smaller motions she revealed an even more terrible fact.

"The males are gone. Every one. The eggs they carried will never hatch."

Akotolp swayed with agony, fought for control, spoke calmly and wisely. "It is not the end. We are only one city. There are other Yilanè cities inland along the great rivers to the north. One even on the inland sea of Isegnet. When the time comes I will visit them and return with males. Yilanè are as one when facing disaster. The city will be grown again."

The Eistaa moved with pleasure when she heard this and took Akotolp's upper arms between her opposed thumbs in the gesture of greatest happiness, highest respect. The fargi murmured with pleasure at this happy sight, pain and despair forgotten for the moment. The city would grow again.

They set to work, under the Eistaa's instruction, clearing away the mud-caked debris. The rain never stopped, pouring darkly from a muddy sky. By nightfall much had been done. They discovered that fish that had been washed in from the sea were still alive in the remaining pools of water. These were gathered and shared out. In the end, tired and wounded, they slept.

The flood of water that had destroyed the coastal plain had also destroyed the civilized, formal way of life of the city. The fish vats were gone, along with the enzyme vats that cured and preserved the flesh of the animals. These creatures were gone too for the most part, the thorn barriers between the fields wiped away, the penned animals drowned or fled. Only a single hunter had survived — though all her weapons had drowned. With teeth and claws alone she could not supply the city with meat. Therefore it was the sea they turned to, the sea they had emerged from, renewing ancient swimming skills, seeking out the schools of fish and herding them into the shallows. Then the ocean churned with silver bodies seeking escape and reddened quickly with blood. It was crude but effective; they would survive.

Many days passed before Akotolp approached the Eistaa where she sat in the newly-cleaned ambesed. All had worked hard. The dead had been cast into the sea, the lightly injured had recovered. The badly injured were dead, for all of Akotolp's healing creatures were gone and she could not aid them.

"Everything is gone," she told the Eistaa. "You must remember that all of the creatures bred by our science are mutations and most cannot survive on their own. Our weapons, the hèsotsan, lose mobility with maturity and must be fed. We need more of them — as well as all the other forms of life that enable Yilanè civilization to survive. I have now done all that I can within the limitations forced upon me. I have taken fargi inland and returned with sharp-thorned vines that have been planted to once again form our fields. I have examined every fargi; the badly wounded are all dead. There is a sufficent supply of fish."

She acknowledged the Eistaa's motions of commonplace and boring food. "I agree, Eistaa. But it enables us to live. To improve our situation I must take fargi with me to Teskhets, the city on the great river beyond the hills. I know all of the things we need, hèsotsan and string-knives, nefmakel — the list is very long. I will return with breeding stock and our city and our lives will be regrown. I ask only your permission to leave."

The Eistaa moved tail and thumbs in the sign of doubt magnified. "Your presence is needed here."

"Was needed. I guided and explained, you ordered. My work is done — unless I get those things that make science possible. Fargi are training as hunters, the meat supply grows. The fishers grow more proficient. Under your supervision the Yilanè will eat, the city live."

The Eistaa radiated displeasure, looked out at the dark and ceaseless rain. "We live, but barely. More like wild creatures than Yilanè."

"But we live, Eistaa, that is what is important. In order to live once again the rich life of Yilanè you must permit this expedition."

"I will consider it. The meat supply must be greater before you go. You must find a way to bring that about."

Akotolp did what she could, which was very little, knowing that it was only the Eistaa's sense of unease that prevented her making any decision. It was understandable. At least six fargi, uninjured and strong, had simply curled up and died. This of course happened when a Yilanè was forced to leave her city, a terminal punishment only meted out after great provocation. Now it happened spontaneously. That even the Eistaa was disturbed by terrible events of this magnitude was understandable.

Still Akotolp was displeased, even angry. There was really nothing more for her to do. The endless clouds, the almost continuous rain, did nothing to change her mood. A second time the Eistaa refused her request; she was hesitant about a third. It was Velikrei, the hunter, who brought a measure of light into her darkness.

"I seek permission to speak as one to one," the scarred hunter said, moving one of her eyes in the direction of the nearby fargi.

"Granted. We will walk along the shore."

"Respectfully suggest forest instead."

There must be a reason for this, Akotolp realized, and signed agreement. They were silent until they had crossed the hardened mud flats and reached the trees beyond.

Here, out of sight of any watchers, Velikrei stopped and spoke.

"You must tell me what to do. I hunt, that I do well. And I follow orders. I serve the Eistaa. Now order and service clash." She brought her fists together with a loud crack; her body writhed with indecision. Akotolp saw she needed quick reassurance.

"The city needs you, Velikrei, at the present time far more than it needs me. Let me help you, for I respect and admire your skill and your strength. My thoughts-rational powers are at your service now. Tell me what disturbs you."

"One comes from the forest with fargi. She will not enter the city, will not see the Eistaa. Asks if a Yilanè of science is here. She knows your name. Orders me to bring you, not the Eistaa..."

The hunter could no longer talk, her mouth gaped wide as she shuddered. Akotolp touched all four thumbs to her arms in reassurance.

"You have done the correct thing. The Eistaa must not be disturbed in her labors. I will talk to this one who comes — then I will tell the Eistaa about the matter. The responsibility is now mine."

"You have decided," Velikrei said, relief draining the tension from her knotted muscles. She was safely back in the chain of command, following orders. "I take you to her."

"Name?"

"Essokel."

"I do indeed know her as she knows me. This is very good — for all of us. Take me to her, quickly."

Akotolp recognized the tall form of the other scientist at once, waiting in the shelter of a large tree. She stepped forward when they approached, made motions of greeting. Velikrei stood hesitantly to one side, signed gratitude when she was dimissed, almost fled from sight. Only when she was gone did Akotolp speak.

"Welcome, Essokel, welcome to what little remains of our city."

"Of many cities," she answered grimly. "I was far inland when this thing happened, returning with fargi to my city. When I saw the destruction along the coast I halted them in the forest, went on alone." There was pain in her eyes now, the wound of memory. "Destroyed, gone, none survived. I came close to dying myself — but I did not. I have willed myself to forget the name of my city, strong-request you do not repeat it."

"You are welcome-magnified here. You are now a part of my city, our city. We were injured, we survive. With your aid we grow anew. You will mend our broken egg. We now have nothing other than the claws and teeth with which we emerged from the ocean."

"Then I can indeed be of service," Essokel said, drawing herself up, pride replacing death in her movements. "Mine was a long expedition to distant cities. My fargi carry everything we needed — that your, our, city needs."

"The fargi are here?"

"Close by and out of sight. I wished to talk with you and you alone."

"Not the Eistaa?"

"Not yet. There are matters of science that are for our knowledge alone. Are you strong, Akotolp?"

"I survived. I will survive. I am needed."

"Good. I must talk with you, share my knowledge and you must query it. For I have fear."

"Of what?"

"Of *everything.*"

There were such overtones of despair and death when she said this that Akotolp cried aloud and recoiled. Then controlled herself and spoke with all the courage she could summon.

"You are no longer alone, my old friend, no longer surrounded by mindless fargi you cannot speak to. Unburden yourself, share your knowledge and thoughts. Fears shared are halved, for we will each carry part of the load now."

"You are a Yilanè of great intelligence and strength, Akotolp. I will tell you what I have seen and reasoned. Then you will query me, perhaps even prove me wrong. It is as you say, a burden shared. First I need information for I only saw what happened from afar. You were here?"

"Indeed — and it is only by chance I can talk to you now for only one in five survived. It was night — and then it was day. A light that hurt my eyes before slowly fading away. Later there was an immense sound and the ground moved. Later still, as I thought it would happen, the ocean rose and enveloped us."

"You thought it would — why?"

"A chain of logic. An incident of great force occurred, the light of which we saw. The sound came much later — and the shock. A force at sea great enough to cause this would also move the ocean as well."

Essokel signed reinforced agreement. "I did not see or experience what you did — though I surmised as much from physical evidence. Important query: what do you think caused all this?"

"Profess lack of knowledge, lack of theory."

"Then listen to mine. Have you any interest in astronomy?"

Akotolp signed negative. "Biology fills all my time and needs."

"But you have looked at the night sky — seen various phenomena there. You have seen the lines of light that cross the darkness from time to time?"

"Assuredly. Though I have never heard an attempt at explanation."

"I have. Our atmosphere grows thinner as one goes higher; this has been proven by those who carried air pressure devices up mountains. If this is true, then logic dictates that if the pressure drop is continuous then at a certain height there is no more air."

"I know of this theory and am in agreement. That air ceases to be and beyond our atmosphere there is a nothingness."

"But matter exists in this nothingness. We see the moon and the stars. Now hold that thought and in parallel entertain another thought. A bird moves faster than a fish because it moves through a less dense medium. If something moves through a medium of no density it could have a speed beyond comprehension. So much so that if there are particles of matter moving through this emptiness, small particles, through the operation of the laws of dynamics they would exchange motion for temperature. And glow with light."

Akotolp closed her eyes, wrapped in intense thought. Opened them and signed agreement. "I cannot argue with facts revealed, extrapolation of idea. Seek relevance."

Essokel was grimly silent for a long heartbeat of time, then spoke quietly. "I suggest to you the possibility that a larger particle from above might strike our atmosphere. A particle the size of a boulder, a tree — perhaps a mountain. What would happen then?"

"Then," Akotolp said, slowly and carefully, "this mountain of speed would cause the air to glow fiercely.

It would strike the ocean. If it were large enough, fast enough, heavy enough, it might even strike down through the water to hit the ground below. This immense shock would be felt through the ground, heard through the air for great distances. The mountains of water pushed aside would innundate the shores of this land. I am in awe of your wisdom and intellect."

"There is more to come. The clouds that have never parted once since that day, the clouds that rain down dirt, that are black with filth undoubtedly thrown up by the impact. How many days have they remained up there?"

"A great number. I have kept count."

"As have I. Now, one last fearful consideration. What if they remain there longer and longer? What if the warmth of the sun never bathes us again? What will happen to us then?"

Akotolp the biologist swayed in pain, almost lost consciousness at the terror of this thought. Recovered to find that Essokel was holding her, that she would have fallen without her friend's support.

"Death will be our lot. Without sunlight the green plants will not grow. When they die the creatures who eat them die. When they die — the Yilanè die. Is this what is to happen?"

"I do not know; I fear for the worst. I have measured carefully. The air temperature is lower each day. We cannot live without heat, without sun."

"The clouds must part!" Akotolp cried aloud. "They must. Or..."

She did not finish the thought. There was no need. It was Essokel who finally broke the terrible silence.

"We will go to the city now. And tell the Eistaa...?"

"Nothing. If these things we talk about come to be then we are helpless, powerless. Instead of bringing them death you will now bring them happiness and pleasure. There will be warmth, shelter, food. If...what we discussed...comes to pass, it will not need discussion. It will soon be obvious to the stupidest fargi."

Akotolp was correct; Essokel and the burdens her fargi carried brought civilization and great happiness back to the city. Hèsotsan for hunting, the pleasure of sweet warm meat for all. There were many cloaks in the bundles, for the expedition had been through the mountain passes where the air was chill. They were needed now: the nights were growing colder, and these flat brainless creatures if kept well fed had high body temperatures. All the city leaders had cloaks and slept well. The fargi did not and could only huddle together at night, draw warmth from one another and shudder in silence.

But the pleasure could not last. Even the stupidest fargi, fresh from the sea and unable to talk, could see that the nights were growing colder, days as well. The fish were no longer as plentiful as they had been. The clouds did not part, the sun did not shine, the plants were dying. The animals they ate were leaner and tougher as the grazing grew harder. Still they ate very well, for the enzyme vats were kept filled with meat. Which was a very bad sign indeed, for they were not being killed — they were dying. This was the time when the Eistaa summoned the two scientists to join her in the ambesed where she waited with Velikrei.

"Listen to what this hunter tells me," the Eistaa said, darkness in her speech.

"The onetsensast that they butcher now, that goes into the meat vats. It is the last one. All others — dead, the fields empty."

"What is happening — what is going to happen?" the Eistaa asked. "You are Yilanè of science, you must know."

"We know," Akotolp said, fighting to keep calmness in her words and motions. "We will tell you, Eistaa." The hunter did not see her quick motion of pointing and dismissal.

"You have brought the information, Velikrei. Return to your forest."

Akotolp waited until the three of them were alone before she spoke. Now she made no attempt to keep the dread and despair from her speech.

"It is the sun that brings us life, Eistaa. If the sun does not shine we die. The clouds kill us."

"I see what is happening — yet I do not understand."

"There is a chain of life," Essokel said. "It starts in the cells of the plants, where the sun's rays are turned into food. The fish and the ustuzou eat them and live. We in turn eat their flesh — and we live." She leaned down and pulled a clump of yellowed grass from the ground and held it out. "This dies, they die, we die."

The Eistaa looked at the grass, immobile, her muscles locked hard as the thought echoed again and again in her brain. In the end she turned to Akotolp and signed a short query.

"True?"

"Inescapable truth."

"Can we not fill the vats, store food, wait until the clouds open up and the sun shines again?"

"We can — and we will. Seed will be stored as well, to plant and regrow when the sun returns."

"This will be done. I will order it. When will the sun return?"

The response to this question was only silence. The Eistaa waited, her anger growing, until she could control it no longer.

"Speak, Akotolp! I order you to speak! When will the sun return?"

"I — we — do not know, Eistaa. And unless it returns soon the world as we know it is dead. Species once destroyed do not return. We are one of those species. We are important only to ourselves. In the totality of biology we are as important — or unimportant — as that clump of grass. It is of no help to us to know that even if the clouds remain forever life will go on. But it will not be the world we know. There exist life-forms that are very persistent and can endure a great range of temperatures and environments. We cannot. We will not survive on this world unless things remain very much as they always were. I fear, Essokel and I have discussed this many times that we have already passed the time of survival...

"That is not true! Yilanè live."

"Yilanè die," Essokel said with grim movements. "Fargi die already of cold. We have examined them."

"We have cloaks."

"The cloaks will die as well. It is already too cold for them to breed." There was great feeling of despair in Akotolp's shuddered movements. "I fear that all will be ended, all Yilanè dead, everything we are, everything that we have done, vanished. It will be as we have never been. When the clouds break, if they ever break, it will be the ustuzou who will live."

"What? These vermin — crawling filthy things underfoot. Your speaking is an insult!"

As though in further insult an ustuzou scuttled through the dead grass close by, paused an instant to glance at them with tiny dark eyes, scratched quick claws through its fur. The Eistaa stamped out with her foot but crushed only dead stems as the creature vanished from sight.

"You say that these vile things will live — why?"

"Because of their nature," Essokel explained patiently. "All complex creatures require regularizing of body temperature, they are all warm-blooded. But there are two ways of staying warm. We Yilanè are exothermic, which means we must live in a warm climate and take in heat from outside. This is very efficient. The ustuzou are very inefficient since they are endothermic, which means they must eat all of the time and turn their food into heat..."

"You speak like this only to confuse me — all this talk of hot or cold, inside and out."

"You must excuse my inefficency-stupidity, Eistaa. I simplify. We will get cold, we will die. That small ustuzou will not get cold. When the air cools it will eat more. It will eat dead plants, dead bodies — it will eat our dead bodies. The corpses of our world will nourish these creatures for a long time. Perhaps until the clouds disperse and the sun returns. If this comes to pass then it will be an ustuzou world and the Yilanè will not even be a memory. It will be as though we never were — "

"A thought I will not have!" the Eistaa roared with anger, tearing at the ground with her claws. "Leave me! Be silent in my presence hereafter. I will not hear these words again."

The scientists left, a cold rain fell, night descended. There was the movement of tiny, furry creatures through the grass and into the dead forest beyond. Tiny creatures that ate seeds, stems, bones, marrow, flesh, grass, insects — anything.

Warm-blooded animals that could survive when ninety percent of all other creatures died.

Survive and evolve for sixty million years.

Whose descendants read these words.

12.
EXTINCTION AND DISCOVERY

ESSAY BY DAVID J. ARCHIBALD

ESSAY BY RONALD RAINGER

SPECULATION BY HARRY TURTLEDOVE

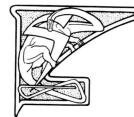
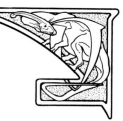

MYTHS, THEORIES, AND FACTS
OF DINOSAUR EXTINCTION

J. DAVID ARCHIBALD

SAY THE WORD DINOSAUR AND AN IMAGE OF A LARGE, LUMBERING SCALY MONSTER IS CONJURED UP BY by almost every person. For most, these creatures are nothing more than lizards with an extreme glandular problem. We owe Hollywood for many of our current perceptions of dinosaurs. Some child psychologists suggest that much of our fascination with these animals is because they are "acceptable monsters." As we become older, most of us leave behind the fairy-tale phantasmagoric, were real flesh-and-blood organisms that trod the planet eons before the most ancient of human ancestors.

As discussed in other essays in this volume, we are rapidly learning more about the lives and evolutionary history of dinosaurs. For many, however, the most fascinating aspect of these creatures is not how they lived, but how they died at the Cretaceous/Tertiary boundary (K/T boundary, for short) some 66 million years ago. Except maybe for the poor dodo bird, dinosaurs have come to epitomize extinction, and for most people extinction equates with failure. This view is not correct. As discussed in the next few pages, there are many inaccuracies, misconceptions, and outright myths surrounding the last days of the dinosaurs and their extinction. Even the view that dinosaurs became totally extinct may not be correct because, as you will see, birds may be considered to be dinosaurs.

EXTINCTION:
COUNTERPOINT OF EVOLUTION

In order to better understand dinosaur extinction, it is first necessary to provide some generalities about our concepts of extinction. Extinction has been receiving bad press lately, and rightfully so. It is estimated

creatures of our youth. Dinosaurs, no matter how that through human agency, we are losing plants and animals at a rate possibly as high as one species every hour. Along with other pending ecological disasters, the extinctions that we are causing will be a tragic legacy to future generations and to the planet. Although we cannot accurately quantify the present and near-future rates of extinctions, there is little doubt among scientists that the current extinctions will make those at the end of the Cretaceous (including those of dinosaurs) look like a picnic. This does not mean, however, that extinction is rare in the geologic past. On the contrary, extinction is the counterpoint to evolution.

There have been episodes during the history of this planet when the number of species increased, sometimes dramatically. During the great majority of the geologic past, however, there has been a rough balance between new species arising and old species disappearing. This should not be viewed as a one-for-one replacement in a given ecological niche or geographic region, but rather a dynamic equilibrium.

Another way to indicate the pervasiveness of extinction through the depths of geologic time is to realize that some 99 percent of all species that have ever lived are now gone. What is true about the cliché concerning life — no one will get out of this alive — is

276

equally true for species. There are only two outcomes in the game of life over the long haul of geologic time: either a species eventually becomes extinct (with no descendants) or it evolves into other species.

It might seem that the difference between extinction and the evolutionary disappearance of a species should be easily detectable in the fossil record. In fact, it is not. In most instances when a species disappears from the fossil record one cannot discern whether it was through extinction or evolution. The only way to determine with any reasonable certainty which of these two events occurred is to estimate the phylogenetic or evolutionary history of the species that are being studied. In this way, the question of whether the disappearance of a given species was the result of its true extinction, or was because of a pseudoextinction, can be answered: that is, did the species disappear or did it evolve into another species or split to form two or more new species.

In addition to eliminating pseudoextinctions from any analysis of true extinction, it is necessary to determine the magnitude and the rate of the latter. The vast majority of the 99 percent of true extinctions that have occurred on earth are within magnitudes and rates that are considered to fall within normal or background ranges. Although extinction may not seem "normal" in the context of human time scales, it must again be emphasized that over geologic time, extinction is the rule and not the exception. On the other end of the scale are extinctions that include so many species over a relatively short geologic time that they qualify as mass extinctions. If in addition the time interval during which they occur is inordinately short in duration, the extinctions are said to be catastrophic. It is precisely the theories of catastrophic mass extinction at the K/T boundary that have captured the imagination of the public and news media. Whether such theories are correct and whether they account for the extinctions of dinosaurs is of course another matter.

Preceding page: Dinosaurs died of various causes, including local cataclysms, such as this ash cloud from an eruption. A herd of Maiasaurs *dies and is buried on the spot. By Doug Henderson.*

DINOSAUR EXTINCTION: SOME COMMON MISCONCEPTIONS

If many newspaper accounts and even books on the subject are to be believed, the evidence argues that dinosaurs disappeared almost overnight along with 75 percent of all other species that were living on earth at the close of the Cretaceous. The fossil evidence of dinosaurs and many other species, however, is not of such a quality to support such drastic scenarios of extinction. Such statements of dinosaur doom are the first of several myths concerning dinosaur extinction.

To confirm that all dinosaurs disappeared in a matter of days, months, or even years from all over the earth would require a fossil record near the K/T boundary from several widely separated areas of the globe. Late Cretaceous dinosaurs are found on every one of the seven continents, yet it is from only one region that we have anything approaching an adequate record of dinosaurs near the end of the Cretaceous. This area is often referred to as the Western Interior of North America. Although this is a large area, stretching from Alberta in the north to Texas in the south, it is a relatively small area of the globe compared to that occupied by dinosaurs in the Late Cretaceous some 66 to 70 million years ago. The record of dinosaur fossils does not show extinction on anything approaching a global scale. Although an overnight demise of dinosaurs cannot be dismissed, neither can it be supported. Accordingly this first myth of dinosaur extinction must remain the purview of supermarket tabloids.

A second related myth of dinosaur extinction concerns how these creatures have been used to establish the K/T boundary. There is a prevalent misconception that rocks and the fossils they encase are usually dated by such means as carbon-14 or radioactive elements found in rocks. Carbon-14 dating is done only on organic material that was once part of living organisms and is only usable for species which died less than about 60,000 years ago. Dating of rocks containing radioactive elements remains almost the only way to date much older rocks, but the dating of fossils is indirect and carried out by dating volcanic rocks that bracket the fossil-bearing strata. Ultimately, the determination of a geochronologic or so-called absolute date must be tied to radiometrically dated volcanic rocks. Estimating the age of most fossils, however, necessitates the intermediate correlation of the fossil-bearing rocks to each other by using the fossils themselves. At first this explanation might seem circular, but when it is realized that evolution is unidirectional, it can be used as a unique sequence of biological events that can tie together, even if imperfectly, rocks from various areas and eras.

It is widely held that the appearance of a species is a better tool for correlation than the disappearance of an organism. This is in part the case because the former constitutes positive evidence of an event while the latter is negative evidence. It is argued, and supported by field studies, that negative evidence should be suspect given the vagaries of the fossil and rock record. The absence of dinosaurs from rocks straddling the K/T boundary is a very good case in point. Recall that at present the only region with a reasonable record of the extinction of dinosaurs is in the Western Interior. Hence the absence of dinosaurs in relatively poorly studied regions or in poorly preserved sequences is not strong evidence that their extinction had occurred in that region or that the K/T boundary had been crossed.

Conversely, the presence of dinosaurs does not necessarily mean that one is dealing with Cretaceous or older rocks. Post-Cretaceous dinosaurs have been reported from poorly understood and/or poorly preserved sequences in China and South America. There also have been recent arguments that in the Western Interior dinosaurs survived the K/T boundary. The problem in the Western Interior is that the dinosaur fossil material may have been reworked. As rivers cut back and forth over their floodplains they routinely exhume older rocks and their fossils, which are later reburied. Although not determined with great certainty, this sort of reworking is likely for dinosaur remains in the Western Interior. If reworked, the fossils will be older than their matrix. Thus, fossils that predate the K/T boundary might be found in more recent sediments.

A third and final myth of dinosaur extinction concerns our knowledge versus our perception of the ecology and relationships of dinosaurs as these factors relate to their extinction. My introductory remarks portraying dinosaurs as "large, lumbering scaly monsters" is probably close to the view of many people. As with many such perceptions, there is more fiction than fact.

Dinosaurs belong to two quite distinct groups, Saurischia or "reptile-hipped" dinosaurs and Ornithischia or "bird-hipped" dinosaurs. These names refer to the morphology of the hip joint and ostentation of the pubis bone, which is more typically reptile-like in saurischians and is superficially like that of a bird in ornithischians. It is from the former group, however, that birds arose. Birds are in fact descendants of saurischian dinosaurs. Shocking as it may seem, the saurischian *Tyrannosaurus* shares a more recent common ancestor with a hummingbird than it does with the ornithischian *Triceratops*. Using overall similarity can be very deceptive in unraveling the evolutionary past. Although all non-avian dinosaurs (the forebears of the bird, if you will) are gone today, there is one living group with which birds share a slightly more ancient ancestry. This group is the Crocodilia. Although these animals seem to be more lizard- than bird-like, their similarities consist of evolutionarily older features such as the presence of scales. Birds share so many special characteristics with the now-extinct dinosaurs that I would argue they *are* dinosaurs. In the final analysis then, dinosaurs, or more precisely the saurischian dinosaurs, did not become extinct but survived as birds.

A counterpoint that is sometimes given to this well substantiated and close relationship of birds to saurischians is that the survival of birds is not germane to the issue of dinosaur extinction because the large, ecologically similar dinosaurs became extinct while the smaller birds did not. Non-avian dinosaurs, however, are not ecologically similar. For example, contrast the large, quadrupedal, tank-like ornithischian, *Edmonia,* to the much smaller, bipedal saurischian *Struthiomimus.* Not only are the large ankylosaur and small saurischian not very closely related, but they are obviously not very similar ecologically. In fact, *Struthiomimus* is ecologically more similar to its closer relative, the ostrich. Any theory of extinction must account for the ecological and evolutionary diversity of dinosaurs.

THE THEORIES OF EXTINCTION

With both a better understanding of extinction and some of the more important misconceptions concerning dinosaurs in mind, it is now possible to explore the various theories that have been suggested to explain their demise. If one were to discuss these theories in any detail, it would be a book-length endeavor, for there are now over 80 hypotheses that have been proposed. Most must be dismissed as either absurd (aliens hunted the ancient dinosaurs to extinction) or untestable (changes in climate affected reproductive fitness). In largely historical sciences such as paleontology, hypotheses cannot be as thoroughly tested as in experimental sciences, but good theories are those that can be framed in such a fashion that permit them to be refuted. This is harder to accomplish than one might at first expect.

Not all theories of extinction can be discussed, but it is possible to examine several classes of theories. Two major ways in which they can be grouped are: 1) whether extraterrestrial or earthbound ultimate causes are invoked, and 2) whether a very short, catastrophic episode of extinction is suggested or the extinctions were drawn out over tens or hundreds of thousands of years.

Arguably the best-known theory is both extraterrestrial and catastrophic in nature. This is the asteroid-impact hypothesis proposed in 1980. In brief, it argues that a six-mile-wide asteroid (or meteor) struck the earth. According to the theory, a dense cloud of debris and smoke quickly blocked the sun. As in a nuclear winter scenario, the reduction in light and presumably temperature would kill most aboveground vegetation. In turn, herbivores would starve, followed by the carnivores.

Some variations on this theory suggest swarms of small meteors or comets struck the earth, and some have suggested that the effects were spread over a much longer interval of time, up to tens of thousands of years.

At present there is not agreement on whether single or multiple impacts are more plausible and what the physical manifestations might have been. Some of the possible scenarios argue for sharp increases in temperature, some a sharp decrease; some show a very acidic rain; a tremendous increase in rainfall has been suggested by some, while others advocate a global fireball. Given these extremes in hypotheses, it is difficult to sort out the realistic possibilities. There are, however, several lines of physical evidence that have been used to support some sort of bolide impact (or impacts).

If such an impact (or impacts) occurred, there should be a crater, which one estimate places at about 100 miles across. Various candidates have been proposed. All have been dismissed as too small or not of the correct age. One site in the Caribbean region is now under investigation and only time will tell if this is a likely candidate. Even without a crater, there are two lines of evidence that are used to support the idea of an impact. These are enrichments in the element iridium in sediments at the K/T boundary and the occurrence in them of shocked quartz grains with double lamellae.

Iridium is a heavy element that probably migrated toward the center of the earth during early stages of planet formation. Although now rare at the surface of the planet, it is present in some meteorites at close to primordial solar system levels. A concentration of iridium at the K/T boundary in a clay within a very thick sequence of limestones near the town of Gubbio in northern Italy was suggested as coming from an asteroid impact. Iridium has now been reported from many sites around the world, although the level of concentration varies considerably and the exact placement at the K/T boundary is not always certain.

The occurrence of shocked quartz is said to be indicative of a tremendous force acting on quartz-bearing rock such as would be generated by the impact of an extraterrestrial body.

Super-vulcanism, a possible terrestrial source for the iridium and the shocked quartz, has been suggested as an alternative. The amount of iridium and the fact that some of the shocked quartz has double lamellae, however, more strongly argue for an extraterrestrial source. Only a truly extraordinary series of eruptions might be sufficient to account for the physical evidence. A tremendous eruption such as that of the Deccan Traps on the subcontinent of India near the K/T boundary is one possible source. Until more

thorough studies are completed, the issue remains unresolved.

There are also paleontologic data that are used to support the impact hypothesis. Most notable are the extinctions of a large percentage of marine microorganisms very close to, if not at, the K/T boundary. In addition, the rapidity with which these microorganisms disappeared from the fossil record such as near Gubbio has been used to argue for catastrophic change.

On land, the paleobotanic data suggest quite drastic changes at least in the more southern and central part of the Western Interior of North America. Rates of extinction are high in this region, and the pollen record also indicates a drastic, rapid change. At or near the boundary in this region of the Western Interior there is a marked increase in fern spores. Paleobotanists suggest that these "fern spikes" are indicative of early colonization following a perturbation to the environment such as could have occurred following an impact.

On the other end of the extinction theory spectrum are the earthbound theories that advocate a more gradual or graded series of extinctions. The most widely cited are those that deal with competition for resources (mainly food), marine regression, and climatic change.

The most widely cited possibility for competition is that between mammals and dinosaurs. Specifically, the model of diffuse competition is suggested. Diffuse competition takes place today, for example, between herbivorous insects and mammals, or between small mammals such as rodents and larger mammals such as antelope. Although such a model for competition between small herbivorous and omnivorous Cretaceous mammals and much larger dinosaurs is plausible, it is untestable. Also, mammals and dinosaurs coexisted from at least the latest Triassic through the Creta-

Following spread: A giant meteor impact may have triggered the extinction of the dinosaurs, many marine reptiles and other marine life. By Doug Henderson.

ceous, an interval of almost 135 million years. Why the mammals would prevail after the long coexistence is problematic for any competition theory.

The ideas of marine regression and climatic change are more amenable to scrutiny because they can be examined using paleontologic and geologic data. In fact, for marine regression, we have almost irrefutable data that such an event took place. Climatic data must be more cautiously analyzed and to date are somewhat contradictory.

Marine regressions have occurred many, times during the history of our planet. During the Late Cretaceous from about 100 million years ago to about 66 million years ago there were at least four major transgressions and regressions of inland seas across the mid-continental area of North America. The last of the regressions occurred near the close of the Cretaceous in North America. There are no continent-splitting seas extant today of Mesozoic scale. During transgressions forming such seas, marine waters covered portions of continents up to depths of about 2,000 feet. Although deep, these seas do not approach the depths of modern ocean basins, which reach tens of thousands of feet in depth. During the time of the last of these great marine transgressions, the sea ran across the middle of North America stretching from Hudson Bay in the north to the Gulf of Mexico in the south. The remaining continents were also undergoing marine transgressions. Somewhere between one-quarter and one-third of all present day continental areas were under water.

Such vast, shallow, warm seas undoubtedly had a profound affect on the climate. Areas in the mid-continent that today experience winter temperatures well below freezing had a much milder Mediterranean-like climate in the Late Cretaceous. With the loss of these seas at the end of the Cretaceous from many parts of the world's continents, there were certainly climatic changes. Of probably greater importance was the loss of habitat. In North America the vast lowland and shallow marine areas bordering both sides of the mid-continental sea were drastically reduced to near their positions of today. Areas around Hudson Bay (although much warmer) and along the southern coast were all that was left. All we need do is look at the profound loss of species that occurs as we fragment and destroy habitats now in order to have some sense of what occurred at the end of the Cretaceous in North America, and prehaps on a global scale.

The very visible proof of the transgressions and regressions of these seaways are found in the marine rocks and fossils that are preserved throughout the central and western part of North America, and in other parts of the world as well. Only the western shores of the last Cretaceous seaway are well preserved. The regressing shoreline can be traced by mapping the successively eastward positions of more and more recent organisms. Especially useful are the ammonites, an extinct, shelled relative of modern octopus, squid, and the chambered nautilus. At or near the end of the Cretaceous the ammonites, like the ancient dinosaurs, became extinct.

The marine regressions almost certainly had an effect upon the climate, but in what manner is still somewhat of a mystery. For areas in the western interior of North America, there have been suggestions of a slight deterioration of the milder climates based upon paleofloral evidence, and an increase in rainfall based upon changes in the sediment across the K/T boundary. How widespread such changes might have been remains unknown.

If some sort of bolide impact occurred, if there were extremely massive volcanic eruptions, or if a combination of the two happened, then the climate may have changed drastically in a very short interval of time. Unfortunately, the rock and fossil records are almost never complete enough to accurately detect extremely short climatic excursions. As noted, there have been suggestions of very sharp, short-lived increases and decreases in temperature, acid rain, and global wildfires caused by such events as impacts and eruptions. Our ability to detect such events remains very poor, but new techniques of analysis are continually being developed so that some of these hypotheses may one day be testable.

THE DINOSAURS WERE NOT ALONE: VERTEBRATE EXTINCTION IN NORTH AMERICA

Another of our perceptions of dinosaurs is that these animals were the only or at least the dominant vertebrates during much of the Mesozoic Era. If the Late Cretaceous of North America is indicative, this is definitely not a correct view of Mesozoic vertebrate life. Birds, squamates (lizards and snakes), and mammals all have more species today than ancient dinosaurs did in their heyday. Living mammals include a greater range of size and diversity of habitat than did dinosaurs. The only way in which dinosaurs can be said to have dominated their world was in size and on land.

We are now beginning to construct a more accurate portrait of vertebrate life near the end of the Mesozoic (and Cretaceous) for at least one region, and that is in the northern portion of the western interior in the northeastern part of Montana. Here are preserved sediments and countless fossil remains of vertebrates that lived and died as the Mesozoic Era was waning. At least 111 species of vertebrates are now known. There is one major group of vertebrates, however, for which we have a very inadequate record — the birds. The traces we do have suggest that birds were probably quite diverse, but we simply do not

and probably never will have a good idea of their true diversity. This is because bird bones are hollow and are accordingly very fragile, with destruction of their remains occurring very soon after death.

Even with this one obvious gap in our knowledge, we do have some idea of the diversity of other vertebrates. Of the other known species, only about 20 are ancient dinosaurs. The remaining species encompass a number of other groups that are still around today. A brief survey will suggest how diverse these vertebrate fauna really were in the time of the last dinosaurs.

Starting in the aquatic realm, there are some 5 species of cartilaginous fishes (sharks, skates, and rays) and 14 species of bony fishes found in the Montana rocks of the era's finale. Today, as was true in the Mesozoic Era, the sharks and their close relatives are mostly marine fishes, although a number of species venture into brackish and even fresh water. The streams and rivers flowing across the low coastal plains during the latest Cretaceous in northeastern Montana provided easy access to the shallow midcontinental sea that lay only tens of miles to the east. The bony fishes also include species that have living relatives who frequent coastal waters. Strictly freshwater bony fishes are fairly uncommon in the latest Cretaceous in Montana in part because many of the groups we recognize today had not yet arrived or had not yet evolved.

Amphibians are also to be found in these ancient waters. Some eight species are recorded from fossil localities in northeastern Montana. Although several species of frogs are reported from latest Cretaceous fauna elsewhere and from younger fauna in Montana, only one species is definitely known from the latest Cretaceous of northeastern Montana. The remainder of the eight amphibian species are salamanders, including some long-bodied giant salamanders measuring several feet in length.

The aquatic realm in northeastern Montana during the waning days of the dinosaurs is not limited to fish and amphibians. Three major lineages of largely aquatic reptiles — turtles, crocodilians, and champsosaurs — shared these waters of the low coastal plain. Only champsosaurs are not familiar to most people, and with good reason. Although they survived the end of the Cretaceous, they died out some 50 million years before our own origin. Champsosaurs superficially resemble crocodilians but belong to a very distantly related group called eosuchians. Only one species is known in the latest Cretaceous of northeastern Montana. There are more species of true crocodilians, including one crocodile, three kinds of alligators, and one form that probably was a terrestrial predator.

By far the most speciose group of largely aquatic reptiles of the latest Cretaceous of northeastern Montana is the turtles. Of particular interest is their considerable diversity as compared to either other fossil fauna or living fauna. With 19 species of turtles in the latest Cretaceous of northeastern Montana, turtle diversity is near its zenith for any time on earth. Some early representatives of living groups of turtles are in these fauna, such as early snapping turtles, while others resemble even more closely their living counterparts, such as the soft-shelled turtles. The most speciose group, however, is the baenids, an extinct family of aquatic turtles. These turtles had tremendously long tails, sometimes reaching 150% of shell length. No living turtle even approaches this tail length. Not all of the turtles are aquatic. At least one is an analogue of living tortoises.

Turning to the terrestrial realm, reptiles found largely in this group of habitats are the squamates and the two groups of dinosaurs, the Ornithischia and Saurischia. If birds could be better surveyed, they would be included with their relatives the Saurischia. Among the 11 squamates, the snakes are very rare, with only one species known. Although vagaries of the fossil record cannot be dismissed, a likely reason for this rarity is that snakes were only just then beginning their modern radiation in the Late Cretaceous. The lizards belong to several living as well as several extinct lineages. Most of the living lineages with latest Cretaceous relatives are now restricted to tropical areas in both the Old and New Worlds. The adult size of these lizards varied from a few inches up to five to ten feet for some of the relatives of living monitor lizards.

As noted, the ornithischians and saurischians combined comprise 20 of the 111 species known from the latest Cretaceous of northeastern Montana. Among the ornithischians are one species each of ankylosaur, nodosaur, and hysilophodont, two species of hadrosaur, and three species each of ceratopsian and pachycephalosaur. It is largely among the ceratopsians and hadrosaurs that the number of species dropped during the last 10 million years of the Cretaceous. Ten million years earlier there were double the number of kinds of ceratopsians and more than triple the number of kinds of hadrosaurs. The 9 species of non-avian saurischians (remember, birds *are* saurischians) are allocated to as many as 8 different families. Although they show some decline in the number of species during the last 10 million years of the Cretaceous, it is not as dramatic as for ornithischians. Ornithischians and non-avian saurischians combined show almost a 45 percent decrease in the number of genera during the last 10 million years of the Cretaceous in North America.

The final group in the Montana K/T rocks are the mammals, the order to which we belong. There are three major lineages of mammals recognizable in these fauna in northeastern Montana — multituberculates, marsupials, and placentals. All are of relatively small size, ranging from that of a shrew to that of a large cat. The 11 species of multituberculates in these fauna represent a very ancient group of mammals that have a long evolutionary history separate from marsupials and placentals. Multituberculates survived the K/T boundary. These mouse- to beaver-sized omnivores and herbivores flourished in the early Tertiary, but disappeared some 30 million years later, probably through competition with rodents and other newly evolving mammals.

The 11 species of marsupials may belong to four or possibly more major lineages. The dentitions of most of these latest Cretaceous marsupials resemble those of the living opossum, suggesting similar diets, but details of the same dentitions do not suggest a close evolutionary relationship.

The word "placental" refers to the fact that mammals in this group develop an unique kind of extra-embryonic membrane for nourishing embryos during uterine development. Humans and most familiar mammals are placental mammals. In the latest Cretaceous of northeastern Montana there are six species of placental mammal. All are quite small, only up to the size of a large cat, and most have sharp crests and cusps on their teeth for dispatching insects.

When combined, the 111 species of vertebrates present a quite diverse assemblage of organisms taxonomically and ecologically. Any viable theory of extinction at the K/T boundary must account for the pattern of extinctions that one observes among these species.

Following the K/T boundary in northeastern Montana, only 32 percent of the 111 species can be found in early Tertiary rocks in the same region. If accepted at face value, this level of extinction certainly would suggest that a dramatic and possibly catastrophic extinction had occurred. This figure of only 32 percent survival is deceptive, however. The figure does not account for at least three artifacts of the analysis and the fossil records.

First, it is known that although some species may not have survived past the K/T boundary in northeastern Montana, they are found elsewhere in lower Tertiary rocks. Thus, the species did not become extinct but only disappeared from northeastern Montana. Including species that survive elsewhere, the survival rate is closer to 42 percent.

Second, although hundreds of thousands of specimens of vertebrates from northeastern Montana have been identified, there are some species that remain exceedingly rare. Some are represented by as few as one specimen. If the survival rates of rare versus more common species are compared, it turns out that only 9 percent of the rare species survived while 46 percent of the common species survived.

Third, as discussed earlier, some extinctions in the fossil record are actually evolutionary events. This is clearly the case in this instance, especially for the mammals. If all mammal disappearances were true extinctions, then only one of 27 mammal species survived the K/T boundary. Yet, we also know that this was the beginning of the greatest radiation of mammals that ever occurred. Although it is very difficult to pinpoint specific species as ancestors, many of these mammal species did survive in the form of closely related species. The apparent massive mammal extinction was actually a massive radiation; thus, apparent extinction actually documents success. A similar but lesser process occurred in other groups of vertebrates, but these are not as well studied.

When all of these factors are included in an estimation of the survival of vertebrates across the K/T boundary in northeastern Montana, we find a survival rate of almost 65 percent, far greater than the uncorrected 32 percent cited above. Still, various major groups of species did not fare as well as others in northeastern Montana. These are the cartilaginous fishes, the lizards, the ornithischians, the saurischians, and the marsupials. This is a phylogenetically and ecologically diverse group of vertebrates. Accordingly, any theory of extinction must account for why these rather than other groups were most affected.

The cartilaginous fishes appear to have been hardest hit, with all 5 species disappearing at the K/T boundary in northeastern Montana. These disappearances are directly tied to the loss of marine influences as the epicontinental seas receded from the region. The marine regression may also have been a factor in the reduction in number of species of lizards. Only 3 of 7 common species survived, possibly because of wetter conditions. The latter occurred because as the sea regressed, large backswamps developed when the pattern of stream drainage changed. Extensive coals found in sediments after the K/T boundary testify to the presence of these swamps. In addition, studies of the ancient soils suggest an increase in rainfall.

The extinction of ornithischians and some saurischians in northeastern Montana may in part have been a result of the extensive marine regressions. As discussed earlier, the regression resulted in the loss of tens of thousands of square miles of coastal habitats in which these dinosaurs lived. Another contributing factor may have been climatic deterioration triggered or caused by bolide impact(s) and/or extensive volcanic eruptions. Of course among saurischians, the birds did survive and later flourish, but without much of a fossil record at the K/T boundary for these creatures we do not know with certainty how they fared at the time.

Locally, marsupials also fared poorly, with only one of 11 species surviving. These animals, however, flourished elsewhere, such as in South America and Australia. Their decline in northeastern Montana may be a result of the appearance of new placental mammals shortly before or just after the K/T boundary. Marsupials had been doing very well for almost 30 million years in the western interior until the appearance of these new placental mammals. Competition for resources between these groups may well have contributed directly to the decline of marsupials in the region.

If nothing else emerges from the studies in northeastern Montana, one thing is clear: there are tremendous variations in extinction patterns for different groups of vertebrates in the region. One single cause cannot yet account for these differences. Only marine regression appears to account for much of the extinction patterns, but it alone does not appear to be sufficient. We still do not know much about the fate of vertebrates elsewhere on the globe at that time, but the patterns of extinction and survival for other organisms (plants and marine invertebrates) suggest that other factors, such as bolide impact and volcanic eruptions, may have been the coup de grace for these organisms.

The pursuit of reasons for past extinctions falls within the realm of historical science. Even if we cannot say with experimental certainty what caused these extinctions, our knowledge and understanding of what probably went on some 66 million years has increased many fold as this scientific quest has become one of the most interdisciplinary in all of science.

THE BONE WARS: COPE, MARSH AND AMERICAN VERTEBRATE PALEONTOLOGY, 1865–1900

RONALD RAINGER

THE SCIENCE OF VERTEBRATE PALEONTOLOGY, INCLUDING THE STUDY OF DINOSAURS, DID NOT ORIGINATE in the United States, but two Americans, Edward Drinker Cope (1840–1897) and Othniel Charles Marsh (1831–1899), contributed significantly to the subject. In the years between 1865 and 1900, these two men discovered and described hundreds of fossils and pushed America to the forefront of vertebrate paleontology. Fieldwork by Cope, Marsh, and their collectors led to the uncovering of the first specimens of sauropod and ceratopsian dinosaurs. Both Cope and Marsh were evolutionists whose work helped to define the evolutionary relationship between birds and reptiles. Marsh also developed a new classification of dinosaurs that had long-lasting signficance.

Despite all of their accomplishments, Cope and Marsh are best known for their "bone war," which began in the early 1870s and lasted for twenty years. It was a nasty affair that created deep divisions between many workers in American vertebrate paleontology. The feud was largely a result of the ambitions of the two men. Both Cope and Marsh were independently wealthy men who sought to dominate the field of vertebrate paleontology. Priority in discovering and naming fossils dominated the bone war in the 1870s, but in later years the Cope–Marsh feud was a highly personalized struggle to gain financial and institutional support for paleontology. In the years after the Civil War, the federal government increased its sponsorship for exploration and research in the western states and territories, and in their quest for preeminence both Cope and Marsh fought for control of that support.

EDWARD DRINKER COPE

Cope began his scientific work studying reptiles, and his ambitions were evident from the outset. Born into a wealthy Quaker family in Philadelphia in 1841, Cope was a precocious child who had an interest in the study of animals from an early age. In 1860 he took courses with Joseph Leidy, a professor of anatomy and naturalist who was the leading vertebrate paleontologist in the United States, and then pursued independent study at museums in the United States and abroad. Cope was eager to establish his reputation, and by the mid-1860s had published almost fifty papers on the reptile and amphibian collections at the Smithsonian Institution and Philadelphia's Academy of Natural Sciences. An energetic and prolific researcher, Cope's work attracted the attention of Spencer Fullerton Baird, Louis Agassiz, and other notable American scientists. Yet Cope was also a hasty and inaccurate worker, as one of his tutors noted, and brash as well as brilliant. In 1864, he referred to the famous Agassiz, whose writings and collections he had examined, as "far from infallible." At an early age Cope emerged as a productive and ambitious scholar who had supreme confidence in his abilities (perhaps overconfidence) and sought to chart his own course in science.

While Cope's early work in museum collections led him to describe some fossil specimens, it is likely that he was attracted to vertebrate paleontology by exciting developments occurring at the Academy of Natural Sciences in Philadelphia. In 1858 William Parker Foulke, a Philadelphia resident, captured the attention of Academy scientists by announcing the discovery of large bones hear Haddonfield, New Jersey. Leidy, who had previously examined fossils from the New Jersey Cretaceous, examined the specimen *in situ*. He described it as an extinct reptile about twenty-five feet in length, claimed it was related to the *Iguanodon*, a dinosaur previously discovered in England, and named it *Hadrosaurus foulkii*. Further fieldwork yielded additional remains, and in 1865 Leidy described the *Hadrosaurus* as a "great herbivorous lizard [that] sustained itself in a semi-erect position on the huge hinder extremities and tail while it browsed on plants growing upon the shores of the ocean in which it lived." Leidy's work aroused scientific and popular interest, including a proposal from Benjamin Waterhouse Hawkins to mount the bones in the Academy's museum at his own expense. Hawkins, a British artist and student of comparative anatomy who had created the first dinosaur restorations in England in the 1850s, was eager to repeat his achievement. He did so, mounting the first dinosaur specimen in the United States at the Academy in 1868.

Such work aroused Cope's interest, and by the mid-1860s he too was working on dinosaurs. In 1867 Cope used his inherited wealth to move to Haddonfield and took up paleontology on a full-time basis.

Working in the New Jersey Greensand, he too found fragments of *Hadrosaurus foulkii*, as well as fossil turtles and mosasaurs, extinct aquatic reptiles. Cope also discovered remains of another dinosaur, a large carnivorous animal that he named *Laelaps*. During the late 1860s he extended his investigations into Delaware, Maryland, and Virginia and published extensively on the fossils and recent vertebrates that he discovered.

Cope also played a role in the Academy's effort to mount *Hadrosaurus foulkii* but he quickly ran into problems with Leidy and Hawkins. He and Hawkins quarreled over the pelvic structure of the dinosaur and the manner in which the creature should be mounted. Cope had also attacked Leidy's views on a number of occasions, and Leidy responded in kind. In 1870 Leidy criticized Cope's determination of a new species he called *Elasmosaurus* as just a variant of another mosasaur, *Discosaurus*, that Leidy had already described. When Leidy pointed out that Cope had restored a specimen of *Elasmosaurus* backwards, Cope quickly sought to confiscate all copies of the journal that contained the mistaken restoration.

OTHNIEL CHARLES MARSH

Marsh, too, did some of his earliest work on fossil reptiles. Marsh had a formal education in the sciences, first at Yale's Sheffield Scientific School and then at several German universities. He also benefited from the largess of his uncle, the philanthropist George Peabody, who provided for Marsh's career by donating $150,000 for the establishment of a natural history museum at Yale. Marsh was interested in quickly outfitting his museum and establishing himself in the American scientific community. In 1866 he and Yale geology professor James Dwight Dana examined fossil footprints previously discovered in the Connecticut Valley, and Marsh purchased specimens for his museum. He visited prominent scientists and scientific institutions and became closely associated with Leidy, Cope, and others at the Academy of Natural Sciences. In 1867 Marsh became a corresponding member of the academy, and over the next five years attended meetings at which he examined specimens and discussed questions on vertebrate paleontology with Leidy and Cope. In 1868 he and Cope jointly investigated fossil deposits in New Jersey, and in addition to exchanging information and discussing plans for future research they named specimens in each other's behalf. Marsh also collected and described remains of *Hadrosaurus*, mosasaurs, and other fossil reptiles.

Although Marsh and Cope worked together and with Leidy for a time, they soon began to go their separate ways. Their early work focused on fossil vertebrates from Cretacous deposits along the Atlantic coast, but both Cope and Marsh realized that greater opportunities existed in the western states and territories. While a student in Breslau, Marsh had learned from one of his professors, Ferdinand Roemer, that the midwest possessed outstanding fossil deposits. More important, he and Cope were well aware of the fossil treasures that came to Leidy from the west. Since the early 1850s Leidy, through contacts with Baird at the Smithsonian, with the Army, and with a network of state survey geologists and collectors, had become a virtual clearinghouse for fossil vertebrates. As a result, he had produced some of the first and most complete descriptions of extinct animals.

Cope and Marsh also realized that they had more opportunity than Leidy to obtain such specimens. Throughout the 1850s and 1860s Leidy had benefited from a system that provided him with specimens for free. Yet he was dependent on his network of underpaid collectors and not able to take full advantage

of the riches that lay in the West. Leidy was not a wealthy man and for much of his career maintained more than one job in order to make ends meet. Financial and teaching obligations did not permit Leidy to undertake expeditions independently, and he had no institutional support of his own. Cope and Marsh, however, were independently wealthy and had both the freedom and the resources to pursue vertebrate paleontology on a full-time basis. Following a three-year teaching stint at Haverford College, Cope devoted himself to vertebrate paleontology. Marsh, although professor of paleontology at Yale, had no teaching obligations and used his personal income from Peabody for full-time collecting and research. Both men not only could afford to outfit expeditions, but also used their money to purchase specimens and hire fossil collectors. In the process Cope and Marsh turned vertebrate paleontology into an expensive and far-flung enterprise. They also turned it into a battleground for their desires to obtain fossils and scientific reputations.

GO WEST!

Beginning in the early 1870s, Cope and Marsh launched successful expeditions in the West for fossil remains. Marsh organized and directed his own surveys made up of students from Yale College. On the first of those trips in 1870, Marsh and his party crossed paths with Ferdinand V. Hayden, a geologist with Philadelphia connections who headed up a government-sponsored Geological and Geographical Survey of the Territories. Hayden, whose survey collected specimens for Leidy, claimed that Marsh was "raging ambitious" and out "to ransack the entire countryside for fossils." Marsh disputed Hayden's right to collect fossil vertebrates and to reserve the study of such specimens exclusively for Leidy. In the five expeditions he led from 1870 to 1874, Marsh and his parties discovered additional specimens of mosasaurs as well the remains of titanotheres, uintatheres, horses, and many other families of fossil mammals. Among the most important were the discoveries of flying reptiles and birds with teeth, both of which were transitional forms that provided important documentary evidence indicating that birds had evolved from reptiles. In 1873 Leidy stated that Marsh's "new subclass of birds is…the most interesting [discovery] yet made in American paleontology."

Cope was not far behind either in expeditions or discoveries. Although most of his early work concentrated on remains from the East coast, Cope had already described some specimens sent to him by collectors in the midwest. In 1871 Cope followed Marsh's lead and traveled to Kansas to search for extinct vertebrates. He too found remains of mosasaurs, extinct fishes, extinct turtles, and flying reptiles.

THE EARLY COMPETITION

Cope and Marsh, eager to take advantage of opportunities, were investigating similar areas and discovering and describing some of the same genera and species of fossil vertebrates almost simultaneously. That situation created an environment for criticism and conflict. Each man claimed priority of discovery, and each employed a different nomenclature and classification for the new specimens he found. Marsh referred to his recently discovered genus of flying reptiles as pterosaurs; Cope defined them as ornithosaurians. For Marsh, extinct sea serpents were part of the mosasaurs; for Cope, who often looked to Greek rather than Latin origins for his designations, they belonged to the order Pythonomorpha. In 1872 Marsh published an article that showed there were errors in Cope's interpretation of mosasauroid bone structure, and in place of Cope's work provided a new and

more comprehensive classification of those animals.

Marsh was therefore already skeptical of the character of Cope's work when he became concerned about Cope's future research interests. Both men planned to spend the summer collecting in the Bridger Basin of Wyoming, an area where Marsh had run into trouble with Hayden when he laid claim to the region's fossils in 1870. Now, in the summer of 1872, Marsh would have to contend with both Leidy and Cope, who would be working for Hayden. Marsh asked both men to agree to an arrangement whereby each would furnish the others and leading scientific institutions with prepublication notices of their discoveries. Marsh hoped to prevent problems. He was also dubious about Cope's work and eager to retain priority for his discoveries in the region.

MARSH ATTACKS COPE

Marsh's arrangement did not work, and with the Bridger Basin expeditions competition and conflict erupted into controversy. Leidy was the first into the field in July and was the first to report new discoveries. The difficulties emerged later that summer when Marsh and then Cope commenced fieldwork in the basin. Marsh accused Cope of stealing one of his collectors, Sam Smith, who was knowledgeable about fossil deposits in the region. More serious were Marsh's accusations that Cope was providing inaccurate information about new specimens discovered in the area, and that Cope was claiming priority for discoveries that Marsh had previously made and reported.

The dispute, in which Marsh clearly was the aggressor, concerned fossil mammals known as uintatheres, peculiar animals whose discovery resulted in conflicting descriptions and classifications. Their foot structure suggested that the uintatheres belonged to the order of odd-toed mammals, the perissodactyls.

Above: Dinosaur and other fossils on display in all their splendor in the Victorian Hall of Comparative Anatomy, Museum of Natural History, Paris. Photo: American Museum of Natural History. Following spread: The social behavior of dinosaurs was large- *ly unknown until a large Maiasaur nesting area was discovered recently at Egg Mountain. It became clear that mothers tended their eggs. By Doug Henderson.*

However, their bizarre skull bones and large size suggested that they might belong to the Proboscidea, which includes the elephant order. Indeed Leidy, Cope, and Marsh all originally claimed that the uintatheres were proboscideans. According to Leidy, the specimens were the remains of a "huge pachyderm" that he classified under the new genus *Uintatherium*. Cope referred them to another new genus, *Eobasilus*, of the same order. Marsh soon changed his interpretation and claimed that the specimens from the Bridger Basin constituted a new order, the Dinocerata. He described what he considered to be the type genus and species for that order, and in turn erected a classification and nomenclature that included the new species and genera claimed by Leidy and Cope.

Marsh was very much concerned about who had been the first to discover and to publish an account of those fossils. Marsh had not received from Cope the prepublication notices that they had agreed upon, and he became suspicious about notices of discoveries that Cope had telegraphed back to Philadelphia in August and September 1872. Marsh, claiming that there were discrepancies in Cope's reports and suggesting that he had backdated a number of reports to claim priority for his work, mounted a campaign to determine precisely the dates of Cope's reports, when those reports were made public, and when and in what form they were published. Marsh queried Baird, Agassiz, and other scientists to determine when they had received Cope's reports. He sought similar information from the Academy of Natural Sciences and the American Philosophical Society. On the basis of his investigations Marsh asserted that Cope had antedated reports, had claimed as dates for the presentation of reports days when the Philadelphia institutions had not met, and had considered as the date of publication the day when telegraphed announcements of discoveries were presented at the societies' meetings.

Obtaining priority for discovering and publishing information about new specimens was important since it gave the discoverer the right to name the specimen, and, in the words of historian James Secord, "Naming was an essential feature in this active process of achievement. To name something was to place it, to possess it, to confer upon it the status of a natural object." Marsh sought to magnify the achievement by maintaining that he had discovered not just a new genus or species but a new order of animals; that would justify his effort to supersede the discoveries and classifications of Leidy and Cope.

In addition to raising serious questions about Cope's character and the nature of his scientific work, Marsh tried to define what he considered acceptable procedures for reporting and publishing scientific discoveries. In his final foray on the issue in 1873, Marsh attacked Cope:

Prof. Cope attempts to gain an important advantage at the start by assuming that mere printing is publication. This he has no right to do, as the usage of the best naturalists is decidedly against it. In the note from which he quotes, I assumed that publication of scientific results means making them known, especially to those interested, and in the case of advance copies, these must be made accessible to those working in the same department. Judged by this well established standard, not one of Prof. Cope's papers was published at the date claimed. The mere printing of these papers has no more to do with their publication than has the invention of the printing press. Both events preceded this publication, but neither of them constitute it.

At both the Academy of Natural Sciences and the American Philosophical Society Marsh then initiated efforts to have Cope's actions investigated and censured. Privately, Marsh pressured individual scientists not to accept the authenticity of Cope's work.

Marsh's aggressiveness, however, did not extend to Leidy, who had first described and classified uintathere specimens. Leidy did not possess Cope's financial resources for fieldwork and therefore perhaps did not represent the same threat to Marsh that Cope did. However, in 1873 Leidy was an active and leading figure in vertebrate paleontology and had plans for additional fieldwork in the west and for further publications in the science. He and Marsh did not feud; on the contrary, they maintained "a long enduring friendship."

Furthermore, the Marsh–Cope controversy in some respects paralleled earlier problems that arose between Marsh and Hayden in 1870. Hayden and Hayden's Survey represented a different tradition from Marsh. Hayden was a physician by training. Marsh was a trained, professional paleontologist. Hayden had worked with geologists John Strong Newberry and James Hall in the 1850s, but for the most part he was self-taught and learned geology and paleontology on expeditions to the West. By the late 1860s, Hayden had established himself as the director of a federal survey that served a multitude of purposes and embraced a diversified approach to the study of the West. He examined geology and stratigraphy, but his survey included zoologists, botanists, ethnologists, paleontologists, and paleobotanists. Annual reports of his survey included monographs on those subjects as well as studies of mining, agriculture and land use. Artists and photographers also contributed. Hayden's Survey served political and economic ends as much if not more than scientific objectives. His letters to Leidy are filled with urgent requests for Leidy to complete his report on fossil vertebrates so that Hayden could make the case to politicians and businessmen to support new and and bigger surveys. He also requested Leidy to provide paleontological essays that the public could

understand. Hayden's surveys were an early vision of the modern team approach to field work. Marsh disagreed with Hayden's team approach and felt threatened by his command of resources.

Similar factors also influenced Marsh's attitude toward Cope. Although Cope had studied with Leidy and abroad, he did not have a formal scientific education. Through the Academy of Natural Sciences, Cope was associated primarily with physicians and naturalists who had a broad interest in science. Cope, who examined a wide range of recent as well as fossil vertebrates, was part of that tradition.

COPE AND EVOLUTION

However, Cope was an evolutionist, again treading on Marsh's territory, though he did not accept Darwin's theory. In Cope's view, Darwin's mechanism of natural selection only eliminated the unfit; it could not account for the origin of favorable variations, or what Cope called the origin of the fittest. He maintained that will or choice led organisms to make movements and to use parts, and the inheritance of those choices, habits, and acquired characters resulted in evolution. Cope employed that neo-Lamarckian interpretation to explain the evolution of the feet, teeth, and other skeletal parts. Yet he sought to explain evolution and inheritance in terms of energies, growth forces, and non-material factors. He also employed a terminology that was confusing and difficult to understand. In short, Cope engaged in a great deal of ill-founded speculation about the causes of evolution.

Cope was also concerned with questions of the habits, physiology, and ecology of prehistoric life. In an 1867 paper, Cope followed an analysis of the teeth, feet, and limb bones of the dinosaur *Laelaps* with the claim: "We can, then, with some basis of probability imagine our monster carrying his eighteen feet of length on a leap, at least thirty feet through the air, with hind feet ready to strike his prey with fatal grasp, and his enormous weight to press it to the earth." A few years later when discussing the ancient marine reptiles of Kansas, he described "a huge snake-like form which rose above the surface and stood erect.... Then it would dive into the depths and naught would be visible but the foam caused by the disappearing mass of life."

Cope was also interested in visually portraying the prehistoric forms that he examined. As indicated, he collaborated with Leidy and Hawkins on the mounting of the *Hadrosaurus*. He sketched illustrations of *Laelaps* and in 1870 presented a pictorial interpretation of the large sea serpent *Elasmosaurus* and its environment. In later years he illustrated the *Eobasilus* from the Bridger Basin, as well as sauropod dinosaurs from Colorado and Wyoming. In those efforts Cope received assistance and at least tacit support from others in Philadelphia. The Academy of Natural Sciences endorsed the *Hadrosaurus* exhibit. Cope's portrayal of the habits and life-styles of flying reptiles was published in an annual report of Hayden's survey.

Marsh, however, cast a critical eye on such efforts. Although it was Leidy who in 1869 pointed out that Cope's restoration of *Elasmosaurus* was completely backwards, it was Marsh who publicly ridiculed Cope for that error in 1873 and 1890. He was also critical of Cope's efforts to reconstruct or mount fossil vertebrates. Although Marsh purchased from Henry A. Ward's Scientific Establishment mounted specimens of *recent* animals for the Peabody Museum, he was skeptical of Ward's offers to mount extinct vertebrates. In 1875 when Spencer Fullerton Baird solicited support to have Hawkins produce restorations of fossil animals for the Centennial, Marsh returned a negative reply. After dismissing Hawkins as a mere draftsman who had little knowledge of anatomy, he asserted: "I

do not believe it possible at present to make restorations of any of the more important extinct animals of this country that will be of real value to science, or the public." In later years Marsh included reconstructions of extinct toothed birds and dinosaurs in his publications, and he was even willing to have mounts of his fossil specimens made for the United States National Museum and the International Geological Congress. But in the 1860s and 1870s he opposed efforts to popularize vertebrate paleontology, especially the work of Cope and Hawkins.

MARSH AND CLASSIFICATION

Marsh, unlike Cope, whose active, fertile mind grappled with theoretical questions, did not usually analyze evolutionary questions. While on some occasions he offered brief comments on the habits and life-styles of mosasaurs, pterosaurs, and dinosaurs, and provided some ideas on the causes and pattern of evolution, he did not engage in sustained analysis of the relationship of form to function or the dynamics of the evolutionary process. For Marsh, matters of description and classification were most important. His publications were usually brief, descriptive accounts of new finds that offered little in the way of functional, phylogenetic, or stratigraphic detail. Marsh's work was definitely narrower than Cope's. Marsh, like Cope, boldly established new species, genera, or even orders on the basis of very little fossil data. His work included errors in morphology and description and was often characterized by taxonomic inflation. Yet he maintained that in his work he provided "the facts I know" and did not engage in "preaching on what might have been." According to Marsh, his work was more empirical, accurate, and professional than the work produced by Cope or Hayden.

Despite Marsh's contempt for Cope and his efforts

*A dinosaur skeleton is revealed and preserved in
place in its rocky matrix for display to visitors. Photo:
Dinosaur National Monument/U.S. Park Service.*

to have Cope's work condemned and stopped, both men concerned research in vertebrate paleontology and continued to snipe at each other in print and in the field. Although Marsh personally abandoned fieldwork after the summer of 1874, he employed a large number of collectors who supplied him with specimens. Following another season with the Hayden Survey in the Bridger Basin, Cope collected for Lieutenant George Montgomery Wheeler's Survey in New Mexico in 1874. He participated in expeditions to Montana and Wyoming over the next two years, but warfare between Cope and Marsh broke out again in Colorado and Wyoming in the late 1870s.

THE MORRISON CONTROVERSY

The controversy centered around discoveries of some of the most magnificent dinosaur deposits ever found. In 1877 two amateur collectors in Colorado informed both Cope and Marsh of the discovery of large fossil remains in the Morrison formations near Morrison and Cañon City, Colorado. After some hesitation, Cope and Marsh quickly engaged the collectors to unearth and ship the specimens, and the two men became involved in a headlong rush to obtain more dinosaurs. Marsh sent Samuel Wendell Williston, one of his assistants at the Peabody Museum, to supervise the collecting operations, but Cope obtained larger and better remains than did Marsh from that region. By August 1877 Cope was describing remains of *Camarasaurus supremus* from near Cañon City. Marsh, however, soon learned that railroad workers in Wyoming were uncovering gigantic fossil remains near a railroad station at Como Bluff. Again he jumped in, and over the next two years Williston, W. H. Reed, Arthur Lakes, and other paid collectors uncovered hundreds of fragments of *Apatosaurus*, *Diplodocus*,

Camarasaurus, *Barosaurus*, *Stegosaurus*, and other dinosaurs. Como Bluff was the richest dinosaur deposit ever discovered, and reinforced the preeminence of American paleontology.

Accompanying the excitement and interest associated with the discoveries of those gigantic remains were continued feuding and the use of questionable tactics by both Cope and Marsh. They had been bitter enemies since their encounter in 1873, and each man sought to ensure that the other did not infringe on his presumed proprietary rights to the fossil deposits and specimens. Marsh made sure that his collectors Reed and William E. Carlin signed contracts pledging not to reveal information about the deposits at Como Bluff or to work for Cope. Both camps hired employees to keep tabs on the other's operations. Despite Cope's and Marsh's precautions and cajolings, a number of collectors defected to the opposite side. When Reed learned that Carlin had gone over to Cope, he destroyed fragments from his quarries so that Carlin would not learn of important deposits. In 1879, when Cope let it be known that he intended to visit the Como Bluff site in 1879, Marsh's assistants made certain to safeguard all specimens. Cope and Marsh also competed for priority in discovery and naming the specimens. Although Marsh defined some genera that have since been determined to be only variants (for example, *Brontosaurus* [1879] is a junior synonym of *Apatosaurus* [1877]), Cope's designations *Agathaumas* and *Amphicoelias* were not recognized then or now.

Although Marsh maintained collectors at Como Bluff until 1889, and profited from later discoveries of ceratopsian dinosaurs in other locations in Wyoming and Colorado, the nature of his dispute with Cope had changed by the late 1870s. Rather than continued confrontations over the discovery, description, and classification of specimens, the Cope–Marsh feud primarily involved a struggle to gain control over political and financial resources for work in vertebrate paleontology.

THE STRUGGLE FOR CONTROL

Marsh had previously sought to undermine his rival's bases of support. In 1873 he protested and sought censureship of Cope's actions at meetings of the Academy of Natural Sciences and the American Philosophical Society. The latter organization agreed to stop accepting telegraphed messages as the basis of scientific publications, but the Academy refused to censure Cope. Marsh requested that Hayden prohibit the publication of Cope's disputed work on the Bridger mammals in the annual report of the survey. Hayden, however, maintained that he was not " competent to decide disputed claims." He also sided with Cope. In 1873 he rehired Cope for another summer's work on his survey and created the *Paleontological Bulletin* as a periodical designed to provide a ready means for publishing information from the field. Having failed in an effort to have Hayden dispense with Cope, Marsh went after Hayden's Survey. In 1874 Congress initiated an investigation into a controversy between the Wheeler and Hayden surveys and the issue of whether the military or civilian agencies should control government science. Most civilian scientists supported Hayden, but when the Yale faculty submitted to Congress a testimonial in opposition to army-sponsored science, Marsh's name was conspicuous by its absence. "Marsh," as Hayden noted, was "working the other way."

Although the government allowed the Hayden Survey to continue, Marsh worked for reform in a related quarter. His fieldwork in South Dakota in 1874 indicated that the Sioux Indians were receiving sub-

standard government provisions. Charging the government with fraud, Marsh played a role in the controversy that forced the resignation of Secretary of the Interior and thus sullied the reputation of the department that sponsored Hayden's Survey.

Marsh also established ties to powerful Washington scientists. In 1874 he was elected to the National Academy of Sciences and became closely associated with government scientists Simon Newcomb, Clarence King, and John Wesley Powell. King had been one of Marsh's colleagues at the Sheffield Scientific School and in the mid-1870s was the director of the government-supported Geological Survey of the 40th Parallel. King agreed to publish Marsh's work on extinct toothed birds he had discovered in Kansas. Through King, Marsh also met other Washington scientists and gradually an alliance emerged of Marsh, Dana, Agassiz, Whitney, and other friends of Clarence King and John Wesley Powell. All were unalterably opposed to army-dominated science and also "upstart" science of the kind represented by Hayden and Cope.

THE GEOGRAPHIC SURVEY

Marsh not only became part of that group, but circumstances thrust him into a powerful position that helped to bring his group to power. In 1878 Marsh became president of the National Academy of Sciences at the time when the government was again considering the question of the nation's geological and geographic surveys. When Congress ordered an investigation into the several separate but competing surveys, King and his supporters moved quickly to place the matter in the hands of political and scientific friends. As geologist J. J. Stevenson told Marsh: "King said... that an excellent idea would be to have some senator move that the whole matter of these surveys be referred to the National Academy to report on the competence of the persons in charge of the several surveys." Representative Abraham Hewitt of New York did just that, and with the issue in the hands of the National Academy of Sciences, Marsh held center stage in the struggle over the control of government work in the geological sciences. The National Academy committee that Marsh created was anti-Hayden and was opposed to military control of science. The committee opposed the continuation of the existing surveys—the position supported by Hayden and Cope—and came out in favor of the establishment of a consolidated civilian survey. By April 1879 King was appointed the first head of the new United States Geological Survey.

Marsh, who had consistently supported his Yale colleague, benefited from the new arrangement. Although King emphasized economic geology and mining and did not provide a place on the survey for vertebrate paleontology, his successor Powell did. In 1882 Powell appointed Marsh vertebrate paleontologist of the Geological Survey and thereby gave him a much greater opportunity for doing work in vertebrate paleontology. Throughout the 1870s Marsh had relied on his money to develop a laboratory and a collection at Yale, but the government position enabled him to expand his operations considerably. Provided with a budget that by 1884 reached $16,000 annually, he commanded an ample personal salary and supported collecting crews in the western fossil fields and a large staff of artists and preparators in New Haven. The government position gave him ready access to fossil deposits and publications outlets, and the means to deny the same benefits to others. Through an agreement with Baird and Powell, the government allowed Marsh to keep all specimens he collected at the private Peabody Museum. Powell also gave Marsh a great deal of autonomy; he readily agreed to the research pro-

posals that Marsh put forth, and required only generalized annual reports of the activities of his vertebrate paleontologist.

As Marsh gained control of valuable resources, Cope's fortunes declined. Although Cope continued to outfit expeditions and collect specimens through the 1870s, the mad rush to obtain dinosaurs put a serious strain on his finances. A series of poor investments created additional economic problems. Cope had relied on some government support for his work in vertebrate paleontology, but the creation of the new Geological Survey brought an end to that. The new survey eliminated Hayden's organization, and with it Hayden's *Paleontological Bulletin* that had served as a means for publication. To compensate, Cope purchased the *American Naturalist*, but that investment only compounded his financial difficulties. With the creation of the Geological Survey, Marsh had control over almost all resources for work in vertebrate paleontology.

Throughout the late 1870s and 1880s Cope tried to obtain support for his work in vertebrate paleontology, but failed. He worked unsuccessfully to change the Academy of Natural Sciences into a research institution that would support paid curatorships in vertebrate paleontology and other fields. By the mid-1880s, when he could no longer afford to pay collectors Charles H. Sternberg or Jacob L. Wortman, he was forced to abandon fieldwork. He then began efforts to sell his collections; however, his original asking price of $100,000 was too high for the Academy or other institutions. Realizing that support for his science required political and financial backing, Cope undertook efforts to obtain funding in Washington. He approached Baird for support but was turned down. He worked to oust Marsh as president of the National Academy of Sciences, again unsuccessfully. Throughout 1884–85 he sought to obtain political backing for a new government appropriation bill that would fund his research. Failing that, he sought to promote government investigations into the Powell survey and its operations.

COPE COUNTERATTACKS

In 1885 Cope took advantage of a government investigation into federal science in general to attack Powell and Marsh. Cope and Alabama Congressman Hilary Herbert wrote a 23,000-word statement condemning Powell's agency and its operation. Cope also capitalized on complaints from Marsh's field and laboratory assistants. In the mid-1880s Williston, George Baur, Otto Meyer, and other Marsh assistants complained that they had done most of the research and writing for the two government monographs that appeared under Marsh's name: *The Odontornithes* (1880) and *The Dinocerata* (1886). They also contended that frequently Marsh had not paid them promptly and did not allow them to publish independently or to pursue scientific careers in vertebrate paleontology. Cope publicized such complaints to those investigating Powell in 1885, along with accusations that Marsh kept government specimens under private lock and key. He also enlisted William Berryman Scott and Henry Fairfield Osborn, two Princeton paleontologists whose work he had supported, in the attack on Marsh. Under the guise of attending a Yale–Princeton football game, Scott traveled to New Haven and interviewed several of Marsh's assistants in the fall of 1885. Osborn, then studying in Karl Alfred von Zittel's paleontological laboratory in Munich, obtained additional information which he and his friends hoped to use to defame "the great man." Scott and Cope hoped to publish an exposé of Marsh's operations, but Osborn was wary of going against the president of the National Academy of Sciences, who was also a powerful figure in the

Geological Survey. Osborn wrote a private paper on Cope's behalf, but no exposé was published and Marsh and Powell remained in power.

Cope's frustrations remained, and five years later he brought the issue to a head. In January 1890 he published his accusations against Marsh in the *New York Herald*. Cope charged that most of Marsh's papers and his major monographs were written by his assistants. He also accused Marsh of plagiarizing from Cope's work and from the work of the Russian paleontologist Vladimir Kovalevsky. And he condemned Powell for failing to publish the concluding volumes of the Hayden Survey and for seeking to have Cope turn over specimens that he had collected on government surveys in the 1870s.

The newspaper controversy did some damage to Marsh. His assistants George Baur and Samuel Wendell Williston left New Haven. John Bell Hatcher, Marsh's premier collector, stepped up his demands that Marsh allow him to prepare and publish himself on the specimens that he was finding in the field. The adverse publicity of the affair created some problems for Marsh in Washington, particularly in 1892 when Congress again launched an investigation of the Powell Survey.

MARSH'S DOWNFALL: RECESSION ECONOMICS

The 1892 investigation was not a direct result of Cope's exposé or the ongoing Cope–Marsh feud, but Cope's accusations had a bearing on Marsh's eventual downfall. The main reason for the investigation was an economic recession that fueled an effort to cut the budget. As Marsh's cousin Congressman Joseph H. Outhwaite pointed out: "This House is extremely utilitarian — and has its teeth sharpened for everything strictly scientific." Congress focused much of its attention on Powell, who by that time commanded a great deal of power in government science. Under Powell the Geological Survey employed dozens of scientists working on hydrology, paleontology, and a vast project for developing a national map. He also headed the Bureau of American Ethnology. In the late 1880s, when Powell tried to create an Irrigation Survey to regulate water use and land settlement, western and southern politicians were outraged. In addition, there were rumors of favoritism in Powell's agencies, and Congressmen Herbert revived Cope's accusations against Marsh and his paleontological operations at Yale. When Herbert pointed out the tremendous expense and little practical value associated with Marsh's study of "such worthless objects as birds with teeth," he was appealing to a utilitarian, economy-minded Congress. To Marsh the attack was a part of personal vendetta led by Herbert but orchestrated by Cope and Cope's colleagues.

The 1892 investigation brought down Marsh and crippled his program in vertebrate paleontology. Powell and his successor Charles Doolittle Walcott retained him as honorary government paleontologist, but his stipend was far below what it had been in the 1880s. By that time, too, Marsh's personal fortune was gone; his estate, said his uncle, was "like a squeezed orange." In late 1892, when he let John Bell Hatcher go, Marsh effectively discontinued fieldwork. He had to release Adam Hermann, his chief preparator, and only managed to retain his other preparator, Hugh Gibb, after much negotiation. Marsh did continue to publish; he completed a monograph on North American dinosaurs in 1896. That same year he received a salary from Yale for the first time and supported fieldwork and research on fossil cycads to obtain information on the locations of dinosaur remains. But Marsh's operations in the 1890s were a far cry from what they had been a decade before.

Cope did not profit directly from Marsh's demise, but his interests were promoted by his colleague Henry Fairfield Osborn, who took up where Cope left off. Osborn, whom Cope had helped when he began work in paleontology in the late 1870s, cautiously supported Cope against Marsh in the 1885 affair. But after 1885, when Marsh refused to allow Osborn to examine his collection of Mesozoic mammals, Osborn became highly critical of Marsh's descriptions and classification of those organisms. By 1890 he and Marsh were engaging in such personal attacks over Mesozoic mammals that some of their scientific papers were rejected for publication. In that year, Osborn, a wealthy and well-connected New Yorker, also began negotiations for a position at the American Museum of Natural History. With extensive financial and political resources at his command, he sought to establish a program in vertebrate paleontology, and in the process to undermine Marsh. In the summer of 1890, Osborn sought to lure Hatcher away from Marsh's employ. Although he did not obtain Hatcher for the museum, Osborn contributed money to allow his colleague Scott to hire Hatcher at Princeton in 1893. Osborn did hire Marsh's preparator Adam Hermann. He also obtained Marsh's collector O.A. Peterson, and in 1891–92 started a controversy with Marsh by sending Peterson and another collector, Jacob L. Wortman, into Eocene deposits in southeastern Wyoming where Hatcher was working. With support from the American Museum trustees, Osborn forced Marsh to back down from his claim that as government vertebrate paleontologist he had the right to control access to public lands.

In 1892 Osborn also contributed to the accusations against Marsh's role as government paleontologist. He joined Cope in claiming that Marsh did not allow vertebrate paleontologists access to his collections at Yale, although Osborn had been permitted to examine those specimens on a number of occasions in the 1880s.

Osborn's argument to the government that vertebrate paleontology was not a practical field and should be supported by private not public funds, was directly aimed at undermining Marsh's position. Osborn not only contributed to Marsh's downfall, but within a year of Marsh's death he had negotiated to have the government position reestablished with himself as vertebrate paleontologist for the Geological Survey and in charge of completing Marsh's unfinished monographs!

BIG PALEONTOLOGY: THE EMPIRE RETURNS

Osborn's efforts provide an appropriate conclusion to the bone wars of the late nineteenth century. Osborn, like Cope and Marsh, was eager to create an empire in vertebrate paleontology. The field had become dependent on large financial and political support, and Osborn, like Marsh, relied on rich and powerful associates to gain control of the resources necessary to do work in vertebrate paleontology. Osborn undermined Marsh not only because Marsh stood in his way, but because Osborn believed that the bone wars of the previous twenty-five years had irreparably damaged the scientific research, career opportunities, and character of his friend and colleague Cope. As he negotiated to take over Marsh's position and proceeded to direct fieldwork, research, and exhibitions on dinosaurs, titanotheres, and fossil horses, Osborn was attempting to supersede Marsh on his and Cope's behalf.

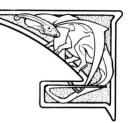

THE GREEN BUFFALO

HARRY TURTLEDOVE

I'M STACKIN' SACKS OF BEANS IN THE BACK OF MY BROTHER PETE'S GENERAL STORE WHEN THE door through the false front opens up and hits the bell a whack. The beans can wait. I hustle out front to see who it is.

"Mornin', Mr. Hatcher," I says, and touch one finger to where my hat brim'd be if I was wearing a hat — Pete, he always says be polite. "What can I do for you today? You haven't come down to Lusk in a while."

"Hello, Joe," John Hatcher answers. He's a little skinny fellow, already mostly bald no matter that he can't be more than thirty. He looks like an undertaker, is what he looks like. Anyway, he goes on, "I came in to send a new shipment off to Professor Marsh, and I figured I'd telegraph to let him know it's on the way."

"Right you are." I go on over to the telegraph clicker off in one corner, set myself down. "Go ahead. You want to write your message out, or can you just talk it to me?"

"I'll talk it," he says, the way he usually does — he knows how to say what he thinks, does John Hatcher. "Let's see, today's the seventeenth, isn't it? All right, here we go, Joe: 'August 17, 1890. To Othniel Charles Marsh, Yale University, New Haven, Connecticut.'"

"Spell me 'Othniel,'" I say. I've sent the man a dozen telegrams, and I never can rightly remember how his name goes.

Hatcher spells it out, then goes on, "'Coming east will be two skulls and other skeletal remains of *Triceratops brevicornus* —'"

"Of *what*?" I say, and I take my hand off the key. "You know you got to spell me out those funny names you throw around." He spells out T-R-I-C-E-R-A-T-O-P-S B-R-E-V-I-C-O-R-N-U-S, nice and slow, and I tap it out a letter at a time. Then I ask him, "Beggin' your pardon, Mr. Hatcher, but what the hell is a Triceratops brevi-whatever?"

"A dinosaur, Joe, a dinosaur with a skull as long as you are and ten times as heavy." John Hatcher's been out here for years, diggin' up old bones and shippin' 'em back east. Damn fool way for a grown man to spend his time if you ask me, especially for a man as good with a deck of cards as Hatcher. Anyways, he goes on, "'— excavated from the Upper Cretaceous'" — I had him spell that one, too — "'Lance Creek beds. More to be forthcoming as discovered. John Bell Hatcher.'"

I send it off, then count up the words and say, "That'll be a dollar twenty, Mr. Hatcher." He tosses down a gold dollar and a couple of dimes. I ask him, "What else can I do for you today?"

"Well, we're running low on beans out at the camp," he says, and it's all I can do to keep from cheering. I'd sooner sell beans than stack 'em, any day. He wants some salt, too, and some flour, as much plaster of Paris as we have, and a couple of other things I misremember. Then he says, "If you want to help get my boxes down from the wagon over at the train station, there's two dollars gold in it for you."

"I'm your man," I say, and we both head out of the

store. I shut the door after me, but Pete comes up just then, all fresh-shaved from the barber shop. "Got some stevedore work from Mr. Hatcher here," I tell him. He waves for me to go on, so I go.

Seems like half the menfolks in Lusk are already gathered round Hatcher's wagon by the time I get there. He needed us, too — we work and we work, and by the time we wrestle this big crate off it and down the ramp to the ground, we're licked, I tell you. "What the devil you really got in there, anyways?" somebody asks Hatcher.

"Dinosaur bones," he answers, the same as he always does. He's been shippin' the things east out of Lusk for years now. 'Most everybody in town's rode out to his digs one time or another, to look things over. Ain't nobody ever caught him minin' gold on the sly yet. Now he says, "I do thank you, gentlemen. Drinks are on me."

Nobody tells him no, either. We're all sweaty from fightin' the crate, and even if we hadn't been, who's going to turn down a free shot? We all troop over to the Rebel Yell, and Hatcher buys, just like he said he would. Then he sits himself down at one of the tables, and five or six of the boys sit down with him.

Me, I knock back my whiskey and get on out of there, before I'm fool enough to try playin' poker with John Hatcher again. That's not a wise thing to do, and I learned it the expensive way. So has every poker-playin' man in Lusk, but it don't stop some of 'em from comin' back after him. Some folks purely ain't got no sense, you ask me.

I go on back to the store and start stackin' up what Hatcher ordered from me. Pete asks me why I'm back so soon and I tell him the same thing I just told you — "Hatcher's in a poker game." Pete, he only grunts. He's stubborner'n me, my brother is, so Mr. John Bell Hatcher won a good deal more money off him than off me before Pete figured out he couldn't lick him. You

throw me in the ocean, I'll tell you pretty damn quick I'm in over my head. My brother, he'd sooner try to wade to China, he would.

Maybe there's some new suckers in the Rebel Yell that day, maybe the cards are even hotter for Hatcher than usual, or maybe he's just plain glad to be in town — even a pissant excuse for a town like I know Lusk is — because he doesn't come in for his supplies all afternoon long. Come to think of it, maybe he went upstairs a time or two, too, instead of playin' cards all that while. Women's another thing you'll find in town that's in short supply diggin' old bones out by Lance Creek.

The sun's close to setting when the telegraph clicker starts to chatter. Pete's closer to it than I am, so he gets the message down. When it's done, he gives it to me. "It's for Hatcher," he says. "Why don't you take it on over to him?"

So I take it. Sure enough, he's still at the poker table when I walk back into the Rebel Yell, and sure enough he's got a nice stack of gold and silver in front of him. He's got a bottle in front of him, too, a bottle he's been workin' on, but it don't look to have made him lose his card sense, not one bit of it.

"Telegram for you, Mr. Hatcher," I says. "It's from New Haven, it is."

"I thank you kindly, Joe." Hatcher takes the telegram from me, reads it through, and then, so help me Hannah, he starts to howl like a coyote, he's laughin' so hard.

"What's funny?" I ask him. He's been comin' into Lusk three, four years now, and I ain't never heard him laugh like that before.

"Listen to this." He picks up the telegram from where he's dropped it on the table, reads it out loud to me and everybody else. It goes like this: "'To John Bell Hatcher. The perfidious Cope may by pure luck have found and described in *Monoclonius* the first of the ceratopsian dinosaurs, but my own' (that's Marsh talking, not me, mind you) 'continued discoveries of these fine specimens of *Triceratops* serve to cast him into the shade which is his natural home. Signed, O.C. Marsh.'"

I'm not the only one inside the Rebel Yell scratchin' my head over all that. "Beggin' your pardon, Mr. Hatcher, but I don't quite see the joke," I say.

"Well, for one thing, Marsh and Cope have hated each other's guts for twenty years now. If Cope were in a firepit of hell and screaming out for water, Marsh would hand him a bottle of kerosene — and the other way round, too. So if I've found a bigger fancier dinosaur that's related to one Cope found first, half the reason Marsh is tickled about it is that he gets to score points off Cope's hide."

"I always thought professors were quiet, peaceable sorts," I says.

Hatcher commences to laugh again, but this time he gets hold of himself before it runs away with him. He goes on, "For another thing, notice they're *his* dinosaurs, even if I'm the one who's excavating them and shipping them off to him. He named the strata — the rock formations — from which we're digging *Triceratops* the Ceratops bed, and traced them eight hundred miles along the flanks of the Rockies, and carefully explored them, too, all in the space of three and a half days' time in the field."

"He did?" I say.

"He says he did." Hatcher lays a finger alongside of his nose.

"This here's a professor? Sounds more like a snake-oil salesman to me."

"He is. And if he were selling, you'd buy, too. He's like that." Hatcher sets down the telegram again, picks up his cards, just like he's forgot what he's holding. He tosses a gold half-eagle and then an eagle onto the middle of the table, careless-like. "See your five dollars, Fred, and I'll raise you ten."

Long as I'm at the Rebel Yell, I figure I'll buy me a drink. So I do, and sure as hell Fred loses that hand. He stomps out, all disgusted, but somebody else with more money'n sense sits down in his seat. John Hatcher, he doesn't even smile.

I go on back to the store, work some more. Hatcher's stuff is all piled up nice and neat, but he doesn't come get it. The fellow who took Fred's seat must be one natural-born greenhorn. Finally Pete and me, we go on up to bed up in the attic.

Hatcher finally shows up the next morning. I hear later he'd played poker all night long, but he doesn't look it. I help him and his people load up their wagon — believe me, what we throw in isn't near as heavy as them bones we'd took out the day before. He pays me off, starts to get up onto the wagon, then stops and rubs his chin like he's just thought of somethin'.

He had, too. He turns around, says to me, "Joe, how would you like to ride out to camp with us. We're short of fresh meat, but we've been too busy digging to do much in the way of hunting. Maybe you and a couple of other folks from Lusk can shoot some for us."

"Three dollars a day, like the last time?" I ask. He just nods. It doesn't faze him a bit. I don't know whether he's spending Marsh's money or what he wins at poker, but he always seems to have plenty. I say, "Let me go in and ask Pete."

I do. Pete says, "Sure, go on. I'll do well enough alone for a few days, and you'll have yourself a good time." So I go get my Winchester and two, three boxes of shells, walk over to the livery stable for my horse, and I'm back to Hatcher's wagon inside half an hour. By then he's not there — he's off gettin' his other people. My pa, he fought in the States War. He always used to say soldierin' was like that — as soon as one thing's ready, another one ain't. So I light up a cigar and I wait.

Hatcher, he comes back before too real long, I will

say. Then up ride Jake Snow and Clancy O'Doole, one after the other. Clancy works for his brother Charlie, the farrier. Jake, he just drifts. Sometimes he rides herd, sometimes he does odd jobs, sometimes he just sits in the Rebel Yell cadgin' drinks. Can't deny he's a good man with a gun, though.

We ride out of Lusk, must have been a little past eight. The sun's right nice that time o' day. It lights up the red cliffs west of town pretty as a penny postcard. And you know what else? The air's a sight fresher out of town too, away from the chimneys and the stables and the privies. I ought to get out more often. I really should.

We rattle along, not in any tearin' hurry but makin' good time all the same. Somewhere around noon, Hatcher goes inside the wagon, lays down, and damned if he doesn't lay himself out on top of the beans and go to sleep. How he can have such a clear conscience after skinnin' so many folks at the card table is purely beyond me. But when he comes out a couple of hours later he's cheery as could be, might as well have slept the whole night long.

By the time the sun goes down, we're every one of us ready for bedrolls. We're still half a day out from where the rest of Hatcher's crew is digging. He wants to talk about his bones, but he's the one had a nap. The rest of us are too worn (and I'm too sore-assed; I hadn't been in the saddle all day for a while) to listen long.

Anyway, we get to Hatcher's camp a little past noon the next day. He set himself up by this outcrop of rock in the middle of nowhere, near as I can see, but seein' the way he knows poker, I figure he knows his own game, too. When we ride up, a couple of his people that was still there come runnin' over and shoutin' like they found gold or somethin' really good.

But it's only more bones. They're carryin' on somethin' fierce about a fibia and tibula or tibia and fibula or whatever the hell the right names of 'em are.

Hatcher gets all excited too. He jumps down from the wagon and goes runnin' over like wolves are after him. Over his shoulder, he says, "Joe, Jake, Clancy, this is what we spend our time doing out here, if you care to see it."

I get down from my horse and go on over after him. Sure as hell, his people've dug a couple of great big bones out of the rock. There's picks leaned up against the outcrop, and chisels, and little awls and things like a dentist uses to poke inside your mouth with.

John Hatcher, he's carryin' on like my sister Betty did after she had her baby. He's as careful with those bones as Betty was with Tyler, too — he touches 'em like they'd break if he looked at 'em sideways. Then one of the fellows who was there when we came in says, "We saved these so you could have a look at them. We'll protect them now."

Well, blast me if they don't start coatin' them old, dead bones with plaster, just like a sawbones would do if I busted an arm. Hatcher sees I'm kind of starin' like, so he says, "We don't want them to break either on the way to the train or going east on it. They can't grow back together again, you know." He's just about readin' my mind. No wonder he's such a blamed good poker player.

Jake hasn't even got off his horse. He shifts his chaw, spits, and says, "Let's get huntin', if we're gonna get huntin'."

"Yeah," Clancy says. So I mount up and the three of us, we ride on out of that camp. When we're out of earshot, Clancy grins and says, "And if we take a little longer to find meat than we reckoned, well, at three dollars a day, who's gonna complain?"

"You got that right," Jake says, and spits again.

Twenty years ago, you ride around in this part of the country and you'd fall over buffalo, there was that many of 'em. They're a lot thinner on the ground nowadays, what with repeatin' rifles and all. Truth is,

I wasn't lookin' to come onto a trail. Pronghorn, I figured, 'd be about the best we can do.

But I'd just stuck a cigar in my mouth late that afternoon when blast me if we don't come across a buffalo track runnin' east, and a fresh one, too. Jake looks at Clancy, Clancy looks at me. "If we take it kind of easy," I say finally, "we won't catch up to 'em tonight. We'll worry about 'em again come mornin'."

"I purely like the way you think, Joe," Clancy says.

So we make ourselves a little fire and gnaw on some jerked beef and hard bread. I brew up a pot of coffee, we all drink some, then we draw straws for who gets first watch. I get the short one, worse luck for me. But what with Indians and outlaws and all, you don't have somebody up at night and you'll wake up with an extra eyehole right in the middle of your forehead.

I wake Clancy and go to bed. When Clancy wakes Jake, he's loud enough so he wakes me too, but not for long. Next thing that wakes me is the sun. We eat some more bread, pour down some more coffee, and off we go.

The buffalo, they haven't been gallivantin' around in the night time either, so we know pretty soon we're gainin' on 'em. Up ahead we see the cloud of dust the herd is raisin'. I peer toward the cloud, tryin' to make out critters through that dust. I just about think I can when the goddamnedest thing happens. I don't hardly know how to put it into words.

One minute I'm ridin' along without a care in the world but for tryin' to spot buffalo, the next I'm so dizzy I almost fall off my horse. He snorts too, like he don't like what's goin' on either, and damn near stumbles, which doesn't make stayin' in the saddle any easier. Jake cusses and Clancy yells, so I'm not the only one who feels somethin' peculiar.

The dizzies go away after a few seconds, thank you Jesus. I guess they do for Clancy too, 'cause he says, "That was right strange."

And it gets stranger, let me tell you. My horse puts his head down to snatch a bite to eat. Everybody knows what Wyoming prairie's like — sagebrush and tumbleweed and grass, all of it dry and yellow by the time August rolls around. Well, may God strike me dead if my horse isn't chewin' on ferns like you'd see if you was by a streambank up in the mountains somewheres, and them just as fresh and green and pretty as ever you'd hope to find.

Not far away is a kind of plant like I never seen before. You take a palm tree — you know, one of those funny ones they have down near the Mexican border, looks like a feather duster for a giant — and forget about the trunk, just have the leaves comin' out of a knobby thing down low to the ground, and you'll get the idea.

Well, I could go on a while long, on account of there's a lot more funny plants around, but I reckon you'd think I was just makin' it up, so I'll leave well enough alone. It was purely perplexin', I tell you that. Like I said, Jake, he's done a deal o' driftin', so I turn to him and say, "Did you ever see the like?"

"Not even close," he answers. Just then a lizard scurries out from under one fern and over to another. I'm not talkin' about some little fence lizard or horny toad, mind you; this critter's big as my arm and half again as thick.

When Jake sees it, I thought he was gonna swallow his chaw. That's always worth a laugh, watchin' a fellow puke up his guts, but he kept it where it belongs. He spits again, and says, "Let's us head on outa here." Nobody argues with him, no sirree.

We ride on about a quarter mile maybe, then the dizzies hit me again. This time, though, they're not so bad as they was before. My horse missteps, but I jerk his head up and he's all right too. When I look down, the prairie's back to bein' the prairie, just like it ought to.

Jake and Clancy, they see that too. Clancy says, "Next time I drink in the Rebel Yell, I'm gonna watch the barkeep closer. I think maybe he put locoweed in my whiskey."

"We all saw the same thing, Clancy," I tell him. Then I stop and think—how do I know that's so? So I say, "The ferns and funny kind of squashed-down palm and that big fat lizard—"

When I talk about the lizard, Jake spits again, so I know he seen it. Clancy nods too. I tell you true, I'm right relieved. I wouldn't want to think I made that stuff up out of my own head.

We ride on after the buffalo. They'd gained some on us—I guess we spent a while gawpin' after we got dizzy the first time. Pretty soon, though, we come close enough to 'em to really start pickin' 'em out one by one. We ride closer, lookin' 'em over. Finally we're within a couple hundred yards, and nobody's sayin' a thing. I got to know if Jake and Clancy see the same thing I do. I just got to, so I say, "Boys, ain't one of them buffalo *green*?"

Clancy, he ups and crosses himself and shouts out, "Jesus, Mary, Joseph, and all the saints be praised, I'm not the only one!" He must be plumb shook up—first time I ever heard him sound like an Irishman. Jake spits twice and nods, so I figure he sees it too.

We don't none of us say anything again for a while, but we don't need to, either. We're all makin' for that green buffalo. The closer we come, the odder it looks. I start to figure the green's some kind of nasty mange, on account of it don't look to have any hair anywhere, just the bare hide. That makes me want to forget about killin' it—the stuff might be catchin'. Then I figure I better kill it, so it can't spread the sickness to the rest of the herd, or to the cattle the ranchers run hereabouts.

And then I get a look at its horns. They're bigger'n any I've ever seen on a buffalo, the ones above its eyes, I mean. But on top of those—not, not on top, in front— oh, hell, you know what I mean—it had another horn,

a third one, right on its snout. I'm not makin' that up, so help me. Never seen one like that before nor since. Never seen a green one before nor since, either, come to that.

The regular buffalo, it's like they don't know what to make of the green one any more'n me and Clancy and Jake do. There's considerable pushin' and snortin' and shovin'. Some of the bigger bulls, they jostle the green buffalo pretty hard. He jostles right back, too. He's as big as any of 'em, bigger if you count his tail, which you ought to do, 'cause it's bigger and fatter than a buffalo tail has any business bein'. A buffalo he jostles stays jostled, if you know what I mean. Those horns have a lot to do with that—he pretty near out-does the rest of the herd put together with 'em.

Those horns! I mean, you'd have to be a natural born fool not to want to kill somethin' with horns as fine as that. I swing up my rifle to my shoulder and fire off a round. Jake and Clancy, they're still right with me, so I don't know to this day if I fired first.

The buffalo, they commence to bellowin', the way buffalo do when you shoot at 'em, and they run like a freight train comin' down out of the Rockies with its brakes gone. I see dust puff up on the green buffalo's flank, so I know we hit him, but he don't go down. Sometimes buffalo, they're purely hard to kill.

Kill? Hell, far as I can tell, the green one isn't even fazed. He runs right along with the rest of the herd. The three of us are gallopin' alongside 'em. I chiefly hope my horse don't stick his foot in a prairie dog hole. If he does, he breaks his own fool neck and mine along with it.

The chase goes on longer than you'd think, because the green one stays in the middle of the herd for a while. Usually in a hunt like that you take whatever critter you can get. Me, Jake, and Clancy, though, we all want him. If we can't get a clear shot at him, we let the others go.

Finally, when I'm startin' to wonder who has more wind, the herd or our horses, the green buffalo commences to drop a little behind the rest. We start shootin' again soon as we see the chance. I reckon we miss a few times, too, or maybe more'n a few. You try aimin' from a runnin' horse at a runnin' buffalo, my friend, before you laugh at us for it.

But we make some hits, too. The green buffalo slows down some more, then comes to a stop. Blood's runnin' down his side in little red streams. His flanks heave like he can't get enough air. His head hangs down the way they do when they're hurt too bad to go on much farther. When he opens his mouth to pant, he drools pink. There's pink froth around his nostrils, too, so he must've been bleedin' in the lungs.

When they stop like that, the kill's easy. You gauge by the hump where to put the next shot right through the heart. But the green buffalo, even his hump isn't right, and he's got a bony frill, I guess you'd call it, that runs up from his neck over the fore part of his back. Growin' something that unnatural must've been a torment to him, so I'd say he's lucky we come along to put him out of his misery.

I ride up close to do what needs doin'. I guess the best I can where his heart is, take dead aim, and squeeze the trigger. I have guessed better, indeed I have. When the bullet hits him, the green buffalo lifts up that big old head of his and out comes a noise like a locomotive with a busted boiler. Then he wheels round and runs right at me.

He's bigger and meaner'n any longhorn you ever seen. I shoot at him again, but you got to be lucky with a head shot on a buffalo, hit him in the eye or somethin' like that. Otherwise the slug 'll just bounce off his skull. That's just what happens here, too. I rowel my horse for all I'm worth. He springs forward like you wouldn't believe, and the buffalo can't quite shift fast enough to spike me with his horn.

He lets out that squealin' bellow again, tries to change the way he's goin' so he can make another run at me. All the while, though, Jake and Clancy keep on pumpin' bullets into him. He takes so many, I reckon when we butcher him he'll be as full of lead as a shotgunned mallard.

I turn around to shoot some more too, but this time I see it really isn't needful. That last charge of his took all the strength he has left in him. He wobbles like a drunk goin' out of the Rebel Yell, then kind of folds up on himself and falls over. He heaves out another breath or two, then he's finally done.

"Thought he was gonna use you for a pincushion there, Joe," Clancy says.

"You're not the only one," I tell him. "I thought he was through. When he came at me, I like to've pissed myself."

"Don't blame you a bit."

Jake says, "Let's cut him up." Jake, he takes care of what needs doin' first and worries about everything else afterwards.

I climb down from my horse, tether him to a clump of sagebrush that sticks up higher above the ground than anything else thereabouts. Then I pull out a knife and walk up to the green buffalo. I'm ready to run like hell, I tell you. After that last scare, I figure he might just be shammin'.

But he's not, not this time. The one eye I can see doesn't blink. It just stares up at the sky. Flies have already started walking along the tracks of blood on his flank. One ambles down into a bullet hole, comes back out a second later and starts wipin' its little thread of a neck with its legs the way they do.

I take out my knife, give the green buffalo a poke. The mange or whatever it is has the hide all rough and scaly, but it's not any thicker than the usual run of buffalo hide. You have to put some arm into what you're doin', but you can cut yourself a good slice.

Once they see I'm not trampled, Jake and Clancy give me a hand with the butchering. We hack off steaks and chops and roasts till we've got as much as we can carry with our pack horse and tied behind us. It's not as easy as it ought to be. Instead of havin' the ribs stop at what'd be the bottom of a man's chest, they keep right on going, down to the critter's hipbones — that green buffalo isn't normal any which way. We're bloody to the elbows and dead beat by afternoon, but we get the job finished.

By the time we're done, the buzzards are already circlin' overhead, waitin' for their share. Soon as we take off, I figure they'll argue it out with the coyotes. Before too long, even the bones'll be gone. That's the way the world is. If it wasn't like that, we'd all be ass-deep in bones, and then what would ornery professors like Hatcher's Marsh and Cope do for fun?

We ride on back the way we came. Followin' our own tracks is the easiest way to get on back to Hatcher's camp. It's gettin' close to sundown when Clancy says, "Ain't this about the place where we all got dizzy?"

I look around. He's right. But there's no ferns there now, no funny plants that look like squashed feather dusters. Just prairie, lots of it. Clancy points. "Look, there's our tracks, right?"

I nod. Sure enough, those are our outbound tracks. Jake spits. Clancy rides on a few more feet. I walk my horse up after him. He keeps pointin' down to the ground. All at once he says, "There!"

I see what he's pointin' at, too. Right at the spot where he said "There!" our tracks just up and disappear. It's not like the wind blew dust over 'em. It's like they never, ever happened. "That's queer, all right," I say. Jake nods.

Clancy looks west, points again, this time toward the horizon. "We came from that way, right?" he says. He knows he's right, and doesn't wait for an answer. He walks his horse real slow and easy westward, lookin'

down every foot of the way. After a quarter mile or so, maybe a tad more, he rides a little ways south, then a little ways north, like a dog castin' about for a scent. Finally he says, "Ha!"

I'm right with him. He's picked up our outbound tracks again. He rides back east just a few feet and goes "Ha!" one more time, and then, "Goddam!" I say "Goddam!" myself, on account of he's found the other side of where our tracks disappear. It's like we didn't ride over the stretch between, the stretch with the ferns and all the other stuff that had no call bein' in the Wyoming praire.

"Hell with it," Jake says. "Let's cook some of this here buffalo meat. We don't stop and cook it pretty soon, I'll eat it raw." Comin' out of Jake, that's a speech.

So we stop, we get a fire goin', and we carve off chunks of meat and toast 'em on sticks over the flames. Before long, my mouth gets to waterin' so hard I can't wait any more. I blow and I blow and I blow on my chunk, then I sink my teeth in.

I've had buffalo a good many times. It's not that far from beef, a little leaner, a little tougher, a little gamier. This green buffalo — not that his meat was green, you understand, or the buzzards and coyotes would've been welcome to it — he doesn't taste like any buffalo I ever ate before. But he's a long way from bad.

Clancy says what I'm thinkin': "Reminds me more of dark-meat chicken than any proper buffalo." Jake doesn't say anything. He just ups and cuts himself off another piece.

We ride out again next mornin', and have as peaceful a trip as you please back to Hatcher's camp. We get there late afternoon, and everyone's right glad to see us, and to see the meat we've fetched. Hatcher's boys, they cook some of it and start smokin' the rest so as it'll keep.

I wait for Clancy or Jake to come out with the story of the green buffalo, and I guess they wait for me too, but nobody ends up tellin' it. I like a tall tale as well as the next fellow, but usually a tall tale, you know the one who's tellin' it is yarnin'. Speakin' not a word but the truth and having it taken for a tall tale, that'll just ruin your day.

Tall tale or no, though, the meat's still good. Me and Clancy and Jake, we sit down around a fire and fill ourselves up again. I'm at the teeth-pickin' stage when Hatcher comes over. He's chewin' on a roasted buffalo rib. While he pays us off, some of his boys start laughin' over by his wagon.

"What's funny?" I ask him.

"I picked up my mail in Lusk, along with supplies," Hatcher answers. "O.C. Marsh sent me a copy of *Punch* with a cartoon of himself in it."

"*Punch*? What's *Punch*?"

"It's a British comic magazine. It has a picture of Marsh as a circus ringmaster. He's standing on a *Triceratops* skull—doubtless one of the ones we've excavated hereabouts—and putting a whole troupe of dinosaur skeletons through their paces, as if they were so many trained bears or lions or elephants. Would you like to have a look?" He uses the rib bone to point back where the magazine is.

I think it over, then shake my head. "I thank you kindly, Mr. Hatcher, but I'll take a miss on that. You're the one knows about these here dinosaur things, not me."

"However you like, Joe. I thank you for the tasty meat you brought back." By now, he's gnawed everything off of that bone, so he tosses it on the ground. Then he reaches into his waistcoat pocket, comes out with a deck of cards. "Care for a little game to make the time go by?"

"I'll pass on that, too, Mr. Hatcher," I tell him. He's just tryin' to skin me out of the wages he paid so next time he needs me, he can give me the same money again. I'm wise to that one, I am. So are Clancy and Jake, when he tries it on them. We may not know these dinosaurs, but we're nobody's fools.

KEY TO THE APPENDIX

The following eight pages show where the major families of dinosaurs lived during the various ages of the Mesozoic era, plus the radiations of the dinosaurs from earliest forms through latest.

"Land and Animal Distribution In The Mesozoic Era" is shown for the Triassic, Early and Middle Jurassic, and the Cretaceous. Each map shows the positions of the land masses at that time. Color keys identify the continents. The major dinosaur families for each period are listed and silhouetted below each map, along with the land masses in which their fossilized remains have been discovered. As the dinosaurs evolved through the Mesozoic, more families appeared, as indicated by the maps.

The next four pages show "The Dinosaur Radiations" through time, and how each family relates to its evolutionary predecessors and descendents. The radiations are given for each of the two main dinosaur lines: saurischia and ornithischia.

The first chart shows the entire Mesozoic, beginning with the early archosaurs, 245 million years ago. (Turn the book for an easier reading of this chart.) The second, third and fourth charts show the dinosaur radiations for the Triassic, Jurassic and Cretaceous, respectively.

Radiation lines for each dinosaur family have lighter and darker tones, in many instances. Darker tones represent familial connections for which there is great evidence. Lighter tones represent best estimates of familial relationships, based on limited fossil records.

Appendix

LAND AND ANIMAL DISTRIBUTION
IN THE MESOZOIC ERA

TRIASSIC

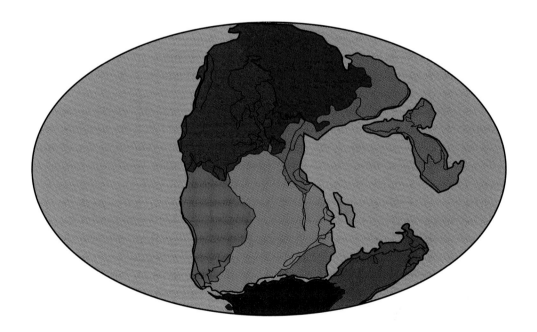

SMALL THEROPODS

NORTH AMERICA
SOUTH AMERICA
AUSTRALIA
AFRICA
EUROPE
ASIA

PROSAUROPODS

SOUTH AMERICA
AUSTRALIA
EUROPE
ANTARCTICA

EARLY ARCHOSAURS

ASIA
NORTH AMERICA
SOUTH AMERICA
EUROPE

HETERODONTOSAURS

AFRICA
ASIA

EARLY/MIDDLE JURASSIC

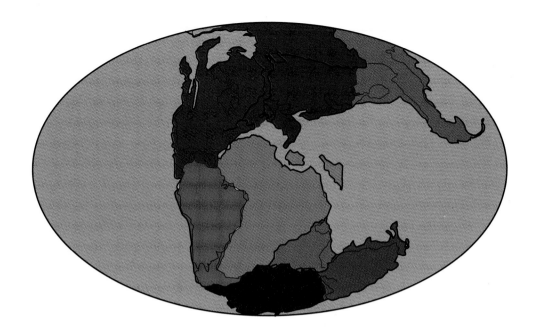

ALLOSAURIDS

SOUTH AMERICA
ASIA
EUROPE

SMALL THEROPODS

NORTH AMERICA
SOUTH AMERICA
AFRICA
EUROPE
ASIA

SAUROPODS

SOUTH AMERICA
AUSTRALIA
AFRICA
EUROPE
ASIA

PROSAUROPODS

NORTH AMERICA
SOUTH AMERICA
AFRICA
ASIA

LESOTHOSAURS

AFRICA

HYPSILOPHODONTS

ASIA

ANKYLOSAURS

EUROPE

STEGOSAURS

EUROPE
ASIA

LATE JURASSIC

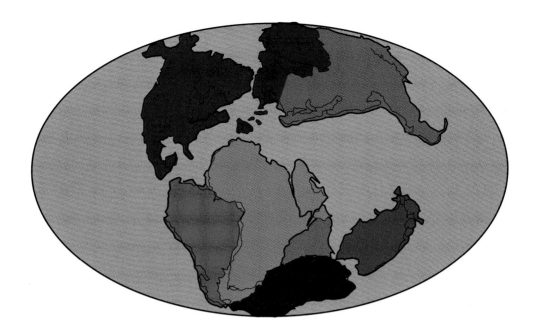

IGUANODONTS

NORTH AMERICA
EUROPE

ALLOSAURIDS

NORTH AMERICA
AFRICA
EUROPE
ASIA

SAUROPODS

NORTH AMERICA
SOUTH AMERICA
AFRICA
EUROPE
ASIA

HYPSILOPHODONTS

NORTH AMERICA
AFRICA

CERATOSAURIDS

NORTH AMERICA
AFRICA

STEGOSAURS

NORTH AMERICA
EUROPE
ASIA
AFRICA

SMALL THEROPODS

NORTH AMERICA
AFRICA
EUROPE
ASIA

ORNITHOMIMIDS

AFRICA
NORTH AMERICA

ARCHAEOPTERYGS

EUROPE

CRETACEOUS

ANKYLOSAURS

NORTH AMERICA
EUROPE
ASIA
AUSTRALIA
ANTARCTICA

STEGOSAURS

EUROPE
ASIA
AFRICA

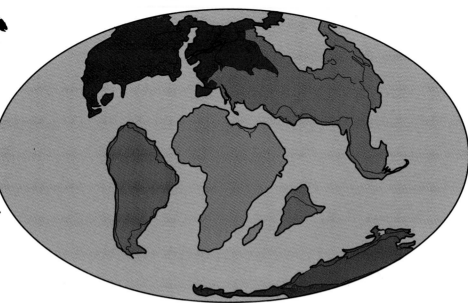

PROTOCERATOPSIDS

NORTH AMERICA
ASIA

ORNITHOMIMIDS

ASIA
NORTH AMERICA

PACHYCEPHALOSAURS

NORTH AMERICA
AFRICA
EUROPE
ASIA

HADROSAURS

NORTH AMERICA
SOUTH AMERICA
EUROPE
ASIA

TYRANNOSAURIDS

NORTH AMERICA
ASIA

DROMAEOSAURIDS

NORTH AMERICA
ASIA

SAUROPODS

NORTH AMERICA
SOUTH AMERICA
AUSTRALIA
AFRICA
EUROPE
ASIA

IGUANODONTS

NORTH AMERICA
AUSTRALIA
AFRICA
EUROPE
ASIA

HYPSILOPHODONTS

NORTH AMERICA
AUSTRALIA
AFRICA
EUROPE

ALLOSAURIDS

NORTH AMERICA
AUSTRALIA
ASIA

SEGNOSAURIDS

ASIA

PSITTACOSAURIDS

ASIA

CERATOPSIDS

NORTH AMERICA
ASIA

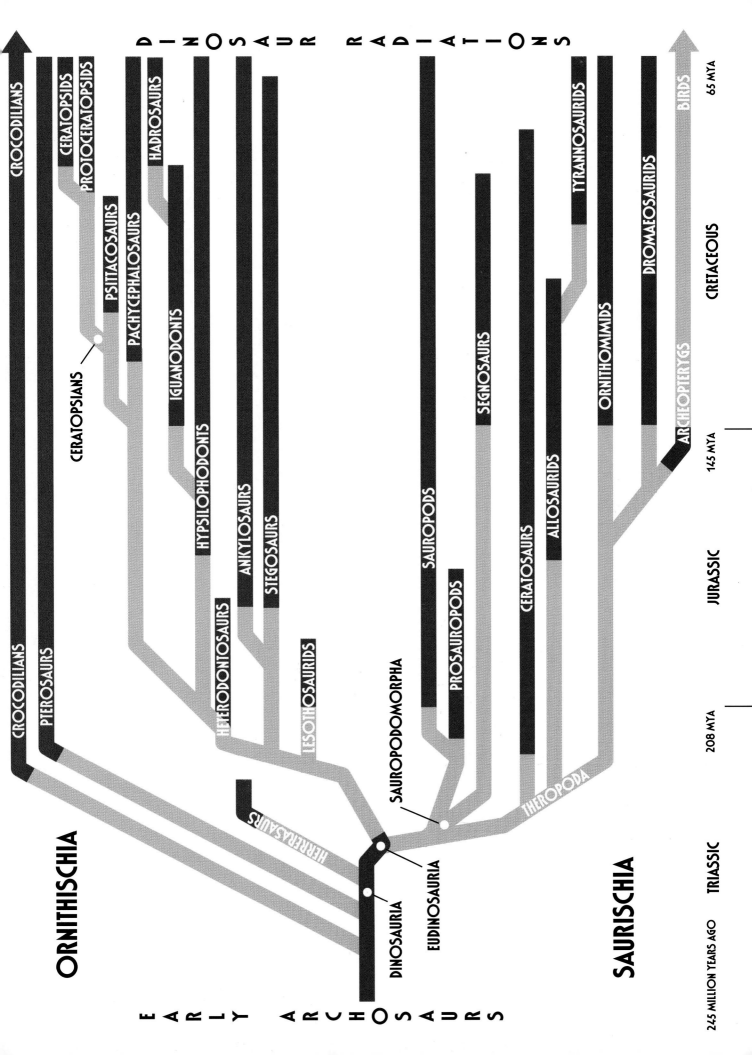

DINOSAUR RADIATIONS

ORNITHISCHIA

SAURISCHIA

CROCODILIANS
PTEROSAURS
CERATOPSIDS
PROTOCERATOPSIDS
PSITTACOSAURS
PACHYCEPHALOSAURS
HADROSAURS
IGUANODONTS
HYPSILOPHODONTS
ANKYLOSAURS
STEGOSAURS
HETERODONTOSAURS
LESOTHOSAURIDS
HERRERASAURS
PROSAUROPODS
SAUROPODS
CERATOSAURS
SEGNOSAURS
ALLOSAURIDS
ORNITHOMIMIDS
TYRANNOSAURIDS
DROMAEOSAURIDS
ARCHEOPTERYGS
BIRDS

CERATOPSIANS

SAUROPODOMORPHA

THEROPODA

DINOSAURIA

EUDINOSAURIA

EARLY ARCHOSAURS

245 MILLION YEARS AGO   TRIASSIC   208 MYA   JURASSIC   145 MYA   CRETACEOUS   65 MYA

TRIASSIC

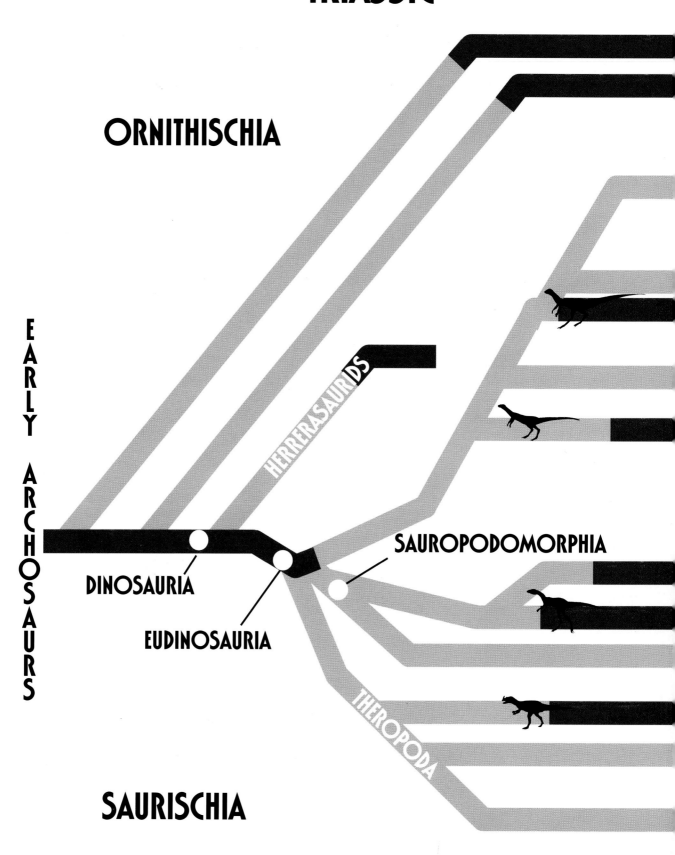

ORNITHISCHIA

EARLY ARCHOSAURS

HERRERASAURIDS

SAUROPODOMORPHIA

DINOSAURIA

EUDINOSAURIA

THEROPODA

SAURISCHIA

245 MILLION YEARS AGO

JURASSIC

CROCODILIANS

PTEROSAURS

PACHYCEPHALOSAURS

IGUANODONTS

HYPSILOPHODONTS

TERODONTOSAURS

ANKYLOSAURS

STEGOSAURS

OTHOSAURIDS

SAUROPODS

ROSAUROPODS

SEGNOSAURS

CERATOSAURS

ALLOSAURIDS

ORNITHOMIMIDS

DROMAEOSAURIDS

ARCHEOPTERYES

YA

145 MYA

CRETACEOUS

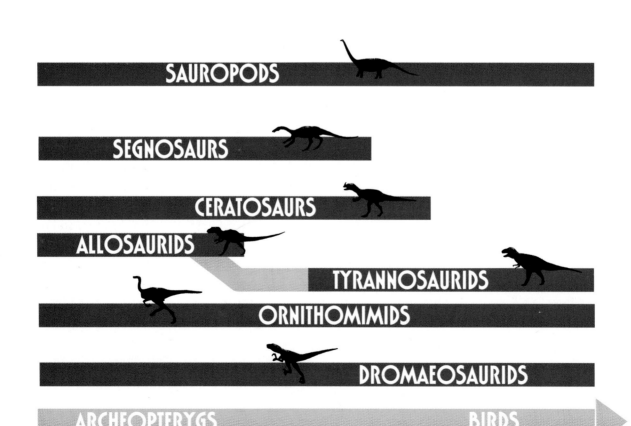

CROCODILLIANS

PTEROSAURS

CERATOPSIANS — CERATOPSIDS

PROTOCERATOPSIDS

PSITTACOSAURS

PACHYCEPHALOSAURS

HADROSAURS

IGUANODONTS

ANKYLOSAURS

STEGOSAURS

SAUROPODS

SEGNOSAURS

CERATOSAURS

ALLOSAURIDS

TYRANNOSAURIDS

ORNITHOMIMIDS

DROMAEOSAURIDS

ARCHEOPTERYGS   BIRDS

145 MYA   65 MYA

CONTRIBUTORS

BYRON PREISS, co-editor of the THE ULTIMATE DINOSAUR, is the editor of the books THE PLANETS, THE UNIVERSE, THE MICROVERSE, and THE DINOSAURS: A NEW LOOK AT A LOST ERA, which was featured in *Life* magazine. He has collaborated with Arthur C. Clarke, Isaac Asimov and Ray Bradbury, and edited the Grammy Award-winning THE WORDS OF GANDHI. His monograph on THE ART OF LEO & DIANE DILLON was a Hugo Award nominee. He holds a B.A. from the University of Pennsylvania and an M.A. from Stanford University. He currently resides in New York.

ROBERT SILVERBERG has been a professional writer since 1953. His work has appeared in *Omni, American Heritage, Horizon,* and many other publications. Among his best known science fiction books are THE MAJIPOOR CHRONICLES, DYING INSIDE, TOWER OF GLASS, and NIGHTWINGS. His non-fiction titles include MOUND BUILDERS OF ANCIENT AMERICA, THE REALM OF PRESTER JOHN, and SCIENTISTS AND SCOUNDRELS: A BOOK OF SCIENTIFIC HOAXES. He is a multi-time winner of the Nebula and Hugo Awards for his science fiction.

Since 1974, science consultant PETER DODSON has taught anatomy in the School of Veterinary Medicine at the University of Pennsylvania in Philadelphia, where he is also adjunct professor of geology. He is a research associate at the Academy of Natural Sciences in Philadelphia. He has extensive field experience in the dinosaur beds of western Canada and the United States, and was a National Academy of Science exchange visitor to Poland in 1988.

In 1986 he described a new genus and species of horned dinosaur *Avaceratops lammersi,* from Montana. He has studied at the Canadian Museum of Nature in Ottawa, the University of Paris VI, and the Paleobiology Institute of the Polish Academy of Science in Warsaw. Dr. Dodson has more than fifty publications to his credit, is co-author of the text EVOLUTION: PROCESS AND PRODUCT (Wadsworth 1985) and is co-editor of THE DINOSAURIA (University of California Press, 1990), a comprehensive scientific treatise on dinosaur systematics and paleobiology.

HOWARD ZIMMERMAN, associate editor, entered the publishing field in 1976 as the editor of *Starlog* magazine, which covers the fields of science fiction and fantasy. He helped create and edited *Future* magazine, an *Omni*-esque publication that preceded *Omni.* He has also written and edited books on cinematic robots, spaceships, and aliens. He joined forces with Byron Preiss in 1987 and has since edited science fact and science fiction books for adults and for young readers.

WILLIAM ALSCHULER, associate editor, is the founder and principal of *Future Museums,* a museum-consulting firm providing program concept through final design for museums and exhibits with a science or technology content. He has a Ph.D. in astronomy from the University of California at Santa Cruz, and extensive university teaching experience in the sciences and energy conservation. He is currently a member of the physics faculty at FIT/SUNY. His books for Byron Preiss Visual Publications include THE MICROVERSE, FIRST CONTACT, and UFOs AND ALIENS.

ALEX JAY is a designer and lettering artist. His design of the BANANA REPUBLIC GUIDE TO TRAVEL AND SAFARI CLOTHING book was exhibited in the 1986 AIGA Book Show, the Type Directors Club 33rd annual competition (TDC 33), and GRAPHIS DESIGN ANNUAL 87/88. TDC 28 displayed his title lettering for the book THE ART OF LEO & DIANE DILLON. He art directed and designed TALES OF THE DARK KNIGHT:BATMAN'S FIRST FIFTY YEARS, and THE MICRO-VERSE, which were published in September 1989.

POUL ANDERSON is a widely published author with over one hundred books and short pieces in print. Besides science fiction and fantasy, his subjects include mystery, historical, juvenile contemporary fiction and non-fiction, and verse. He has received seven Hugo and three Nebula Awards, the Gandalf Award, and investiture in the Baker Street Irregulars.

J. DAVID ARCHIBALD, was born and raised in the Midwest. He received his undergraduate degree with honors in geology from Kent State University in 1972. He completed his Ph.D. in paleontology at the University of California, Berkeley in 1977. For two years he was a J. Willard Gibbs Instructor in Yale University and then an assistant and associate professor in the Department of Biology at Yale for four years.

At Yale, he was also Curator of Mammals at the Peabody Museum of Natural History. In 1983 he became a professor of biology at San Diego State University. He has done extensive paleontological fieldwork in the American west and overseas. His numerous articles, essays and reviews include research on the systematics, anatomy, and evolution of early mammals and other vertebrates, studies of the Cretaceous and Paleogene vertebrate faunas, and analyses of patterns of origination and extinction.

After attending the Art Students League and Cooper Union in New York, WAYNE BARLOWE apprenticed in the Exhibition Department of the American Museum of Natural History. In 1979, his first book, BARLOWE'S GUIDE TO EXTRATERRESTRIALS, was published by Workman Publishing. The book received nominations for The American Book Award and the Hugo, and was chosen Best Book for Young People by the American Library Association.

Barlowe's second book EXPEDITION, consisting of forty paintings and one hundred black and white illustrations, was published in late 1990. Barlowe's artwork has appeared on over two hundred paperback and magazine covers. His paintings have been exhibited at The Bronx Museum of the Arts, the New Britain Museum, and the Hayden Planetarium.

DR. GREGORY BENFORD is professor of physics at University of California, Irvine. He conducts research in plasma turbulence theory and astrophysics, and has advised the Department of Energy NASA, and the White House Council on Space Policy over the last decade. He is a Woodrow Wilson Fellow and a visiting fellow at Cambridge University.

Dr. Benford was host and scriptwriter for the television series *Galactic Odyssey*, describing modern physics and astronomy, with the perspective of the evolution of the galaxy. His articles have appeared in *Smithsonian*, *Natural History*, *New Scientist* and *Omni*. He is also the author of over a dozen novels, among them *Timescape* (a Nebula Award winner) and his most recent, BEYOND THE FALL OF NIGHT, written with Arthur C. Clarke. He has won the Nebula Award twice, the John W. Campbell Award, the Australian Ditmar Award and the United Nations Medal in Literature in 1989.

MICHAEL BISHOP is currently an editor of the NEBULA AWARD ANTHOLOGY, VOLUMES 23-25. His book NO ENEMY BUT TIME won the Nebula Award in 1982. He has two books forthcoming, COUNT GEIGER'S BLUES and BRITTLE INNINGS.

RAY BRADBURY has published four hundred short stories and eighteen books, including novels, short stories, poems, and plays. He created the basic scenario for the United States Pavilion at the New York World's Fair in 1964/65, and did similar creative work at Walt Disney's EPCOT in Florida, where he was writer-consultant for Spaceship Earth. His *Windows on the Universe,* a multi-media history of astronomy, is now appearing at the Air and Space Museum in Los Angeles. His latest book is DEATH IS A LONELY BUSINESS, his first suspense mystery novel.

KENNETH CARPENTER received his undergraduate degree in geology from the University of Colorado. He is now chief preparator at the Denver Museum of Natural History, and has overseen the mounting of over fifty fossil skeletons. Most of his research has been on dinosaurs and marine reptiles. He has spent fifteen years collecting marine reptiles and pterosaurs in Wyoming and South Dakota.

DR. SANKAR CHATTERJEE is professor of geosciences at Texas Tech University, Lubbock, and is curator of paleontology and director of Antarctic research of that institution's museum.

He studied vertebrate paleontology under Dr. Pamela L. Robinson at London University and graduated from Calcutta University in 1970. He held a postdoctoral fellowship at the Smithsonian Institution for one year. He taught geology and paleontology at the Indian Statistical Institute, University of California, Berkeley, and George Washington University before he moved to Texas Tech.

Dr. Chatterjee has led several expeditions to Antarctica, China, India, and Texas, following the trail of dinosaurs. His research was funded by the National Science Foundation and National Geographic Society. He has been actively involved in many of the new fossil finds in recent years including an array of thecodonts, lizards, dinosaurs, plesiosaurs, mosasaurs, pterosaurs and what may be the world's oldest bird, Protoavis. Dr. Chatterjee's major research interests are the anatomy and relationships of Mesozoic reptiles and birds, plate tectonics, and K/T extinction event. He is the author of fifty technical papers and a book. In 1982, he received the Antarctic Service Medal from the Department of State.

PHILIP J. CURRIE is head of dinosaur research at the Royal Tyrell Museum of Palaeontology and adjunct associate professor at the University of Calgary.

As the manager of the Dinosaur Research Programme at the Royal Tyrell Museum of Palaentology, Drumheller, he has published more than thirty scientific and twenty-five popular publications, focusing on the growth and variation of extinct reptiles, the anatomy and relationships of carnivorous dinosaurs, and the origin of birds. Fieldwork connected with his research has been concentrated in Alberta, British Columbia, the Arctic and China. He received the Sir Fredrick Haultain Award for significant contributions to science in Alberta, 1988. He has given numerous popular and scientific lectures on dinosaurs all over the world.

A trained engineer who brings a serious scholar's attention to his fiction, L. SPRAGUE DE CAMP has been entertaining readers since 1938. In addition to numerous works of heroic fantasy and science fiction, he has written many non-fiction books including important biographies of H.P. Lovecraft and Robert E. Howard. Among his most noted science fiction and fantasy works are such classics as LEST DARKNESS FALL, THE INCOMPLETE ENCHANTER (with Fletcher Pratt), and THE WHEELS OF IF. He has had a lifelong interest in dinosaurs.

BOB EGGLETON is an award-winning astronomical artist and Hugo-nominated science fiction illustrator who has recently turned his interests to comics and graphic novels. He is currently illustrating an adaptation of *Aliens 3* for Dark Horse Comics. His humanistic goal is to convey through astronomical art that planets like Earth are rare and need to be treated with care.

ANTHONY R. FIORILLO is on staff at the Carnegie Museum of Natural History in Pittsburgh, Pennsylvania. He received his bachelor's degree in geology from the University of Connecticut, his master's degree in geology from the University of Nebraska, and his Ph.D. in vetebrate paleontology from the University of Pennsylvania. Although his research interests have varied from issues concerning early terrestrial vertebrates of the Paleozoic to issues focused on modern vertebrates, he has spent most of his time concentrating on the evolution of terrestrial ecosystems during the age of the dinosaurs. These studies have led him to examine the origin of fossil deposits, the possible paleoecological interactions between different dinosaurs and between various herbivorous dinosaurs and plants, and the biogeographic patterns of dinosaur distributions in western North America. As a result of these research interests he has spent numerous field seasons in western North America, particularly in Montana and Utah, collecting dinosaur fossils.

DR. CATHERINE FORSTER's interests focus on the evolutionary biology of dinosaurs. In particular, she has examined the pattern of descent of the *ceratopsids*, or horned dinosaurs, as well as the early evolution of ornithopods and the origins of the duck-billed lineage. She has also studied allometry and shape change in the skulls of horned dinosaurs using modern morphometric techniques. Her field research has resulted in discoveries of ceratopsians in the Late Cretaceous of western North America and to new finds of the earliest dinosaurs in the Late Triassic of Argentina. Her current research is centered on the evolution of horned and duck-billed dinosaurs in the Late Cretaceous.

WILLIAM B. GALLAGHER was born in Philadelphia, and started collecting fossils when he was eight years old. He obtained his first job in paleontology when he was seventeen, working for the Academy of Natural Sciences. Gallagher did his undergraduate studies at Rutgers University, and received his doctorate in geology from the University of Pennsylvania.

His current research interests include the paleoecology of mass extinction events. He has traveled extensively in the American west, Europe and the Middle East while doing field work. He is presently employed as a paleontologist with the New Jersey State Museum.

Since graduating from the School of Visual Arts in 1987, JOHN PAUL GENZO has pursued a career in freelance illustration, working for a variety of publications. He has illustrated a number of covers for Penguin Books, including AND LEAVE HER DYING, THE MAN WHO MURDERED GOD, and the SNIPER'S MOON. He has also worked on cover art for *The New Republic, National Review* and *Chemical Week Magazine*.

DAVID D. GILLETTE received his Ph.D. in geology from Southern Methodist University in 1974, and worked in their geological sciences department from 1981 to 1983. He held the position of Curator of the New Mexico Museum of Natural History from 1983 to 1988.

Currently, Gillette is the State Paleontologist of Utah, as well as the chief scientist for the Southwest Paneontological Foundation, Inc., and consultant to Los Alamos National Laboratory. His research interests include dinosaur anatomy, taxonomy, and geographic distribution, especially of sauropods. His interests also include the geochemistry of bone preservation, remote sensing of fossils, dinosaur tracks and traces, and the history of paleontology.

JOHN GURCHE, whose art is part of many museum exhibits, works at the Smithsonian Institution in Washington, DC. He is world renowned for his photo-realistic illustration of dinosaurs in their natural habitats.

MARK HALLETT is a painter of prehistoric animals and their environments. His art has been published in many books including DINOSAURS, RIDDLE OF THE DINOSAUR and DINOSAURS, PAST AND PRESENT. He has also contributed to various periodicals such as *Life*, *Smithsonian*, and *Natural History*. His work has been incorporated into internationally televised programs including *Smithsonian World*, *Nova* and a series on prehistoric life by David Attenborough. He is currently investigating the neck biomechanics of the giant sauropod dinosaurs, such as Diplodocus, in order to understand their behavior. His paintings can be seen in the traveling exhibit, Dinosaurs, Past and Present. It has toured to all the major North American natural history museums for the past four years and has been extended to Europe for the fall of 1991.

HARRY HARRISON has been an artist, art director, and editor. As a writer, he had a career as the author of numerous true confessions and men's adventures before leaving New York for Mexico in order to write his first novel. He has since written thirty-two novels, and has lived in nearly as many countries. His books have been translated into twenty-two languages. He was founding president of World SF. He received the Nebula Award and the Prix Jules Verne for his novel MAKE ROOM! MAKE ROOM! which was made into the film SOYLENT GREEN.

DOUG HENDERSON is a self-taught artist who learned how to draw by sketching landscapes when hiking. His main interest lies in illustrating earth history, and he has worked with a number of paleontologists. He illustrated MAIA—A DINOSAUR GROWS UP, DAWN OF THE DINOSAUR and LIVING WITH DINOSAURS. His work has also appeared in several national touring exhibits of prehistoric life.

PHILIP HOOD has been a freelance book and magazine illustrator as well as designer and contributor to the humor magazine *Punch* since 1974. Included in his book illustrations is the trilogy by Dougal Dixon, AFTER MAN, THE NEW DINOSAUR and MAN AFTER MAN. He trained in graphic design at the London College of Printing, and currently lives in North London with his wife and children.

KEVIN JOHNSON is a native of Washington State. He started painting science fiction book covers in 1978, and has done well over a hundred of them. He is the co-inventor of "The Supernaturals" toy line for Tonka Toys.

Author and journalist DON LESSEM is a former Knight Science Journalism Fellow at M.I.T. and a frequent contributor to *The Boston Globe* and *Smithsonian Magazine*. As the most widely published journalist on dinosaurs, Lessem has written on new discoveries` in dinosaur science for *Life, Discover, Omni, Rotunda* and *Smithsonian*. He is the host and narrator of *T. Rex Exposed*, a *Nova* documentary aired in 1990, and an originator, writer and scientific advisor for two other 1990 dinosaur documentaries on PBS.

Lessem has spent the last two years researching dinosaur fieldwork from Mongolia to Arctic Alaska for his forthcoming book, AT THE DINOSAUR FRONTIER.

A powerful writer who has successfully combined the literature of the mainstream with the conventions of science fiction, BARRY N. MALZBERG is the author of some seventy-five novels and collections including such landmark works as BEYOND APOLLO, HEROVIT'S WORLD, GATHER IN THE HALL OF PLANETS, GUERNICA NIGHT, THE MAN WHO LOVED THE MIDNIGHT LADY, THE CROSS OF FIRE, and THE REMAKING OF SIGMUND FREUD. Such noted critics as Joyce Carol Oates have praised his work, and he is no mean critic himself, producing in THE ENGINES OF THE NIGHT one of the most insightful volumes on the meaning and importance of science fiction.

After attending Otis/Parsons in Los Angeles, MICHAEL MEAKER worked at DIC animation for one season of the television show *Alf*. He is currently working as the staff illustrator at the Museum of Natural History of Los Angeles and also illustrates several traveling exhibits around the nation. He has developed and directed many museum products such as posters, books, and cards, as well as worked on various museum publications and scientific journals.

DR. RALPH E. MOLNAR is currently a senior curator with the Queensland Museum in Brisbane, Queensland, Australia, where he pursues a vigorous research program in the biogeography of southern hemisphere dinosaurs. He has published more than fifty scientific papers in *Nature, Geobios* and the *Journal of Paleontology*, as well as other journals worldwide. In addition, he writes a popular column on current developments in evolutionary theory for *Australian Natural History* magazine.

As a scientific illustrator, lecturer and writer, BILL PARSONS has had much practical experience in the field of dinosaurs and other related areas. From 1985–1990, he illustrated the paleontological specimens displayed in the DINOSAURS & CO. exhibit at the Buffalo Museum of Science. He has participated in dinosaur digs all over the nation, and has conducted on-site research for illustration of Paleo-Indian habitations, geological formations and fossils remains.

PAUL PREUSS began his successful writing career after years of producing documentary and television films. Since 1980 he has published five novels in addition to those in the VENUS PRIME series, most recently STARFIRE. His articles and reviews have appeared in the *Washington Post, New York Newsday*, the *San Jose Mercury News*, and other newspapers, and he has written numerous science articles for national publications. He frequently works as a science consultant for film companies in the San Francisco Bay area, where he lives when he is not walking in the mountains of Crete.

RONALD RAINGER is assistant professor of history at Texas Tech University. He has published a number of articles on the history of biology and paleontology and has co-edited THE AMERICAN DEVELOPMENT OF BIOLOGY (Philadelphia: University of Pennsylvania Press, 1988) and THE EXPANSION of AMERICAN BIOLOGY (New Brunswick, N.J.: Rutgers University Press 1991). His book, AN AGENDA FOR ANTIQUITY: HENRY FAIRFIELD

OSBORN AND VERTEBRATE PALEONTOLOGY AT THE AMERICAN MUSEUM OF NATURAL HISTORY, 1890 – 1935 is forthcoming from the University of Alabama Press.

MICHAEL ROTHMAN is a freelance natural science illustrator based in Ridgefield, Connecticut. He has painted exhibition murals for the Atlanta, Detroit, and Philadelphia Zoos. Two of his paintings on the subject of the French Guianan rainforest ecology are in the collections of the Massachusetts Horticultural Society and the Fund for Neotropical Plant Research at the New York Botanical Gardens. He also illustrates for *The New York Times* science section, and has illustrated four children's books: WHITE BEAR, ICE BEAR, CATCHING THE WIND, LIZARD IN THE SUN, and WINTER WHALE, to be published in August. He has just completed his first book, MOON ON THE ALLIGATORS, published by HarperCollins.

As an illustrator, BILL SANDERSON has worked with a variety of publications, ranging from *Esquire* and *Discover,* to *New Scientist* magazine, for which he is a regular contributor. In the last few years, he has illustrated Harry Harrison's trilogy, WEST OF EDEN an alternative-earth saga depicting an intelligent dinosaur race competing with stone-age humans.

DR. CHARLES SHEFFIELD is a vice president of The Earth Satellite Corporation, president of the Science Fiction Writers of America, and past president of the American Astronautical Society. He holds bachelor's and master's degrees in mathematics and a Ph.D. in theoretical physics. His written works include five novels, four short story collections, the best-selling nonfiction volumes EARTHWATCH and MAN ON EARTH, and the reference work *Space Careers.*

JOHN SIBBICK has been a professional illustrator for eighteen years. His dinosaur reconstructions have appeared in publications such as THE ILLUSTRATED ENCYCLOPEDIA OF DINOSAURS with Dr. David Norman. He has also illustrated the companion volume, THE ILLUSTRATED ENCYCLOPEDIA OF PTEROSAURS, published in the summer of 1991. His work has appeared on the BBC television series *Lost Worlds, Vanished Lives* and will soon be featured in *Dinosaurs* for Granada Television. Some of his paintings can be seen in a traveling exhibition, Dinosaurs Past and Present and in another exhibition, Dinosaurs – A Global View.

EVAN TENBROECK STEADMAN received his BFA from the University of Denver in 1975 and attended Parson's School of Design in 1976. As a freelance illustrator, his clients include such companies as Coca Cola, Subaru, Nissan, TWA, and General Foods. He has also illustrated books for many publishers, including Doubleday, Zebra, Macmillan and Scholastic.

WILLIAM STOUT earned his degree at the California Institute of the Arts. In 1977 he had his first one-man show, "The Prehistoric World of William Stout." In 1981, Stout received acclaim for his book THE DINOSAURS — A FANTASTIC VIEW OF A LOST ERA, a major contribution to the renewed interest in dinosaurs. Stout's children's book collaboration with Byron Preiss, THE LITTLE BLUE BRONTOSAURUS, resulted in a 1984 Children's Choice Award. Stout's paintings were included in the six-year, international, museum-traveling exhibition "Dinosaurs Past and Present." His travels to Patagonia and Antarctica led to the creation of his one-man show "Dinosaurs, Penguins and Whales — The Wildlife of Antarctica," currently touring the major natural history museums of the world through 1996. Stout was recently chosen by the National Science Foundation to participate in their Antarctic Artists and Writers Program.

HARRY TURTLEDOVE began publishing science fiction in the late 1970s under the name "Eric Iverson." The holder of a doctorate in history, he has enjoyed success in the sword-and-sorcery field with novels like WEREBLOOD and WERENIGHT; in the fantasy genre with the successful "Legion" series of novels; and in science fiction with the highly acclaimed AGENT OF BYZANTIUM. Two recent novels are A WORLD OF DIFFERENCE and KRISPOS RISING.

CONNIE WILLIS first published in 1978, and in 1982 won two Nebula Awards and a Hugo Award. Her work was described by *The New York Times* as "fresh, subtle, and deeply moving." Her story, *Schwarzchild Radius* in THE UNIVERSE was a Nebula nominee, and she won for her novella *The Last of the Winnebagos*. She recently received a Nebula for her short story At the Rialto in THE MICROVERSE, the previous book in this series.

JOHN DAVID WOLVERTON is the author of the acclaimed *On My Way To Paradise*, an expanded short story which won the Writers of the Future Grand Prize and was first published in WRITERS OF THE FUTURE, VOLUME 3 (1986). His latest book, SERPENT CATCH, was published earlier this year.

SELECTED READINGS

BAKKER, Robert T. *The Dinosaur Heresies.* New York: Morrow, 1986.

BENTON, Michael J. *The Reign of the Reptiles.* New York: Crescent Books, 1990.

CZERKAS, Sylvia and OLSON, Everett. *Dinosaurs Past and Present*, vols. 1 and 2. Seattle: University of Washington Press and Natural History Museum of Los Angeles, 1987.

DIXON, Dougal *et al. The Macmillan Illustrated Encyclopedia of Dinosaurs and Prehistoric Animals.* New York: Macmillan, 1988.

GILLETTE, David. "Seismosaurus," the Earth Shaker from New Mexico. Abiquiu, N.M.: Ghost Ranch Journal, vol. 5, no. 1, pp. 26-28, 1990.

LAMBERT, David. *A Field Guide to the Dinosaurs.* New York: Avon/The Diagram Group, 1983.

NORMAN, David. *The Illustrated Encyclopedia of Dinosaurs.* New York: Crescent Books, 1985.

STOUT, William G. *The Dinosaurs.* New York: Mallard Press, 1981.

ART AND PHOTO CREDITS

SECTION TITLE PAGES

Page 1:   A crocodilianlike phytosaur roars across a Triassic rain forest. By Doug Henderson

Page 27:   Among the earliest of meat-eaters, these *Coelophysis* are hunting along a Late Triassic forest floor. By Brian Franczak

Page 49:   Giant sauropods wander down a damp stream bed, making a trackway in Jurassic Colorado. By Doug Henderson

Page 77:   *Stegosaurs* in a Late Jurassic wetlands. By Doug Henderson

Page 101: A giant sauropod flees tornados on a Cretaceous plain of the Old West. By Doug Henderson

Page 121: An *Allosaur* pauses to scan for prey at a Cretaceous stream-bank. By Doug Henderson

Page 143: A courting pair of *Stygimoloch spinfer.* By Brian Franczak

Page 183: *Deinonychus* were swift, clever hunters as depicted in this scene of a hunting party stalking across a Middle Cretaceous swamp. By Doug Henderson

Page 209: The predator *Troodon formosus* pursuing a small mammal. By Brian Franczak

Page 231: A "sea monster" (a *Pleisiosaur*) swimming and feeding alongside of Cretaceous sharks. By William G. Stout

Page 253: The Late Cretaceous hadrosaur, *Parasaurolophus*, walking on a river bank. By Brian Franczak

Page 275: A duckbill dinosaur, *Anatotitan copei*, browsing in a Cretaceous swamp. By Brian Franczak

TEXT CREDITS

Kingdom of the Titans, © 1992 Agberg Ltd.

Dinosaurs for Adults, © 1992 Peter Dodson

The Dawn of the Age of Dinosaurs, © 1992 Sankar Chatterjee

Crocamander Quest, © 1992 L. Sprague de Camp

The First Dinosaurs, © 1992 Catherine Forster

The Feynman Saltation, © 1992 Charles Sheffield

The Dinosaur Radiations, © 1992 Teresa Maryanska

Siren Song at Midnight, © 1992 Dave Wolverton

The Jurassic Period: A Time of Great Change, © 1992 David Gillette

Rhea's Time, © 1992 Paul Preuss

The Age of Giants, © 1992 Anthony Fiorillo

Shakers of the Earth, © 1992 Gregory Benford

Dinosaur Predators, © 1992 Halszka Osmolska

Hunters in the Forest, © 1992 Agberg Ltd.

The Cretaceous Dinosaurs, © 1992 Don Lessem

In the Late Cretaceous, © 1992 Connie Willis

Major League Triceratops, © 1992 Barry N. Malzberg

Migrating Dinosaurs, © 1992 Philip J. Currie

Herding with the Hadrosaurs, © 1992 Michael Bishop

The Behavior of Predatory Dinosaurs, © 1992 Ralph Molnar

Besides a Dinosaur, Whatta Ya Wanna Be When You Grow Up? , © 1983 Ray Bradbury

Monsters of the Sea and Air, © 1992 Kenneth Carpenter

Unnatural Enemy, © 1992 Poul Anderson

Becoming a Modern World, © 1992 William Gallagher

Dawn of the Endless Night, © 1992 Harry Harrison

Myths, Theories, and Facts of Dinosaur Extinction, © 1992 David J. Archibald

The Bone Wars: Cope vs. Marsh, © 1992 Ronald Rainger

The Green Buffalo, © 1992 Harry Turtledove

ABOUT DINOSAUR PRINTS

Some of the dinosaur paintings by William G. Stout are also available as prints. For information on his prints, please send a self-addressed stamped envelope to William Stout, 1468 Loma Vista Street, Pasadena, CA 91104.

The "Art Dino" border designs used on the opening pages of each chapter were designed and executed by William Stout.

The beautiful Wayne D. Barlowe painting that appears on the front cover of *The Ultimate Dinosaur* will be available as a high quality full color print. Entitled *Velociraptor*, it portrays one of the most provocative of all predatory dinosaurs. For information on the print, please send a self-addressed stamped envelope to Byron Preiss Visual Publications, Inc., 24 West 25th Street, New York, New York 10010, Attention: Dinosaur Print.

Hallett '78

You are the bone, she said. You are the bone which talks to us. Take me home and show me the bone.

He turned away from her but his other hand was reaching, clutching for her waist. She felt the icy, encircling touch. In old Montana, he said. They must have had a time.

They always had a time. Time was nothing for them. They cruised through the dirt like boats. Take me out of here, she said. I have heard enough of Montana and the ranches and time. I don't want to look at the dead things anymore. Now, she said, or not at all.

Am I too *de-ca-dent* for you, Maria? Is that what you are telling me?

She looked at the spaces up and down, the crucifixes of bone assembled now in small wedges up and down the spines of the reconstructed tyrannosaur. I don't know, she said. Am I supposed to?

Back then, back here, he said. His grasp tightened and they were moving then toward the door, he leading, she guiding, the two of them reaching but at the exit they stood for a while, first one then the other pointing at the creatures looming before them. When they were gone at last, the fog, cleared slightly by their respiration, closed on the emptiness and obscured what neither had seen: the small, round skull, shiny and neat as an ornament, lying at the reconstructed rear left foot of the tyrannosaur, the eye hollows glinting in the received light.

In the light my bird, the paleontologist cried later. But that had nothing to do with the gallery, he insisted. Nothing to do with it at all. Her hands on his head were fire.

THE ROBLES TRANSCRIPTS

I am going to keep notes on this. Testimony is going to be kept. There will be some records of the disaster, if disaster it will be. Going back to torment *Tyrannosaurus*, shoot *Triceratops*, explore the flora of the Cretaceous and sight the huge, dying beasts. We promised Dix a kill and a kill it is going to be, one saved from paradox by this world. It will change nothing. (Perhaps it will change everything. But we wouldn't know, would we?) Consider the *Triceratops*.

Consider that beast. Weight up to five and a quarter tons, more than four thousand kilos, then. Thirty to thirty-five feet in length full grown, flourished or at least lurked in this latest part of the Cretaceous (Latin derivative, *chalk*). One of the largest and meanest of the horned dinosaurs, not like scuttling *Struthiomimus* or businesslike tyrannosaur but rather this is an animal with its own program. Put it down, give it to Dix tomorrow, the number of the beast. With photographs. Three sharp, pointed horns on that bland, boxy rhinoceros face, the horns measuring more than three feet. The mottled cores encircled by a series of occipital bones. Am I doing this right? Ten species, more or less, slightly varied.

Those bony horn cores survive into our era in the form of rhinoceroses and some of the great horned birds. The Great Montana Dude Ranch. Point the launcher, Dix, and let it fly, *unseat the beast*, make his bones run like water. Perhaps overdramatizing but then again, melodrama is the last connection the servant class can attempt toward a sense of their consequence. I think I just made that up now.

It is cold here, the small arc of light, the pungent blasts of heater do not really help, do not conceal the cold. Dix, the winner of the contest, sleeps quietly, gathering himself against his great opportunity. I gather myself *too*. Gather myself in this prehistoric plunge toward — toward what? Reconception and redevelopment to be sure and all the revisions of time. In latter years the *Triceratops* shot by Dix will decompose along with all this era, the living too, steam slowly into the mists. None of it will remain but that small testimony I can leave or that at least I think is the insistence which drives me forward, drives me back, takes me through this busy and circumstantial time.

Dix, poised on the rim of the impossible, leveling the stick of fire and the great beast, confused, stumbling in the chalk and doom.

MORNING LIGHT

The notes locked away, his schedule set, insistent sleep craved, Robles stumbled toward awareness quickly, rising through the flickering levels of illumination, reaching toward the weight of sixty-seven million crushing years and found himself lying tangled on the earth, the ropes of the tent a geometry of madness spattering shadows. Cry of prehistoric birds in the distance, the strange, dry whooping of a beast, then. He reared to a seated position, arched away from the sleeping Muffy, fully clothed yes as he had prepared but with the feeling that he had nonetheless fallen helplessly behind, lost all grip and sense of what he had come to do, knew only the falling sickness. But peering through the tent he could see that the little camp was silent, the other tents undisturbed, Dix's tent falling in even folds, this dense time still wrapped heavily around the sleepers. His terror must have come from dreams, not circumstance, some atavism of displacement, of having been taken by time to this utter and dismaying disconnection.

Back in the tent he struggled to move from dreams of wounded reptiles and death then, suppressed the dream sounds of carnage to come, breathed slowly in the clammy silence, his breath curling before him. Muffy sighed, a pretty woman, a pretty distracted woman, no courtesan but a friend, a part of the tour, yes, but more than that to him now, she insisted, and he looked at her momentarily without desire, without any intimation of need, remembering the places his hands had found in that scurrying time earlier when he had been driven from a need he could no more

articulate than he could decipher those dim whoops. Let her sleep, yes, he thought, there was enough and a different aspect of time to come.

Standing there, back to the embankment, he could see the reflection of the floodlights spilling through the protected zone, framing the sleeping Muffy Carter, he could see the Cretaceous refracted as panorama, *dio*rama, hurtled dogwood and the swamp having the aspect of the museum. It was a "natural habitat," Robles thought, and put the quote marks in, the biggest and goddamndest habitat of then all, a Cretaceous replicate and just the most remarkable thing. Scratching his ass in the curling sunlight, trying to bring himself to some kind of accommodation, Robles peered at his strange and attractive partner, then turned to see the mesh fences in the distance, the fences walling off the compound, holding it through paradoxical electrification and wire from the gigantic animals that would otherwise in their ignorance blunder through. Protect the animals, protect the travelers, a mutuality of indifference. That was the point of the tour, wasn't it? Buy they had promised Dix one kill. A major-league *Triceratops*. That was where the center lay now.

He didn't want to think about it. Killing *Triceratops* was not Robles' ticket, he would direct the fire, whisper words of encouragement to Dix, estimate the windage and the burn ratio and the number of meters toward the beast but the kill was all Dix's responsibility, the Combine had made that quite clear, a line had been drawn (just like that for the dinosaurs) and Robles would not have to cross it. I'm here safe, he said, you hear that Muffy? Muffy sighed, clutched a pink pillow in her pretty hands, rubbed her face in the crease, then gave a long, purling groan. I know you don't want to talk about it, he said. No one wants to talk about it. We all have our jobs, we're all safe, aren't we? Dix is the major-league *Triceratops* hunter while you and I make sweet, sweet love under the dogwoods, isn't that right? He listened, heard the catch in her breath, the tiny acquiescence in her exhalation. Right, he said, that is exactly right.

He strode toward the flat, peered out again. Past the enclosure: past the abyss dug into this hollow by Camp Paradox itself (that was Muffy's name for it, it would stay, it was the right term) was the landscape. The shallow depressions, curved mountains, all of this curiously without color like the beasts themselves; small puffs from hidden volcanoes and buttes, those commas and exclamation points of nature. Later, much later, the strata would accumulate: these would be mines, the strata valleys and mountains, over there perhaps downtown Helena. The volcanoes, attended to, the fix of attention, gurgled like beasts, made little whickering sounds in the darkness, and the beasts hidden by the arc and incline of the landscape gurgled like volcanoes. In and out, that shuddering identity.

Robles shook his head, not in awe, awe was not the proper term for any of this. On your sixth voyage back, now much more than a guide (if less than a hunter), you either internalized some of this and put it away or you perished through the implications of the circumstance, just let it carry you under. No, it was the *lack* of anticipation, his strange indifference in this first dawn which was stunning; never had he felt this way before, now the period had no effect upon him. He was rising to confront fire and the beast but he might as well have been in Brooklyn Complex, working out some kind of appropriations plan. That was how much it meant to him now. Even burrowing within Muffy had had that blandness — her deeps which once had seemed magnificent, arching now gave him back only small and splintering visions of himself, little feathered mysteries in the dark. Here in what would become Helena sometime, the mines were yet to be cast from this crystal unrest, the strata and volcanic ash lay millennia in the future as did his own unspeakable conception. To this place, which should have been sacred

— Robles felt that this was the only sanctity which could be grasped, all the rest of it was ritual — had come the crowd of travelers with Dix, host and moderator at their front, to sight the huge beasts for the promised international, televised, major-league kill. What fearful symmetry, Robles said. Who would have dreamt that? Hand or eye? Are you up yet?

Amphibian noises from the pallet, water and earth. She flipped a cover at him. I'm up, she said, thanks. What are you talking about?

Poetry, Robles said. Old poetry.

You mean unwritten poety, Muffy said. Won't be written for ages.

Camp Paradox, Robles said. Camp out of time.

You said it, she said. I didn't. Why don't you come here and lay with me? Create some more paradox.

He looked at her, the shadows dressing her nakedness, casting arrows and curvatures of shape. Better not, he said, everyone will be up soon. What if they saw us locked to ground, playing the old sniffle-snaffle? What then, Muffy?

She yawned. Part of the tour, she said.

I'm a guide, Robles said. You're a counselor. Not professional, it wouldn't look right at all.

What do you think they're doing? Any different than we?

Dix doesn't, Robles said. He doesn't do anything like that at all, ever. Remember? He said that once. A violation of the temple of the holy spirit. He's a fanatic too, not just a great group mind.

You're too serious for me, Muffy said. You're too much of a speculator. I don't have that kind of stuff going on in my head. To me it's all green thoughts, everywhere. Whatever you say, then.

Robles walked to the pallet, looked down at her, then knelt, touched her elbow gently, felt the yielding of the flesh, watched as her mouth opened slightly for entrance or reproof, it hardly mattered, with Muffy Carter they mingled, they were all the same. Everything mingled and intermixed deep in the sweet probe. Murder coming, yes, anachronism aplenty in the deep Cretaceous, but it was all the same to her and everything would come out even in those dark, sweet depths. No copulation, nothing like that in the sendback, the Administrators had said, but Muffy paid as much attention to that as any guide, which was none at all. With good contraception and a tight, banging constraint, what was the difference? she had asked. A pregnancy would be silly, bad luck for all of them, but really, who was to know? What was the difference? There would be no pregnancy and everything happening here then, even the kill, would be an abstraction. The death of the dinosaurs was as diminished as the pregnancy which would not occur: they became in that cosmic accident fungi, heaps of bone trapped in that fungus, then ash, then fossils, trapped in the clumsy and insistent onrush of time. In the new millennium, only a few bones and suggestions then to mark their passage. Come on, she said, get right aboard. Ride me like a hobby horse, ride me like before. Come, come.

Robles felt himself rolling toward her, then yanked himself away. No, he said, not now. It wouldn't work out, it wouldn't be right.

Then go away, she said. She stared at him. I mean it. Just go. Don't *hover*.

Yes, he said, you're right. He tried to stand, felt his knees lock, sank into the dirt, vertigo pulling at him then. You never get used to it, he said. Do you? I can't take it. But it's never been like this before.

Don't get sentimental on me, Muffy said. I'm just a guide.

Maybe you never get used to it, he said. It's all the cartage outside. Hundreds of thousands of tons. How do you get used to it?

Maybe you should pass me my clothes, let me pull myself together then.

You can be blasé, Robles said. That's because you don't have to think about it. You just point and give

figures. But I'm supposed to be able to give *interpretation*. It's the intellectual part of me.

You're a deep fellow, she said. You're beyond me. If fate and circumstance hadn't thrown us together, who knows how we might have been? Is it too late for us now? Will we survive? Time will tell, two hundred million years of it.

I'm afraid of Dix, Robles said. Can you understand that? I don't like him. I don't know what he wants.

He wants to shoot *Triceratops*, dummy. That's why he's here.

Not *Triceratops*, Robles said. That's just a symbol, whatever you call it. He wants something else. I don't know where your clothes are. You're going to have to get them yourself.

You're the one who threw them somewhere.

This isn't a hotel, Robles said fiercely. This isn't a one-night stand. We're buried in this place, now, not in the past, can't you see that? It's no joke.

Sure, she said, you're always so right, I'll find my own clothes. See if I care. You throw, I go. He's just a tourist, she said in a different tone. Maybe a host, maybe a personality with an entourage, but he wants what the rest of them do. A few pictures, a little admiration, a thrill to touch his insulated life.

The others didn't want to kill.

We didn't let them, remember? We changed the rules for Dix, that's all. They wanted to kill, all right. That was the lure all along, don't you know that?

He curled an arm over the floor, found a shirt half crouched beneath the pallet, tossed it to her. You're not all dumb, he said. You play that way but you can figure things out pretty good.

Muffy took the shirt from his hand, ran a hand through her hair, patting it down, then pushed her head through. They're all the same to me, she said. Man with a plan, man on a mission, one way or the other.

In the distance, a tyrannosaur screamed, that odd,

trapped sound arcing to penetration, then began to whoop with the regularity of a siren. The sound was bucolic at this moment, fed not his apprehension but what Robles wanted to take as heightened perception. The sound mixed into foliage, became oddly comforting. Trees in the diorama rustled harmlessly. Muffy squeezed his hand, peered over his shoulder. Here he comes, she said, there he comes, for heaven's sake. Look at him break water.

Break water it did. Not a tyrannosaur then but a major-league *Triceratops*. Robles had seen them in the distance many times but this emergent *Triceratops* in the near bog was something different, was a *stunning* son of a bitch, disproportionate but elegant in the sudden proximity. Thirty feet long, half that high, three discolored horns, greenish at this angle, the huge, comic neck frill, those horns jutting at odd angles above the eye and yet at the center of that movement an odd stillness. The gray-brown mass stolid, almost bovine then as it emerged from a crouch, shoot itself toward land, nuzzled at the ground then closed in on a magnolia so furiously leaved that the trunk was invisible. Began to pull at the discolored flowers.

Cute, isn't he? Muffy said.

Oh yes, Robles said, that's the word.

Makes you want to go over and pet them. Ride the *Triceratops*, Daniel? Want to take another seat? I'm not the only hobbyhorse around.

Go to hell, Robles said without anger. Take it on the tour.

A short-frilled ceratopid, Muffy said in a measured voice, tending to have large, unpaired nose horns. The horns are more defensive than instruments of hostility, however, and to avoid injury resulting from combat, the *Triceratops* relies heavily upon bluff displays and evasive maneuvers.

You do that well.

They pay me in time and experience, Muffy said. It's all hypnotic therapy anyway. All those misspent, unspent nights.

My nights weren't so great either, Robles said. I think we all had a pretty bad time. Why else would we show up at Camp Paradox?

Because it's what we're paid to do. See the mountains and ride the beast. And stay out of the way of anachronism.

Smart, Robles said, you're real smart.

You learn something in the service, Muffy said. They watched the *Triceratops* chew contentedly, leaves and twigs tumbling into its throat, no drop at all. The *Triceratops* ate with great delicacy, stripped the magnolia, then seemed to shrug and sink into the bog again. Shoulder high, it wobbled colorlessly away.

Full of purpose, Robles said. More purpose than we have.

Colbert theorizes, Muffy said professionally, that the horns represent individual, random solutions to a common problem of display and protection, that they may indeed represent selectivity by being a kind of sexual lure. Hey, she said, you're not listening. This is very interesting. You ought to pay attention.

I'm paying attention, Robles said. I paid attention to *Triceratops* and now I'm listening to you. And thinking of Dix. The man is dangerous. He wants more than a kill, he wants the beasts to suffer. I can tell that from his face.

You're a perceptive guy, aren't you? How did you get to know so much? It's just a job. You're not responsible for what goes on here, that decision was made by the administration. I think that Dix just wants a trophy like the rest of us. Maybe *Triceratops* is *his* hobbyhorse, that's all.

He came out as if on cue, Robles said. That one seemed to be performing *for* us. Did you ever think that maybe they were waiting, that all this is some kind of show they've set up for the tourists and we're the ones being watched?

I think you are showing symptoms of needing a rest, Muffy said. Maybe you can take one. But not until this is finished.

You don't think maybe that all of this is programmed? The dinosaurs too? That we're being watched and observed?

You're too deep for me, Muffy said. She adjusted her shirt, stood gracefully. Halfway there, she said. Now I have to look for some pants.

There's too much going on, Robles said. I never thought it out until now, I just took it for granted. But it's impossible, he thought. It's impossible, that was it. Camp Paradox in fact as well as in name, *none* of this should be happening, not by the rights they had established.

A bell clattered behind them, hardly dinosaur sound, but a technological, post-op summons. In the light they lived by bells and those cruising forms. Turning, Robles peered past Muffy, past the transparent arc of the tent wall, and could see beyond them the low structures of the ranch, the five or six tents which with the Transporter comprised Camp Paradox. Small puffs of smoke vented from those tents, little puffs of light and the suggestion of movement within. Reveille. Inside the domed structure at an oblique angle from the tents, Dix himself would be standing now, pacing on the curved ground, staring through the aperture, looking for his *Triceratops*, measuring for the kill. Well, Robles said when the clattering had ceased, I guess today's the day.

Hunting time, Muffy said. Get a square into the belly and onto the range. Poor little warrior.

Dix? He's a contest winner.

No, Muffy said, not Dix. He's got what he'll be getting. You. You're the one. All suffering because of your rhinoceros out there.

It isn't that, Robles said, it isn't that at all. Can't we forget this? Can't we let it be?

That was your decision all the time. You can come and play inside if you want. It isn't all dead things.

No, Robles said. He shook his head. I told you, I can't. But we're doing something wrong, Muffy. It isn't right, not what we're doing here. This is not the way it was supposed to be. Bringing Dix to Camp Paradox, giving him a gun, setting him loose here.

This is hardly the time, she said. That was all decided a long time ago, worked out by people like you. Let's make reveille and go out on the trails and watch Dix a-hunting go. Then we'll be out of here.

We're never out of here.

You're out of me. Wouldn't you like to get back inside? You can, you know. It's what you want to do. What do you want? She grasped his hand, bent it suddenly at the wrist, sent a splinter of pain up his arm. Robles shrieked. Come *on*, she said. Say it, do it. What do you *want*?

Anachronism, Robles said, rubbing his arm, shaking the wrist. Time out of time. I want it to mesh. I want confluence, can you understand that?

Do business, she said, keep your eye on the sparrow. Go sparrow-hunting, let Dix take primordial rhinoceros over there.

Business, he said. There seemed nothing more to say. Not introspective under the best conditions, the convolutions of the tour had made him utterly unable to cope. Big business.

Not for Dix, Muffy said, taking his hand, rubbing the arm expertly, working blood into the sprain. Not for him though.

Pleasure?

Try again, Muffy said.

FURTHER OBSERVATIONS

Rhinolike as they might have been, *Triceratops* nonetheless dropped eggs. The cutting edge theories had been wrong: they weren't warm-blooded, they did not carry or suckle their young. Robles had taken it badly, seeing his teleology upset. He had envisioned *Triceratops* as a pinnacle: first the fire-breathers, then the vegetarians, then the long, galumphing *Struthiomimus*, big as hangarports, dense as earth, two brains, one prick. They all laid eggs, Robles believed, except *Triceratops*, the advance model, major-league *Triceratops* had vaulted to the next stage. Except that it hadn't. Like all the rest, it laid its seed in the cold, cold ground, abandoned it there. No home on the range for *Triceratops*, no family life at dusk. They were no different than all of the others. In that first expedition, his fragile hold upon evolution had disintegrated, the *Triceratops* had fallen from its distant height to the deserts of inanition and stupidity with all the rest of them. In a sense, Robles felt he had never survived that knowledge. There was no evolution then, no discrimination, only accident and the huge, dark, scuttling forms.

Robles continued to write: An enlarged fragment of shell mounted in the Crete Musée des Beaux Arts, tyrannosaur suspected as keeper, the outer surface not smooth but stucco-like, brought from the Wyoming wastes, one of eighteen preserved for the new and refurbished Musée. Nothing within, the most sophisticated radiology had indicated, but of course it was early in cycle. What would one do with a tyrannosaur? Lady Carter, I seem to have a tyrannosaur on the premises, he is consuming the wallpaper and has most discomfited the butler. What would we do, Lady Carter? Oh never mind, James, the little creature will find its way back to the nest at last. Let us have some stucco.

He struggled to put it down, relying upon primitive implements and means otherwise unacceptable. Oh, to stroll those wastes, to go egg-gathering in the weak Cretaceous sun, return then to Paradox, on what careful and exquisite omelette we could dine. To dine on unhatched *Triceratops*, essence of *oeuf*, to curl with Muffy amongst the dogwood and magnolia, concealed from the prowlings of Dix, safe from his scatterings, to chow down this thrifty forerunner of our modern rhinoceros and ostrich. This is not merely a prize but an opportunity unafforded by *Triceratops* who granted no such leavings. Joint by joint, inch by inch, one can surely chow down this unspeakable history.

And so he continued—

THE NEST

It had been a stunt, in fact. Rig a contest, get someone like Dix to win, bring him to Camp Paradox with appropriate publicity, let equipment film good times here. A television personality, Dix carried his own equipment and crew. It had seemed acceptable at the start, had in fact seemed a brilliant plan. Robles had no objection. Robles, knowledgeable, was all for it. Something had to be done and soon, otherwise they would lose the post.

It was time to alter the situation. Business in Cretaceous Montana had collapsed, Camp Paradox was no longer pulling its new millennial weight. Sour clumps of travelers drifted amongst the chuck wagons and the anachronistically styled riding enclosures, looking grim. The dinosaurs, shy even in better times, could hardly be prevailed upon to circle the ranch and were often unavailable for days while the travelers stared glumly at one another and disdained the holos. Bring back a celebrity to go track the dinosaurs in habitat, it had seemed an audacious conception, yes, but what else was there? There were simply very few new ideas and administration had its own problems, had left them more or less to deal with themselves.

Ultimately, the idea had come from Robles. He could fix responsibility at no other point, it had to be his. What wouldn't work as vista might if it were given some aspect of plot: the quest of a celebrity figure to unravel the secrets of his past. Of course Dix could not be enlisted straight off, that would not work, he would have to be taken in the guise of a contest winner but contests themselves were easy enough to manage. Robles had rigged more than his share in another profession, at another time. And Dix had looked good, he had seemed at the start to be precisely what they had needed, personable, jaunty, a quizzical tilt to the head that bespoke intelligence, irony, and a serious interest in the problem of Camp Paradox. Because it is both there and not there, am I right? Dix had said. Because it exists both in and out of time, the only millionaire tourist trap in Montana that is ecologically sound, is that right? They had laughed. Dix had seemed quite reasonable at the start, it had been a pleasure to tilt the contest toward him, make the business of a celebrity winner credible, test things out then.

Who could have known then how it would turn out? Who knew that Dix had an assassin's eye, a hunter's deisre? There was no way to tell, not until the announcement. Not until Dix had started to go public with his plans to land a big one back there and carry it back so that the world could share in the meat of his accomplishment. Grinning, showing sketches of *Triceratops* to the cameras, Dix had been Everyman's version of a winner, smiling at them. We'll bring 'em back alive, Dix said. Oh, not the dinosaurs, he said, winking. They'll be dead as tumbleweed. But the *hunters*, the expeditionaries, we'll be alive and we'll have film the likes of which we'll never have again to play for you.

Let's call it off, Robles had said to Arness, who had played the role of the Committee then. Let's just annul the whole thing. I'll take the blame, we can say that we hadn't calculated the paradoxical effect of a shooting or of transporting someone without special

biological delousing. I don't care what we say, we can figure out something.

Can't do it, Arness said, you wanted publicity, we have it now. There's too much. We call it off in public, we look bad.

We can say that there are dinosaur eggs in the machines, that the transporter is clogged. What the hell do I care? Robles had said. He had been eager to concede fault, compelled in fact, the need for self-abnegation had seized him, made him shake. This guy is no good, he said. And no good gets worse.

A contest is a contest, Arness had said. We got too much attention, you did even better than we hoped. We can't break it now without looking even worse.

But killing the beast! Killing a *Triceratops*—

Arness said, We've studied this. There's no anachronism, no risk. If we can go stomping around there sixty-seven million years back, we can kill a *Triceratops*. All of this will be fossilization in no time.

We can't be sure of that, Robles said. We can't be sure of anything. Maybe the *Triceratops* he kills is the grandfather of Gawaine. Maybe he misses and kills a tyrannosaur who found Atlantis.

All subsumed, Arness said, all of it eaten up by the million of years. The dinosaurs left no trace, remember. We don't even know what they looked like. We don't know if they had pricks or cunts or how the males sniffed each other out. No trace means no risk. So let him shoot one. It will be good for business and we need business. Private enterprise, remember?

Yes, Robles remembered. He knew everything about private enterprise back then, hadn't he been living it back and forth for all these years? Muffy Carter was private enterprise, so was the transporter, so was all of it. You took your chances, you stayed outside the system and made the best of it you could and the rest of it was bullshit, that was his motto. But this is different, he said to Arness. This is a dangerous guy, someone who thinks that the shadow and the act are the same, like all these communications types. I tell you, I don't like it, Robles said.

We don't like it either, Arness said, but we're into the situation and that's all. It's too late. He'll murder us if we back out now what with the exposure he has. He'll make us the laughing stock of late night. He'll say that the whole thing is a studio job and there's no prehistory there, just some hanging loops and video machines. We can't take it. We can't put up with it. So we go through and hope for the best.

Trusting, Robles said, we've always been so trusting. But it's going to catch up with us. We're going to have real trouble.

You and that little Muffy, Arness said, you can keep an eye on him. Muffy can control him, maybe. He likes women, he likes them small.

He better keep his hands off Muffy, Robles said, surprising himself. He just better leave her alone. To Dix later, at their briefing session, he had said, All right, you got to do it, you go ahead and take care of it. Shoot one, get your pictures. But we're going to be careful, you hear me? We're going to watch this all the way. This isn't a safari, it isn't *The African Queen*. You get into real trouble here and you don't back out.

The transporter's going to fail? Dix said. Is that the deal? And we'll be trapped back there then?

The transporter never fails and we got six backup for any problem. No, Robles said, I mean other stuff. Stuff you better be aware of.

Your stuffed animals going to eat me alive?

No, Robles said, it isn't that. I won't let you bait me, he thought. That is your skill, baiting guests into reactions, but it won't happen to me. I can deal with this, I can control the situation.

You better pay attention, he said. You better watch what's going on there and you'd better listen to me.

I listen to everyone, Dix said. That's my own zone of operations, mister, and you better leave that to me.

Leave that to him. Everything in the end got displaced, then. In the night, the tyrannosaurs ran in spasms, small gasps of effort, ran like horses down the rutted streams of the Cretaceous. The grunts of the *Triceratops*, the glide of *Struthiomimus*, the whine of tyrannosaur splitting the weak sun. He was, he knew then, absolutely dedicated, part of the period, unable to see Dix as the others might. The situation had overtaken them.

CAMP PARADOX DOWNRANGE

Once, Robles had had clearly defined plans, before the ethos of it began to crawl into him. The plans were two years with the dinosaurs, just two years shuttling in the transport, pushing tourists around the swamps and bogs of that impossible, riotous past and then he would be done with it, would have enough in hand to make something of himself in the tried and true third millennium.

He didn't have to be a range bum like some of them turned out to be, those who got prehistoric and future all mixed up and spewed it all in the transporter. No, Robles had had a sense of command, more command than that when Muffy had moved in and had attracted his attention, the third of the hostesses but the one that had fully caught his attention. He knew that he and Muffy had a connection, could amount to something, but only if they kept it in defined context. But it was palpable, the trade was clear, you gave them your skills and risk — and your sense of balance too because who could sup with *Struthiomimus* and return to Texas fully sane? — and tried to hold on and at the other side of the pipeline you had security.

He agreed with Muffy: they all started that way and some of them even held on to it but it was hard. Camp Paradox broadened your perspective, broadened it perhaps too much, showed you the end of things disguised as the beginning. It isn't the anachronism though, Muffy said, or the fear of getting tangled in a branch and lying down for good, it isn't the fear of one of these shy beasts gobbling you down . . . no, it's something else.

Maybe that we're not supposed to screw here, Robles said. Could that be it?

Yeah, sure, Muffy said, I sure do like to screw and maybe that's it. Celibacy will get you in the midst of rut, right?

But that wasn't it, of course. They both knew that, had agreed not to discuss it. It was the intimation front and back that got you, that poised and terrible certainty as you clutched your way through prehistory, taking the tourists around and showing them this or that out of the guidebook, the sense that you were at all times at some dense and thrilling flashpoint and that everything else, all of it further or later, was of no consequence whatsoever. The beasts were too huge, the tourists too stupid, the thunder of the transporter shattering in its impact. There were only extremes, it would turn a dead man into an ironist. This crawled in, centered you after a while, simply would not go away.

The idea had been—he tried to talk this out with Muffy now and then but somehow he could not make it right, maybe they had never been meant to understand one another—that the dinosaurs would change his life. Not Camp Paradox, not the tours, but the beasts themselves. Wasn't that it? If circumstances, if this malevolent and despairing twenty-first century crowding in on him and his wouldn't do it for him, if he had become misfit amidst the holgraphy and the apocalyptic recreation, then perhaps the Cretaceous would make things different. Here on the trails he could dance with *Triceratops*, leap the fantastic with *Tyrannosaurus*, go trapping for *himself* in that primeval, casual ooze, learn from the nesting of these peculiar and intransigently shy beasts how he might make his own nest finally.

You don't want to nest, Muffy said. No man does. You want to fly, to scatter, to kick the nests down. Any man who doesn't know that hasn't found himself yet. But that's okay, she said. I have my own troubles too. We're all in flight. You want biography, I've got as much as yours and more disastrous.

What they didn't tell you, he wanted to point out to her but he couldn't, there was simply too much he could not discuss, what you didn't know until you learned it agonizingly yourself, slogging every step of it, was that oldest of truths: that darkness you carried within yourself was your own, *yours*. Wherever you were, there was that prehistoria of the spirit and it was of a numbing equalization. Under that ancient but familiar dark with Muffy, cheating a little (but all of them did, everyone knew that, it was the most laughable rule of the service), soaring and bucking and snaffling like the *Triceratops* which obsessed him, Robles had had his little moments now and then, his flickers of possibility. Certainly in the earlier period when the tourists with money and cameras came to open their eyes to the past and gamble at night it had been kind of fun, before Camp Paradox had begun to dwindle—like its age, like all apocalyptic hobbies—into disuse. That had been fun then, screwing Muffy within hairsbreadth of the tourists when the sun went down, sharing information on the beasts during the day as if none of the other part existed and they were truly in the service of the tourists. But as that and the travelers went away, as the harder necessities of the doubled advancing time stream (moving one to one, there was no other way that the committee could manage, the situation would have been uncontrollable otherwise) closed in, that feeling of possibility, the sheer illicitness of all connection drained. Robles began to understand why the guides looked as they did and why most of them never got out. It was as dense and troubled, as empty and desperate here as in the twenty-first when you turned inward to the situation and it was impossible to project it upon the beasts as had been managed at the outset.

But you couldn't tell the males or females apart, not at a distance. As Muffy had said, that most central information, at least for the explorers, was a mystery along with the private lives of dinosaurs. All you knew were that they clumped together and that the species did not seem to really intermingle. These animals were helpless to the elements, protected only by their size. Surely the stupidest of all creatures, stupid as the trees they ate, they cruised the landscape like distended toys, parodies of the barnyard. Even if you could ship them back, even if there was a way to risk all the rules of time and circumstances: who would want them? What could they possibly yield?

But that had been earlier. That was when Robles had still been fighting for some sense of possibility, some kind of function, before it had all collapsed and he realized that he was just another staring, stricken guide, nothing else. Those thoughts, that concern for polarities had been before the idea of the contest, before they had rigged it for Dix, before the intrepid Dix had appeared, filled with guns and plans. We'll kill one and film the whole thing. The first prehistoric hunt, Dix had said. It will be a sensation. At last they'll see something so big, such a piece of work that they'll be able to give up their own problems and watch the general collapse. That is *media*! Dix had said, and I am your media star.

Well, he had been through that before. He had given his warnings for all the effect they had, and could do no more. Gonna get me one of those, Dix said, and let the folks at home share it all. Give them a good time, let them follow along. Maybe he was right. Maybe that was the truth and Dix had the final and absolute handle. Maybe so, and it was Robles, trapped with his barnyard and with Muffy's sly anomalies, who was the fool. Maybe it was Robles then who was the guy really out of time, more millennial detritus, that was all.

So there came a time when you had to let go, had

to let matters take their course, reasonable or unreasonable, there was no other way. If Dix was right, then all of Camp Paradox from the start had been an entertainment device, a dude ranch set up for home movies. When he said that to Muffy she had been extra calm, another layer of disdain coming over her as if she had been prepared for more of Robles's silliness. Let's see what he gets, she said. Maybe he'll run at the first sign of tyrannosaur. These aren't guys of will and courage, she said, they get off from performing behind glass.

We're all behind glass. They ship us back that way in the transporter.

Don't get sophisticated on me, she said. Let's just see what will happen. It doesn't make any difference any other way, does it? I mean, nothing could be worse for business than what we have. So they would see, that was the arrangement. This will end too, Muffy pointed out, Camp Paradox was a fad, a phase like almost everything else. Dix himself would be back in the studios in just a little time.

Think of the litter here, Robles said. Think of what we're leaving behind. I mean that makes some kind of difference, doesn't it?

No it doesn't, Muffy said. She smiled at him. If the centuries ate the dinosaurs then they'll gobble up even the non-degradables. A sensible woman. But everyone was sensible by this time, fixed on outcome. Matters had counseled rationality, Dix too was a businessman. A *Triceratops* shoot was another diversion, that was all.

It was this reasonableness which had left all of them so unprepared, Robles came to think later. They had watched not only sense but passion leached from them here, had left the passion to the beasts, had identified the beasts then with display and had themselves curled in. By assuming control, they had lost control. Early, early on they had learned to screw quietly, emit no sounds, trouble neither downrange anachronism nor the tourists nor the night, wheezing out perfectly controlled, soundless orgasms, teeth sheathed in the other's neck. Oh Muffy had given acquiescence in that prehistoric night but never voice, there was no voice for any of them and that perhaps was the problem. *Tyrannosaurus* had that whine but the others made no sounds, only the clumping and crush of vegetation, the deep well of their impression to mark passage. Not barnyard but dirigible, not dinosaurs but huge, misaligned aircraft, Muffy had said.

But had not said this thrashing beside him; during those times she had — ah, correctness! — said nothing at all.

THE HUNT

Oh paradox! Dix thought, paradox, most ingenious paradox; leaving the thin straggle of tourists back at the camps, coming hard on *Triceratops*, his body curled to the stalk. Free, free! free for the moment of those controlling bastards in the tent, free of Robles who wanted to abort everything, he could now and at last concentrate on this dreadful and necessary task.

The Magnum, he knew, would more than distort the hapless rhinoceros before him. No, it would *reassemble* the beast, turn the rhino head to pulp, send those stupid eyes, by globule, to the far distance. Bring a video for this, track it for permanence? Hardly likely, this would destroy his audience and he was not there for that, he was to lend comfort to them. Maybe he should have saved this for his private collection but no, no, he wanted no record of slaughter, simply its evidence. Not too long now, he thought. He had the bastard leveled. It stood downrange fifty or sixty yards, shyly bobbing its head, giving him greedy little glances in the sudden adopted frieze, then poking and snaffling at the flowered branch. Dead meat on the hoof then, waiting for him.

Somewhere behind, in what they called Camp Paradox, Dix supposed that Robles and his Muffy were locked to their own task, thrashing away in the bush. He would never ask them, never say anything about it either, but really, what else could they be doing? What was the point of being a loser and blasted back to this kind of convict's exile unless at least you could hump among the beasts, feel the floor of the forest primeval? At least that was the way that Dix figured it. Think of it, he said, talking for the sake of talking, *Triceratops* did not respond to sound, was probably congenitally deaf, gobbling on the leaves anyway, what if Robles loaded her up, got her pregnant? What if the transport failed, not that such a thing was possible, they said? What if the child could get dropped off here sixty-seven million years or whatever behind the timeline? What about that, folks, hey? he said, practicing a riff which would work sooner or later on the concentrated channel. Would the child become its ancestor? Or would the comet due in pretty swift just wipe them out without sunken trace, just as promised? It was something to investigate, he thought, something that might be worth discussing when he brought his true adventures back for them and as he thought of the two of them humping, the leafy violation amidst the beasts, a splinter of envy torqued Dix, spun him, made him grunt with the savagery, the *bullet* of his own need until he put it behind, focusing then on the more immediate circumstance.

Oh paradox, paradox! That was a major-league *Triceratops* all right and as he laid it out in fire on the hot, grabbing flora of this diminished prehistory, so he would lay out *himself*, justify this trip, his life, his circumstance, his sudden and disgraceful need. Camp Paradox had become a cartoon, a vision of stuffed animals and farmyard greenery but this fucker taking the flowers in the sun, that was not a cartoon, that was a big one, the biggest one he could bag and in so doing, change everything. I want him, Dix thought, I want him badly, don't ask why, that's a different thing but

I am going to have him. Somewhere in the distance he could dream that they were nesting, could glimpse the other *Triceratops* this had left behind, a family of *Triceratops*, Muffy had said, gathered together and the hell with that. The vision twinkled, was clear for a moment, even clearer than the beast before him: there were those rhinos massed with one another like Robles and Muffy, blinking and seizing in the light. Dix began to move then with small, persistent steps, focused upon his own rhinoceros in the distance, feeling the morning, the vast Cretaceous now draped on him like a cloak. Oh, those creatures would grunt and mutter from indeterminate distance but here, focused, it would be different. Just him and his rhino then, making that oldest of equations.

The animal stood calmly, poised for him in its careful and sonorous fashion, the weight of the Magnum both jarring and comforting. Prowling through the damp plain, the Magnum against his palm, Dix saw that the low dogwood had already shed its blossoms, was stripped to a bark which had the blandness of an uncovered bog, prowling toward the major-league *Triceratops* downrange, he stepped on pink, white and red petals which marked a path swatched carelessly, almost defiantly. The sassafras trees with their leaves of star or circle stood slender and delicate as the legs of *Struthiomimus*, past the trees and the other foliage Dix could see less trodden paths lead from the compounds.

He wasn't the only one who had been on these trails. But he was the first, he knew, to have the courage of the kill, that was something of which he was convinced. He came to a small rise, casting *Triceratops* slightly to his left and then, in the distance, just past what had been his downrange, he saw the nests.

There they were after all, just as he had always known there would have been. Family life in the rhinos. Of course he had been right. At intervals that seemed to be the length of *Triceratops* itself, maybe thirty feet, were five or six sites and as he peered through the foliage he could see a suggestion of bodies clumped, the animals massed then toward some purpose. Here was a crevice and in the distance another, those crevices nests, all occupied, and Dix felt that if he could focus in the most determined way, could squint, could find some utter concentration he would see friendly *Triceratops* emerge to stare, head bowed, showing the frills. How crazy *was* he? Was this hallucination or had he merely contrived a story around real nests? It was a serious question, something to consider but only later on. When this was over. He had better do something soon, though, nests or whatever, because his customer down there in the distance was going to get nervous soon, real nervous, and would start charging one way or the other very soon. So that was it then, you had to attack the situation at its source, go back to the tangled roots of your history, sixty-seven million years back there. Get into a machine and go to Camp Paradox, seek it there and if you found it—well, if you found it, what then? What next? That was impossible to judge. There was such indeterminacy of circumstance that you had to *kill* your way out of it, had to hack your way through this and that, simply to render some kind of explanation. Well, so much for that dog in the distance. He crouched, dropped to a hunter's position, alertness, sighted the animal. Oh, this is going to make a good one, he said. This is going to make the best, I'm going to *spatter* the son of a bitch, I'm going—

He hadn't heard Robles or Muffy behind, there was no way from the constancy of his self-absorption that he would have tracked them. He hadn't heard them, they had been cut off suddenly, not only in space but from his mind, a clean sheet dropping between his perception and their actuality but now, suddenly, he was aware of the movement behind him, a clash of figures who in no way belonged (like him) in that landscape. He had forgotten them, had crept out on his own and, locked to himself, had forgotten and now he was going to pay for it. He could see them coming up behind him but at the same time he had to keep the damned beast focused, get it in his sights or lose it altogether, try to defend two opposed sights then. Fascinated by a close-up view of the dead eye of *Triceratops* caught in sudden magnification, Dix could feel all within himself tumbling toward that death, that blind, reaching stupidity. Get back! he shouted. Get back or I'll shoot you first! But that was bluff, he was gripped by that dead eye, felt himself arcing toward the bottom of that sensibility and then slowly the transfer lifted just enough to enable him to flex his finger, lock in the sight. Now, he thought, *now* before they catch me, before it's sixty-seven million years later, *now* I've got him and began to count out the seconds while trying to calculate windage, calculate the sudden and frantic movement of the beast which at last, possessed by its stupidity, had sensed something going on there, not the gun but Robles thrashing through vegetation, bringing the animal to attention. Too late, almost too late then.

Dix fired.

The beast *exploded*, even as Robles's hands reached him, he could feel *Triceratops* slowly atomizing through the corridors of the trees, liquid and fire dancing away from the shattered bone and then, one horn uptilted as if in salute, the *Triceratops* plunged.

ROBLES TRANSMOGRIFIED

He did it, Robles said and sprinted away from Muffy, I didn't think the son of a bitch would but he *did*, he said, moving frantically, pushing her away, scuttled then through the mud and greenery, feeling himself moving not toward Dix but at some odd cross-angles to his own purpose. Blood had exploded in geysers from the beast but the *Triceratops* was moving none-

theless, moving with uncommon speed, rushing toward Dix with a determination that Robles could not have calculated. Dix hurled the Magnum, began to scream, words that Robles could not make out. Get *down*! Robles shouted, although he wanted the son of a bitch to die. It was reflexivity, it was the good stuff they had been taught in training. He needed to save Dix if only to protect his own position. *Roll*, he shouted, roll away from it!

But Dix, down and yelling could not move and the *Triceratops* was upon him. Robles scrambled, fell to his knees, lurched toward Dix, was able to get a hand on him, felt their connection in the sucking ooze and as he did so, knew with the absolute and perfect perception he had sought in and out of time all his life that Dix was not going to die, that Dix would get away with this, would live to tell the tale and that it would be *Robles* who was going to perish. Get away, he shouted, this time to Muffy, for God's sake, save *yourself*! knowing that it had all been set from the beginning, their own scuttling copulations too, and then as he tried to raise Dix hopelessly, use the man as a shield, the beast was already on top of him, hurling Dix with its snout to the side, seizing Robles in its huge grasp. There was blood all over him, all over them and then pressure and Robles felt suddenly transcendent, not like the transporter which yanked you here and yanked you there but different, a true conquest, a true sense of control then masked as the greatest pain he had ever known. Dix was screaming something again but it was Muffy's voice to which Robles, dying, felt attuned: she was saying something to him, something which would explain everything and if he could only attend he would understand but she had become very old, she had become older than the pyramids, than the dawn of man, than the ascent of the great beasts, she had receded from him at great and greater speed and he could not hear her, could not reach.

Somehow, it no longer mattered. It didn't matter at all.

AFTER THE GALLERY

Later, deep in the darkness, the paleontologist asleep beside her, Maria remembered what she had seen in the gallery, that sudden awareness before he had pulled her away. At the skeletal foot, shiny and neat as an ornament (had anyone else seen this?) a cylindrical skull, the eye hollows glinting in the received light.

Now what would that mean? the Japanese wondered and thought of the skull for a moment and the haiku the paleontologist had made for her:

In the light the bird
Caught in Cretaceous flight as
The bone talks to us.

The haiku suddenly in the sleep toward which she descended curling around the skull, a ribbon around tht little ornament and she wanted to push that ribbon aside and look more closely, see the final and evident truth she knew was there — but it was impossible, she was too tired, she could not make that separation. Sleep took her, the holovision playing on soundlessly in the room showing described images of the host amidst the dinosaurs.

The bone did not talk to her anymore, then.